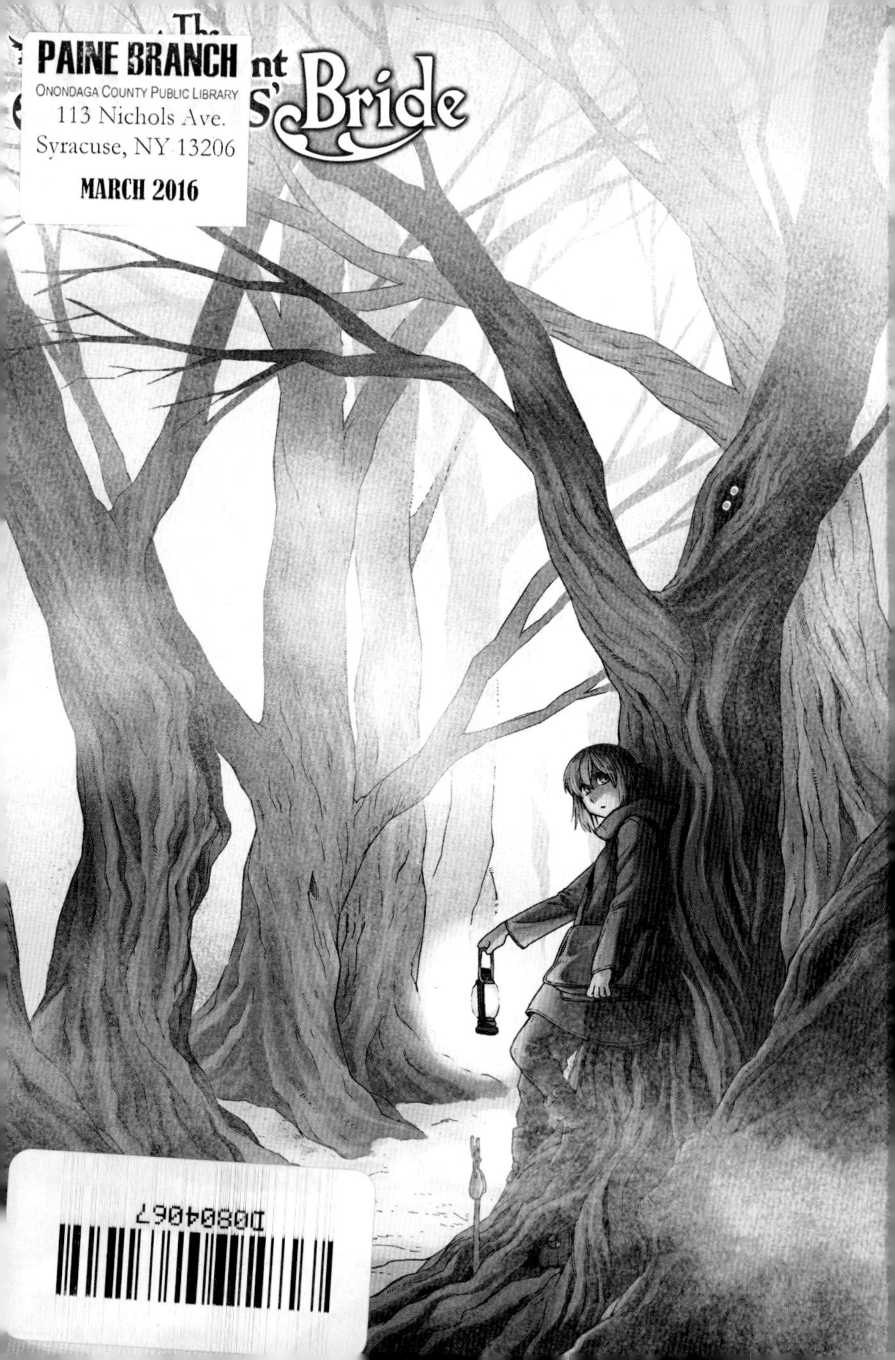
Th
nt
s' Bride

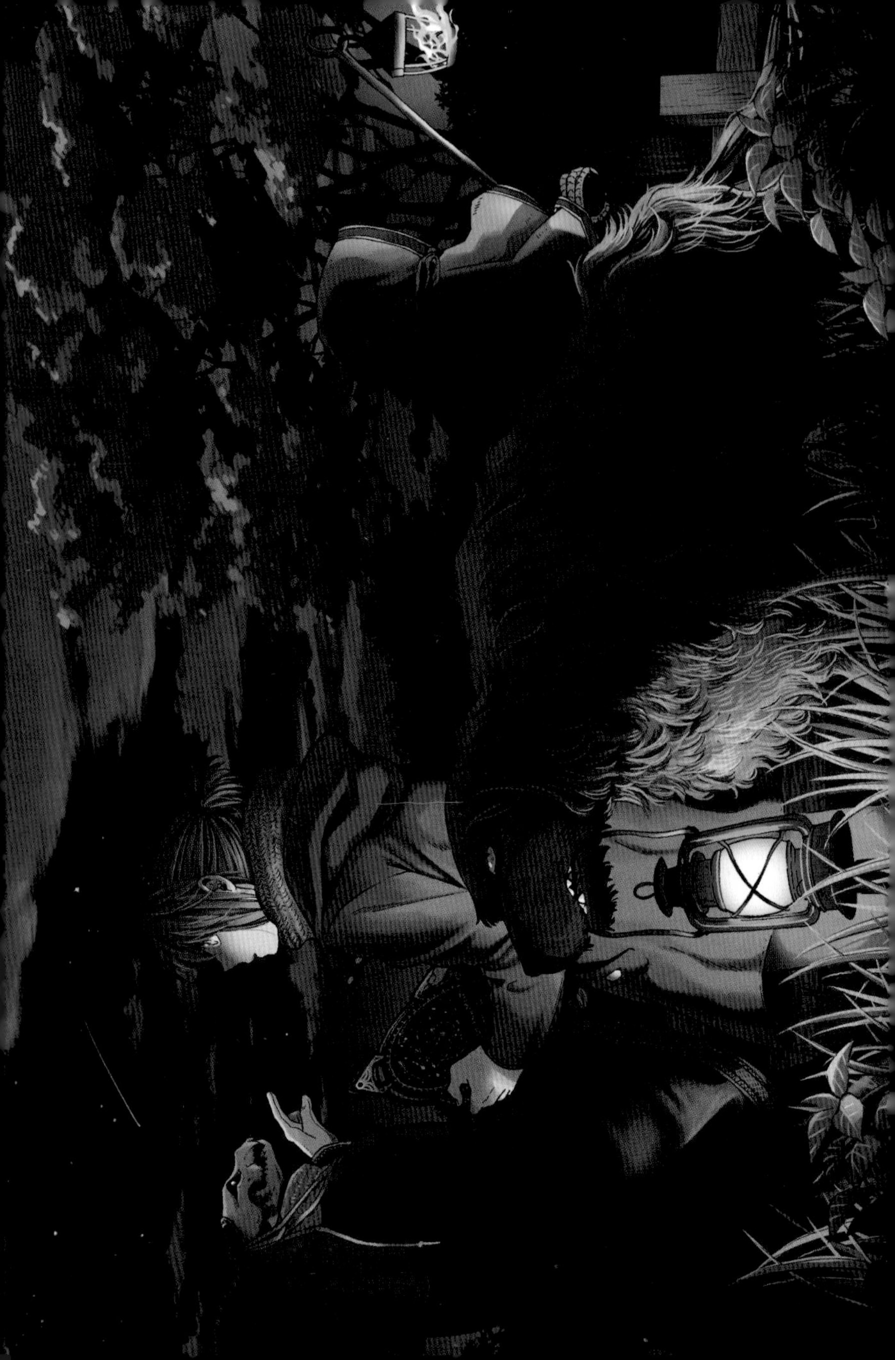

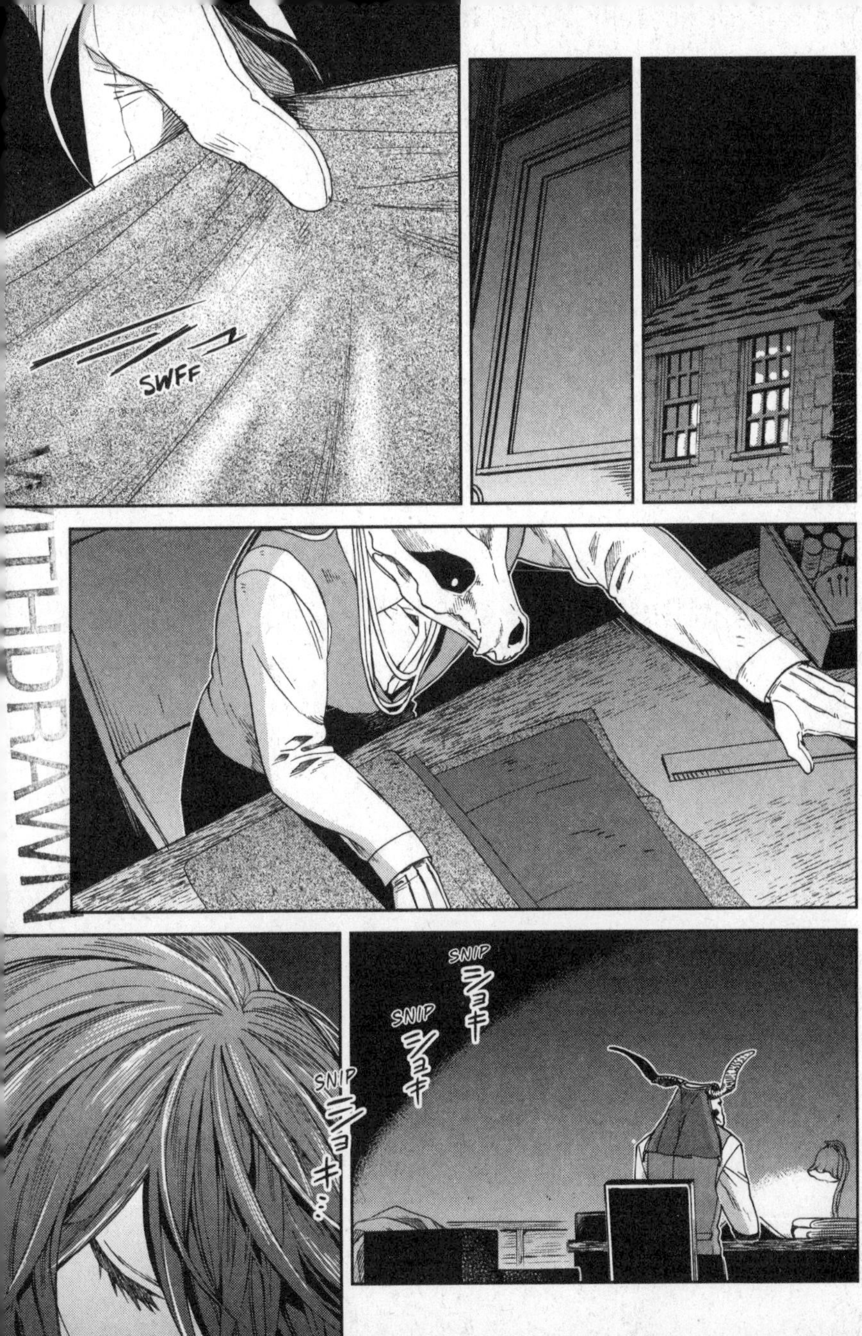
SWFF
SNIP
ショキ
SNIP
ショキ
SNIP
ショキ…

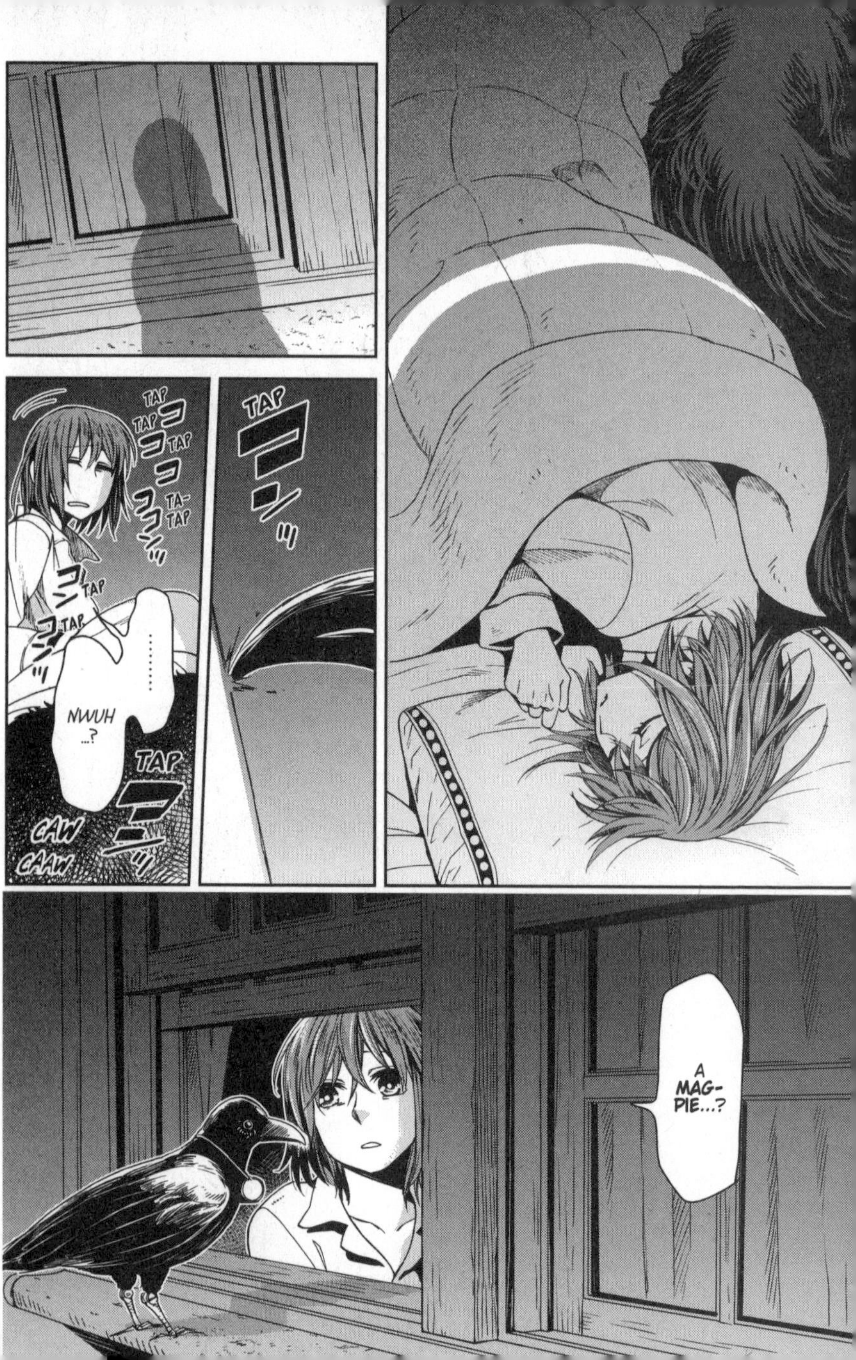
TAP
TAP
TAP
TAP
TA-TAP
TAP
TAP
......
NWUH ...?
TAP
CAW
CAAW
A MAG-PIE...?

Chapter 26: God's mill grinds slow but sure. I

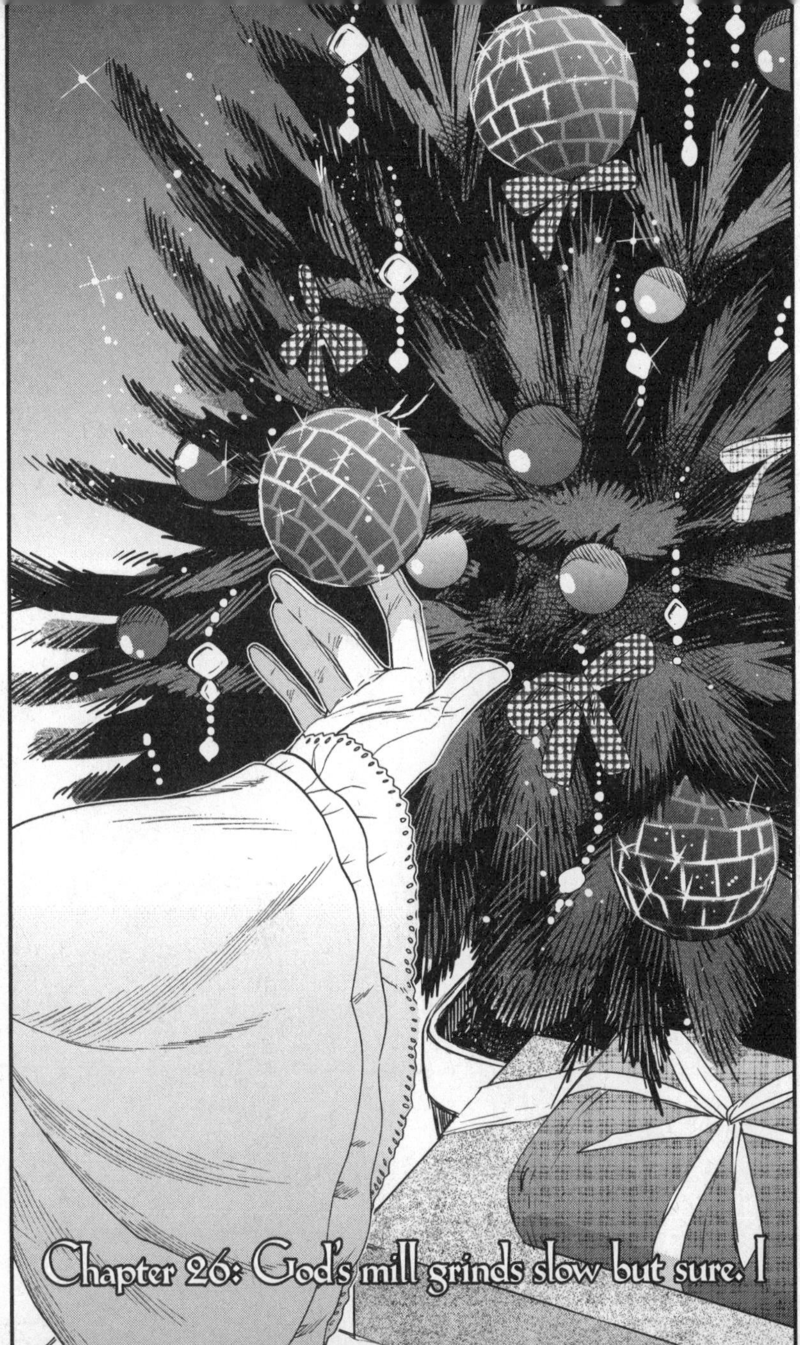

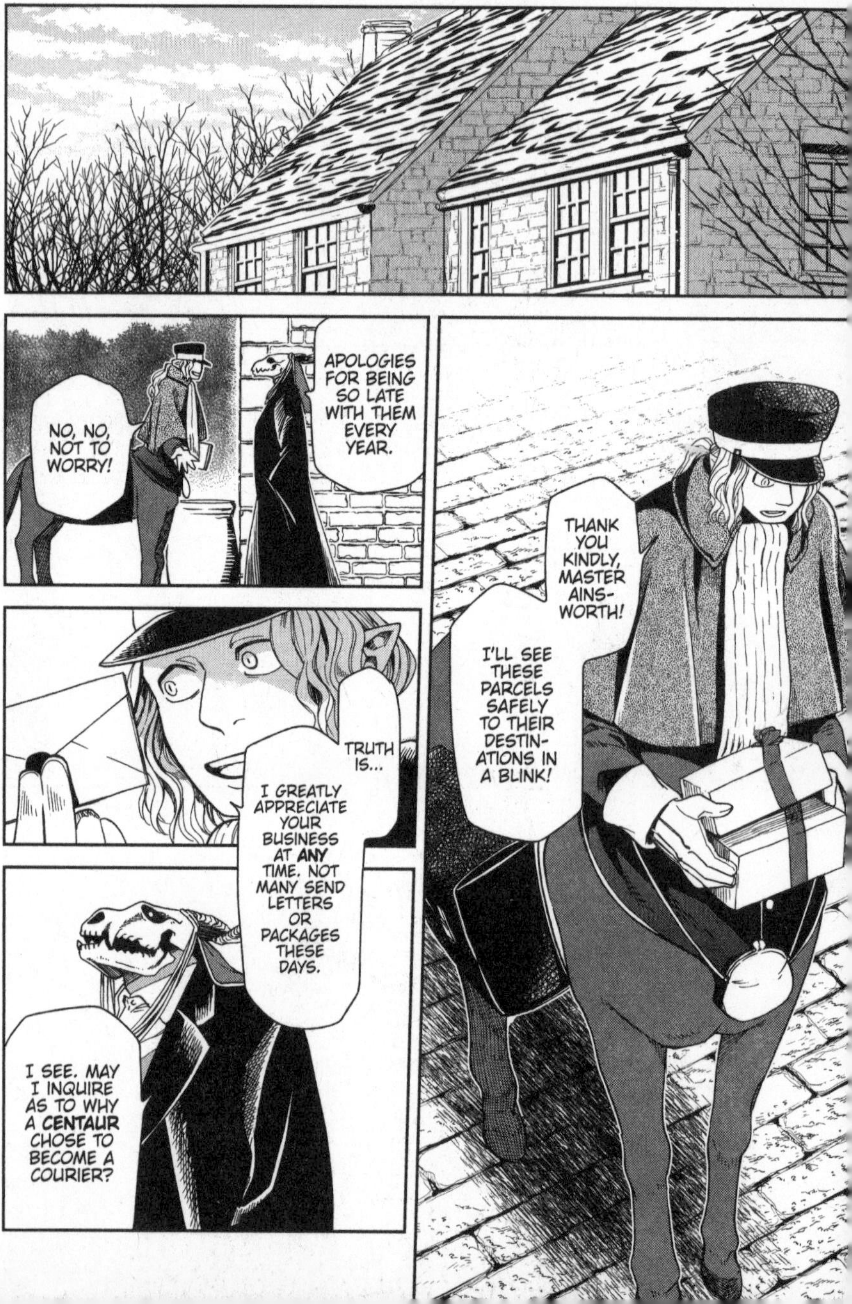
THANK YOU KINDLY, MASTER AINS-WORTH!
I'LL SEE THESE PARCELS SAFELY TO THEIR DESTIN-ATIONS IN A BLINK!
APOLOGIES FOR BEING SO LATE WITH THEM EVERY YEAR.
NO, NO, NOT TO WORRY!
TRUTH IS...
I GREATLY APPRECIATE YOUR BUSINESS AT ANY TIME. NOT MANY SEND LETTERS OR PACKAGES THESE DAYS.
I SEE. MAY I INQUIRE AS TO WHY A CENTAUR CHOSE TO BECOME A COURIER?

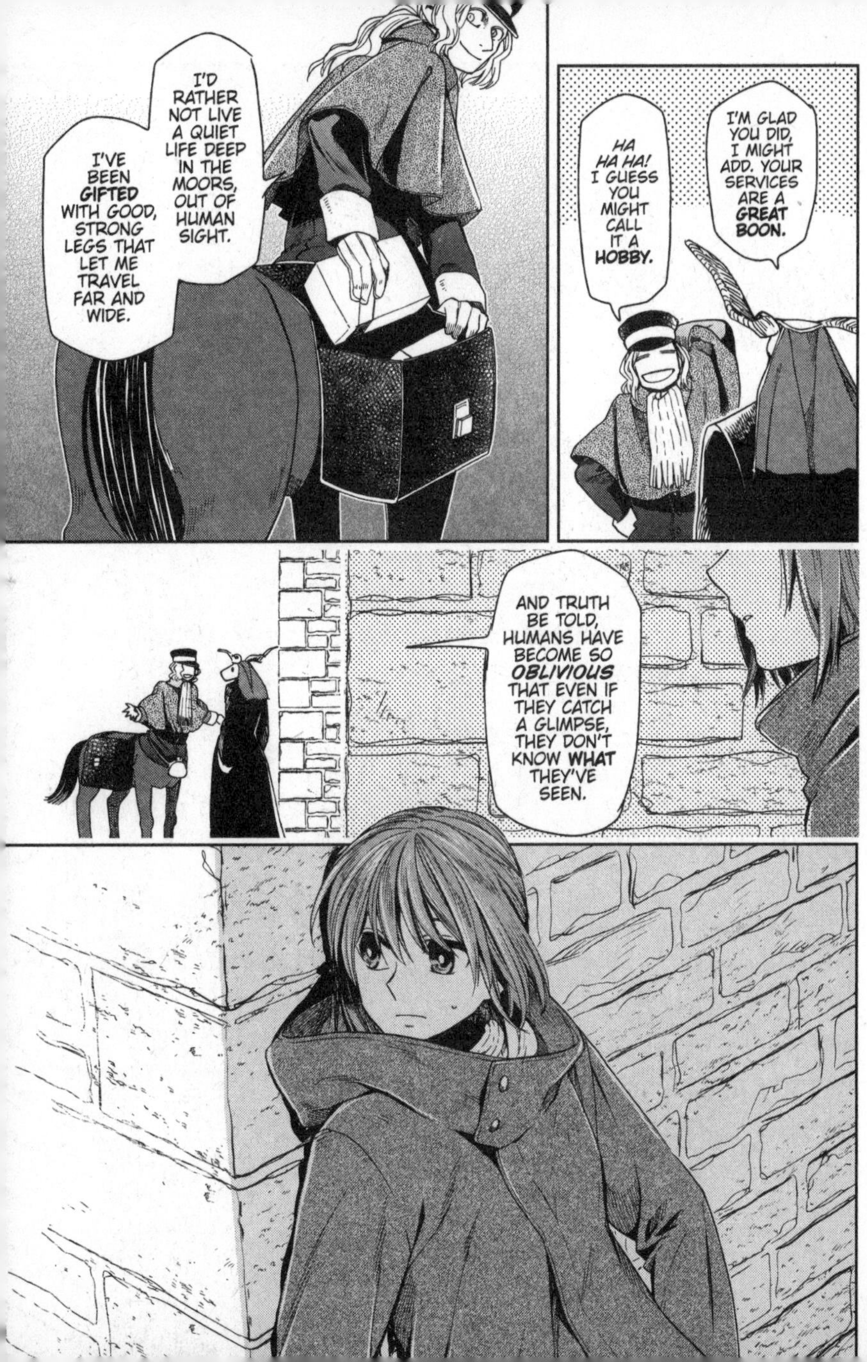

I'M GLAD YOU DID, I MIGHT ADD. YOUR SERVICES ARE A GREAT BOON.
HA HA HA! I GUESS YOU MIGHT CALL IT A HOBBY.
I'D RATHER NOT LIVE A QUIET LIFE DEEP IN THE MOORS, OUT OF HUMAN SIGHT.
I'VE BEEN GIFTED WITH GOOD, STRONG LEGS THAT LET ME TRAVEL FAR AND WIDE.
AND TRUTH BE TOLD, HUMANS HAVE BECOME SO OBLIVIOUS THAT EVEN IF THEY CATCH A GLIMPSE, THEY DON'T KNOW WHAT THEY'VE SEEN.

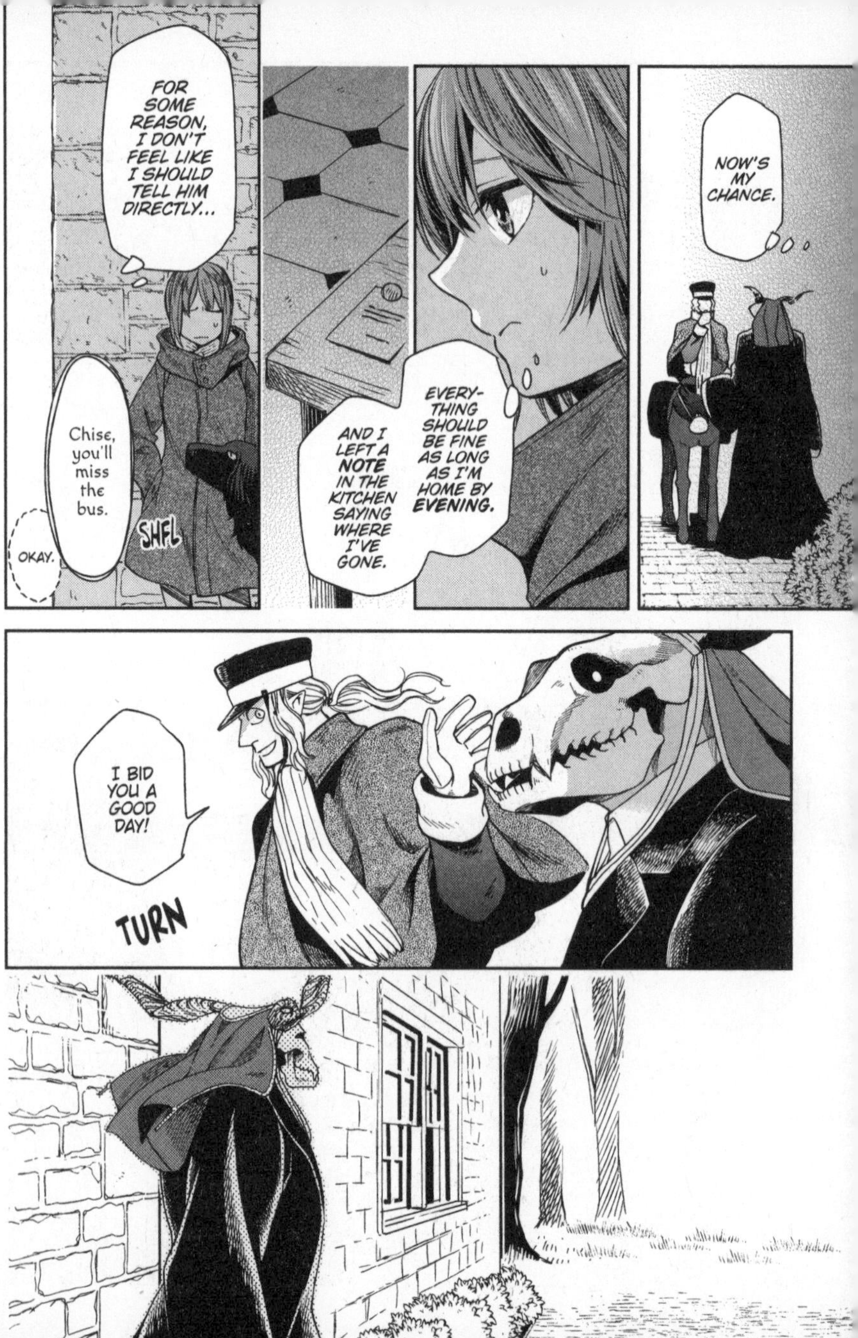
NOW'S MY CHANCE.
EVERYTHING SHOULD BE FINE AS LONG AS I'M HOME BY **EVENING.**
AND I LEFT A **NOTE** IN THE KITCHEN SAYING WHERE I'VE GONE.
FOR SOME REASON, I DON'T FEEL LIKE I SHOULD TELL HIM DIRECTLY...
Chise, you'll miss the bus.
SHFL
OKAY.
I BID YOU A GOOD DAY!
TURN

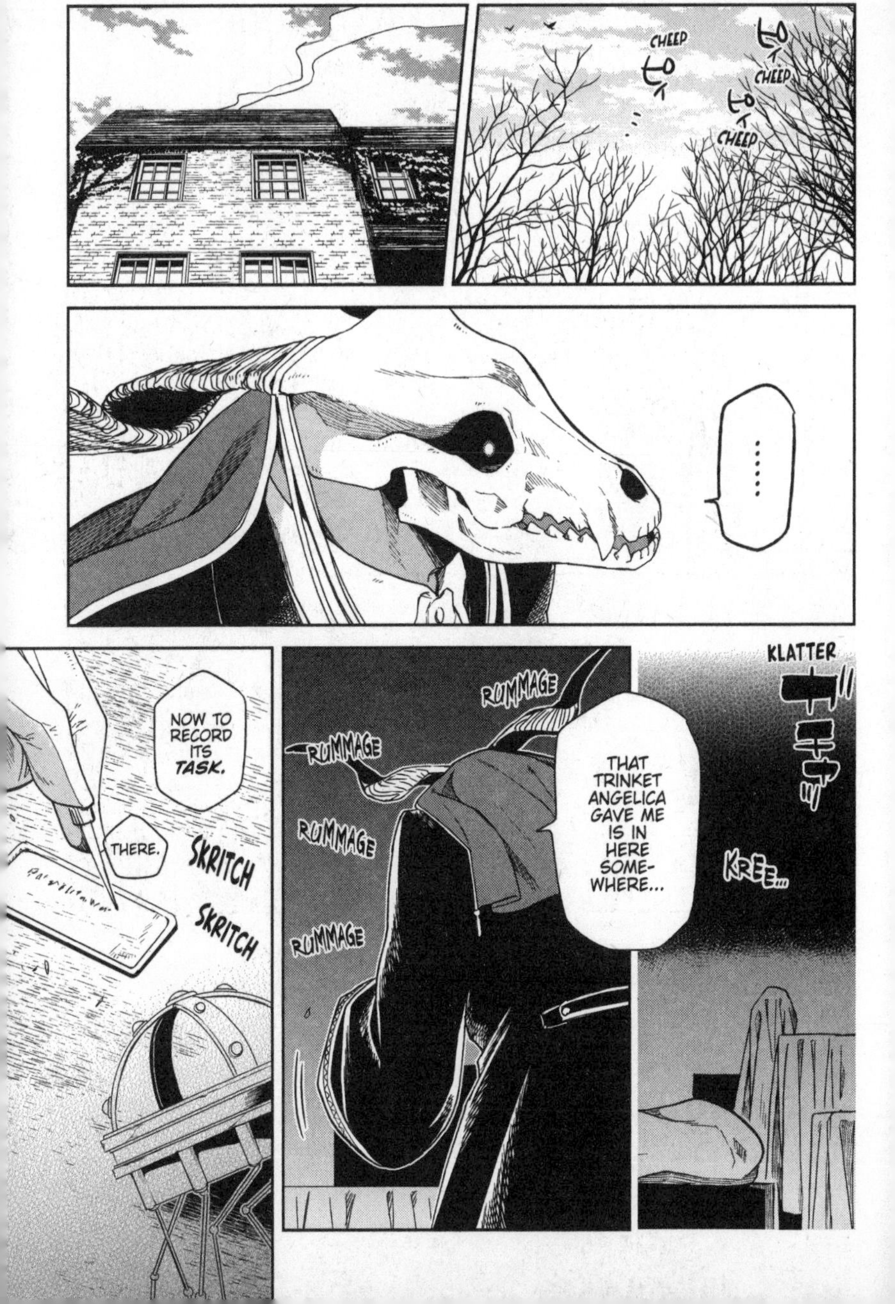
CHEEP
CHEEP
CHEEP
......
KLATTER
KREE...
RUMMAGE
RUMMAGE
THAT TRINKET ANGELICA GAVE ME IS IN HERE SOMEWHERE...
RUMMAGE
RUMMAGE
NOW TO RECORD ITS *TASK*.
THERE.
SKRITCH
SKRITCH

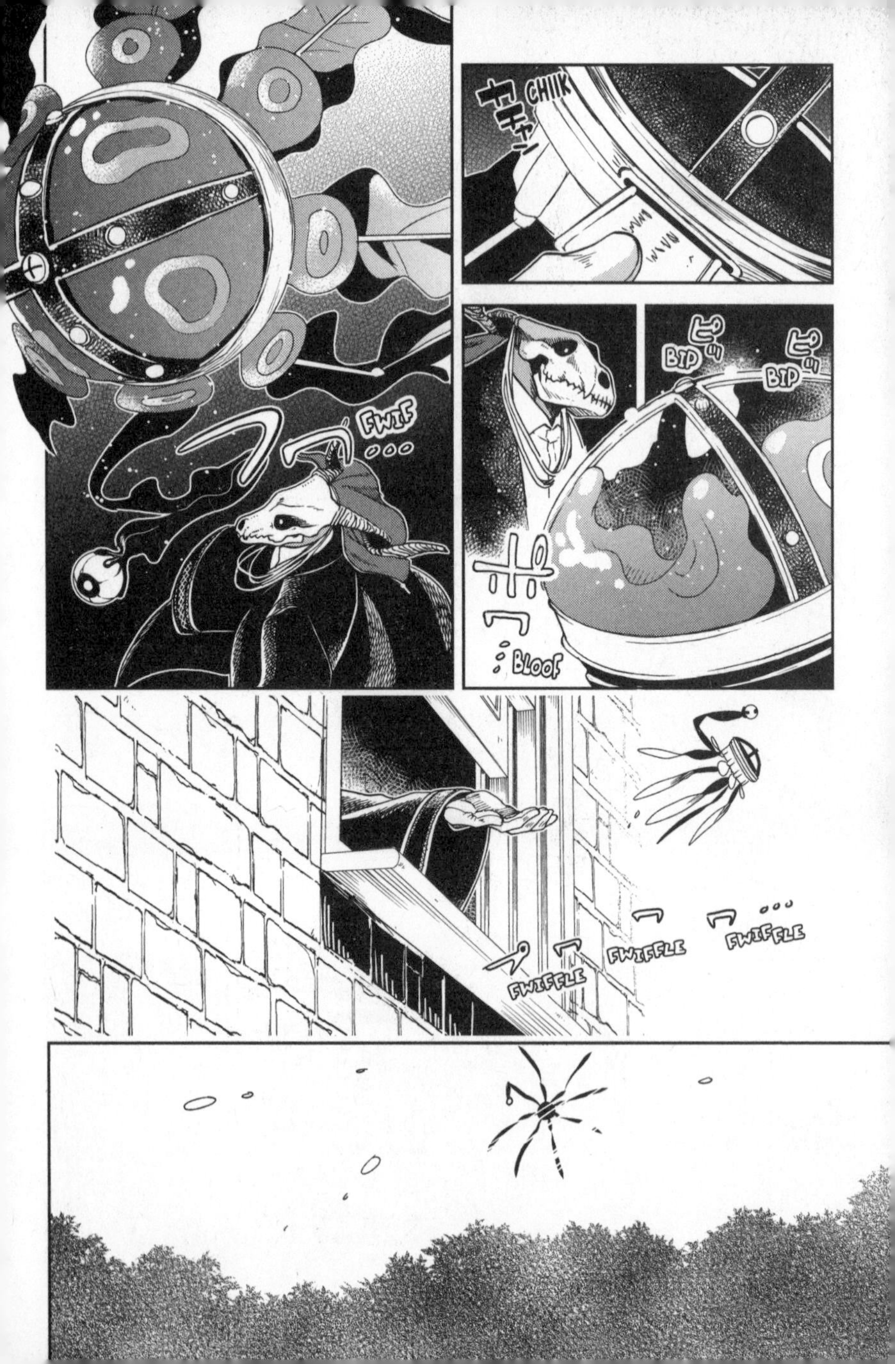

CHIIK
BIP
BIP
BLOOF
FWIF...
FWIFFLE...
FWIFFLE
FWIFFLE

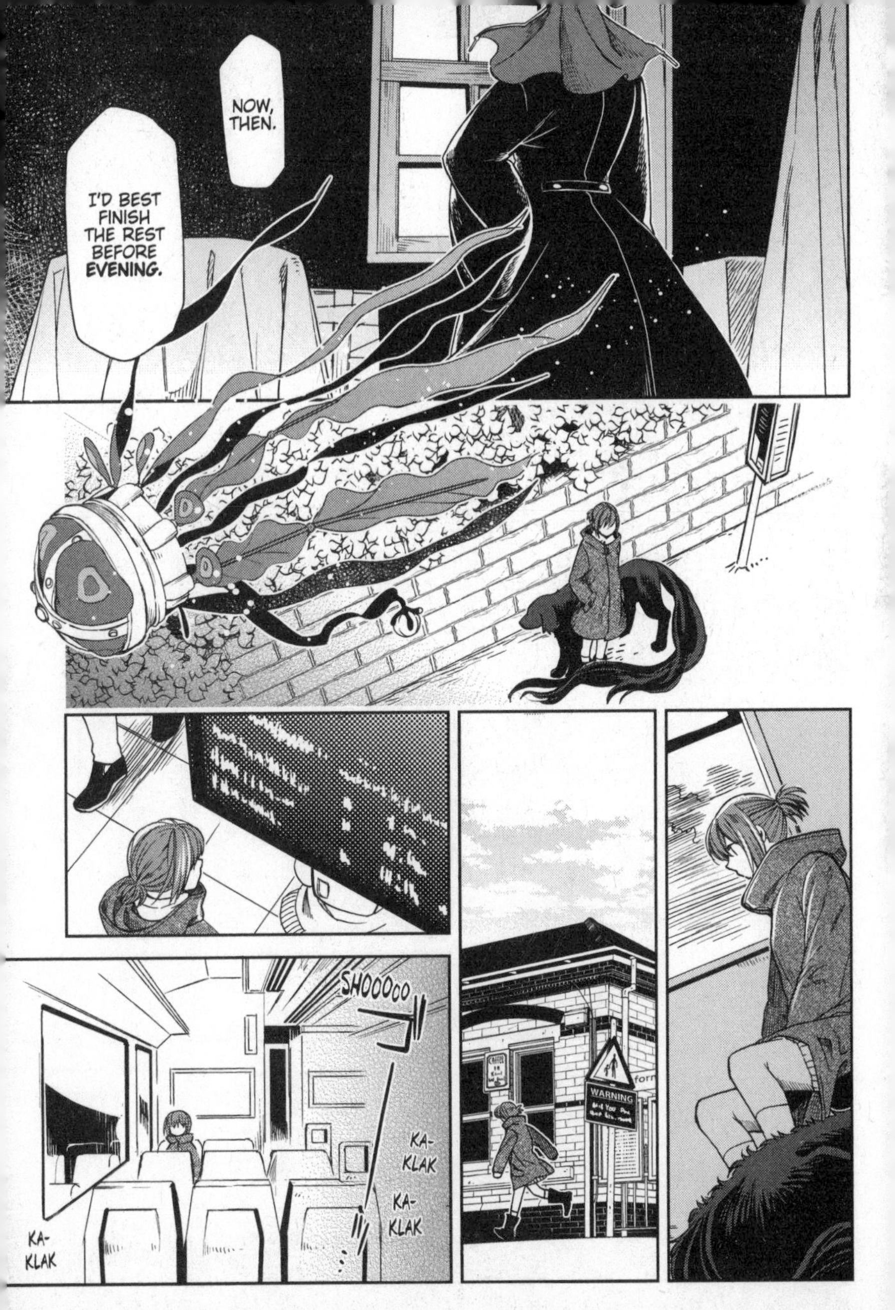
NOW, THEN.
I'D BEST FINISH THE REST BEFORE EVENING.
WARNING
SHOOOOO
KA-KLAK
KA-KLAK
KA-KLAK

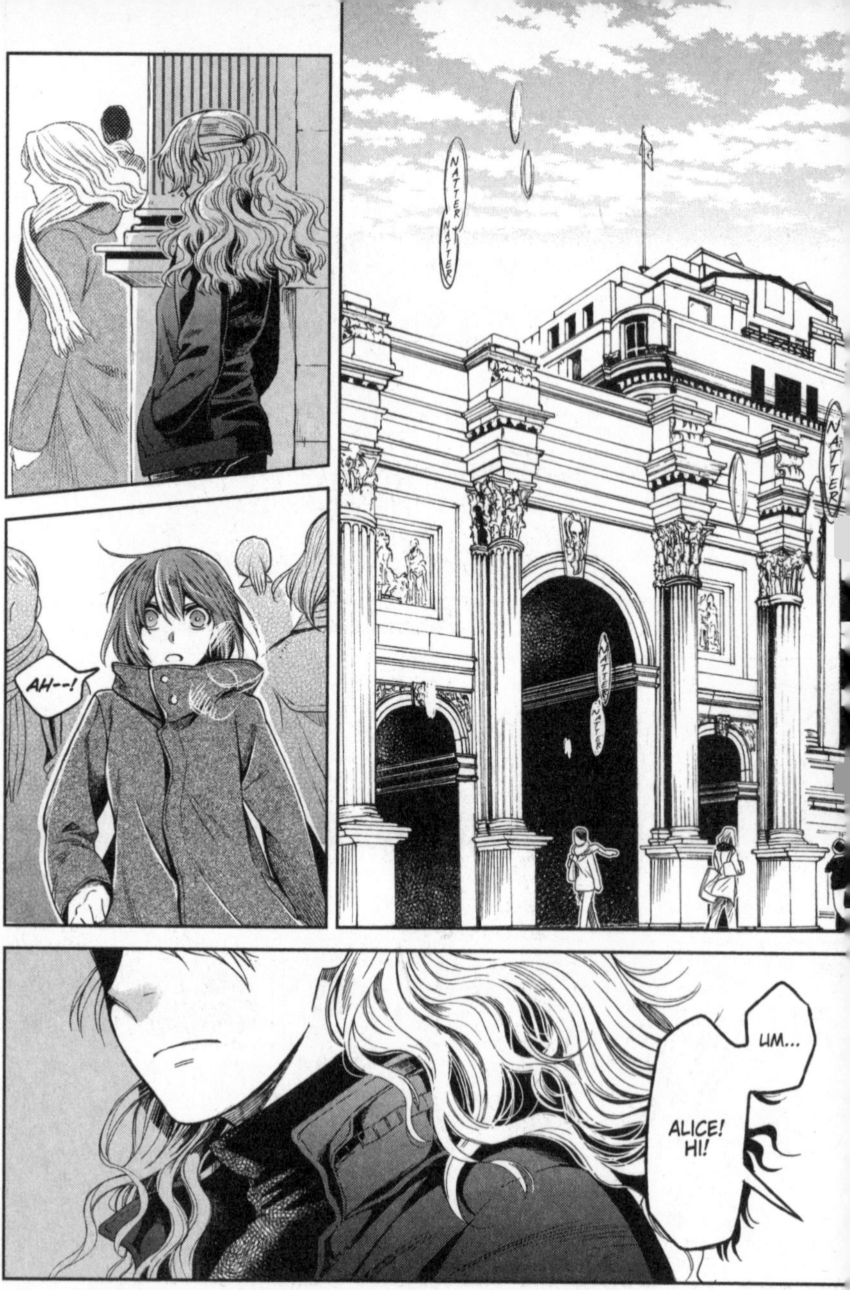
NATTER NATTER
NATTER
NATTER NATTER
AH--!
UM...
ALICE! HI!

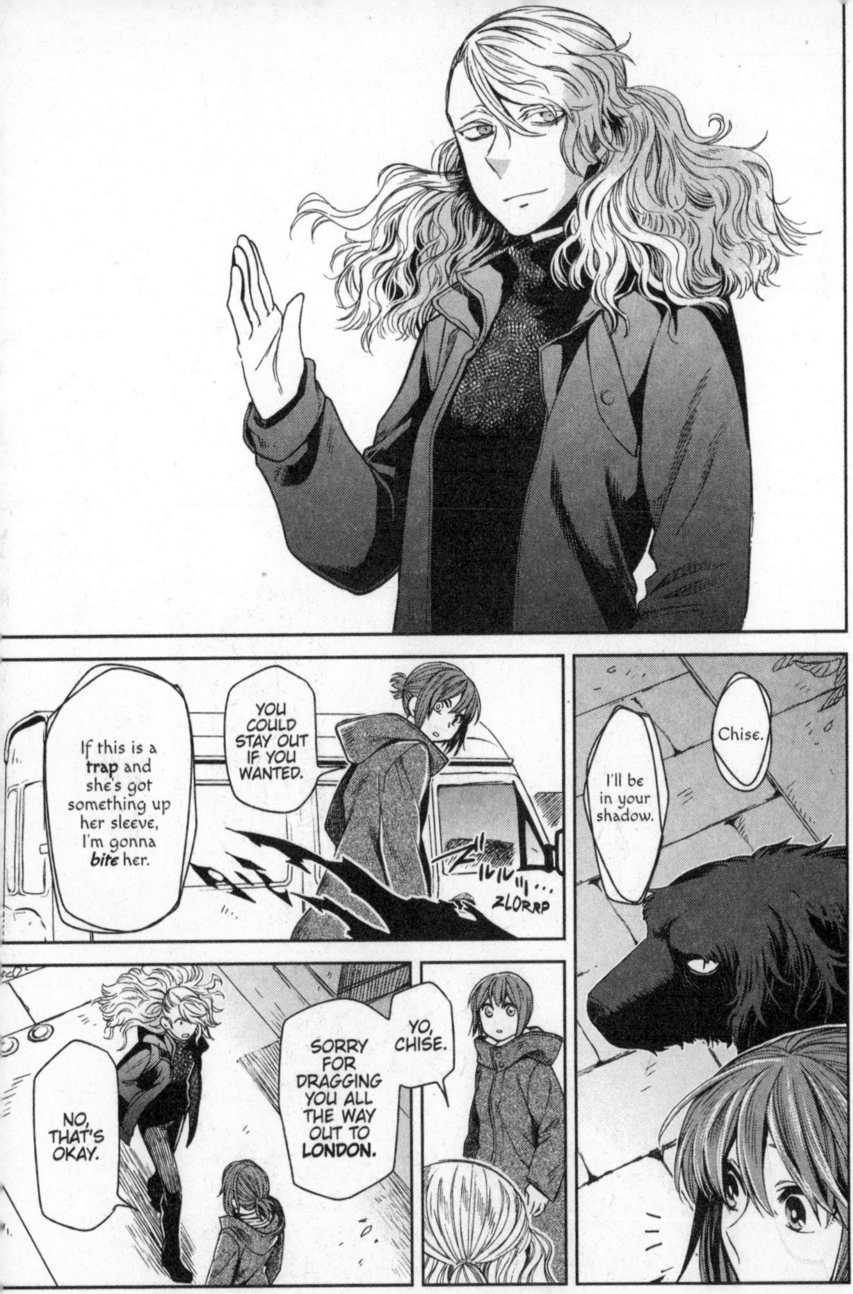
Chise.
I'll be in your shadow.
YOU COULD STAY OUT IF YOU WANTED.
If this is a trap and she's got something up her sleeve, I'm gonna bite her.
ZLORRP
YO, CHISE.
SORRY FOR DRAGGING YOU ALL THE WAY OUT TO LONDON.
NO, THAT'S OKAY.

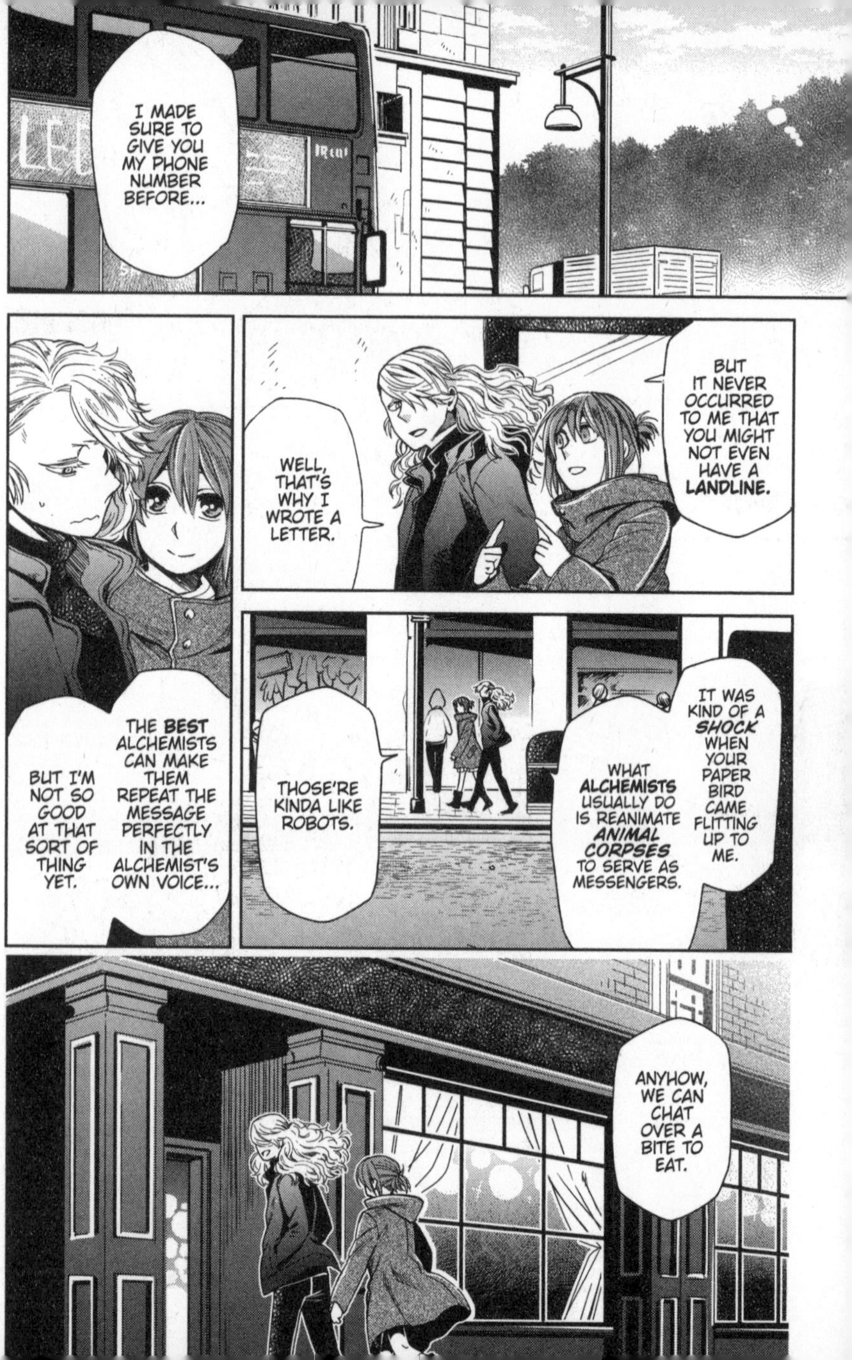
I MADE SURE TO GIVE YOU MY PHONE NUMBER BEFORE...
BUT IT NEVER OCCURRED TO ME THAT YOU MIGHT NOT EVEN HAVE A **LANDLINE.**
WELL, THAT'S WHY I WROTE A LETTER.
IT WAS KIND OF A ***SHOCK*** WHEN YOUR PAPER BIRD CAME FLITTING UP TO ME.
WHAT **ALCHEMISTS** USUALLY DO IS REANIMATE ***ANIMAL CORPSES*** TO SERVE AS MESSENGERS.
THOSE'RE KINDA LIKE ROBOTS.
THE **BEST** ALCHEMISTS CAN MAKE THEM REPEAT THE MESSAGE PERFECTLY IN THE ALCHEMIST'S OWN VOICE...
BUT I'M NOT SO GOOD AT THAT SORT OF THING YET.
ANYHOW, WE CAN CHAT OVER A BITE TO EAT.

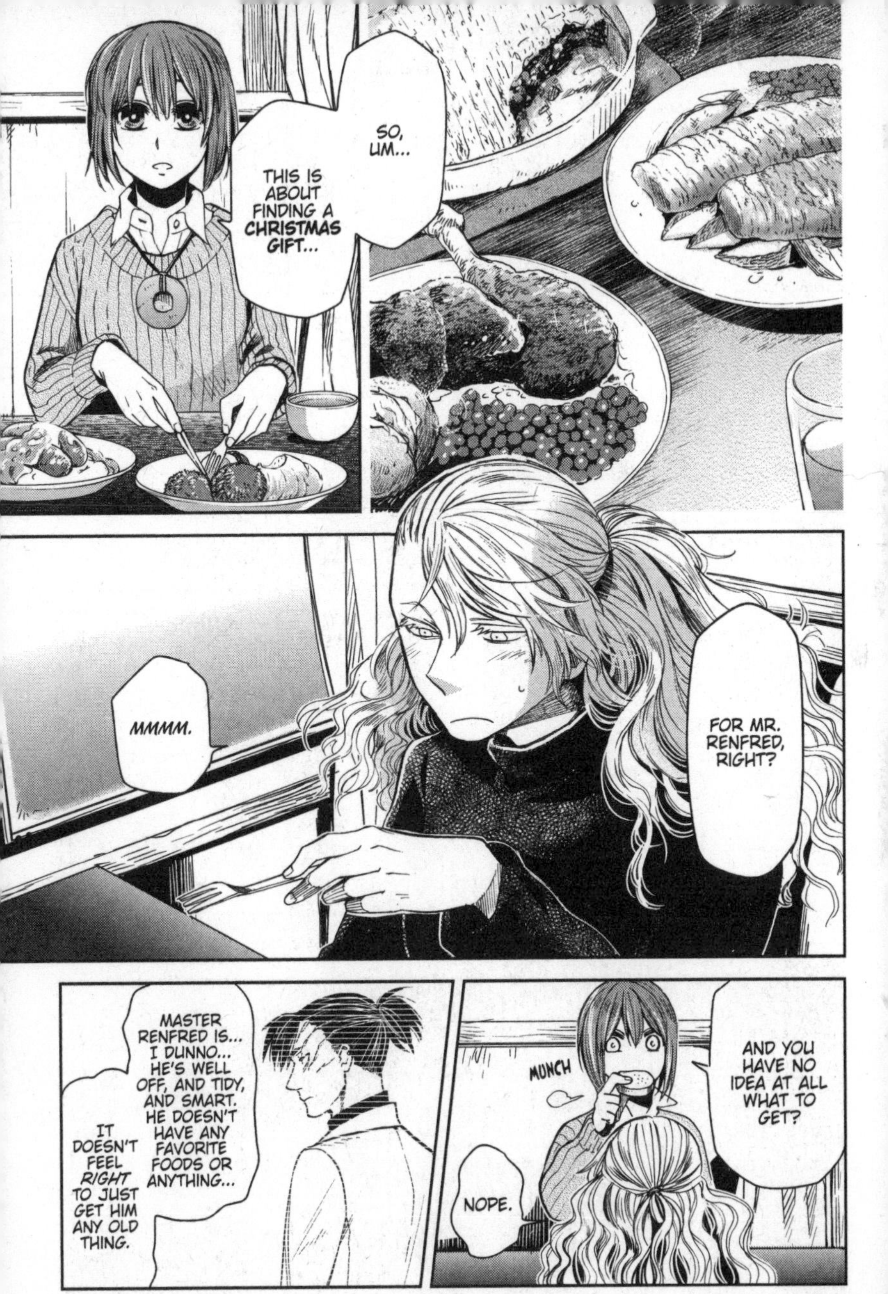
SO, UM...
THIS IS ABOUT FINDING A CHRISTMAS GIFT...
FOR MR. RENFRED, RIGHT?
MMMM.
AND YOU HAVE NO IDEA AT ALL WHAT TO GET?
MUNCH
NOPE.
MASTER RENFRED IS... I DUNNO... HE'S WELL OFF, AND TIDY, AND SMART. HE DOESN'T HAVE ANY FAVORITE FOODS OR ANYTHING...
IT DOESN'T FEEL RIGHT TO JUST GET HIM ANY OLD THING.

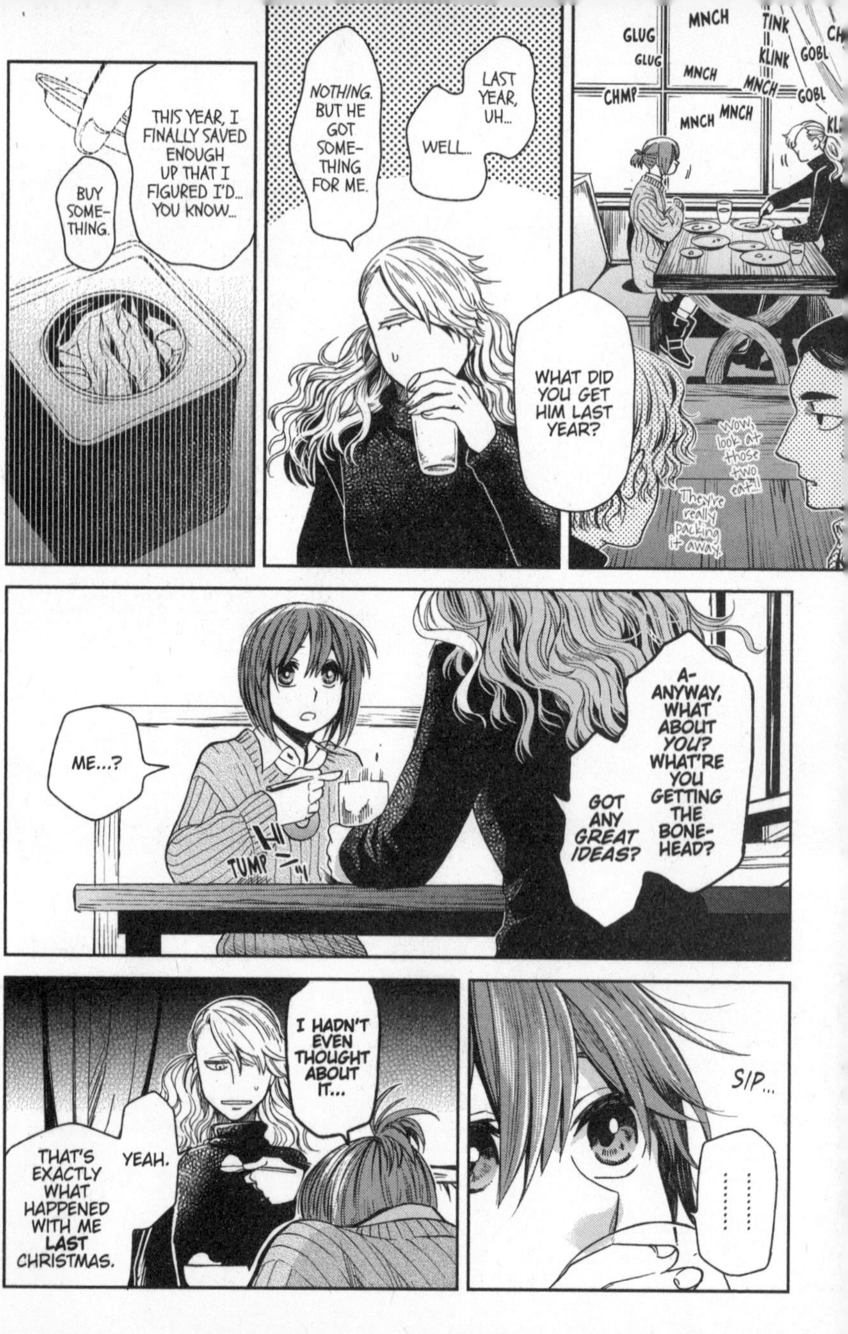
GLUG
GLUG
MNCH
MNCH
TINK
KLINK
MNCH
GOBL
GOBL
CHMP
MNCH
MNCH
WHAT DID YOU GET HIM LAST YEAR?
Wow, look at those two eat!!
They're really packing it away.
LAST YEAR, UH...
WELL...
NOTHING. BUT HE GOT SOME-THING FOR ME.
THIS YEAR, I FINALLY SAVED ENOUGH UP THAT I FIGURED I'D... YOU KNOW...
BUY SOME-THING.
A-ANYWAY, WHAT ABOUT *YOU*? WHAT'RE YOU GETTING THE BONE-HEAD?
GOT ANY GREAT IDEAS?
TUMP
ME...?
SIP...
......
I HADN'T EVEN THOUGHT ABOUT IT...
YEAH.
THAT'S EXACTLY WHAT HAPPENED WITH ME **LAST** CHRISTMAS.

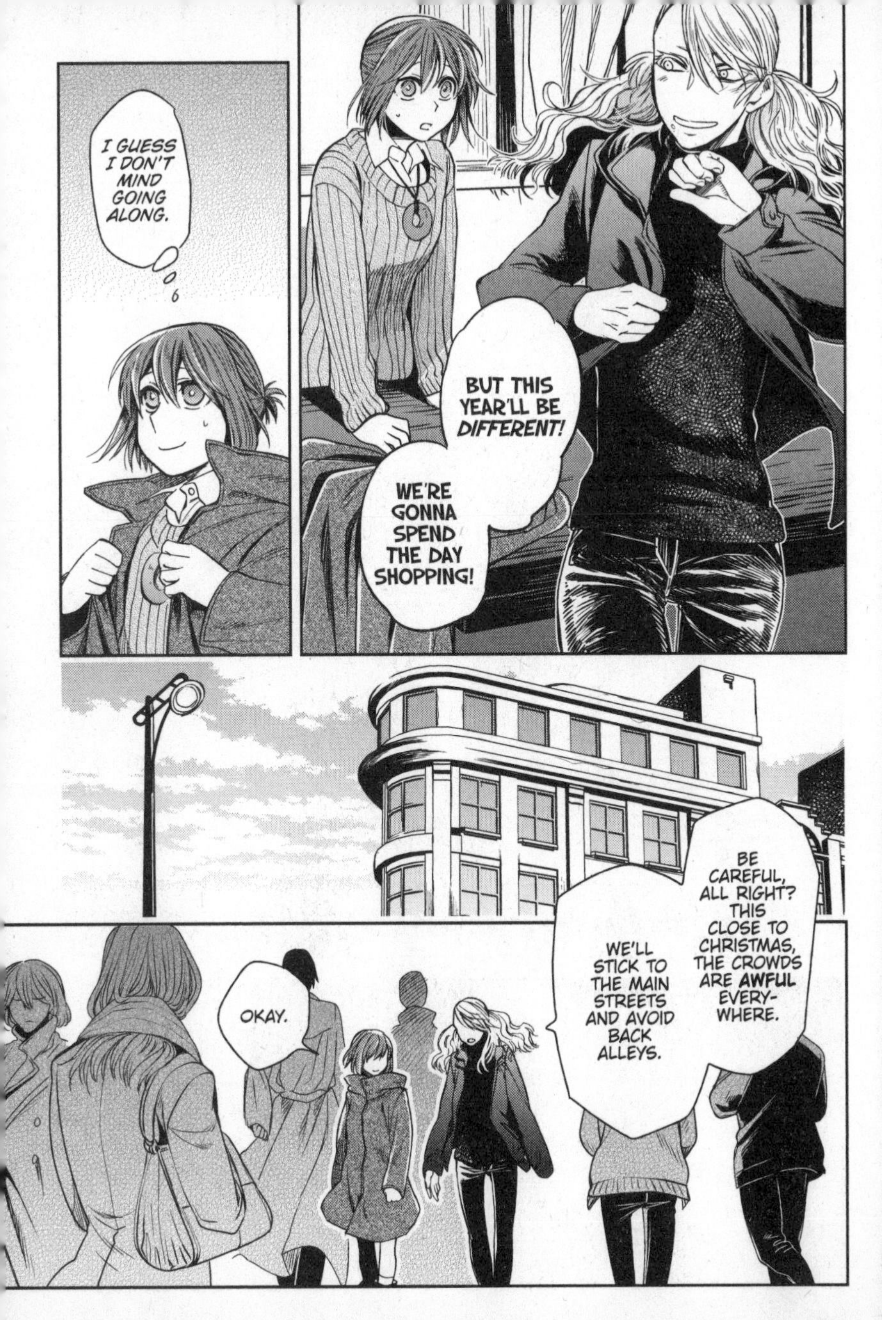
BUT THIS YEAR'LL BE *DIFFERENT!*
WE'RE GONNA SPEND THE DAY SHOPPING!
I GUESS I DON'T MIND GOING ALONG.
BE CAREFUL, ALL RIGHT? THIS CLOSE TO CHRISTMAS, THE CROWDS ARE **AWFUL** EVERY-WHERE.
WE'LL STICK TO THE MAIN STREETS AND AVOID BACK ALLEYS.
OKAY.

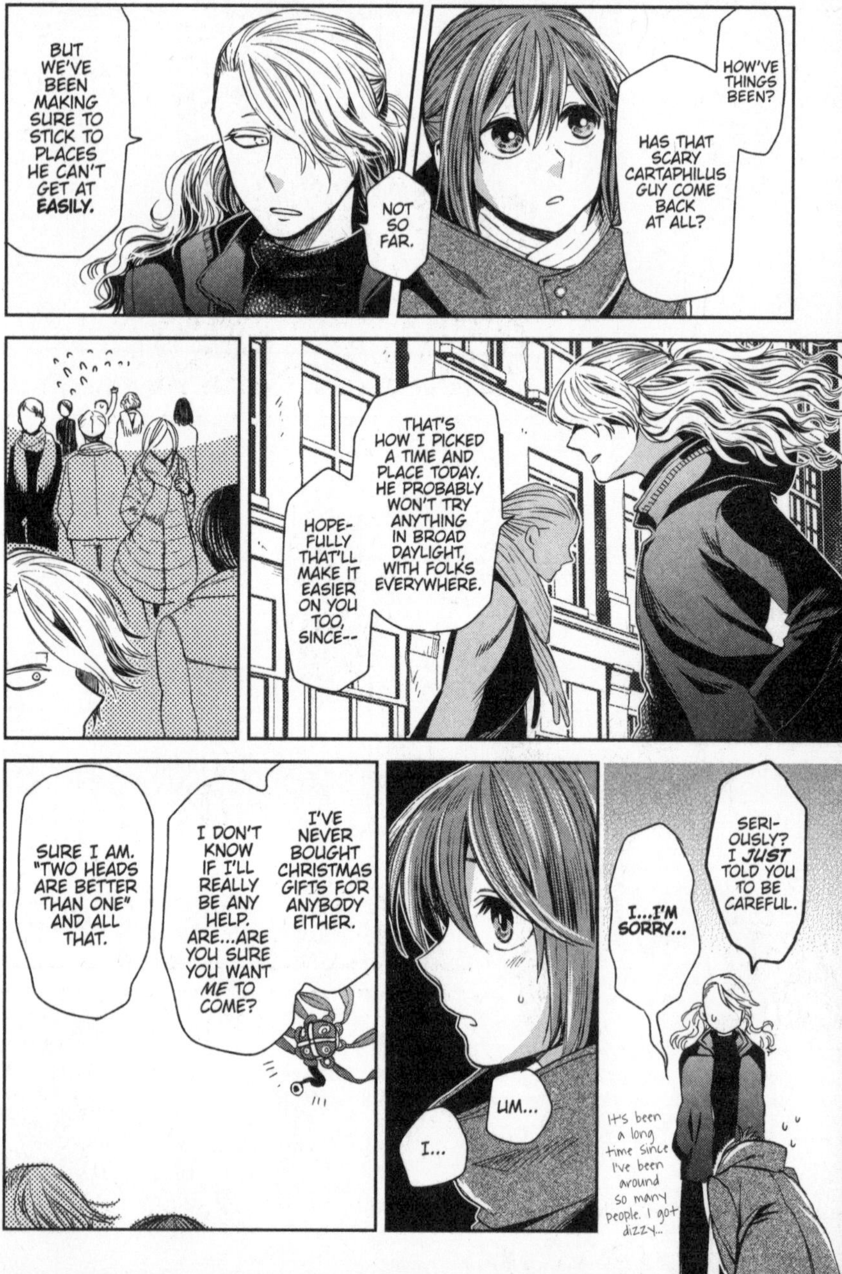
HOW'VE THINGS BEEN?
HAS THAT SCARY CARTAPHILUS GUY COME BACK AT ALL?
NOT SO FAR.
BUT WE'VE BEEN MAKING SURE TO STICK TO PLACES HE CAN'T GET AT **EASILY.**
THAT'S HOW I PICKED A TIME AND PLACE TODAY. HE PROBABLY WON'T TRY ANYTHING IN BROAD DAYLIGHT, WITH FOLKS EVERYWHERE.
HOPEFULLY THAT'LL MAKE IT EASIER ON YOU TOO, SINCE--
SERIOUSLY? I *JUST* TOLD YOU TO BE CAREFUL.
I...I'M SORRY...
It's been a long time since I've been around so many people. I got dizzy...
UM...
I...
I'VE NEVER BOUGHT CHRISTMAS GIFTS FOR ANYBODY EITHER.
I DON'T KNOW IF I'LL REALLY BE ANY HELP. ARE...ARE YOU SURE YOU WANT *ME* TO COME?
SURE I AM. "TWO HEADS ARE BETTER THAN ONE" AND ALL THAT.

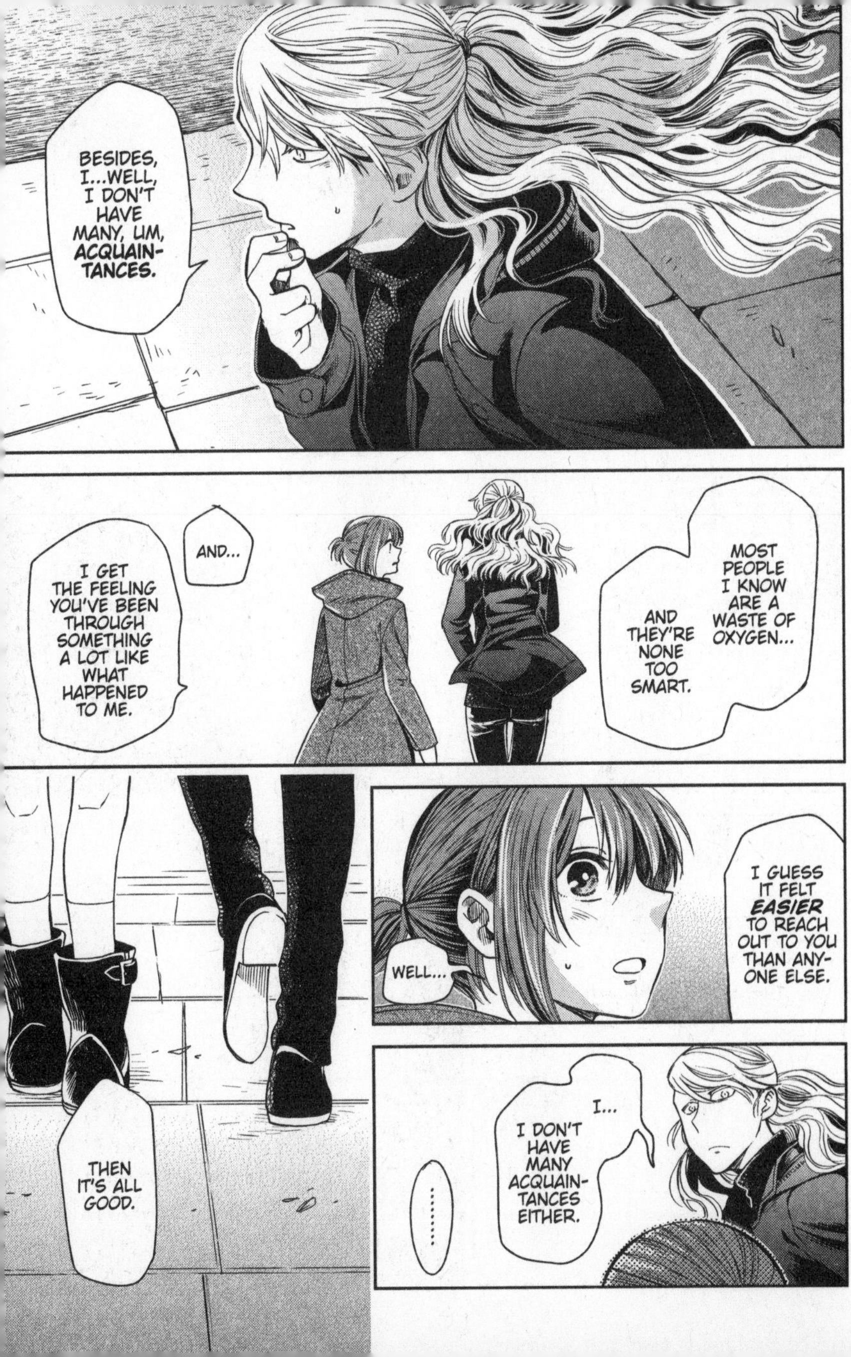
BESIDES, I...WELL, I DON'T HAVE MANY, UM, ACQUAIN-TANCES.
MOST PEOPLE I KNOW ARE A WASTE OF OXYGEN...
AND THEY'RE NONE TOO SMART.
AND...
I GET THE FEELING YOU'VE BEEN THROUGH SOMETHING A LOT LIKE WHAT HAPPENED TO ME.
I GUESS IT FELT EASIER TO REACH OUT TO YOU THAN ANY-ONE ELSE.
WELL...
I...
I DON'T HAVE MANY ACQUAIN-TANCES EITHER.
......
THEN IT'S ALL GOOD.

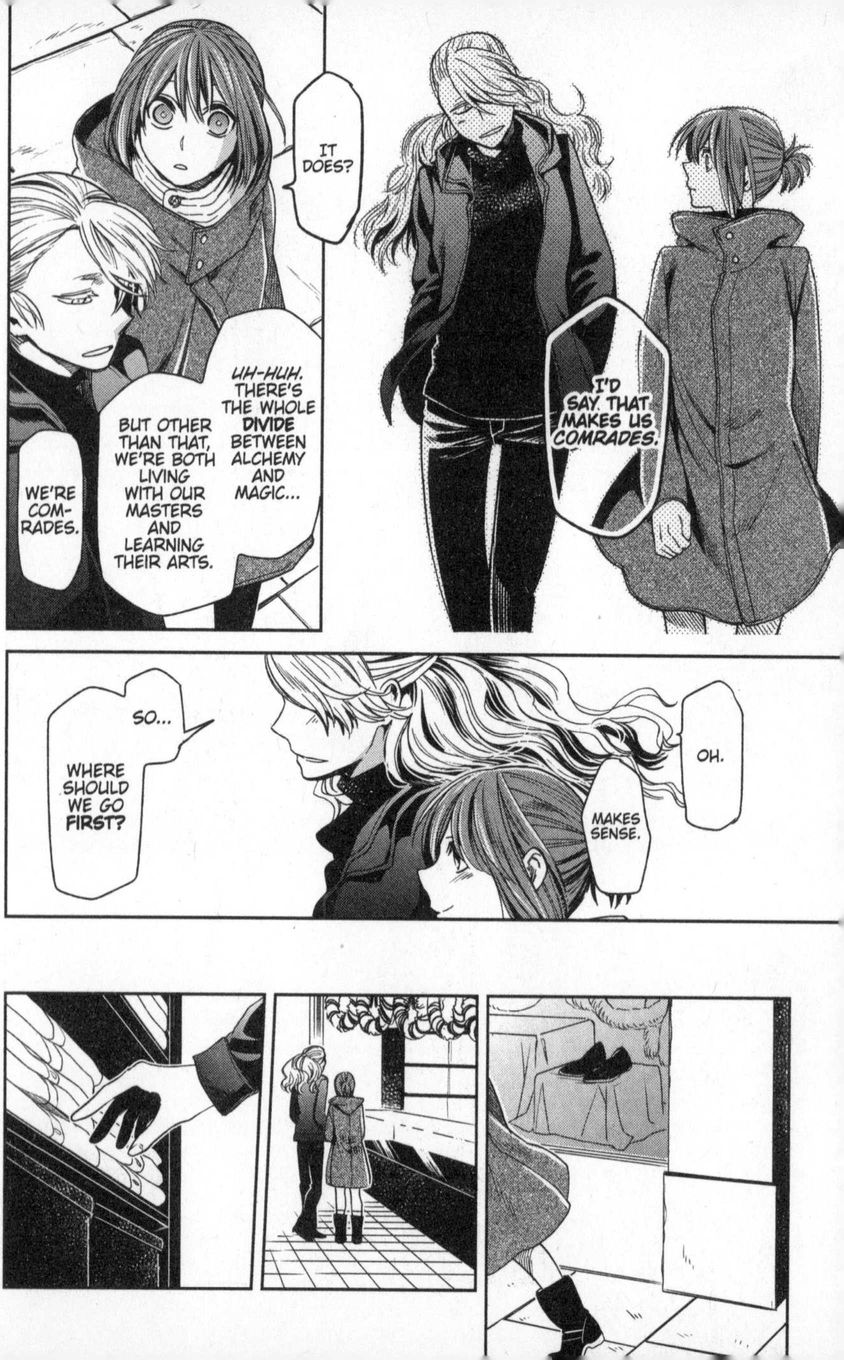
I'D SAY THAT MAKES US COMRADES.
IT DOES?
UH-HUH. THERE'S THE WHOLE **DIVIDE** BETWEEN ALCHEMY AND MAGIC...
BUT OTHER THAN THAT, WE'RE BOTH LIVING WITH OUR MASTERS AND LEARNING THEIR ARTS.
WE'RE COM-RADES.
OH.
MAKES SENSE.
SO...
WHERE SHOULD WE GO **FIRST?**

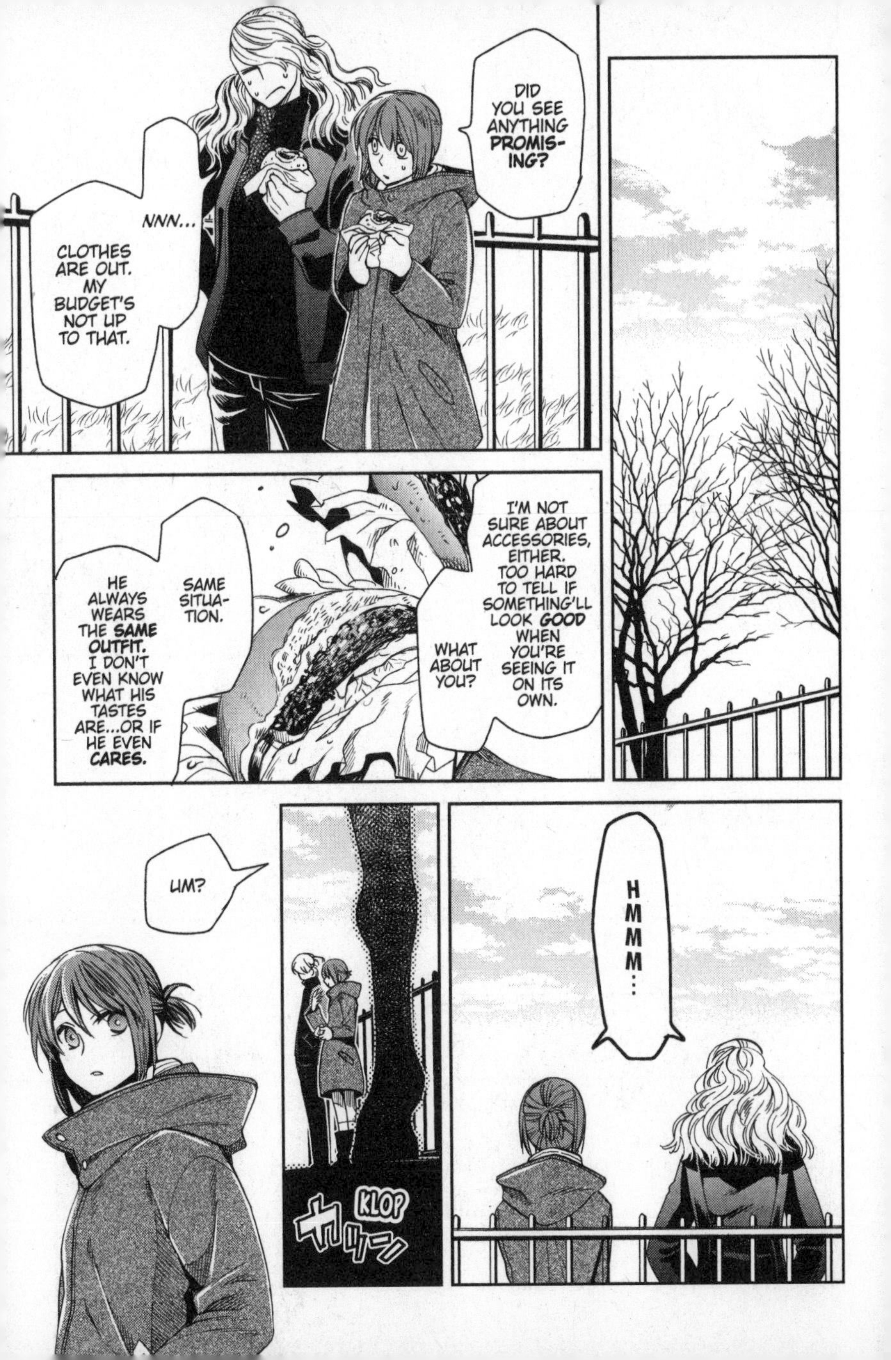

DID YOU SEE ANYTHING PROMISING?
NNN...
CLOTHES ARE OUT. MY BUDGET'S NOT UP TO THAT.
I'M NOT SURE ABOUT ACCESSORIES, EITHER. TOO HARD TO TELL IF SOMETHING'LL LOOK GOOD WHEN YOU'RE SEEING IT ON ITS OWN.
WHAT ABOUT YOU?
SAME SITUATION.
HE ALWAYS WEARS THE SAME OUTFIT. I DON'T EVEN KNOW WHAT HIS TASTES ARE...OR IF HE EVEN CARES.
HMMM...
KLOP
UM?

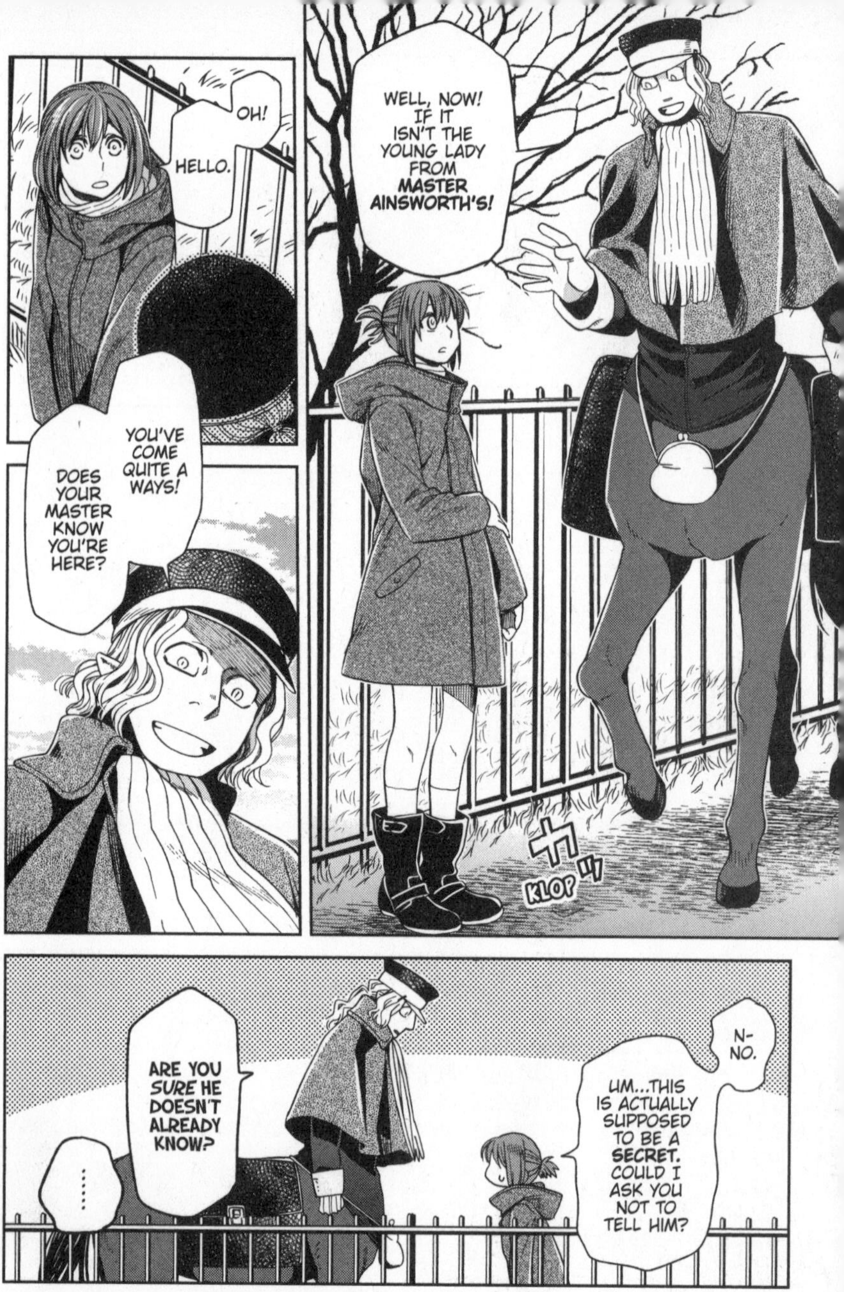
WELL, NOW! IF IT ISN'T THE YOUNG LADY FROM MASTER AINSWORTH'S!
KLOP
OH!
HELLO.
YOU'VE COME QUITE A WAYS!
DOES YOUR MASTER KNOW YOU'RE HERE?
N-NO.
UM...THIS IS ACTUALLY SUPPOSED TO BE A SECRET. COULD I ASK YOU NOT TO TELL HIM?
ARE YOU *SURE* HE DOESN'T ALREADY KNOW?
......

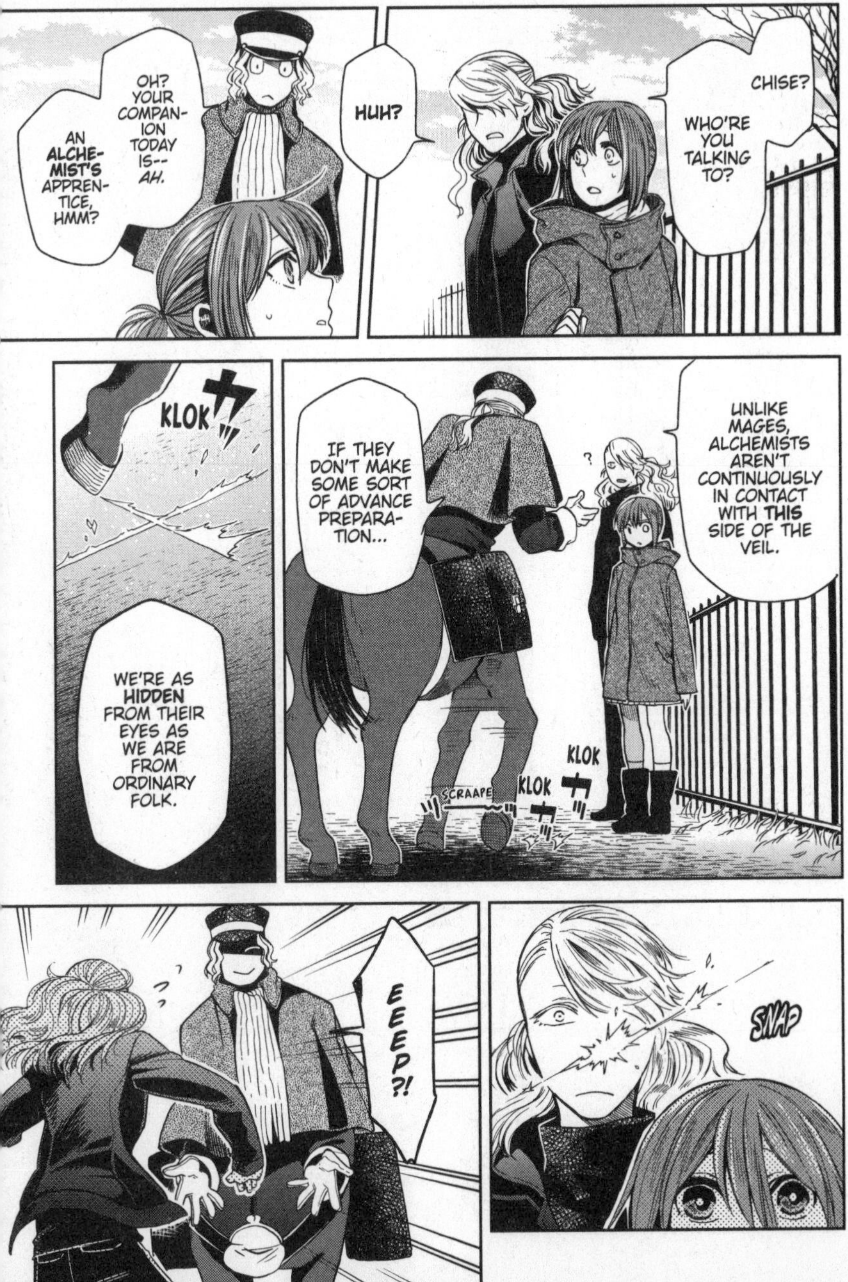
CHISE?
WHO'RE YOU TALKING TO?
HUH?
OH? YOUR COMPANION TODAY IS-- AH.
AN ALCHEMIST'S APPRENTICE, HMM?
UNLIKE MAGES, ALCHEMISTS AREN'T CONTINUOUSLY IN CONTACT WITH THIS SIDE OF THE VEIL.
IF THEY DON'T MAKE SOME SORT OF ADVANCE PREPARATION...
KLOK
KLOK
SCRAAPE
KLOK
WE'RE AS HIDDEN FROM THEIR EYES AS WE ARE FROM ORDINARY FOLK.
SNAP
EEEEP?!

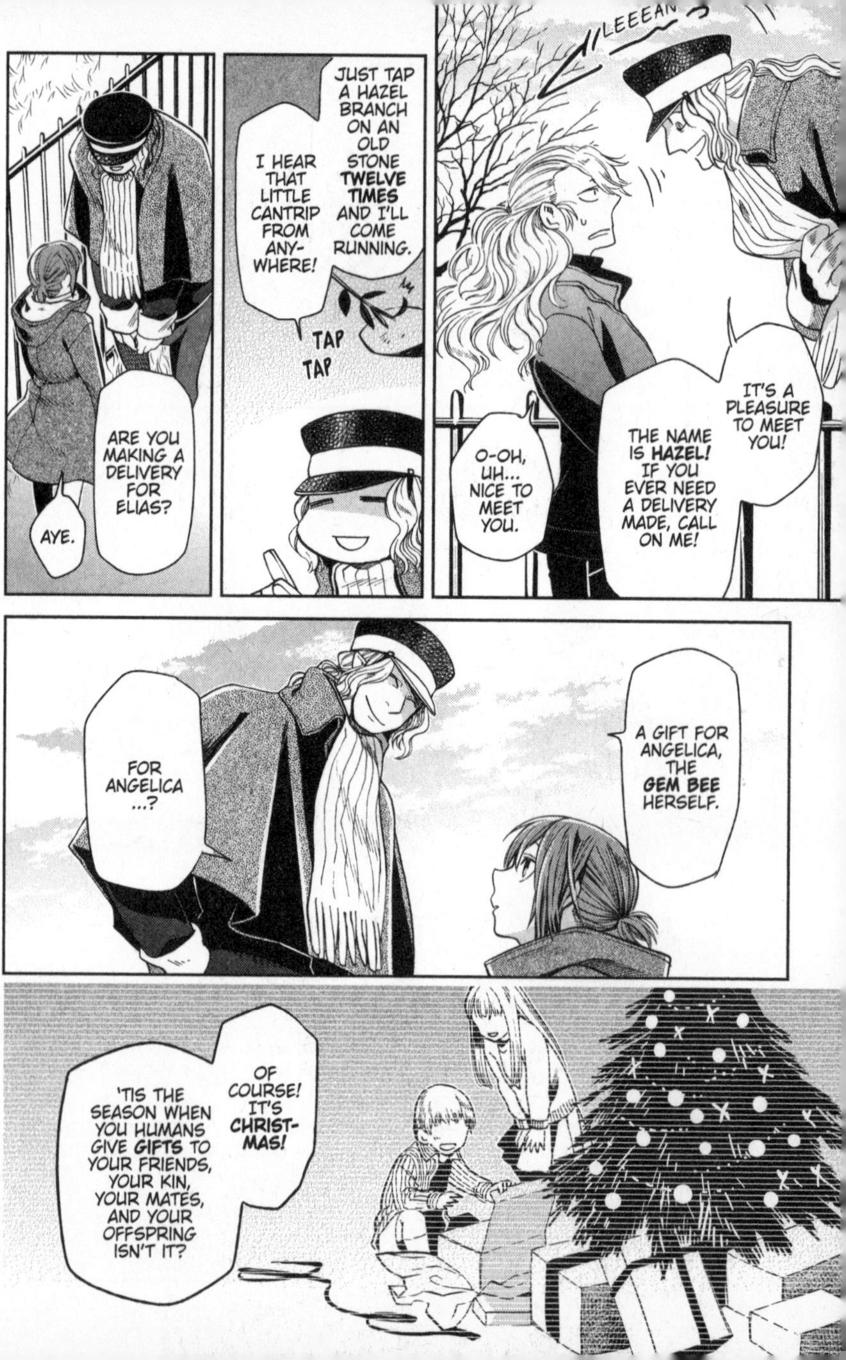
LEEEAN~
IT'S A PLEASURE TO MEET YOU!
THE NAME IS HAZEL! IF YOU EVER NEED A DELIVERY MADE, CALL ON ME!
O-OH, UH... NICE TO MEET YOU.
JUST TAP A HAZEL BRANCH ON AN OLD STONE TWELVE TIMES AND I'LL COME RUNNING.
I HEAR THAT LITTLE CANTRIP FROM ANY-WHERE!
TAP TAP
ARE YOU MAKING A DELIVERY FOR ELIAS?
AYE.
A GIFT FOR ANGELICA, THE GEM BEE HERSELF.
FOR ANGELICA ...?
OF COURSE! IT'S CHRIST-MAS!
'TIS THE SEASON WHEN YOU HUMANS GIVE GIFTS TO YOUR FRIENDS, YOUR KIN, YOUR MATES, AND YOUR OFFSPRING ISN'T IT?

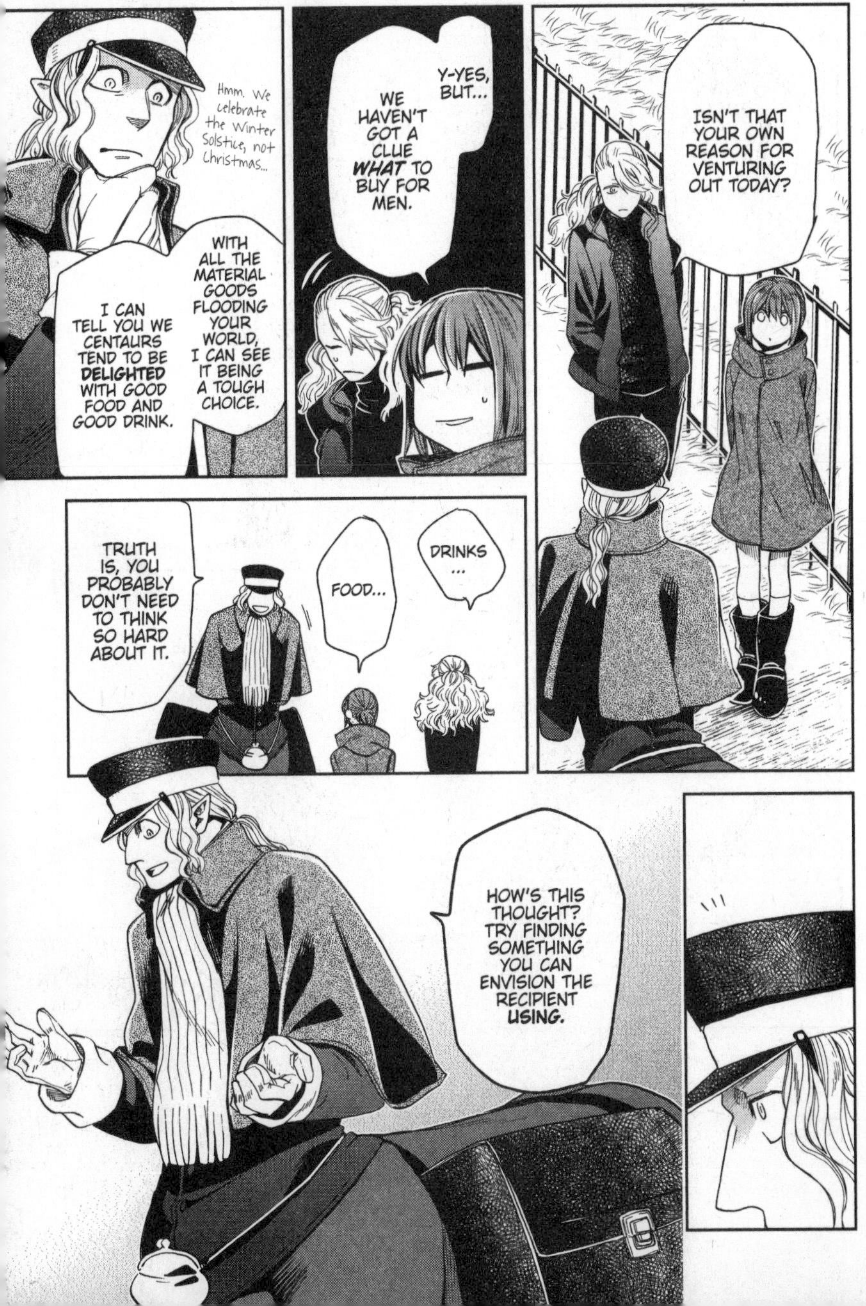
ISN'T THAT YOUR OWN REASON FOR VENTURING OUT TODAY?
Y-YES, BUT...
WE HAVEN'T GOT A CLUE **WHAT** TO BUY FOR MEN.
Hmm. We celebrate the Winter Solstice, not Christmas...
WITH ALL THE MATERIAL GOODS FLOODING YOUR WORLD, I CAN SEE IT BEING A TOUGH CHOICE.
I CAN TELL YOU WE CENTAURS TEND TO BE **DELIGHTED** WITH GOOD FOOD AND GOOD DRINK.
DRINKS...
FOOD...
TRUTH IS, YOU PROBABLY DON'T NEED TO THINK SO HARD ABOUT IT.
HOW'S THIS THOUGHT? TRY FINDING SOMETHING YOU CAN ENVISION THE RECIPIENT **USING.**

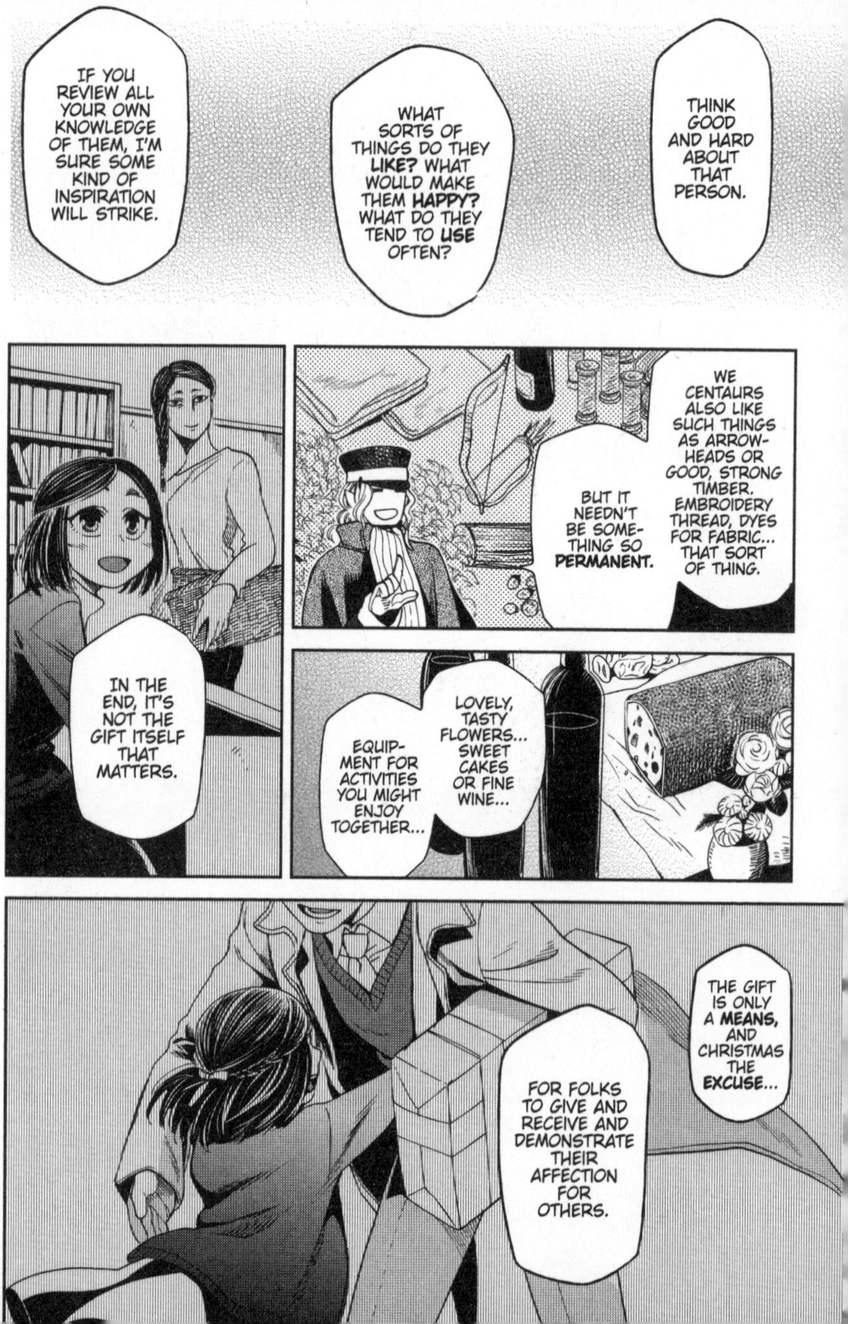
THINK GOOD AND HARD ABOUT THAT PERSON.
WHAT SORTS OF THINGS DO THEY **LIKE?** WHAT WOULD MAKE THEM **HAPPY?** WHAT DO THEY TEND TO **USE** OFTEN?
IF YOU REVIEW ALL YOUR OWN KNOWLEDGE OF THEM, I'M SURE SOME KIND OF INSPIRATION WILL STRIKE.
WE CENTAURS ALSO LIKE SUCH THINGS AS ARROW-HEADS OR GOOD, STRONG TIMBER. EMBROIDERY THREAD, DYES FOR FABRIC... THAT SORT OF THING.
BUT IT NEEDN'T BE SOME-THING SO **PERMANENT.**
LOVELY, TASTY FLOWERS... SWEET CAKES OR FINE WINE...
EQUIP-MENT FOR ACTIVITIES YOU MIGHT ENJOY TOGETHER...
IN THE END, IT'S NOT THE GIFT ITSELF THAT MATTERS.
THE GIFT IS ONLY A **MEANS,** AND CHRISTMAS THE **EXCUSE...**
FOR FOLKS TO GIVE AND RECEIVE AND DEMONSTRATE THEIR AFFECTION FOR OTHERS.

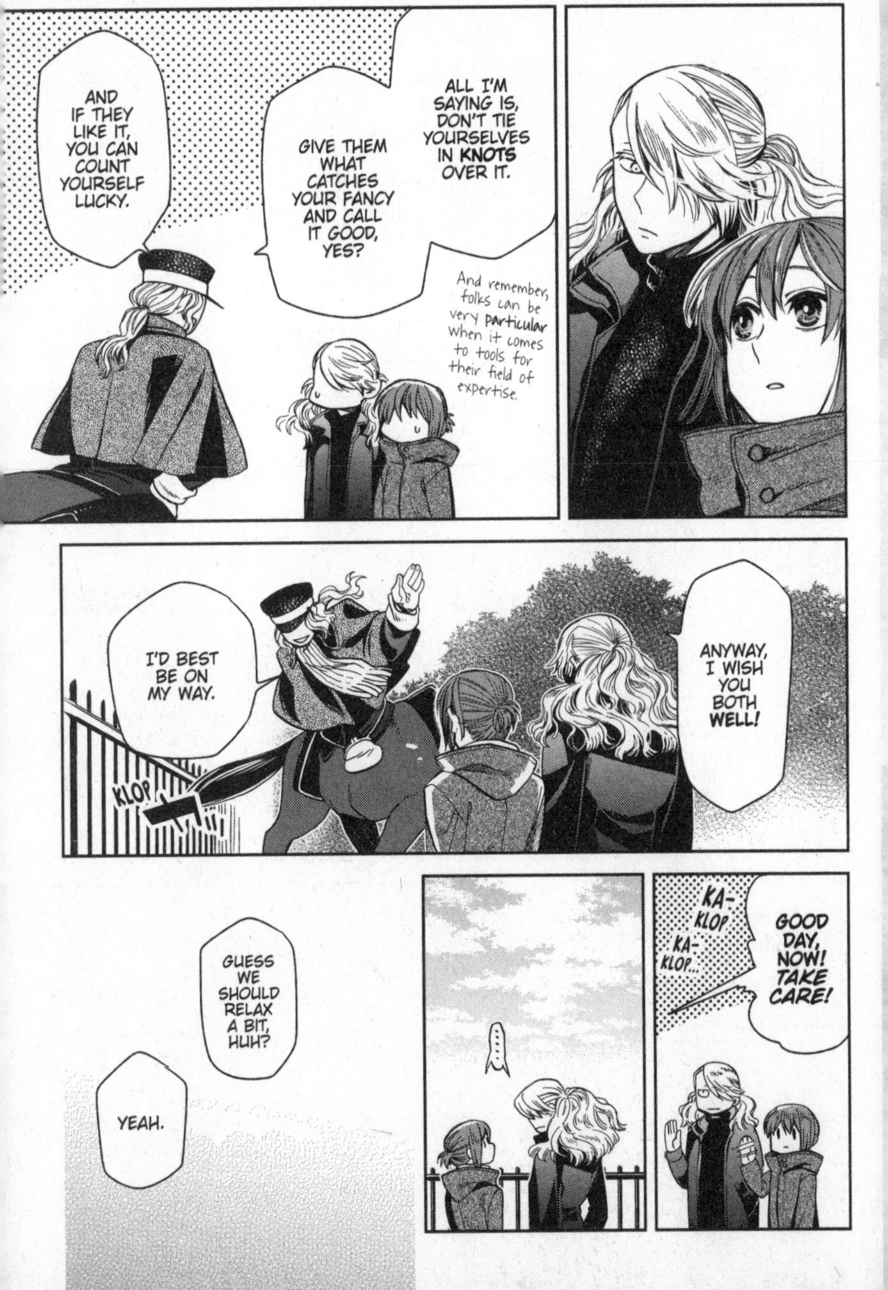
ALL I'M SAYING IS, DON'T TIE YOURSELVES IN KNOTS OVER IT.
GIVE THEM WHAT CATCHES YOUR FANCY AND CALL IT GOOD, YES?
AND IF THEY LIKE IT, YOU CAN COUNT YOURSELF LUCKY.
And remember, folks can be very particular when it comes to tools for their field of expertise.
ANYWAY, I WISH YOU BOTH WELL!
I'D BEST BE ON MY WAY.
KLOP
GOOD DAY, NOW! TAKE CARE!
KA-KLOP
KA-KLOP...
......
GUESS WE SHOULD RELAX A BIT, HUH?
YEAH.

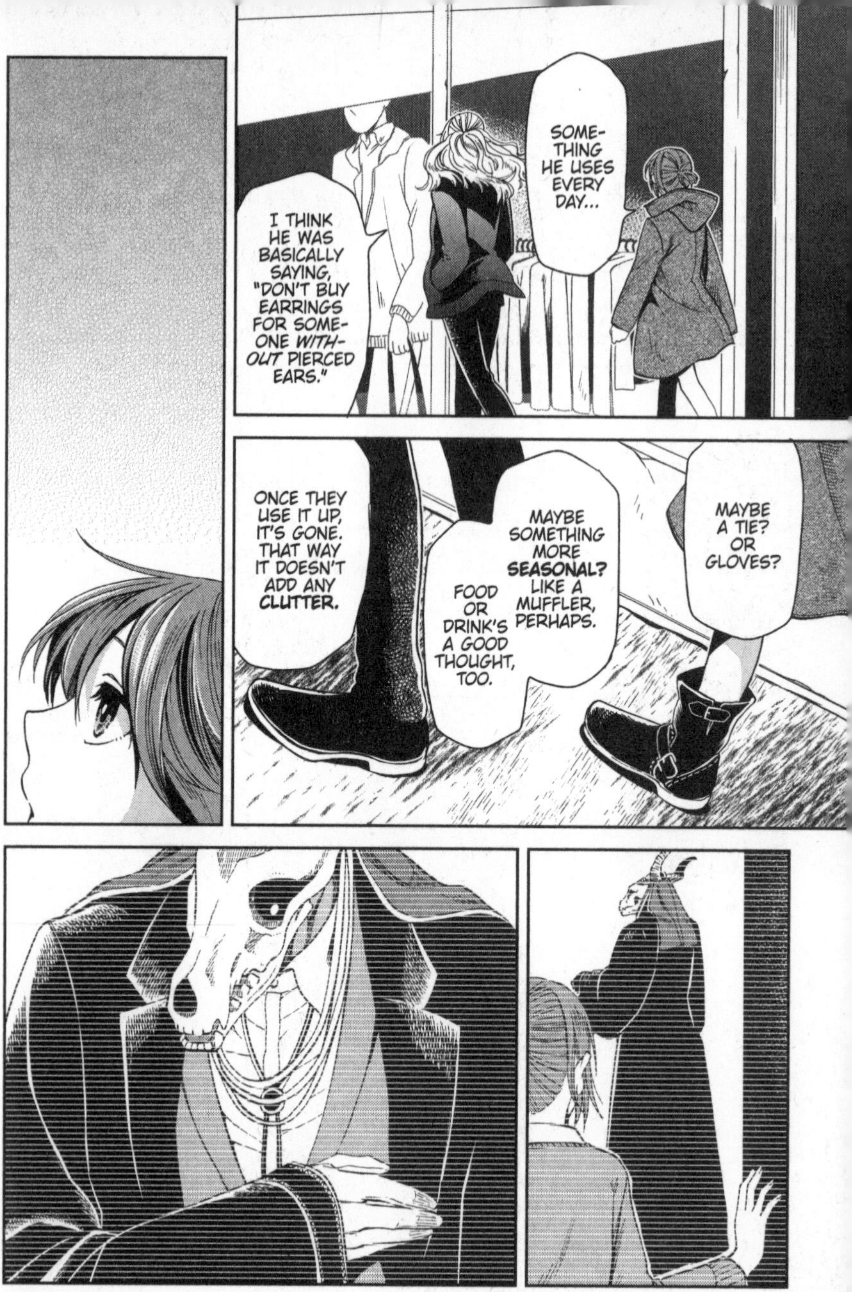
SOMETHING HE USES EVERY DAY...
I THINK HE WAS BASICALLY SAYING, "DON'T BUY EARRINGS FOR SOMEONE *WITHOUT* PIERCED EARS."
MAYBE A TIE? OR GLOVES?
MAYBE SOMETHING MORE **SEASONAL?** LIKE A MUFFLER, PERHAPS.
FOOD OR DRINK'S A GOOD THOUGHT, TOO.
ONCE THEY USE IT UP, IT'S GONE. THAT WAY IT DOESN'T ADD ANY **CLUTTER.**

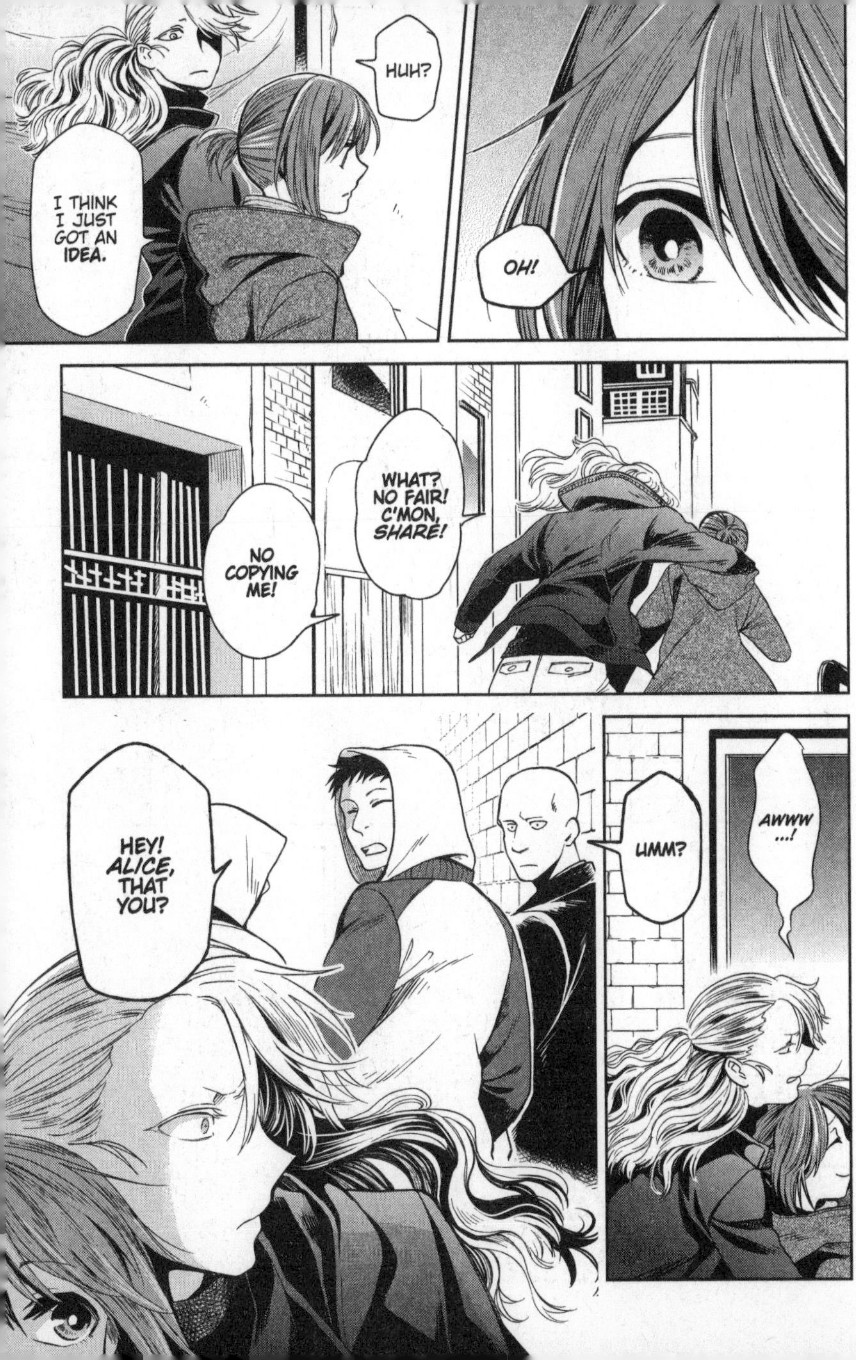
OH!
HUH?
I THINK I JUST GOT AN IDEA.
WHAT? NO FAIR! C'MON, SHARE!
NO COPYING ME!
AWWW ...!
UMM?
HEY! ALICE, THAT YOU?

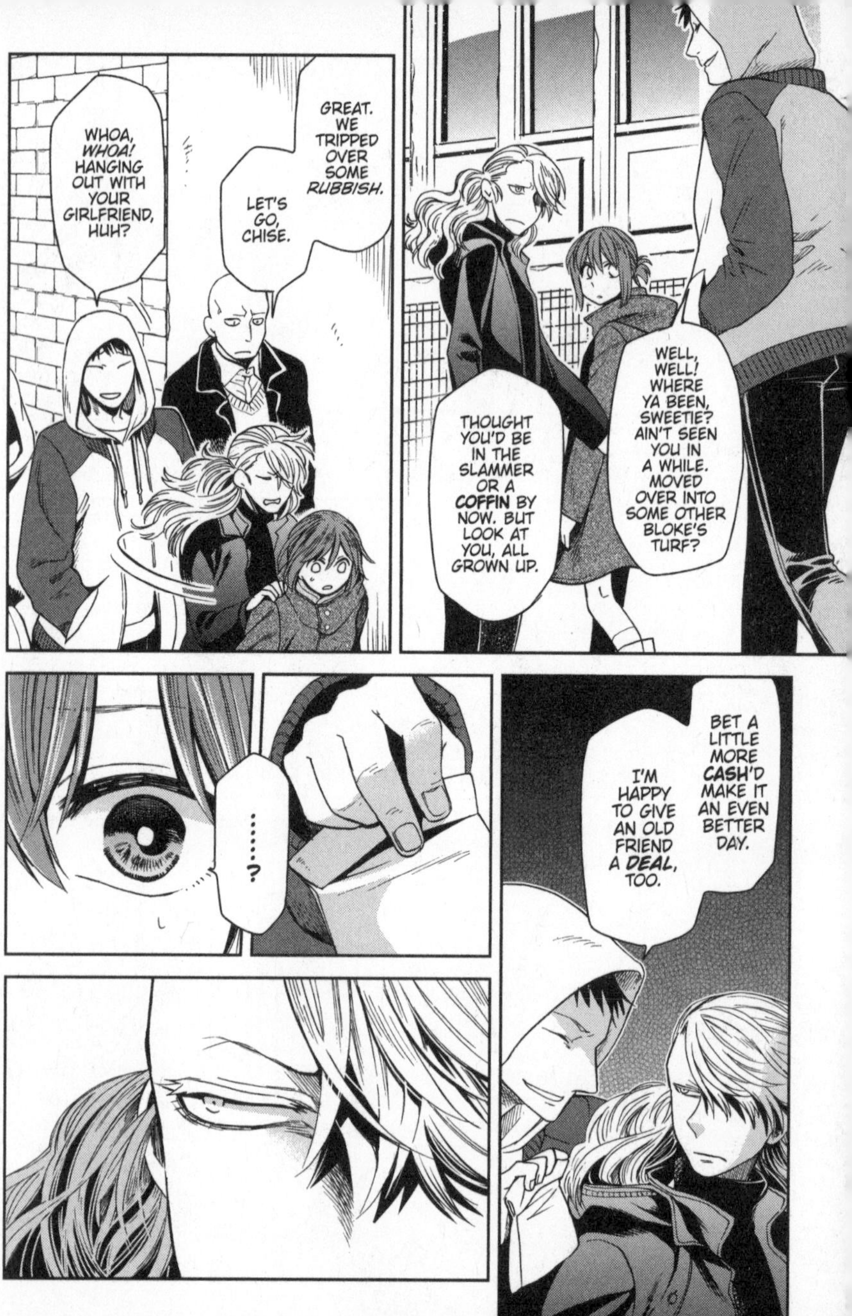
WELL, WELL! WHERE YA BEEN, SWEETIE? AIN'T SEEN YOU IN A WHILE. MOVED OVER INTO SOME OTHER BLOKE'S TURF?
THOUGHT YOU'D BE IN THE SLAMMER OR A **COFFIN** BY NOW. BUT LOOK AT YOU, ALL GROWN UP.
WHOA, *WHOA!* HANGING OUT WITH YOUR GIRLFRIEND, HUH?
GREAT. WE TRIPPED OVER SOME *RUBBISH.*
LET'S GO, CHISE.
BET A LITTLE MORE **CASH**'D MAKE IT AN EVEN BETTER DAY.
I'M HAPPY TO GIVE AN OLD FRIEND A **DEAL**, TOO.
......?

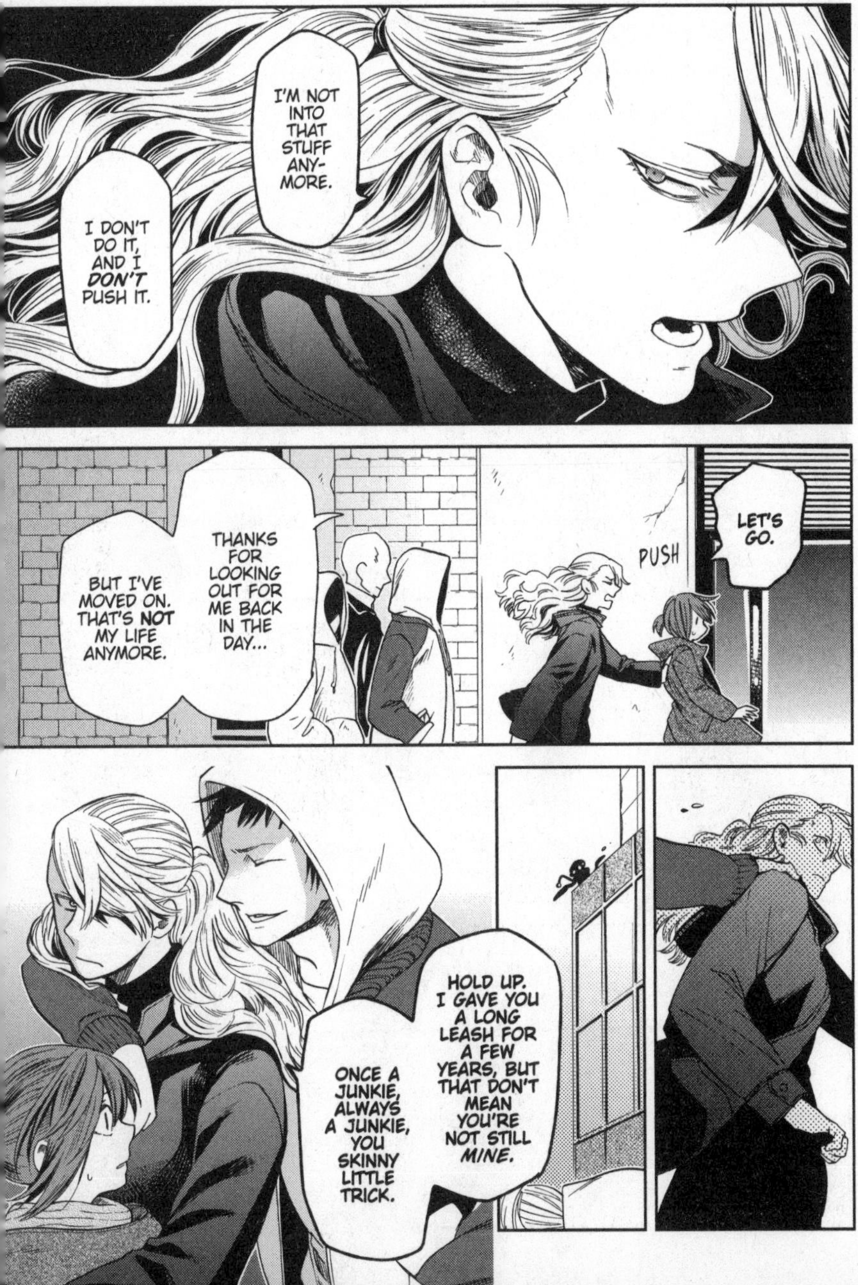
I'M NOT INTO THAT STUFF ANY-MORE.
I DON'T DO IT, AND I *DON'T* PUSH IT.
LET'S GO.
PUSH
THANKS FOR LOOKING OUT FOR ME BACK IN THE DAY...
BUT I'VE MOVED ON. THAT'S **NOT** MY LIFE ANYMORE.
HOLD UP. I GAVE YOU A LONG LEASH FOR A FEW YEARS, BUT THAT DON'T MEAN YOU'RE NOT STILL *MINE*.
ONCE A JUNKIE, ALWAYS A JUNKIE, YOU SKINNY LITTLE TRICK.

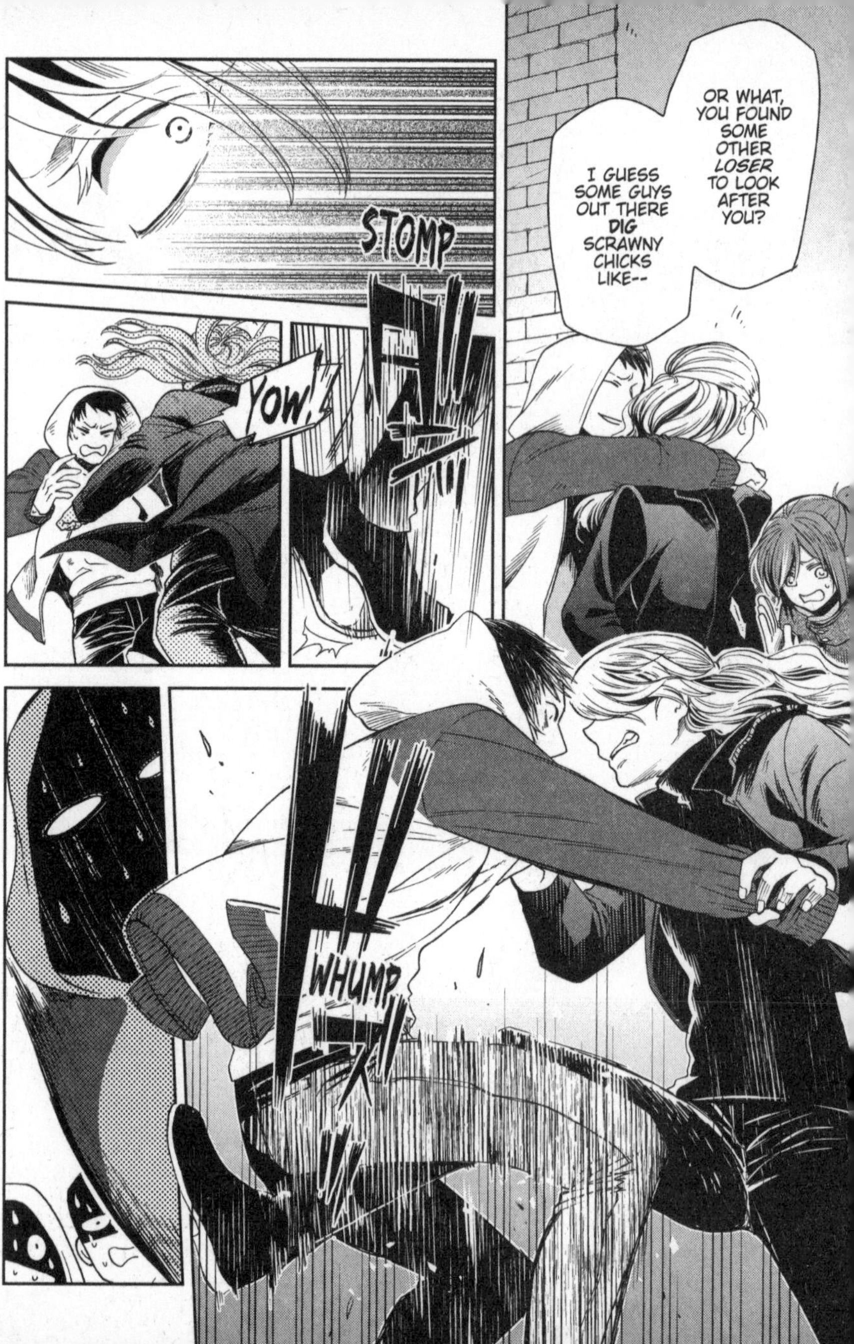
OR WHAT, YOU FOUND SOME OTHER LOSER TO LOOK AFTER YOU?
I GUESS SOME GUYS OUT THERE DIG SCRAWNY CHICKS LIKE--
STOMP
YOW!
WHUMP

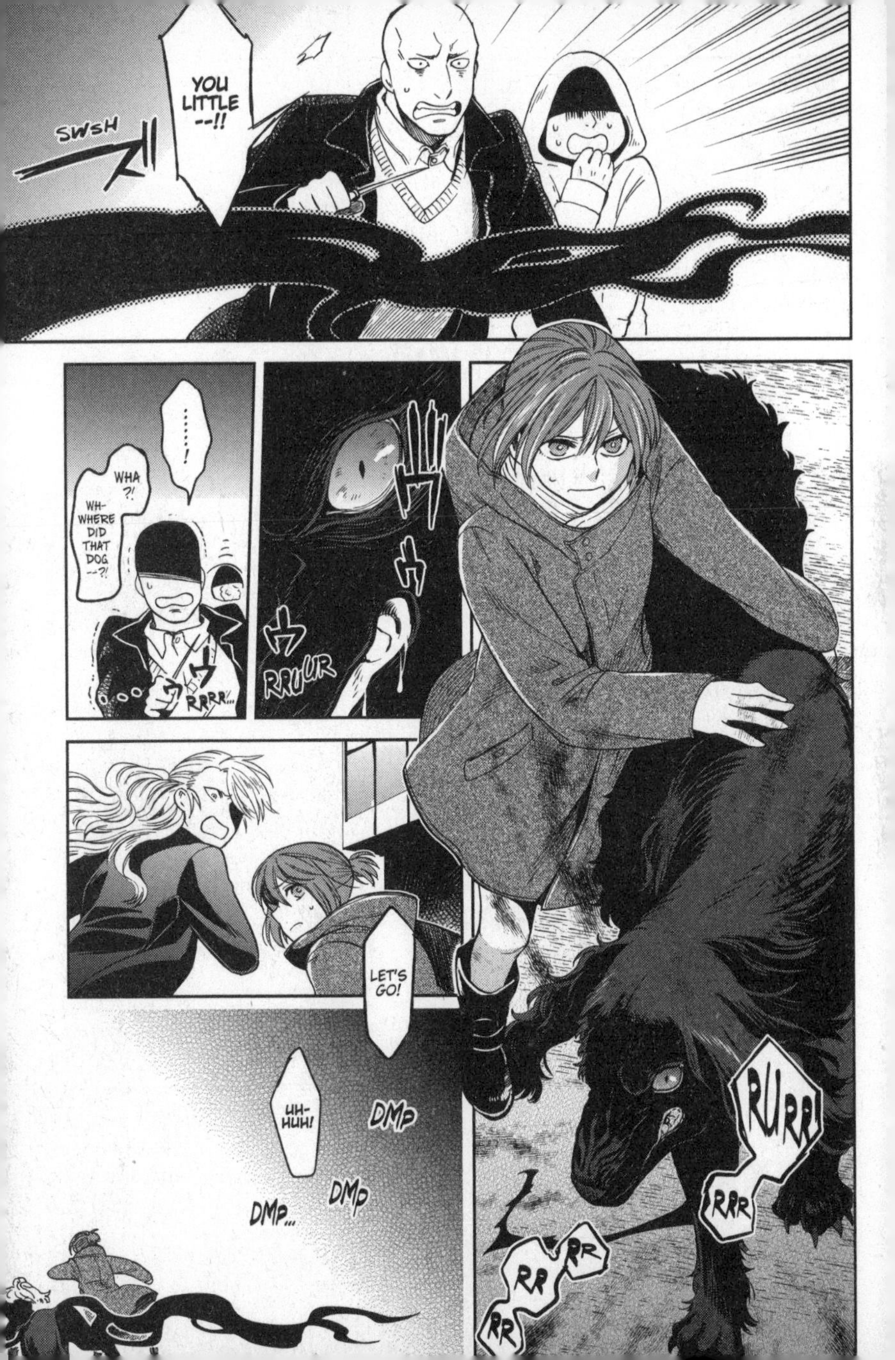
YOU LITTLE--!!
SWSH
RURR
RRR
RR
RR
RR
RRUR
......!
WHA?!
WH-WHERE DID THAT DOG--?!
RRRR...
LET'S GO!
UH-HUH!
DMP
DMP
DMP...

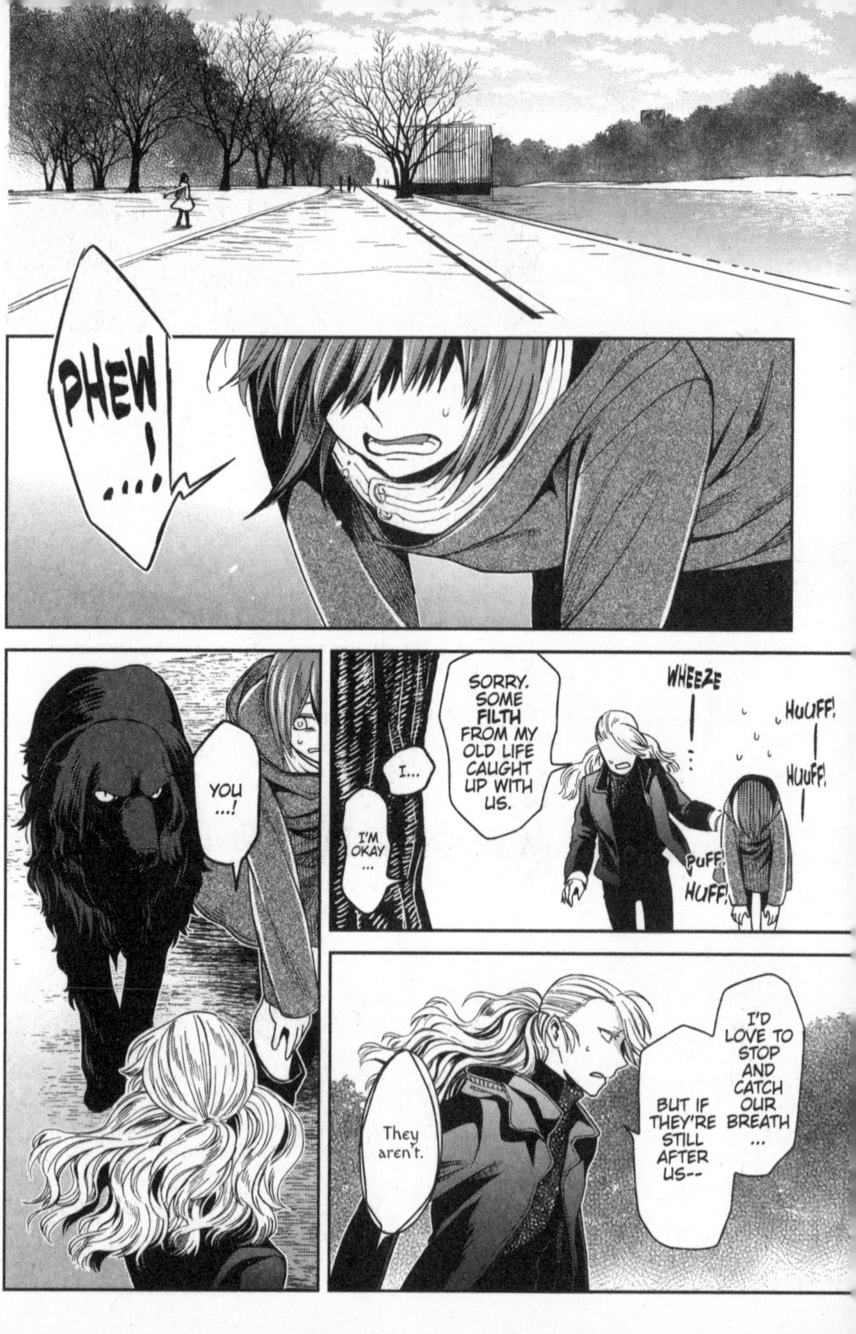
PHEW...!
HUUFF! HUUFF!
WHEEZE
SORRY. SOME FILTH FROM MY OLD LIFE CAUGHT UP WITH US.
PUFF! HUFF!
I...
I'M OKAY...
I'D LOVE TO STOP AND CATCH OUR BREATH...
BUT IF THEY'RE STILL AFTER US--
They aren't.
YOU...!

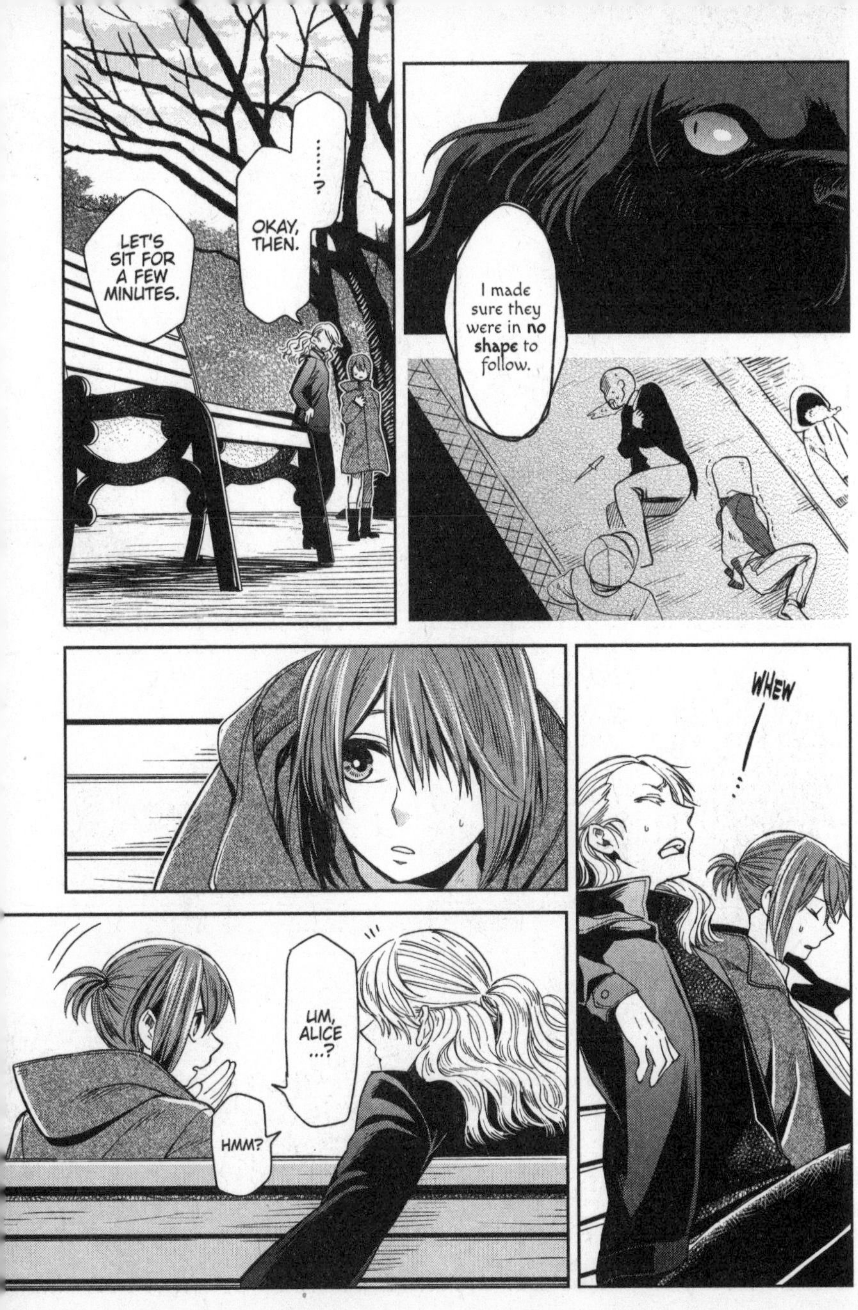
I made sure they were in **no shape** to follow.
......?
OKAY, THEN.
LET'S SIT FOR A FEW MINUTES.
WHEW
...
UM, ALICE ...?
HMM?

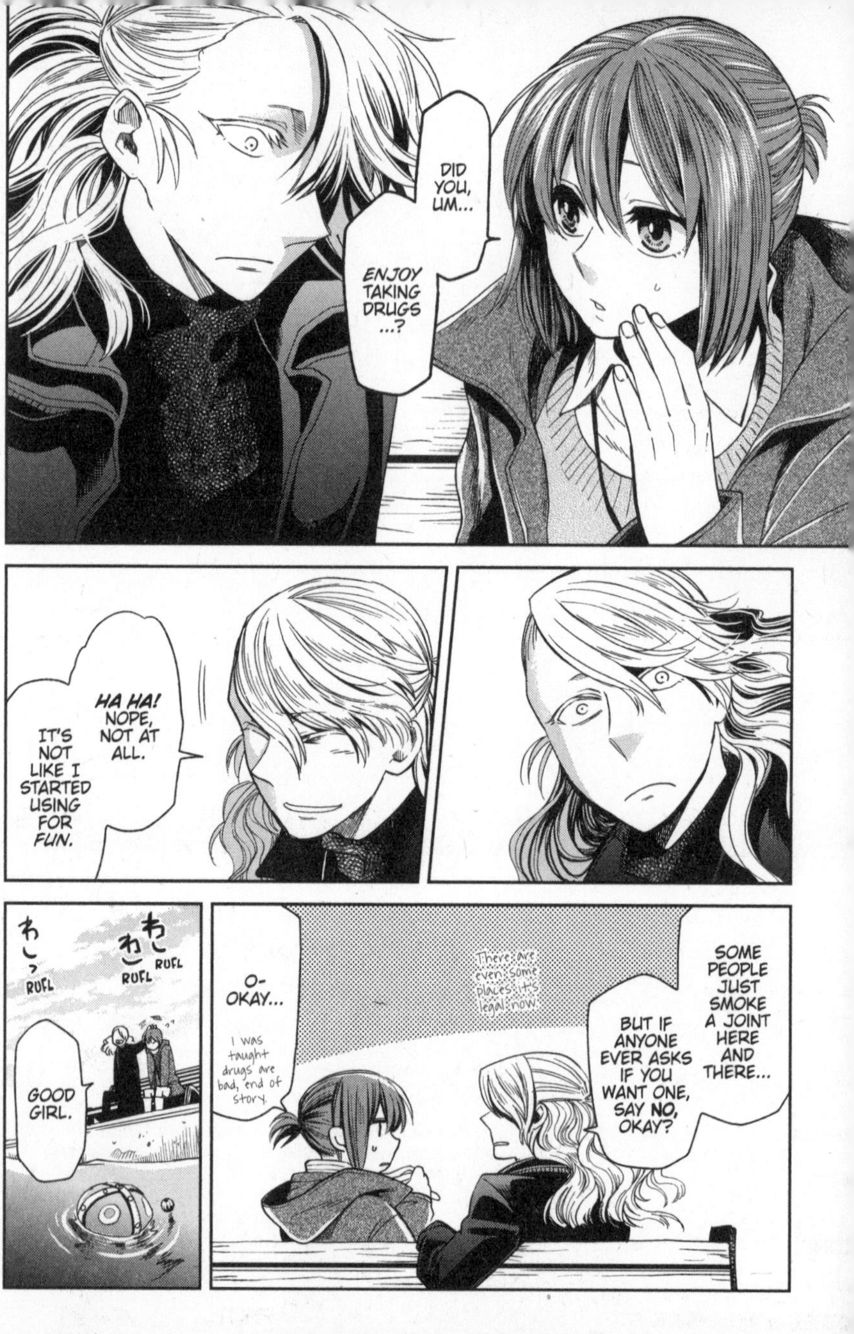
DID YOU, UM...
ENJOY TAKING DRUGS ...?
HA HA! NOPE, NOT AT ALL.
IT'S NOT LIKE I STARTED USING FOR FUN.
SOME PEOPLE JUST SMOKE A JOINT HERE AND THERE...
BUT IF ANYONE EVER ASKS IF YOU WANT ONE, SAY NO, OKAY?
There are even some places it's legal now.
O-OKAY...
I was taught drugs are bad, end of story.
RUFL
RUFL
RUFL
GOOD GIRL.

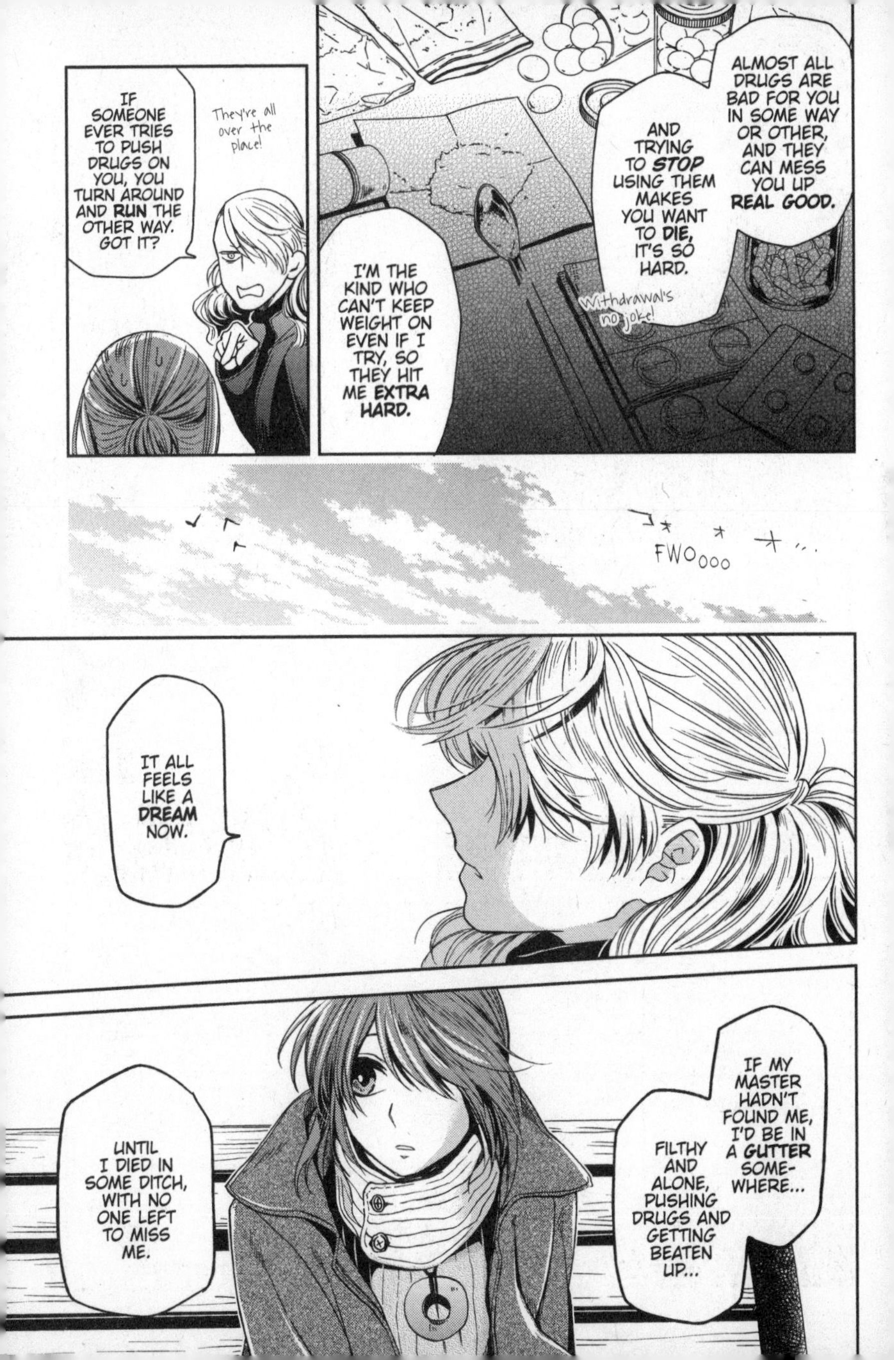
ALMOST ALL DRUGS ARE BAD FOR YOU IN SOME WAY OR OTHER, AND THEY CAN MESS YOU UP REAL GOOD.
AND TRYING TO STOP USING THEM MAKES YOU WANT TO DIE, IT'S SO HARD.
Withdrawal's no joke!
I'M THE KIND WHO CAN'T KEEP WEIGHT ON EVEN IF I TRY, SO THEY HIT ME EXTRA HARD.
IF SOMEONE EVER TRIES TO PUSH DRUGS ON YOU, YOU TURN AROUND AND RUN THE OTHER WAY. GOT IT?
They're all over the place!
FWOooo
IT ALL FEELS LIKE A DREAM NOW.
IF MY MASTER HADN'T FOUND ME, I'D BE IN A GUTTER SOME-WHERE...
FILTHY AND ALONE, PUSHING DRUGS AND GETTING BEATEN UP...
UNTIL I DIED IN SOME DITCH, WITH NO ONE LEFT TO MISS ME.

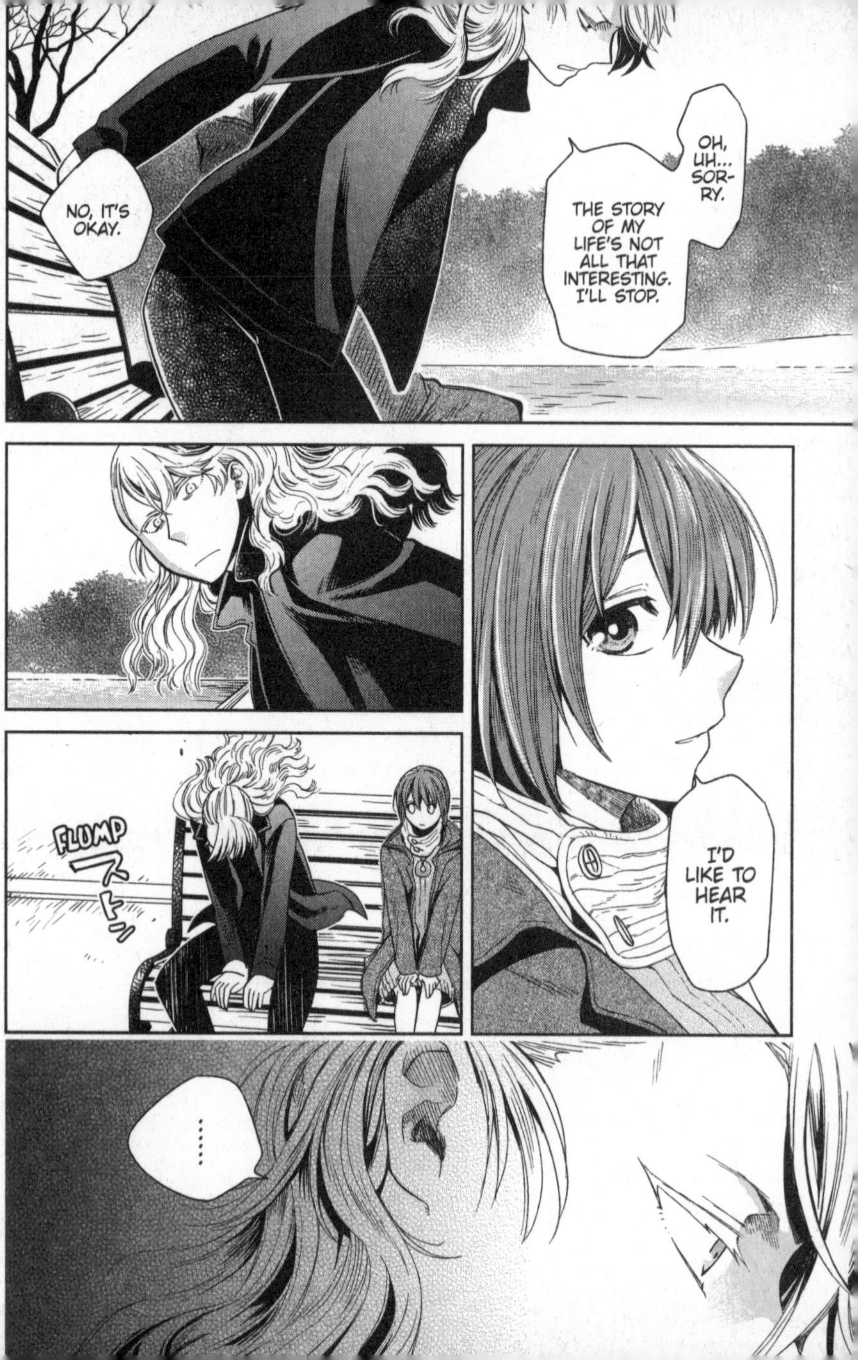
OH, UH... SORRY.
THE STORY OF MY LIFE'S NOT ALL THAT INTERESTING. I'LL STOP.
NO, IT'S OKAY.
I'D LIKE TO HEAR IT.
FLUMP
......

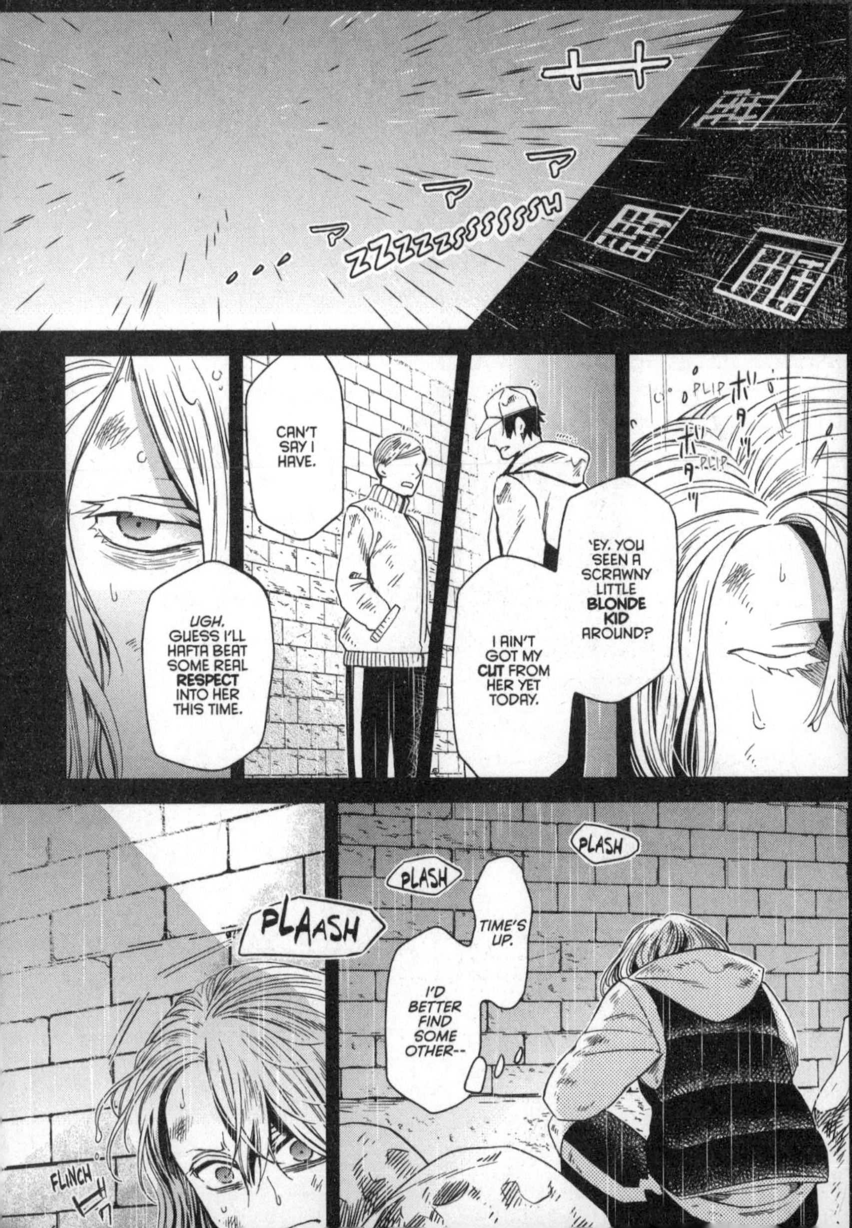
ZZZZZzssssssSH
PLIP
PLIP
'EY. YOU SEEN A SCRAWNY LITTLE **BLONDE KID** AROUND?
I AIN'T GOT MY **CUT** FROM HER YET TODAY.
CAN'T SAY I HAVE.
UGH. GUESS I'LL HAFTA BEAT SOME REAL **RESPECT** INTO HER THIS TIME.
PLASH
PLASH
TIME'S UP.
I'D BETTER FIND SOME OTHER--
PLAASH
FLINCH

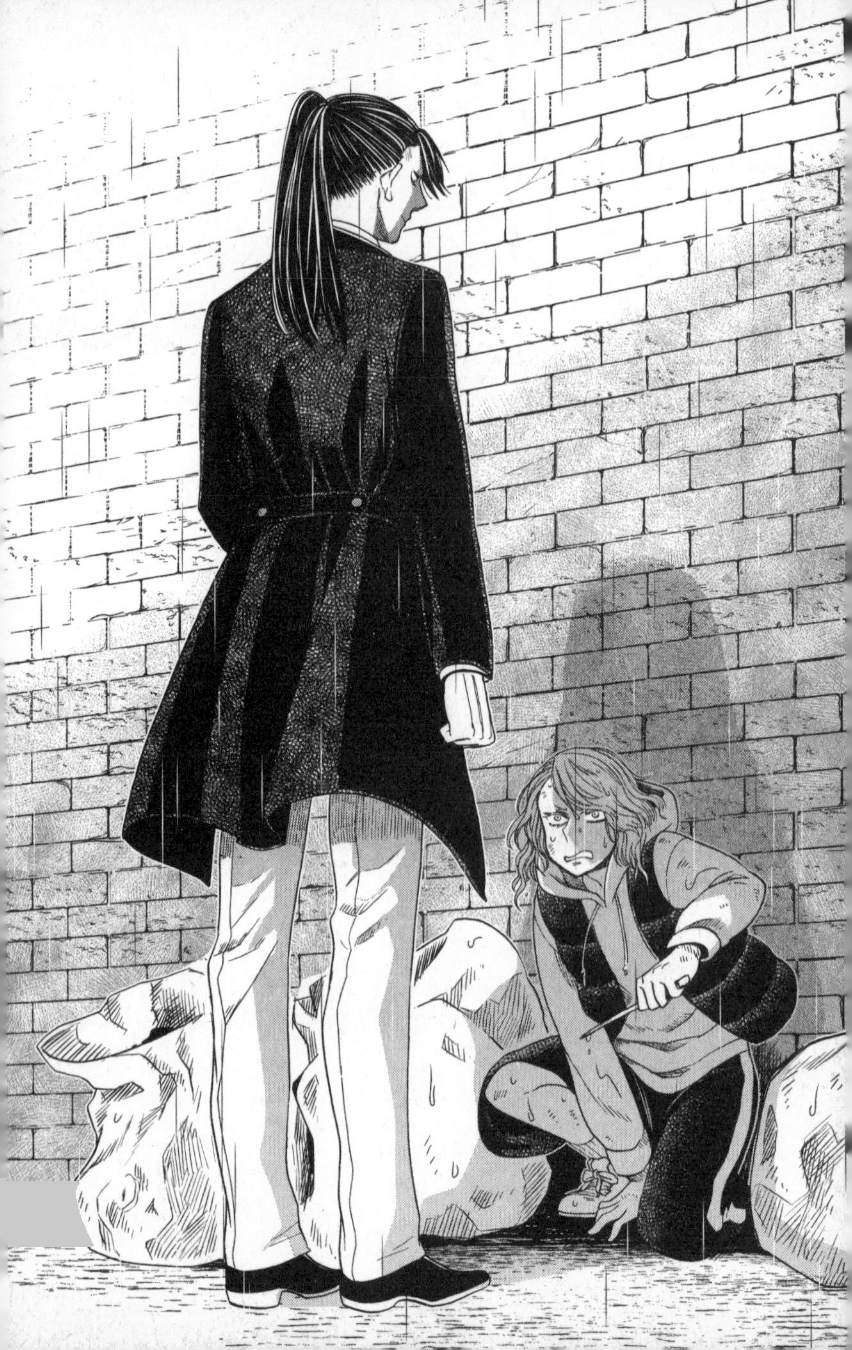

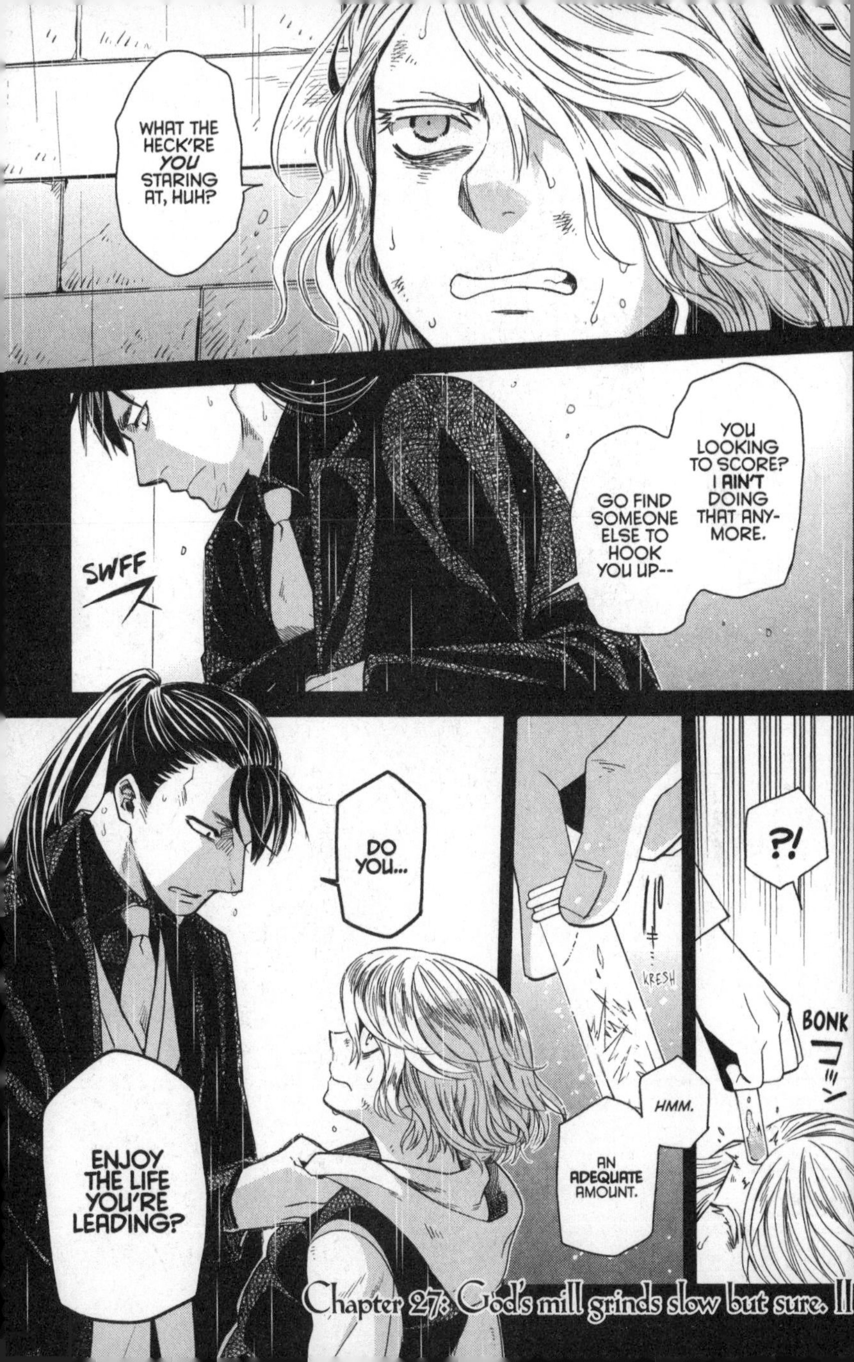
WHAT THE HECK'RE *YOU* STARING AT, HUH?
YOU LOOKING TO SCORE? I AIN'T DOING THAT ANY-MORE.
GO FIND SOMEONE ELSE TO HOOK YOU UP--
SWFF
?!
BONK
KRESH
HMM.
AN ADEQUATE AMOUNT.
DO YOU...
ENJOY THE LIFE YOU'RE LEADING?

Chapter 27: God's mill grinds slow but sure. II

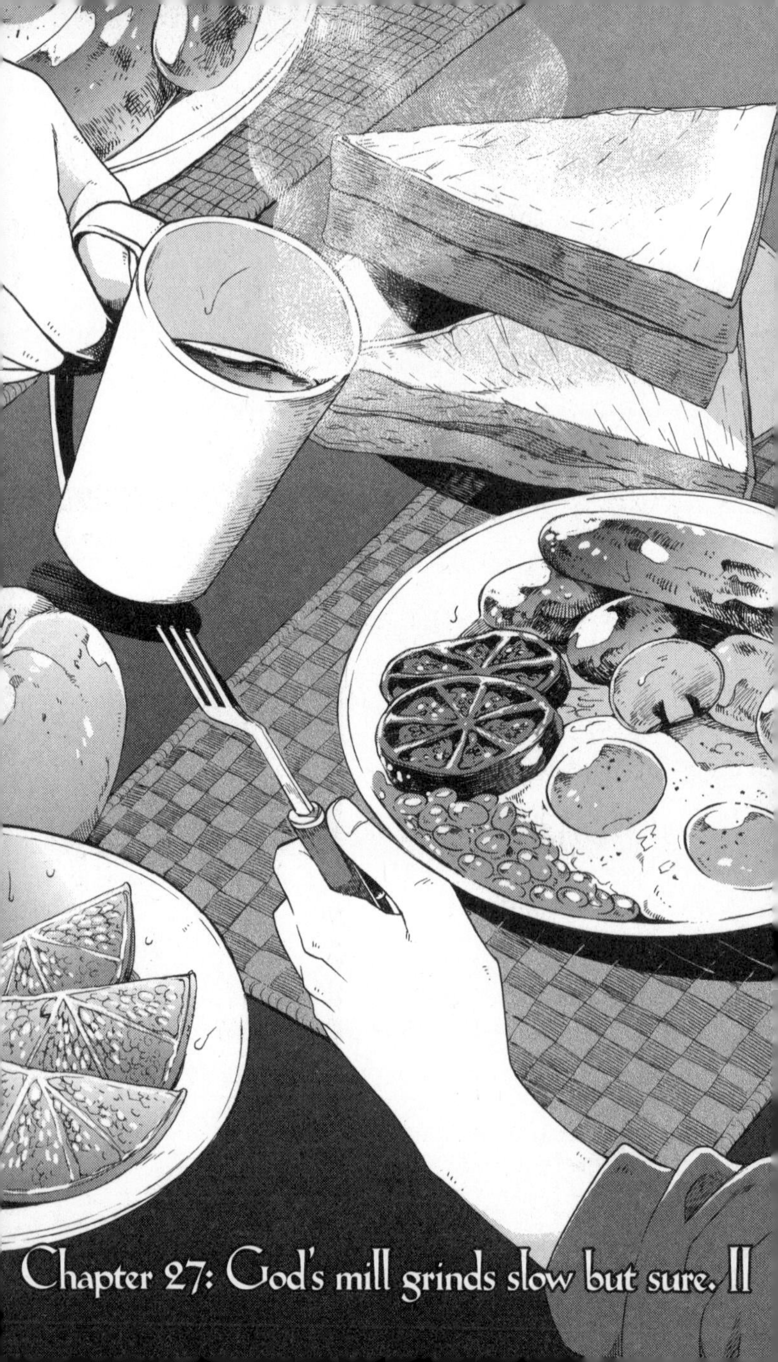

Chapter 27: God's mill grinds slow but sure. II

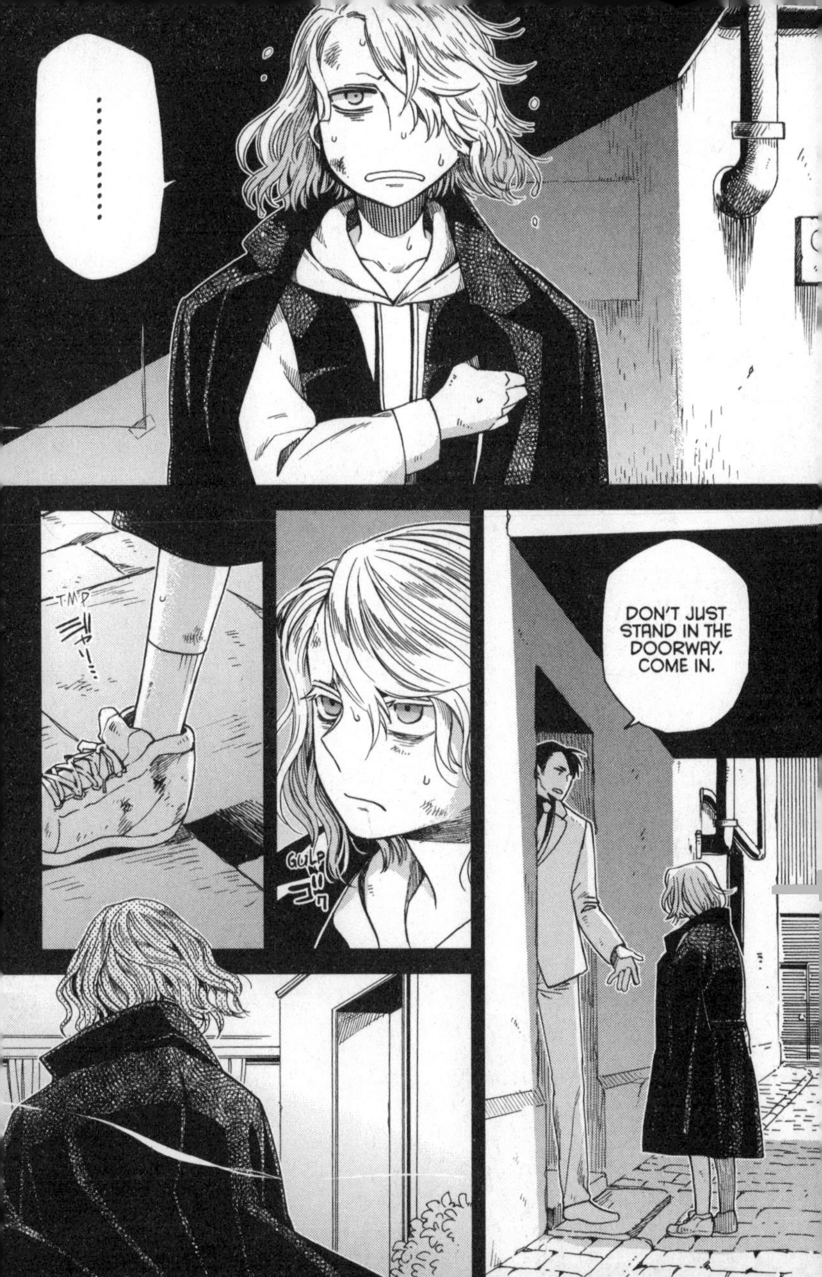
……
DON'T JUST STAND IN THE DOORWAY. COME IN.
GULP
TMP

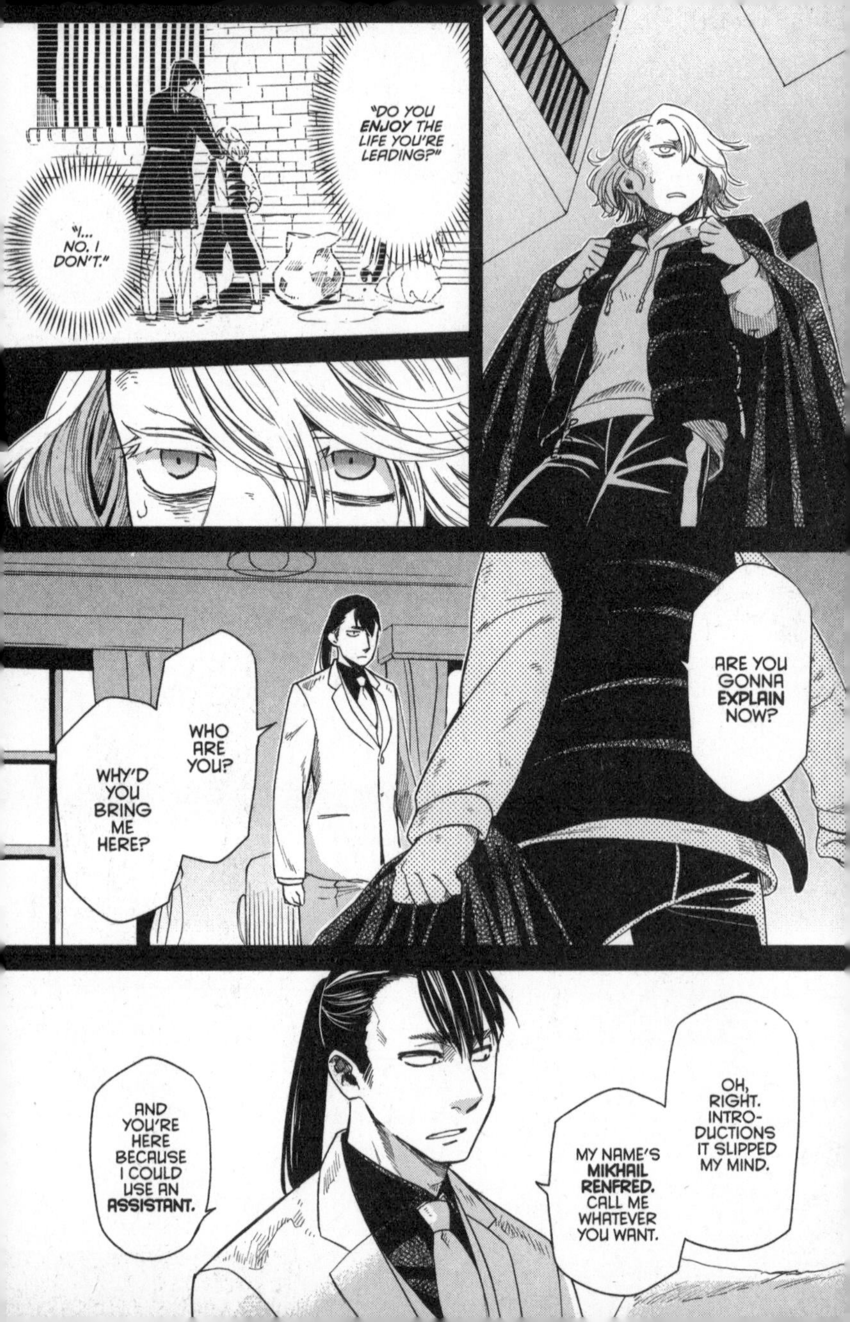
"DO YOU ENJOY THE LIFE YOU'RE LEADING?"
"I... NO. I DON'T."
ARE YOU GONNA EXPLAIN NOW?
WHO ARE YOU?
WHY'D YOU BRING ME HERE?
OH, RIGHT. INTRO-DUCTIONS IT SLIPPED MY MIND.
MY NAME'S MIKHAIL RENFRED. CALL ME WHATEVER YOU WANT.
AND YOU'RE HERE BECAUSE I COULD USE AN ASSISTANT.

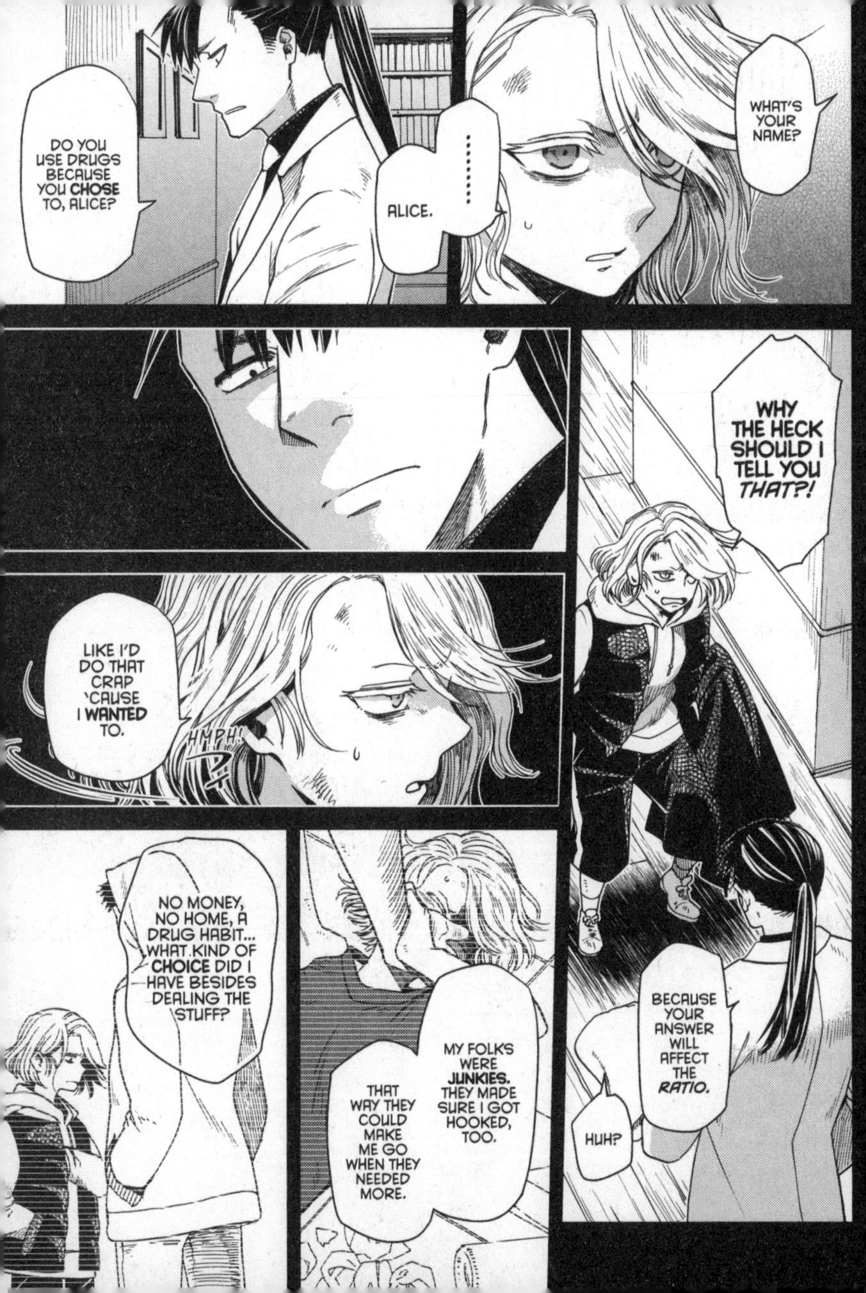
WHAT'S YOUR NAME?
....
ALICE.
DO YOU USE DRUGS BECAUSE YOU CHOSE TO, ALICE?
WHY THE HECK SHOULD I TELL YOU THAT?!
BECAUSE YOUR ANSWER WILL AFFECT THE RATIO.
HUH?
LIKE I'D DO THAT CRAP 'CAUSE I WANTED TO.
HMPH!
MY FOLKS WERE JUNKIES. THEY MADE SURE I GOT HOOKED, TOO.
THAT WAY THEY COULD MAKE ME GO WHEN THEY NEEDED MORE.
NO MONEY, NO HOME, A DRUG HABIT... WHAT KIND OF CHOICE DID I HAVE BESIDES DEALING THE STUFF?

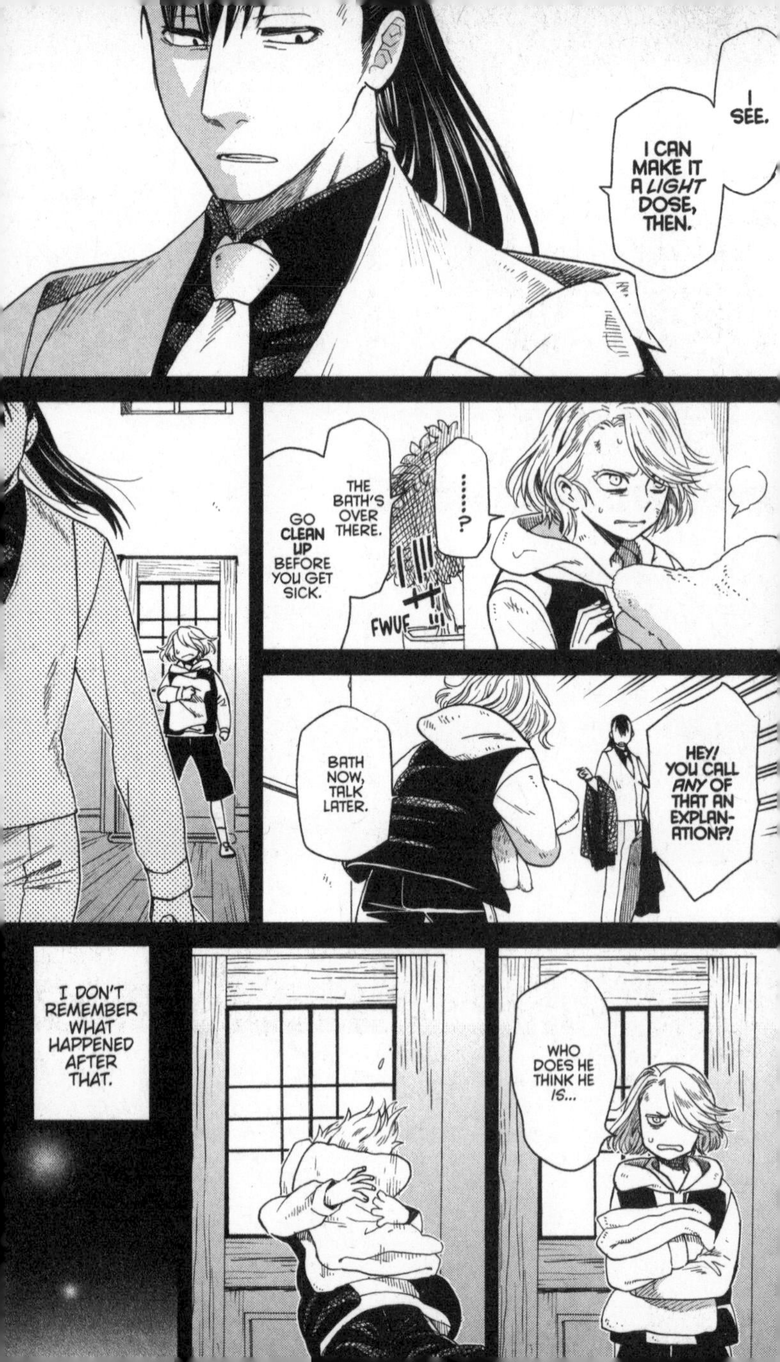
I SEE.
I CAN MAKE IT A *LIGHT* DOSE, THEN.
......?
THE BATH'S OVER THERE.
GO **CLEAN UP** BEFORE YOU GET SICK.
FWUF
HEY! YOU CALL *ANY* OF THAT AN EXPLANATION?!
BATH NOW, TALK LATER.
WHO DOES HE THINK HE *IS*...
I DON'T REMEMBER WHAT HAPPENED AFTER THAT.

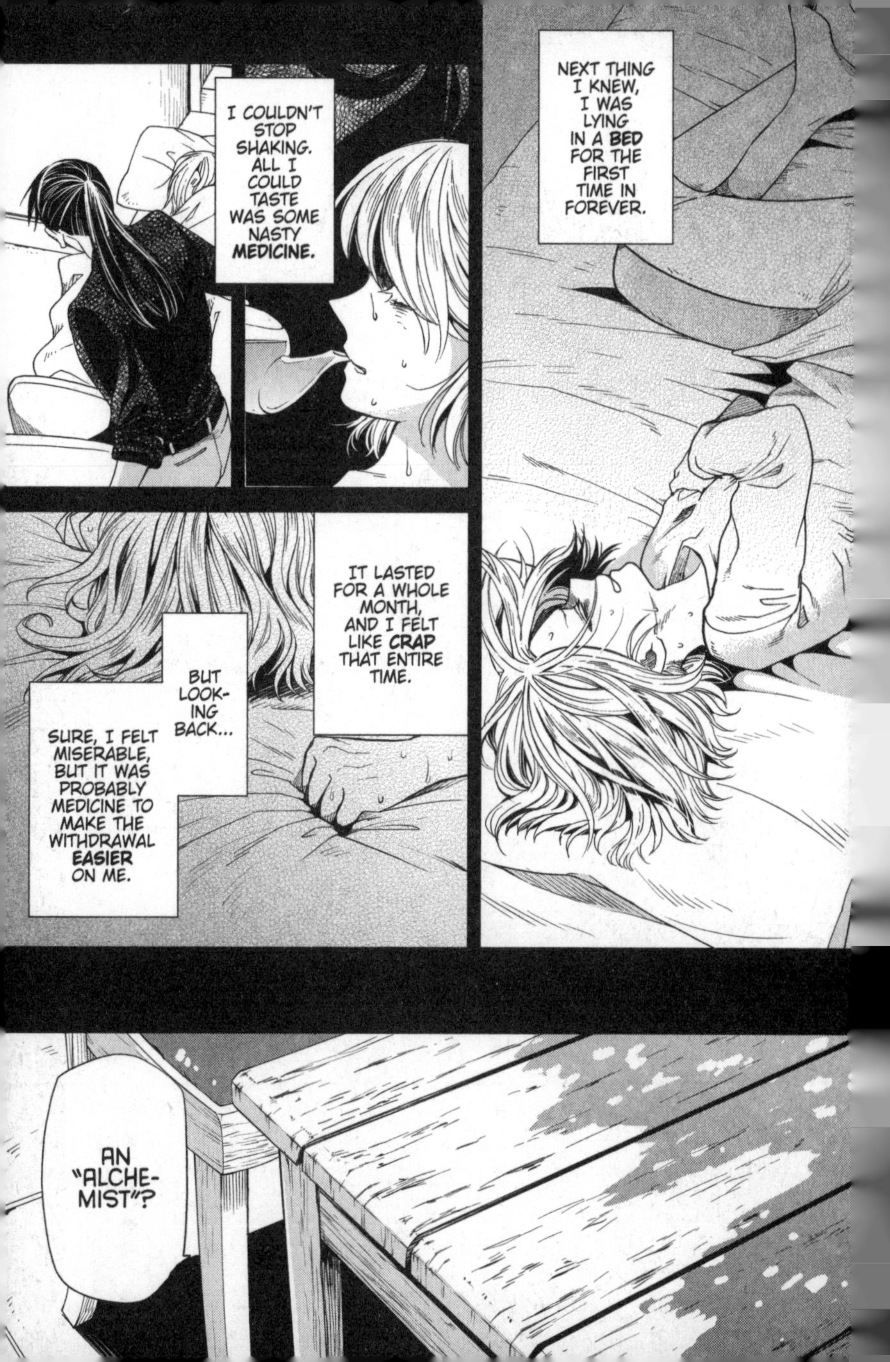
NEXT THING I KNEW, I WAS LYING IN A BED FOR THE FIRST TIME IN FOREVER.
I COULDN'T STOP SHAKING. ALL I COULD TASTE WAS SOME NASTY MEDICINE.
IT LASTED FOR A WHOLE MONTH, AND I FELT LIKE CRAP THAT ENTIRE TIME.
BUT LOOKING BACK...
SURE, I FELT MISERABLE, BUT IT WAS PROBABLY MEDICINE TO MAKE THE WITHDRAWAL EASIER ON ME.
AN "ALCHEMIST"?

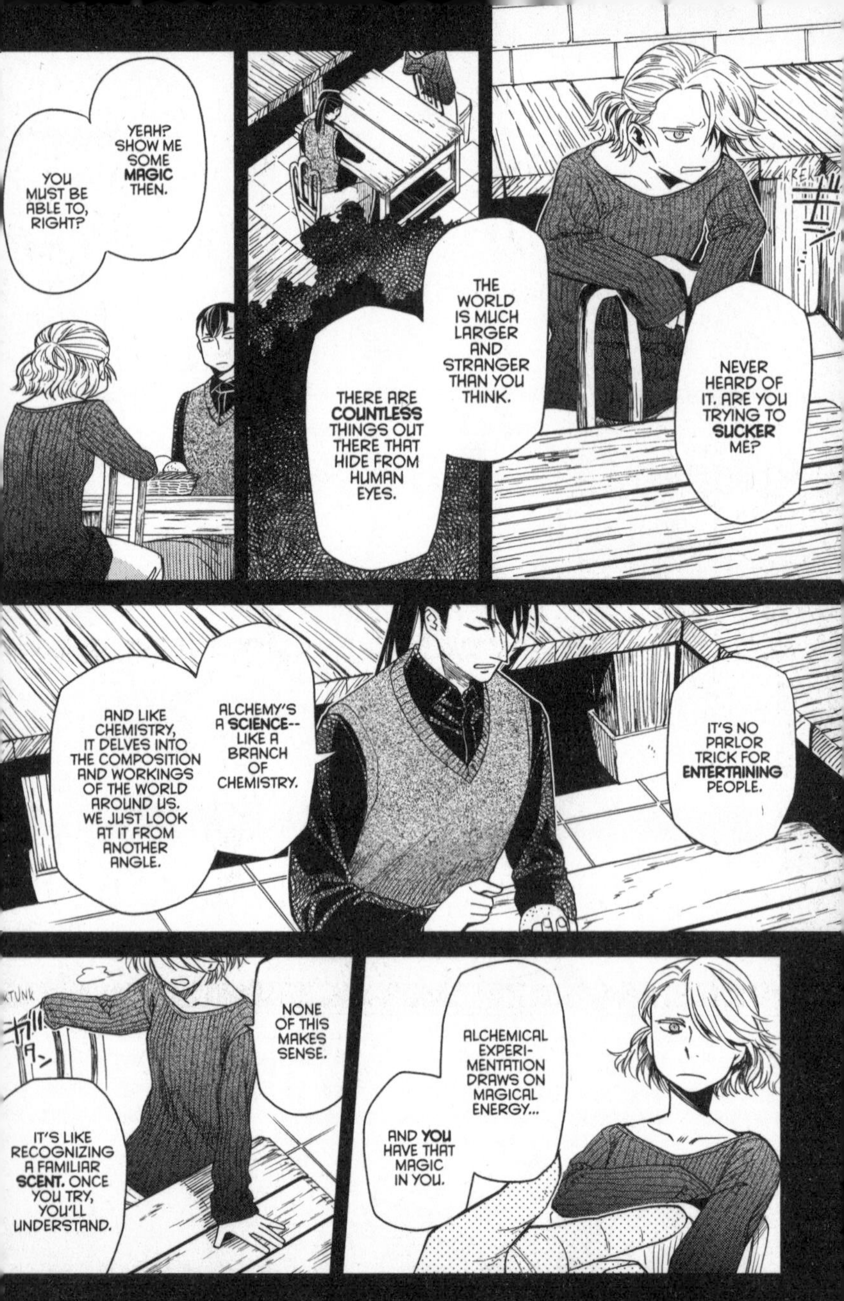
KREK
NEVER HEARD OF IT. ARE YOU TRYING TO **SUCKER** ME?
THE WORLD IS MUCH LARGER AND STRANGER THAN YOU THINK.
THERE ARE **COUNTLESS** THINGS OUT THERE THAT HIDE FROM HUMAN EYES.
YEAH? SHOW ME SOME **MAGIC** THEN.
YOU MUST BE ABLE TO, RIGHT?
IT'S NO PARLOR TRICK FOR **ENTERTAINING** PEOPLE.
ALCHEMY'S A **SCIENCE**-- LIKE A BRANCH OF CHEMISTRY.
AND LIKE CHEMISTRY, IT DELVES INTO THE COMPOSITION AND WORKINGS OF THE WORLD AROUND US. WE JUST LOOK AT IT FROM ANOTHER ANGLE.
ALCHEMICAL EXPERI-MENTATION DRAWS ON MAGICAL ENERGY...
AND **YOU** HAVE THAT MAGIC IN YOU.
NONE OF THIS MAKES SENSE.
KTUNK
IT'S LIKE RECOGNIZING A FAMILIAR **SCENT.** ONCE YOU TRY, YOU'LL UNDERSTAND.

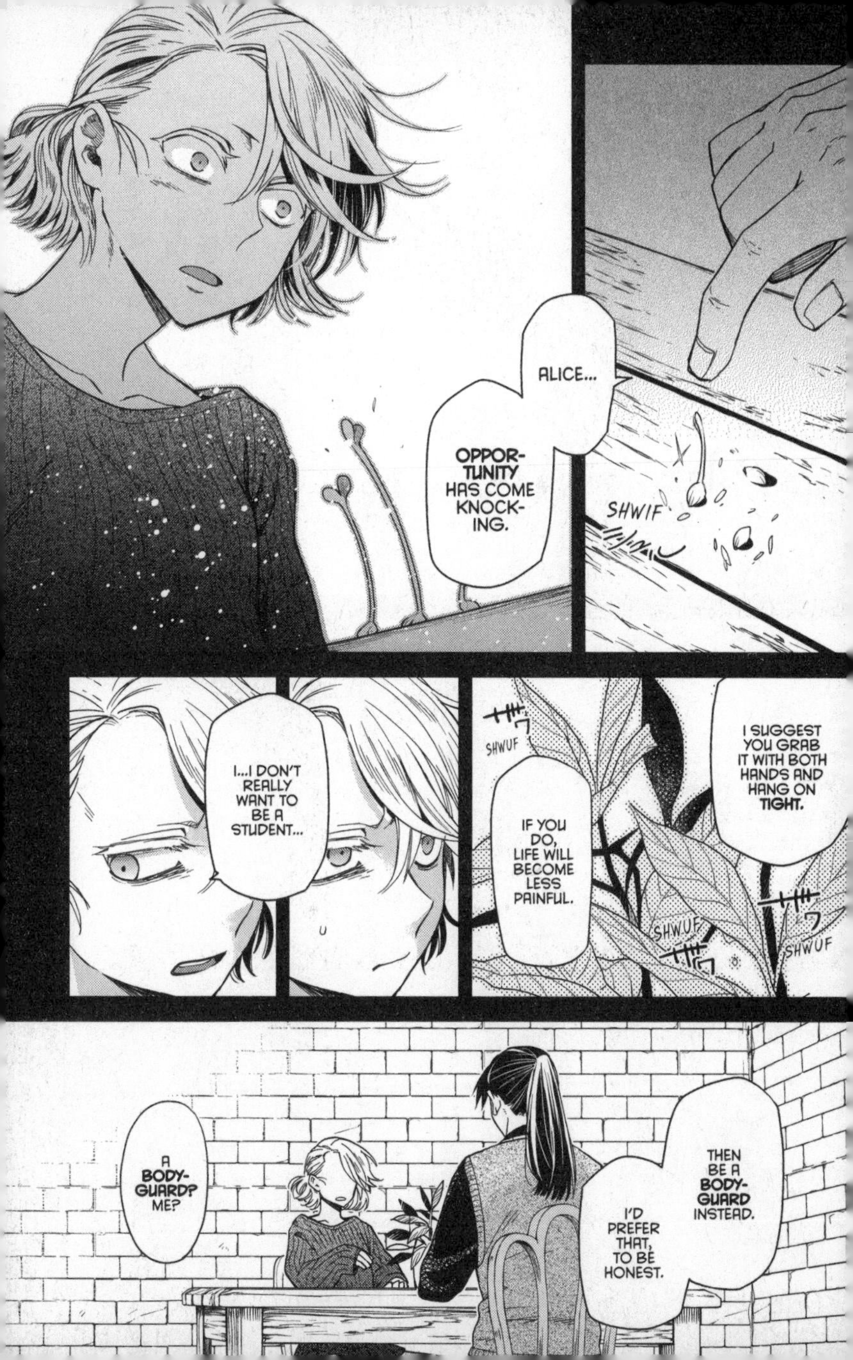
SHWIF
ALICE...
OPPORTUNITY HAS COME KNOCKING.
I SUGGEST YOU GRAB IT WITH BOTH HANDS AND HANG ON TIGHT.
SHWUF
SHWUF
SHWUF
IF YOU DO, LIFE WILL BECOME LESS PAINFUL.
I...I DON'T REALLY WANT TO BE A STUDENT...
THEN BE A BODYGUARD INSTEAD.
I'D PREFER THAT, TO BE HONEST.
A BODYGUARD? ME?

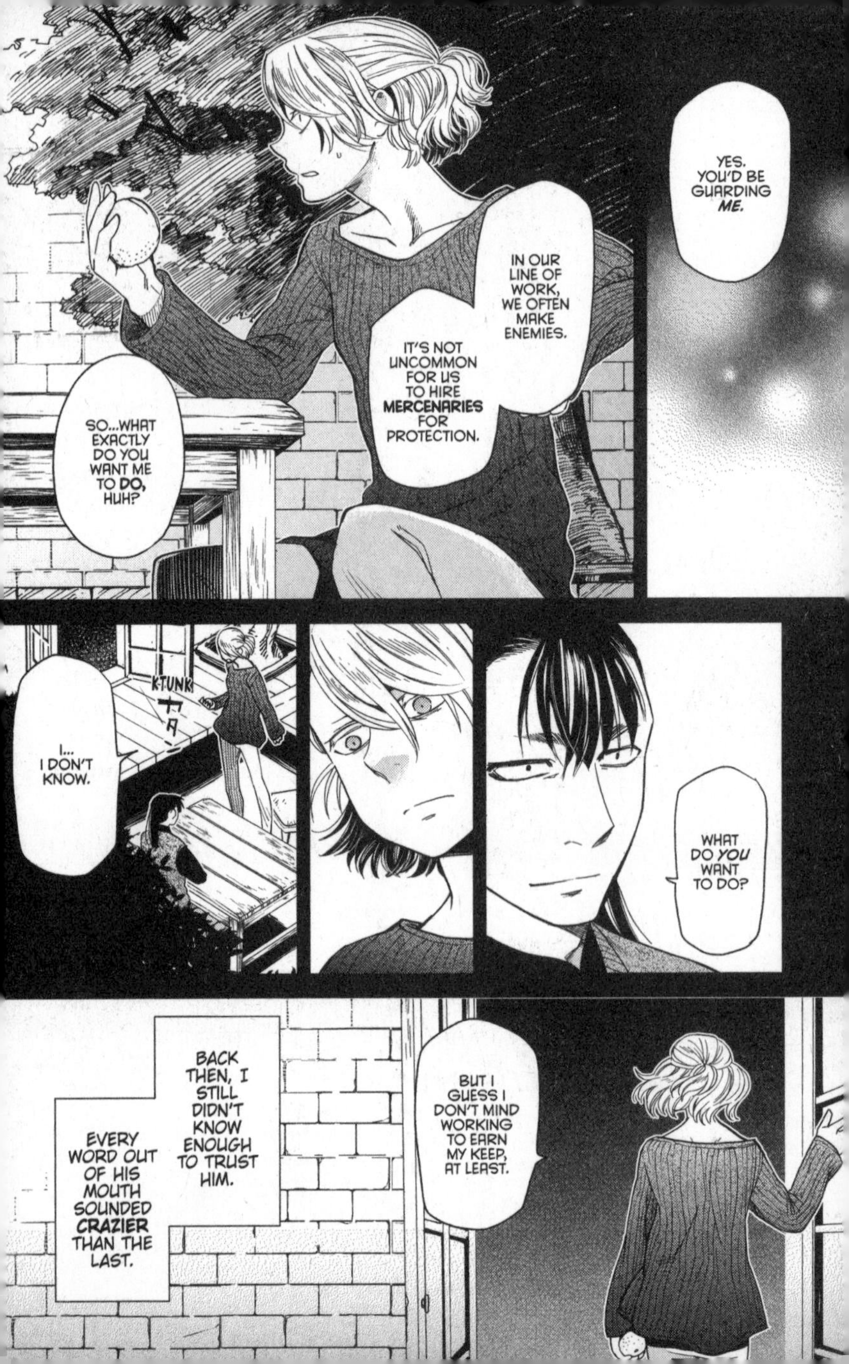
YES. YOU'D BE GUARDING ME.
IN OUR LINE OF WORK, WE OFTEN MAKE ENEMIES.
IT'S NOT UNCOMMON FOR US TO HIRE MERCENARIES FOR PROTECTION.
SO...WHAT EXACTLY DO YOU WANT ME TO DO, HUH?
WHAT DO YOU WANT TO DO?
KTUNK
I... I DON'T KNOW.
BUT I GUESS I DON'T MIND WORKING TO EARN MY KEEP, AT LEAST.
BACK THEN, I STILL DIDN'T KNOW ENOUGH TO TRUST HIM.
EVERY WORD OUT OF HIS MOUTH SOUNDED CRAZIER THAN THE LAST.

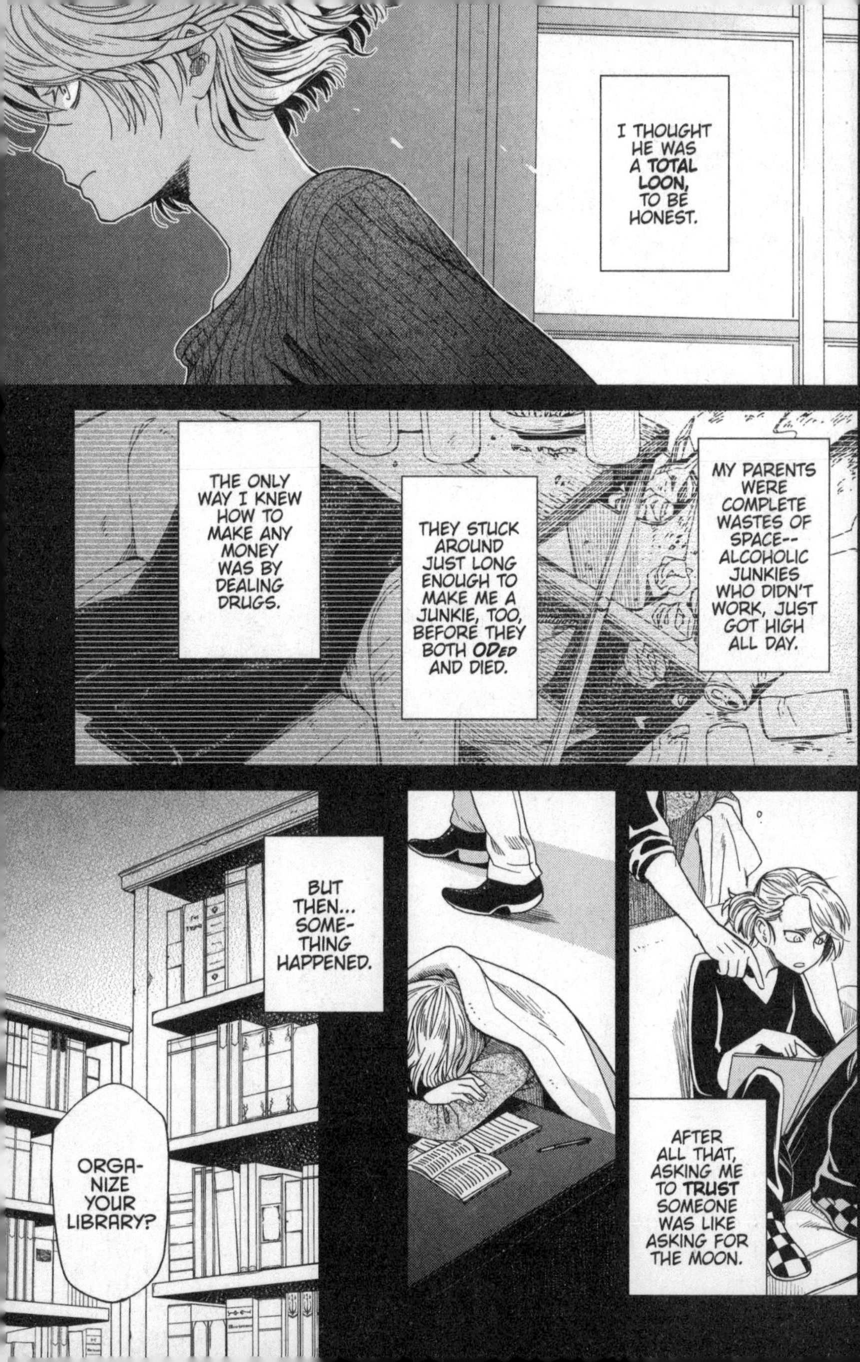
I THOUGHT HE WAS A TOTAL LOON, TO BE HONEST.
MY PARENTS WERE COMPLETE WASTES OF SPACE--ALCOHOLIC JUNKIES WHO DIDN'T WORK, JUST GOT HIGH ALL DAY.
THEY STUCK AROUND JUST LONG ENOUGH TO MAKE ME A JUNKIE, TOO, BEFORE THEY BOTH ODED AND DIED.
THE ONLY WAY I KNEW HOW TO MAKE ANY MONEY WAS BY DEALING DRUGS.
AFTER ALL THAT, ASKING ME TO TRUST SOMEONE WAS LIKE ASKING FOR THE MOON.
BUT THEN... SOME-THING HAPPENED.
ORGA-NIZE YOUR LIBRARY?

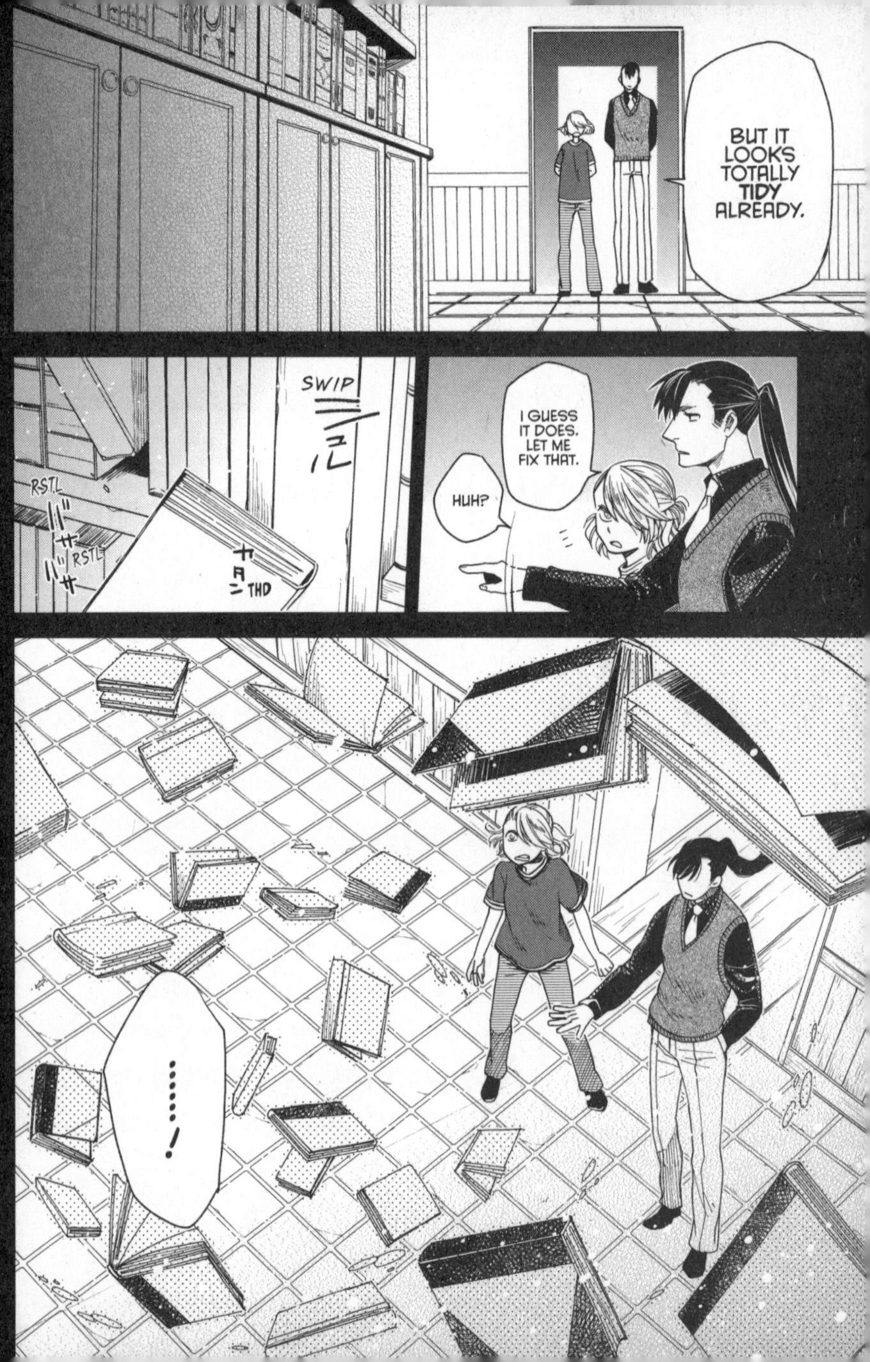
BUT IT LOOKS TOTALLY TIDY ALREADY.
I GUESS IT DOES. LET ME FIX THAT.
HUH?
SWIP
RSTL
RSTL
THD
......!

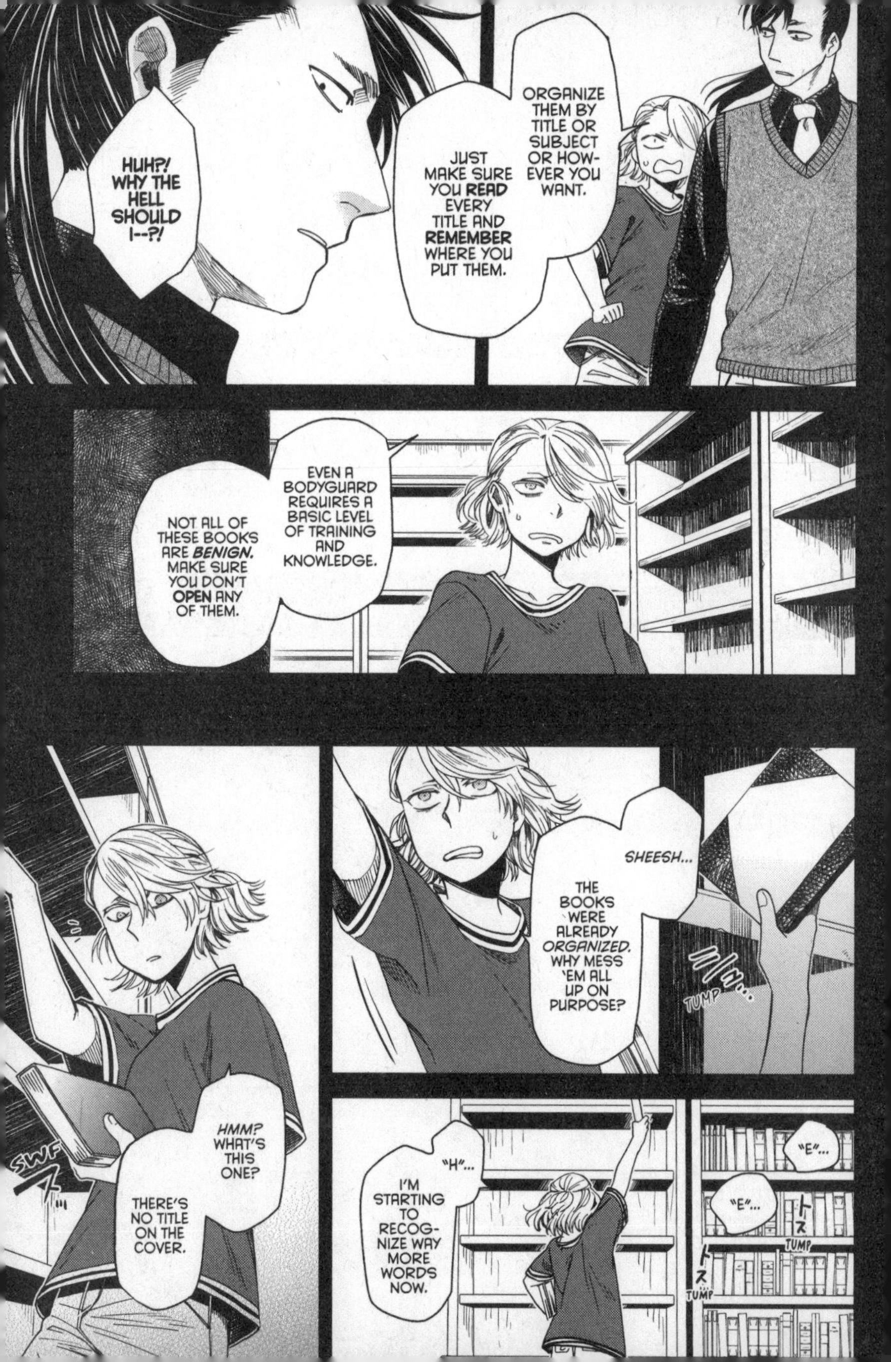
ORGANIZE THEM BY TITLE OR SUBJECT OR HOWEVER YOU WANT.
JUST MAKE SURE YOU **READ** EVERY TITLE AND **REMEMBER** WHERE YOU PUT THEM.
HUH?! WHY THE HELL SHOULD I--?!
EVEN A BODYGUARD REQUIRES A BASIC LEVEL OF TRAINING AND KNOWLEDGE.
NOT ALL OF THESE BOOKS ARE ***BENIGN.*** MAKE SURE YOU DON'T **OPEN** ANY OF THEM.
SHEESH...
THE BOOKS WERE ALREADY *ORGANIZED.* WHY MESS 'EM ALL UP ON PURPOSE?
TUMP
"E"...
"E"...
TUMP
TUMP
"H"...
I'M STARTING TO RECOGNIZE WAY MORE WORDS NOW.
HMM? WHAT'S THIS ONE?
THERE'S NO TITLE ON THE COVER.
SWF

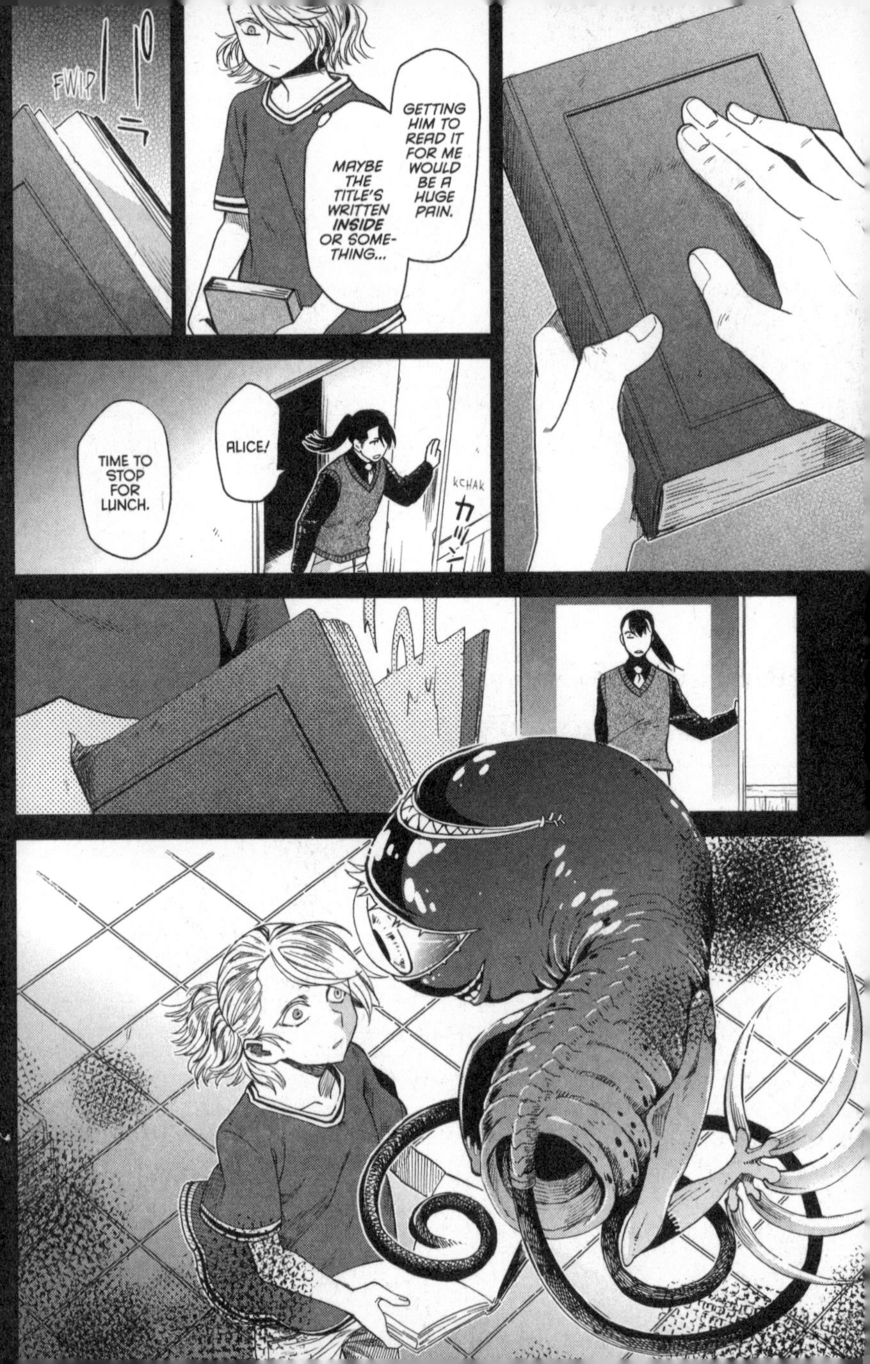
GETTING HIM TO READ IT FOR ME WOULD BE A HUGE PAIN.
MAYBE THE TITLE'S WRITTEN INSIDE OR SOME-THING...
FWIP
ALICE!
TIME TO STOP FOR LUNCH.
KCHAK

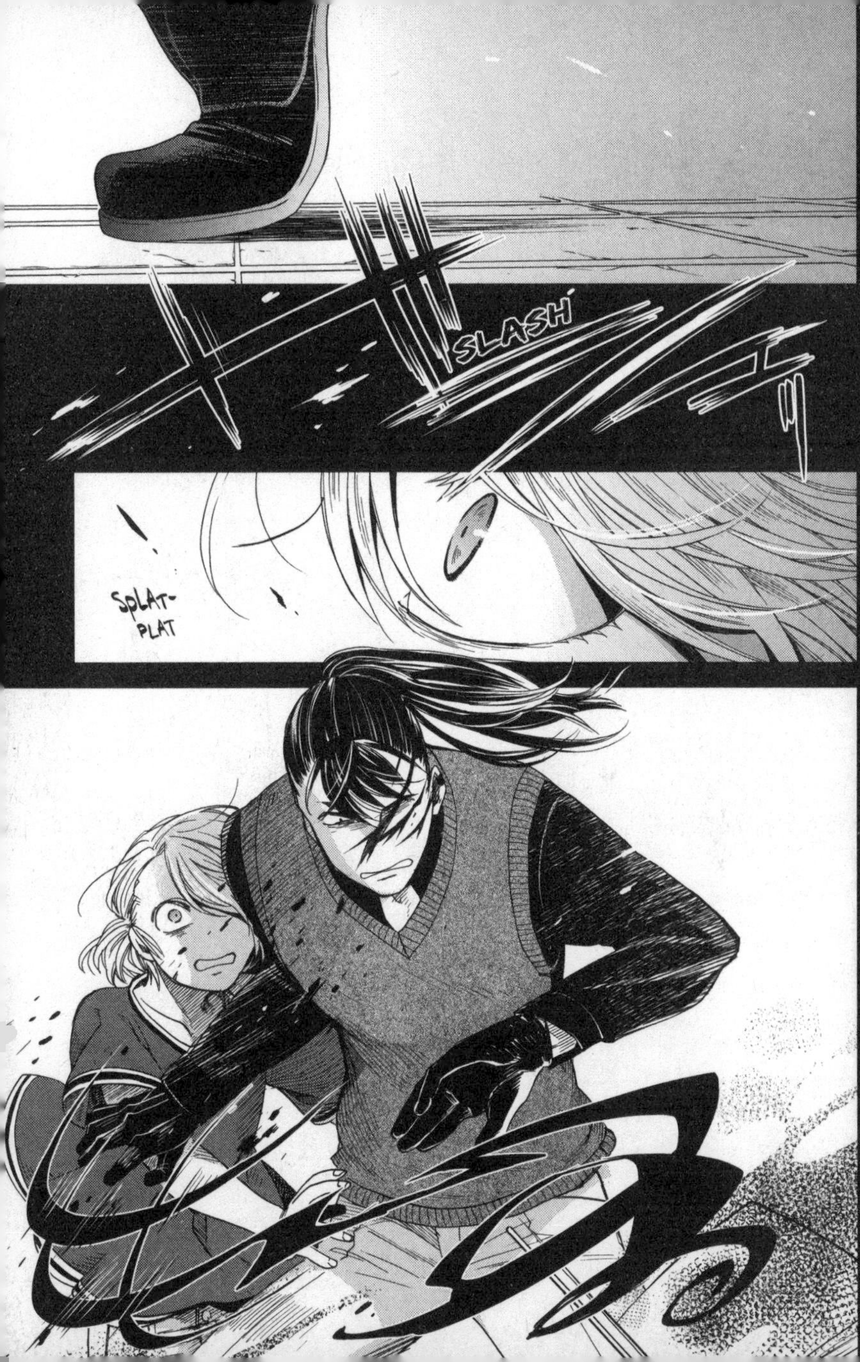
SLASH
SPLAT-
PLAT

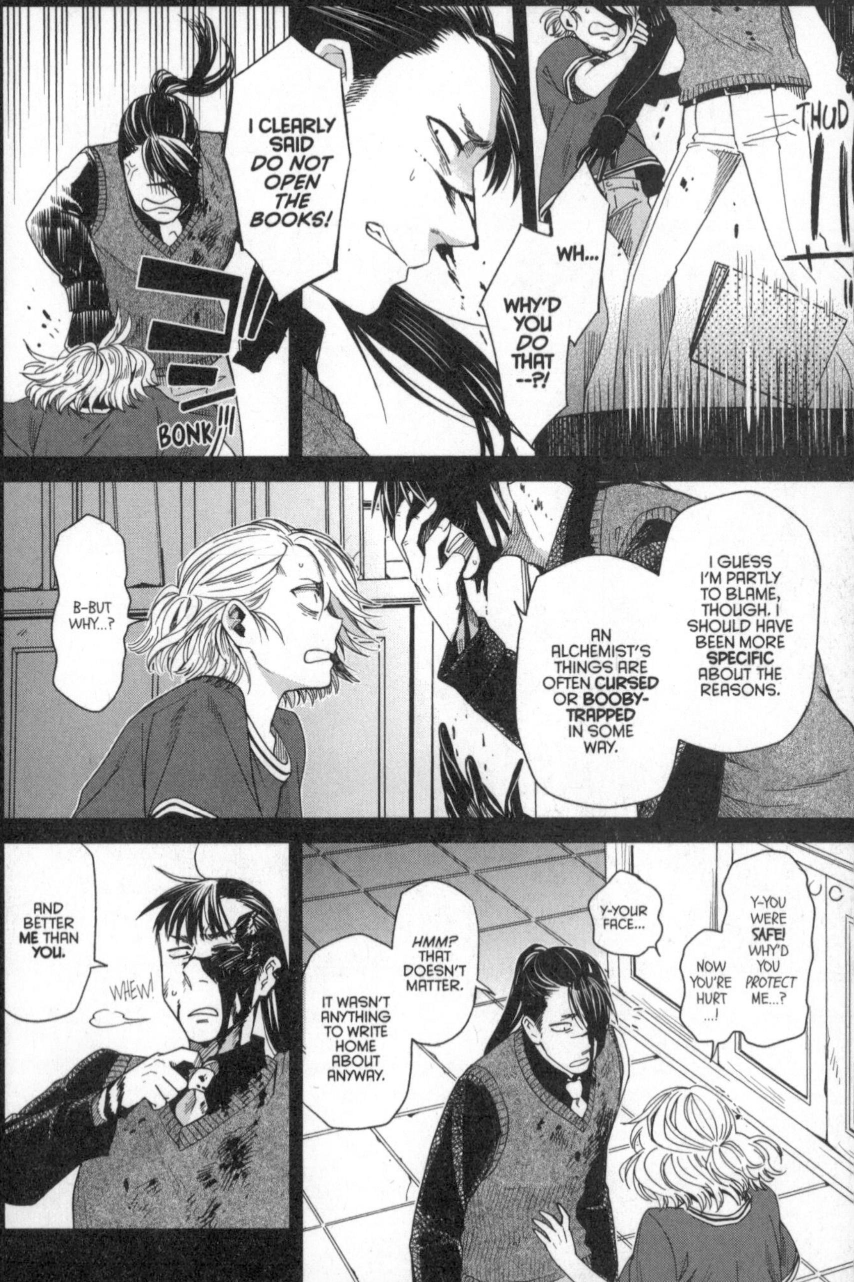
THUD
WH...
WHY'D YOU DO THAT--?!
I CLEARLY SAID DO NOT OPEN THE BOOKS!
BONK!!!
B-BUT WHY...?
AN ALCHEMIST'S THINGS ARE OFTEN CURSED OR BOOBY-TRAPPED IN SOME WAY.
I GUESS I'M PARTLY TO BLAME, THOUGH. I SHOULD HAVE BEEN MORE SPECIFIC ABOUT THE REASONS.
Y-YOU WERE SAFE! WHY'D YOU PROTECT ME...?
NOW YOU'RE HURT...!
Y-YOUR FACE...
HMM? THAT DOESN'T MATTER.
IT WASN'T ANYTHING TO WRITE HOME ABOUT ANYWAY.
AND BETTER ME THAN YOU.
WHEW!

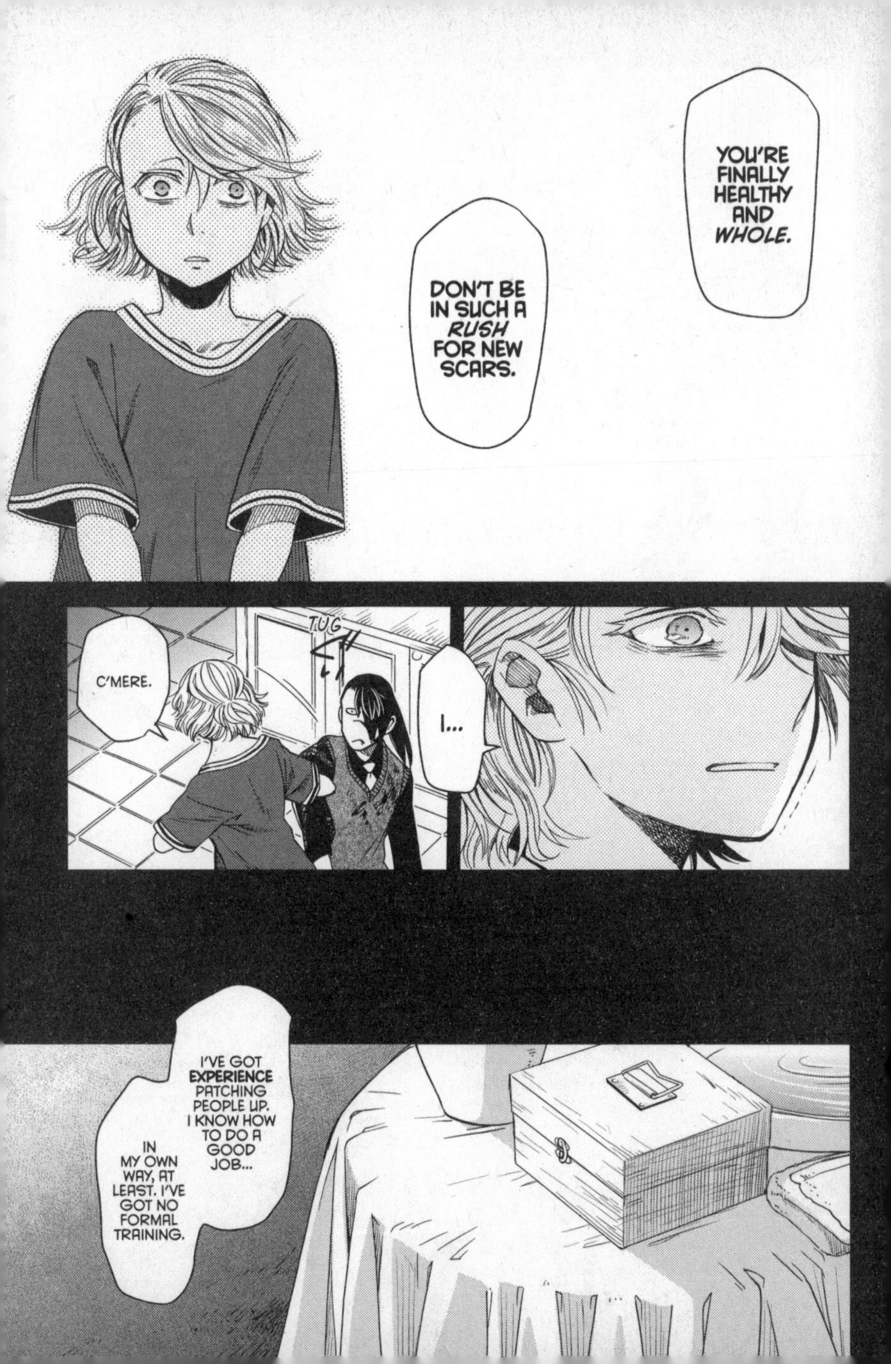
YOU'RE FINALLY HEALTHY AND *WHOLE.*
DON'T BE IN SUCH A *RUSH* FOR NEW SCARS.
I...
TUG
C'MERE.
I'VE GOT **EXPERIENCE** PATCHING PEOPLE UP. I KNOW HOW TO DO A GOOD JOB...
IN MY OWN WAY, AT LEAST. I'VE GOT NO FORMAL TRAINING.
...

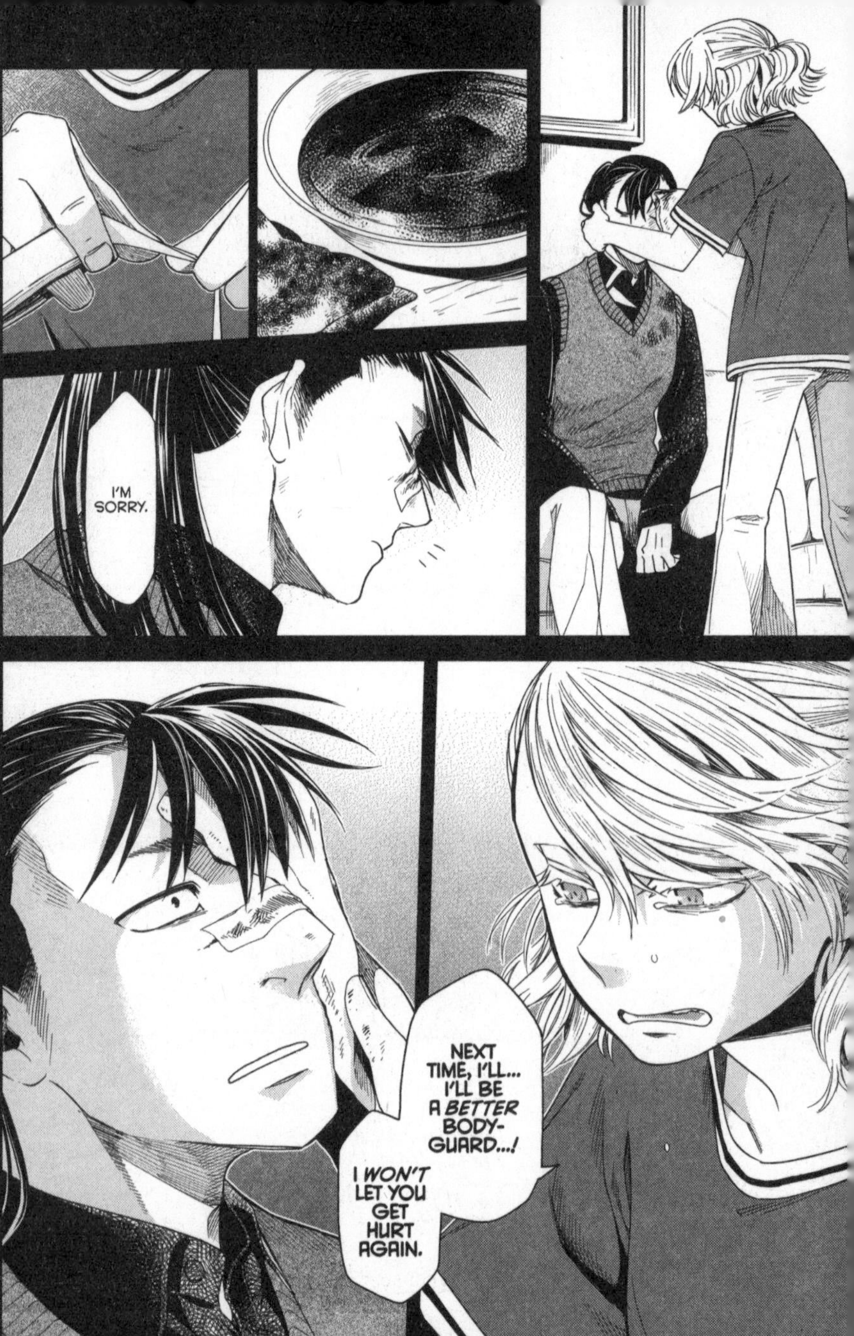
I'M SORRY.
NEXT TIME, I'LL... I'LL BE A *BETTER* BODY-GUARD...!
I *WON'T* LET YOU GET HURT AGAIN.

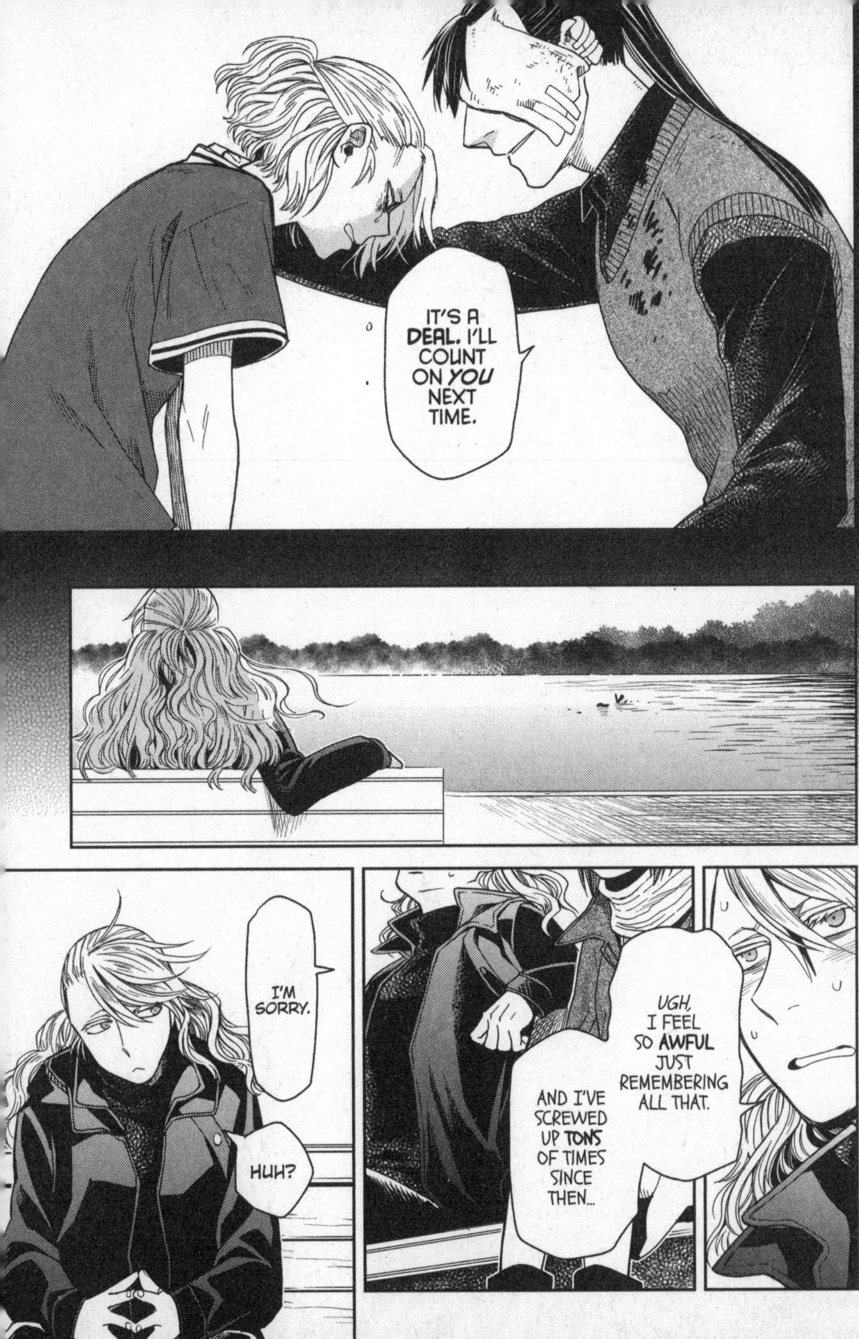
IT'S A DEAL. I'LL COUNT ON YOU NEXT TIME.
UGH, I FEEL SO AWFUL JUST REMEMBERING ALL THAT.
AND I'VE SCREWED UP TONS OF TIMES SINCE THEN...
I'M SORRY.
HUH?

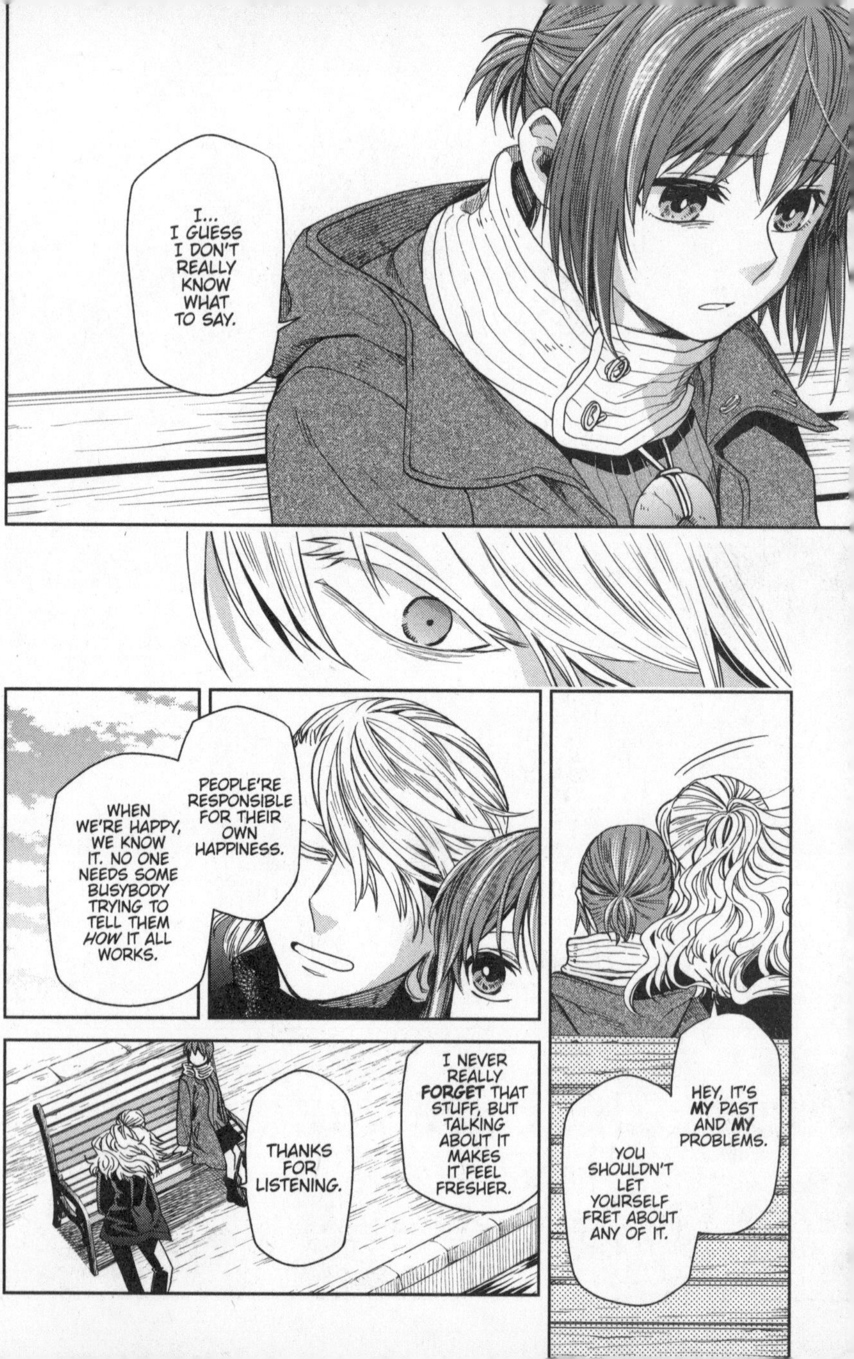
I... I GUESS I DON'T REALLY KNOW WHAT TO SAY.
PEOPLE'RE RESPONSIBLE FOR THEIR OWN HAPPINESS.
WHEN WE'RE HAPPY, WE KNOW IT. NO ONE NEEDS SOME BUSYBODY TRYING TO TELL THEM *HOW* IT ALL WORKS.
HEY, IT'S **MY** PAST AND **MY** PROBLEMS.
YOU SHOULDN'T LET YOURSELF FRET ABOUT ANY OF IT.
I NEVER REALLY **FORGET** THAT STUFF, BUT TALKING ABOUT IT MAKES IT FEEL FRESHER.
THANKS FOR LISTENING.

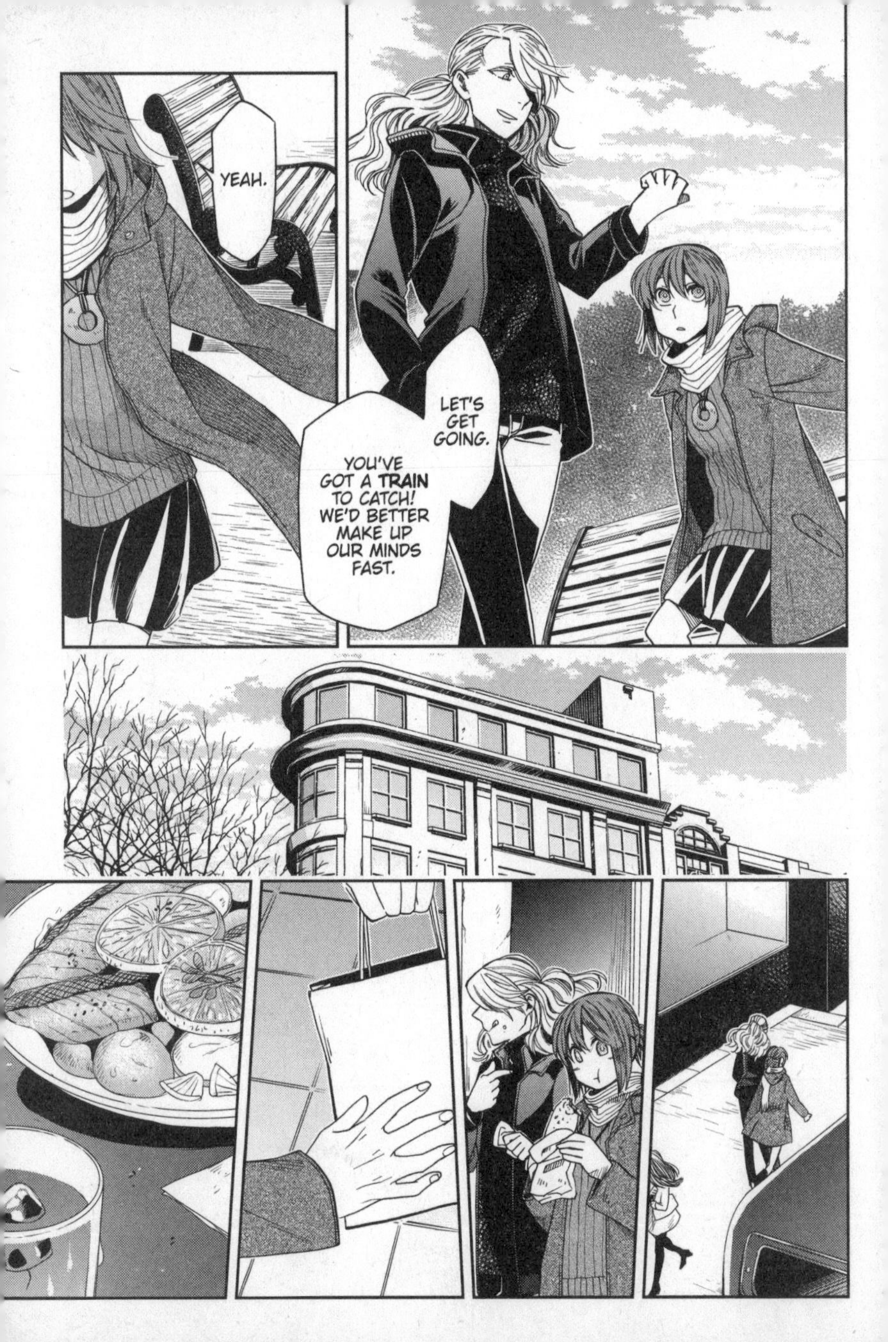
LET'S GET GOING.
YOU'VE GOT A **TRAIN** TO CATCH! WE'D BETTER MAKE UP OUR MINDS FAST.
YEAH.

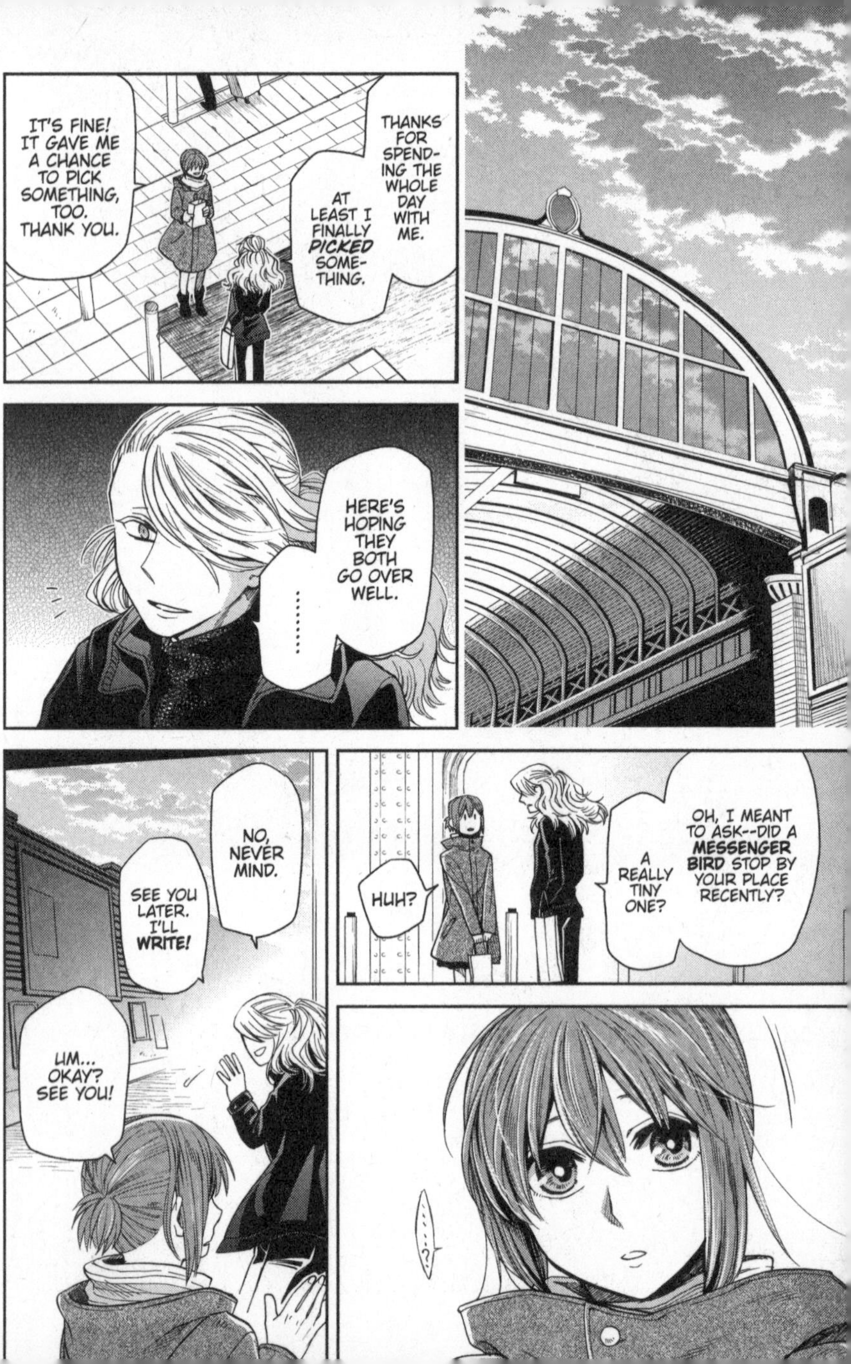
THANKS FOR SPENDING THE WHOLE DAY WITH ME.
AT LEAST I FINALLY **PICKED** SOMETHING.
IT'S FINE! IT GAVE ME A CHANCE TO PICK SOMETHING, TOO. THANK YOU.
HERE'S HOPING THEY BOTH GO OVER WELL.
......
OH, I MEANT TO ASK--DID A **MESSENGER BIRD** STOP BY YOUR PLACE RECENTLY?
A REALLY TINY ONE?
HUH?
......?
NO, NEVER MIND.
SEE YOU LATER. I'LL **WRITE!**
UM... OKAY? SEE YOU!

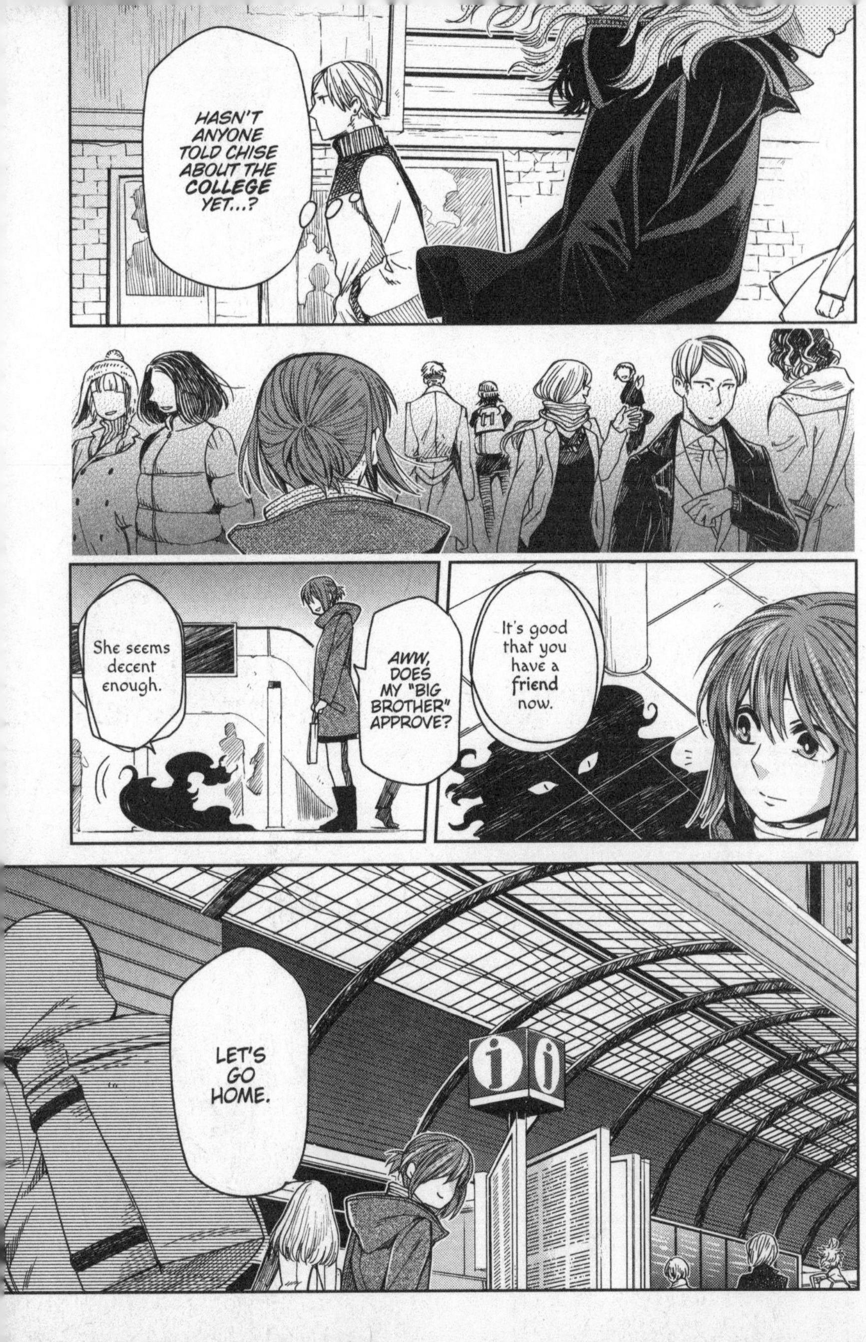
HASN'T ANYONE TOLD CHISE ABOUT THE COLLEGE YET...?
It's good that you have a friend now.
AWW, DOES MY "BIG BROTHER" APPROVE?
She seems decent enough.
LET'S GO HOME.

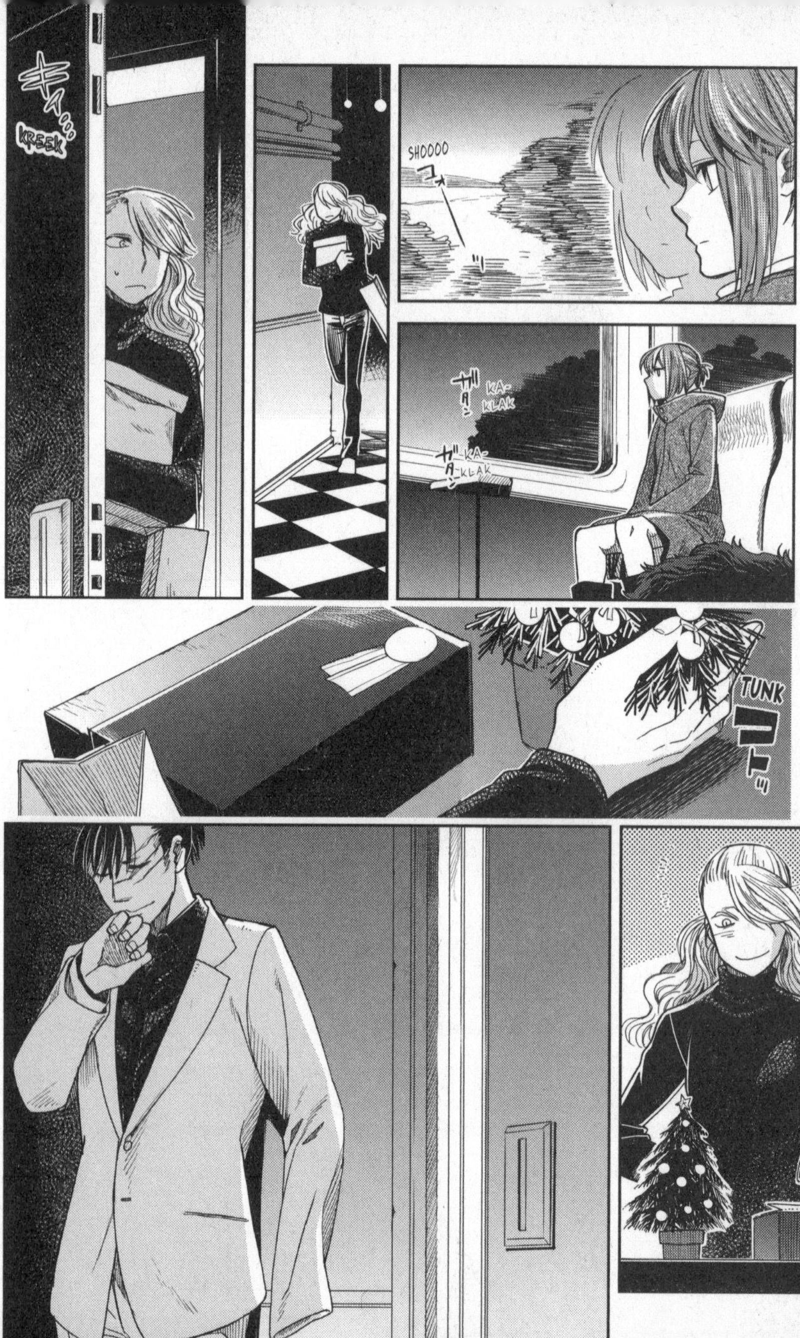
SHOOOO
コォ
KA-KLAK
KA-KLAK
キィ…
KREEK
TUNK
コトッ

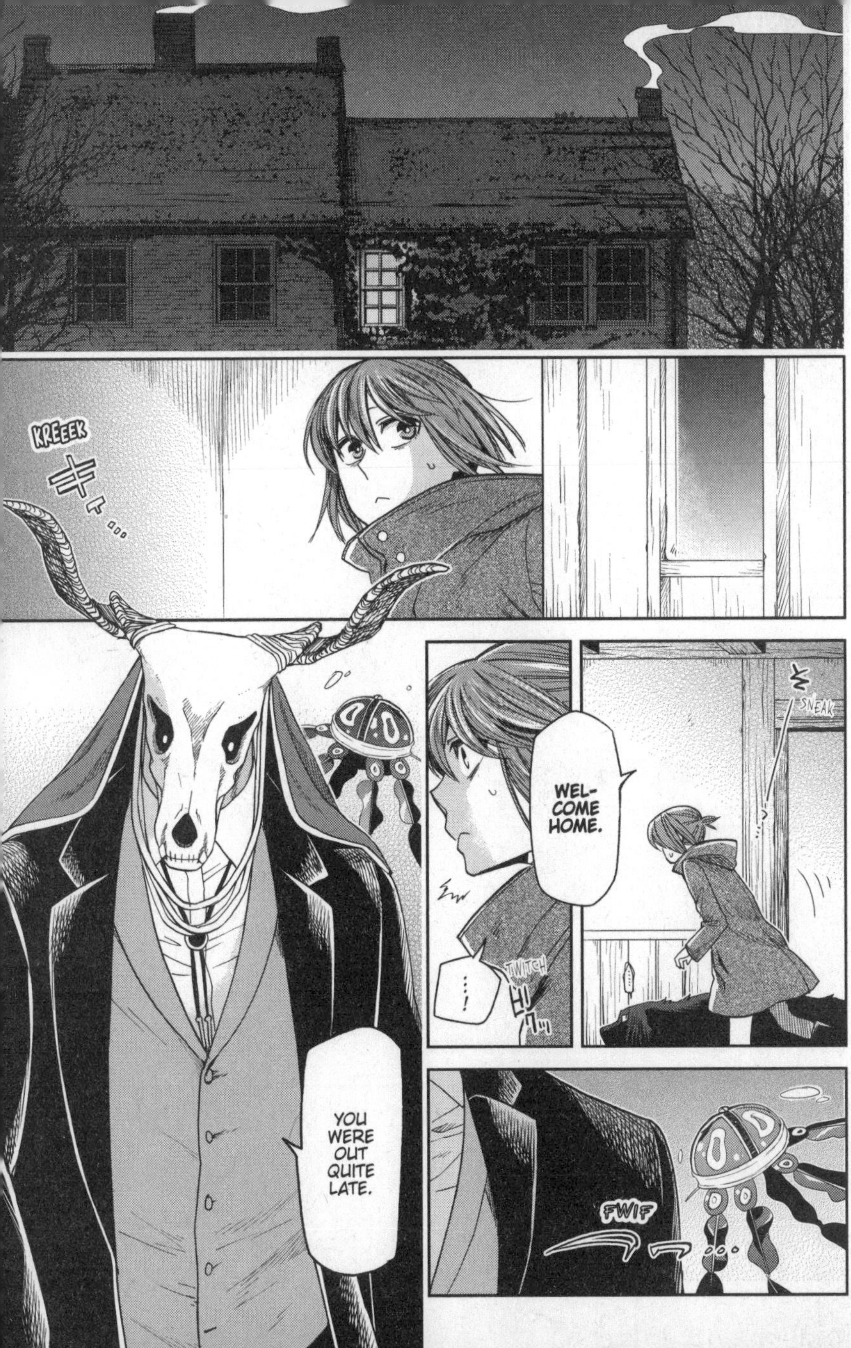
KREEEK
SNEAK
WEL-COME HOME.
TWITCH
...!
FWIF
YOU WERE OUT QUITE LATE.

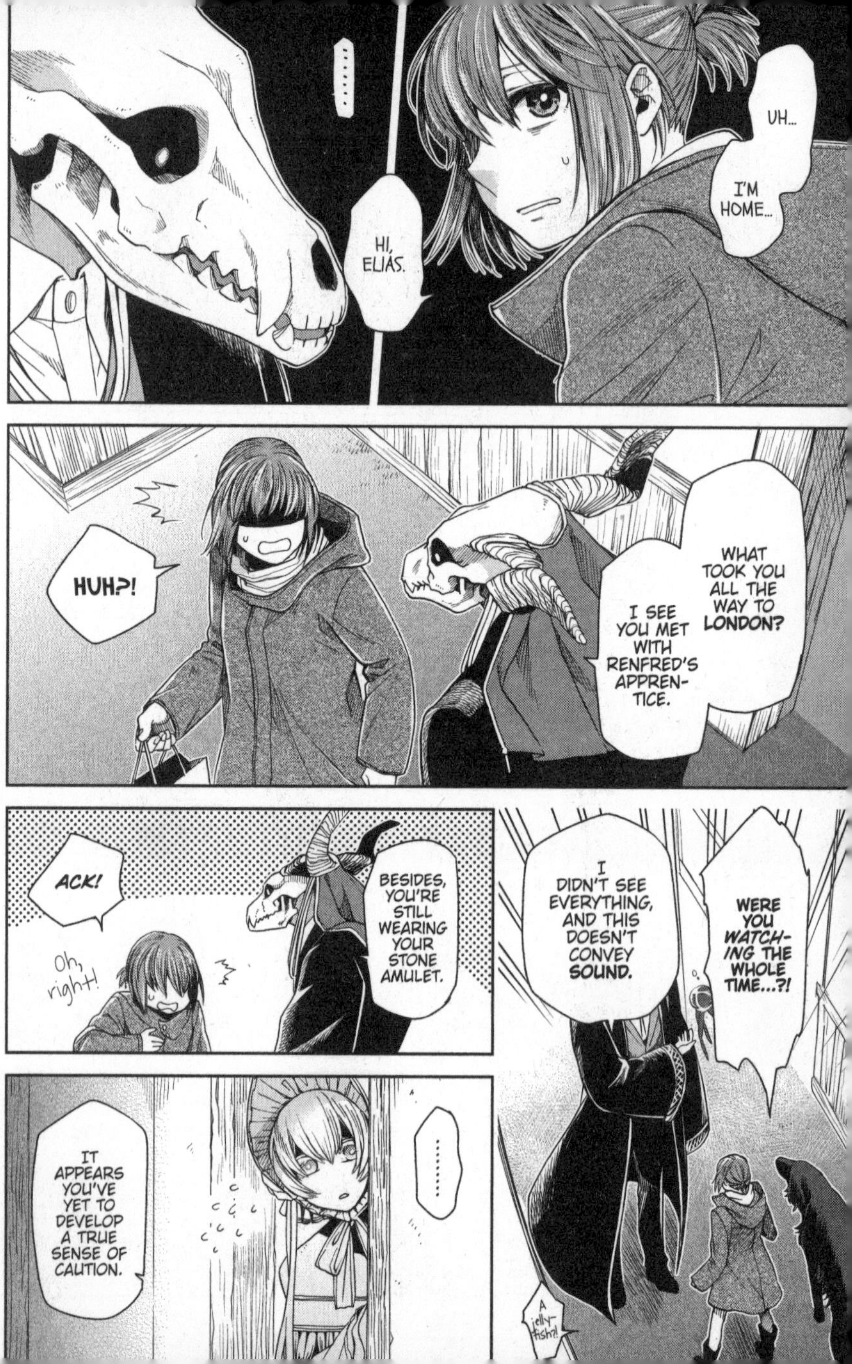
UH...
I'M HOME...
HI, ELIAS.
......
WHAT TOOK YOU ALL THE WAY TO LONDON?
I SEE YOU MET WITH RENFRED'S APPRENTICE.
HUH?!
WERE YOU WATCHING THE WHOLE TIME...?!
I DIDN'T SEE EVERYTHING, AND THIS DOESN'T CONVEY SOUND.
A jelly-fish?!
BESIDES, YOU'RE STILL WEARING YOUR STONE AMULET.
ACK!
Oh, right!
....
IT APPEARS YOU'VE YET TO DEVELOP A TRUE SENSE OF CAUTION.

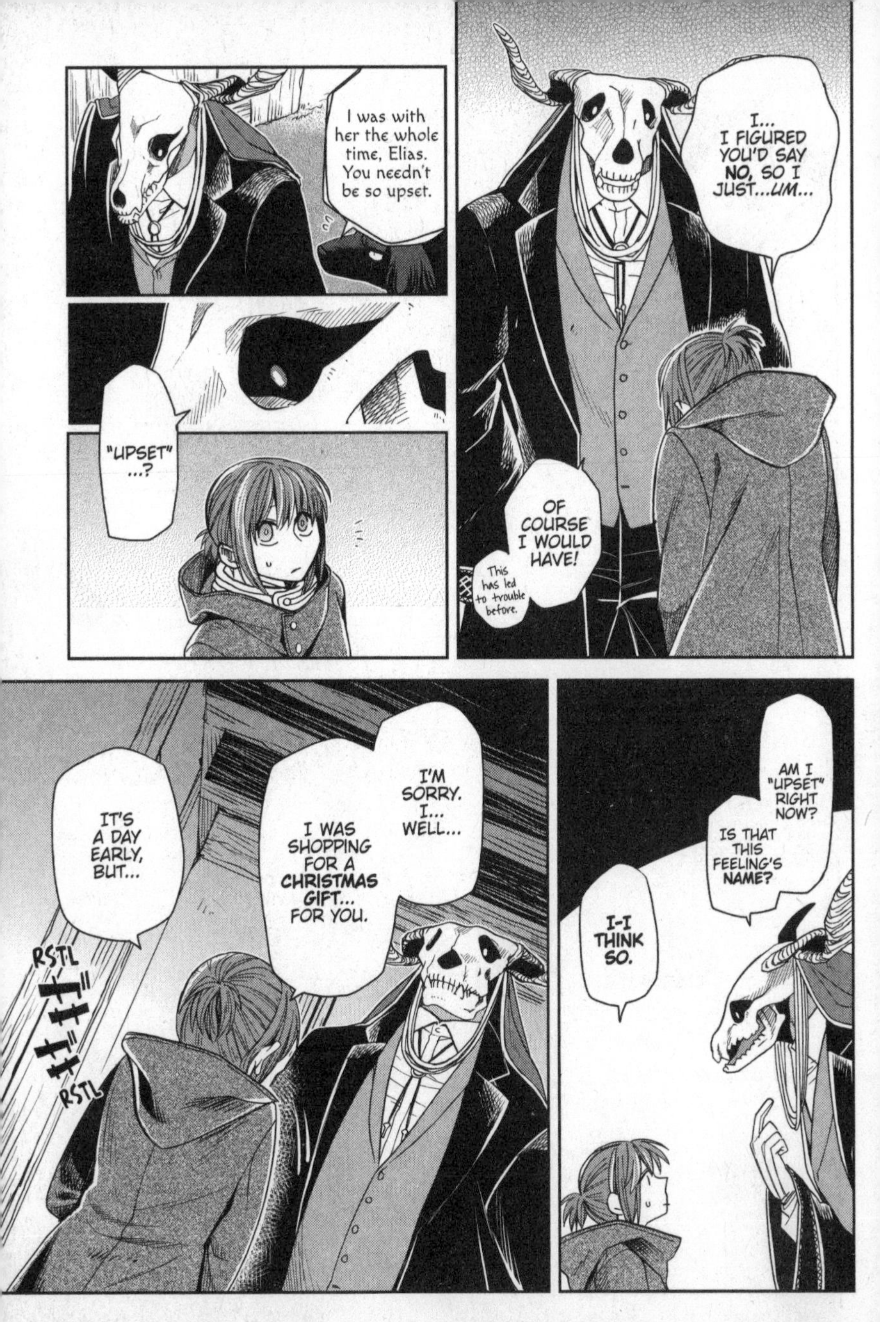
I... I FIGURED YOU'D SAY NO, SO I JUST...UM...
OF COURSE I WOULD HAVE!
This has led to trouble before.
I was with her the whole time, Elias. You needn't be so upset.
"UPSET" ...?
AM I "UPSET" RIGHT NOW?
IS THAT THIS FEELING'S NAME?
I-I THINK SO.
I'M SORRY. I... WELL...
I WAS SHOPPING FOR A CHRISTMAS GIFT... FOR YOU.
IT'S A DAY EARLY, BUT...
RSTL
RSTL

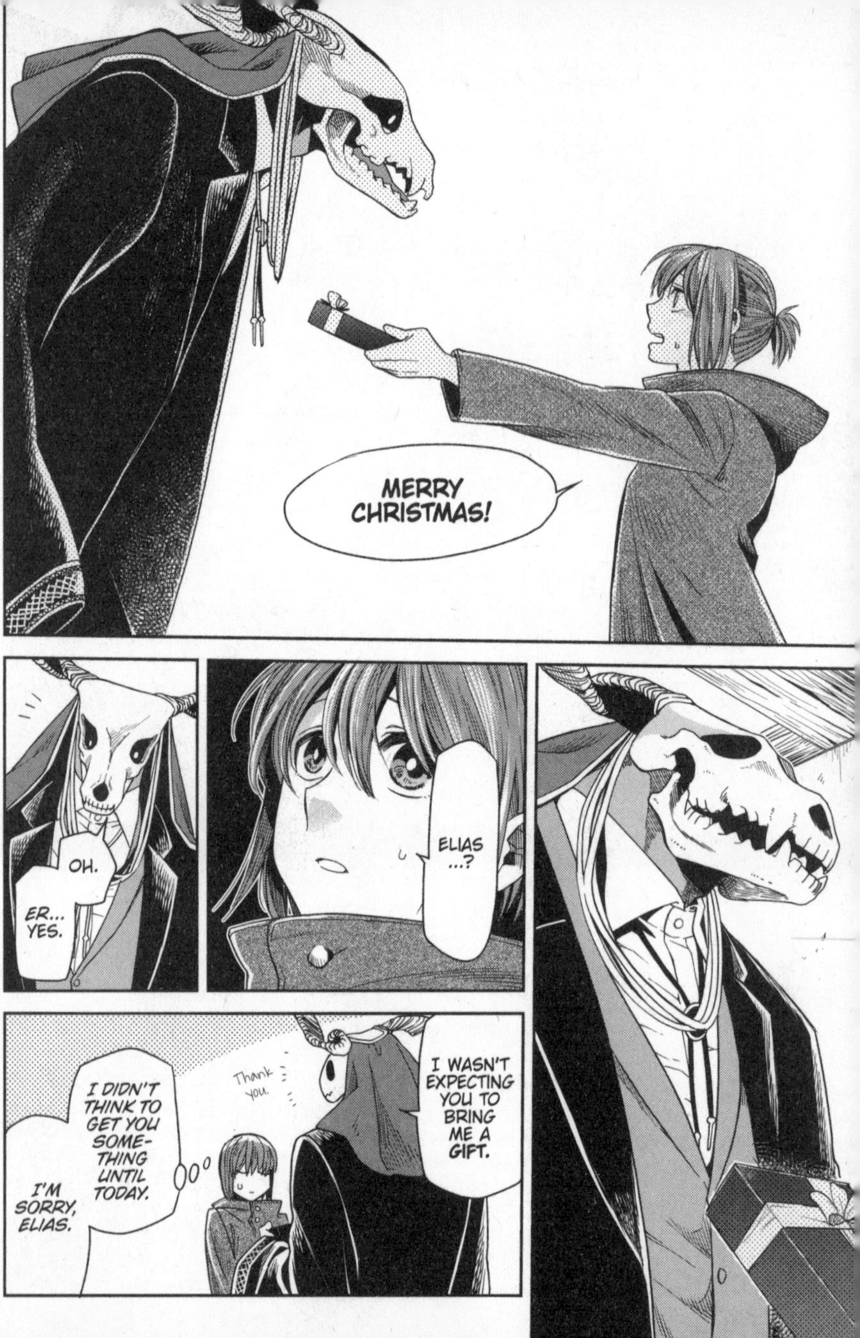
MERRY CHRISTMAS!
ELIAS ...?
OH.
ER... YES.
I WASN'T EXPECTING YOU TO BRING ME A GIFT.
Thank you.
I DIDN'T THINK TO GET YOU SOME-THING UNTIL TODAY.
I'M SORRY, ELIAS.

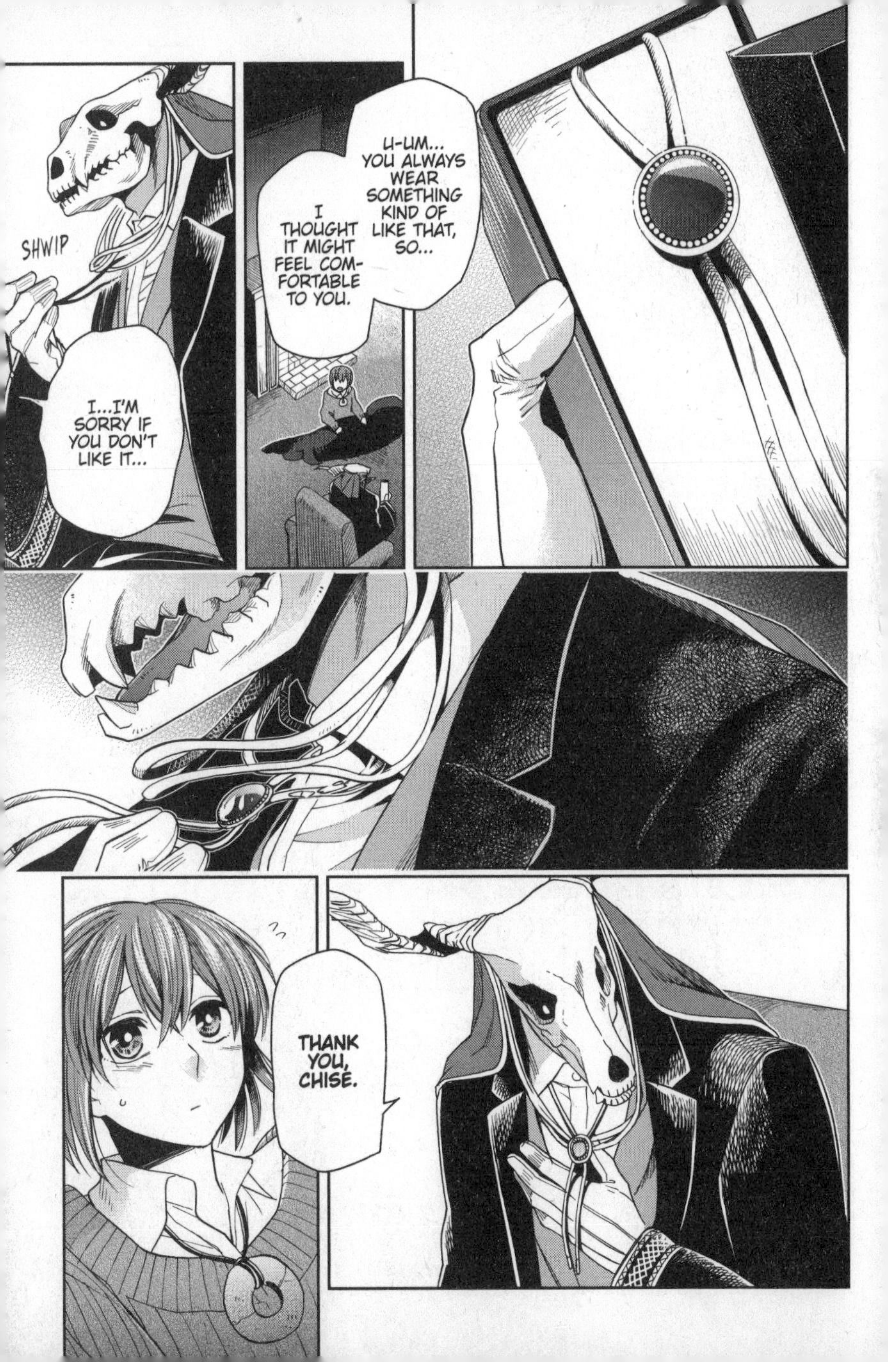

U-UM... YOU ALWAYS WEAR SOMETHING KIND OF LIKE THAT, SO...
I THOUGHT IT MIGHT FEEL COM-FORTABLE TO YOU.
SHWIP
I...I'M SORRY IF YOU DON'T LIKE IT...
THANK YOU, CHISE.

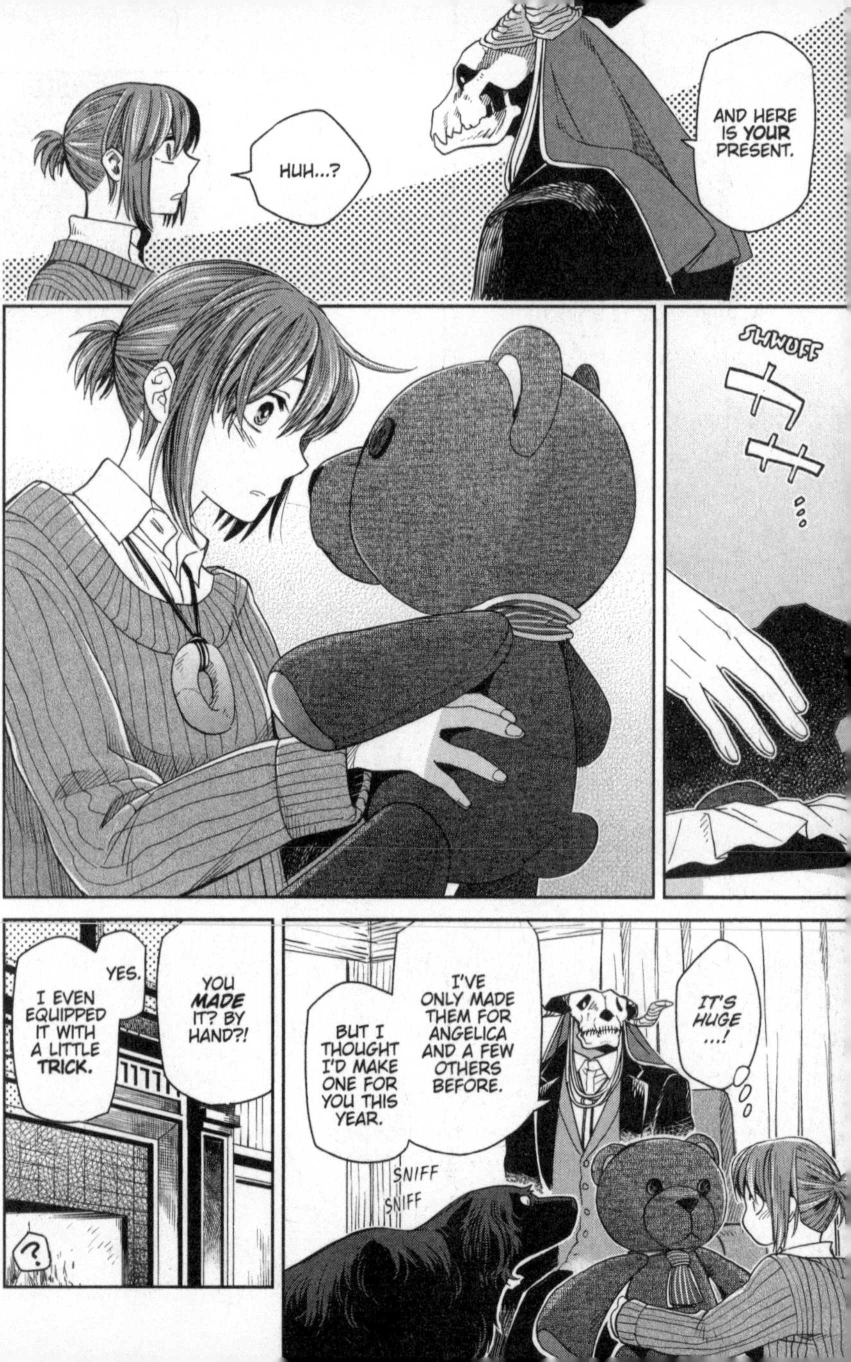
AND HERE IS YOUR PRESENT.
HUH...?
SHWOFF
IT'S HUGE ...!
I'VE ONLY MADE THEM FOR ANGELICA AND A FEW OTHERS BEFORE.
BUT I THOUGHT I'D MAKE ONE FOR YOU THIS YEAR.
SNIFF
SNIFF
YOU MADE IT? BY HAND?!
YES.
I EVEN EQUIPPED IT WITH A LITTLE TRICK.
?

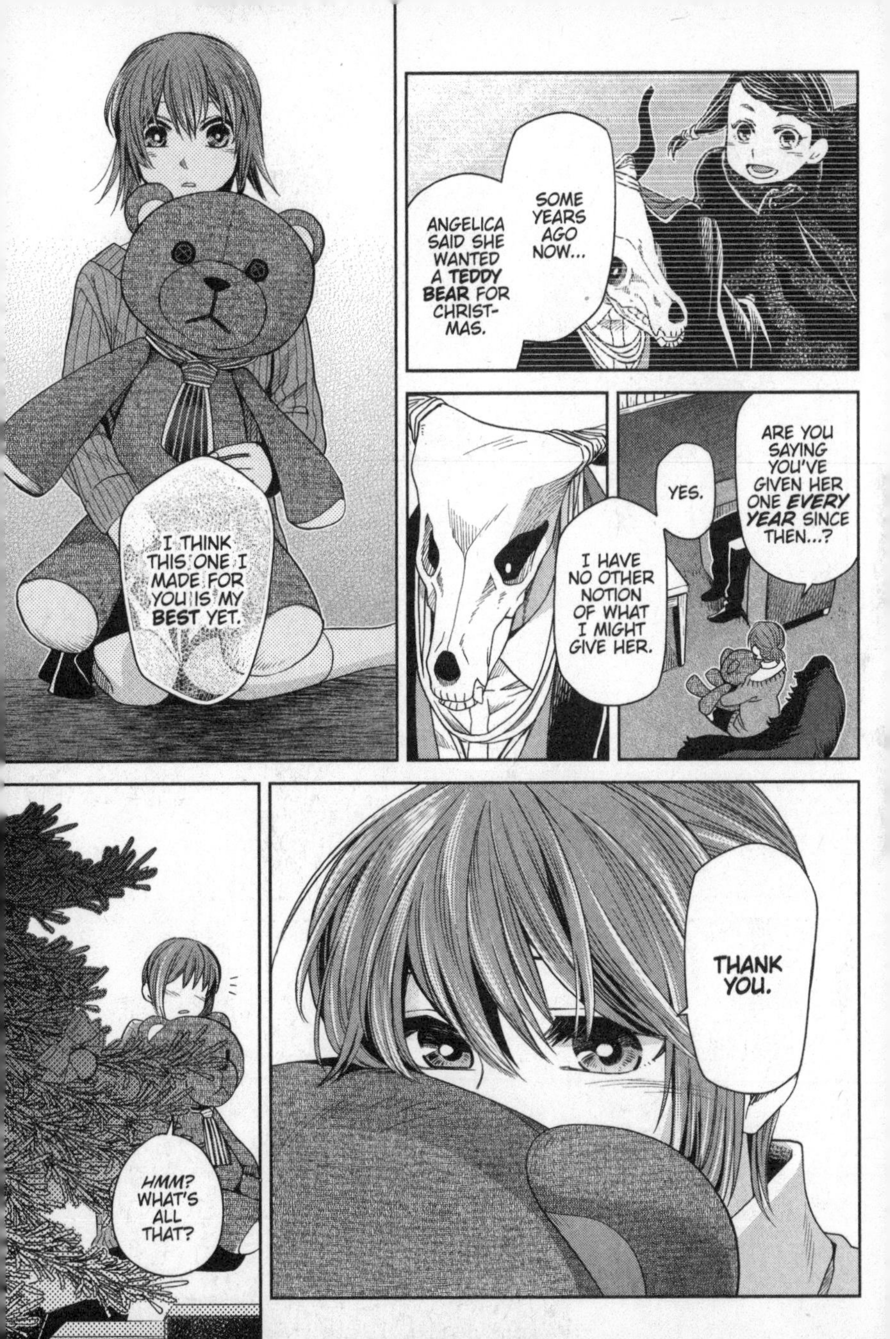
SOME YEARS AGO NOW... ANGELICA SAID SHE WANTED A TEDDY BEAR FOR CHRIST-MAS.
ARE YOU SAYING YOU'VE GIVEN HER ONE EVERY YEAR SINCE THEN...?
YES.
I HAVE NO OTHER NOTION OF WHAT I MIGHT GIVE HER.
I THINK THIS ONE I MADE FOR YOU IS MY BEST YET.
THANK YOU.
HMM? WHAT'S ALL THAT?

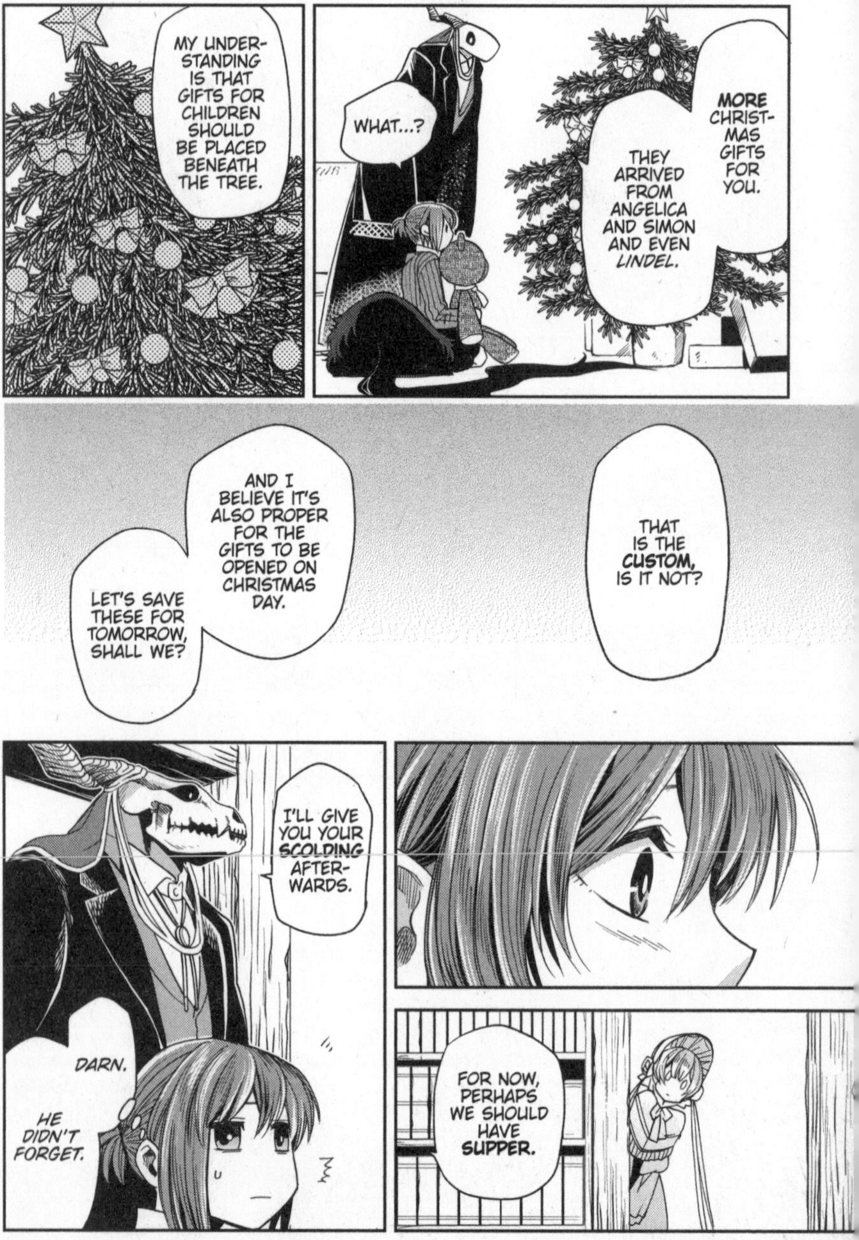
MORE CHRISTMAS GIFTS FOR YOU.
THEY ARRIVED FROM ANGELICA AND SIMON AND EVEN LINDEL.
WHAT...?
MY UNDERSTANDING IS THAT GIFTS FOR CHILDREN SHOULD BE PLACED BENEATH THE TREE.
THAT IS THE CUSTOM, IS IT NOT?
AND I BELIEVE IT'S ALSO PROPER FOR THE GIFTS TO BE OPENED ON CHRISTMAS DAY.
LET'S SAVE THESE FOR TOMORROW, SHALL WE?
FOR NOW, PERHAPS WE SHOULD HAVE SUPPER.
I'LL GIVE YOU YOUR SCOLDING AFTERWARDS.
DARN.
HE DIDN'T FORGET.

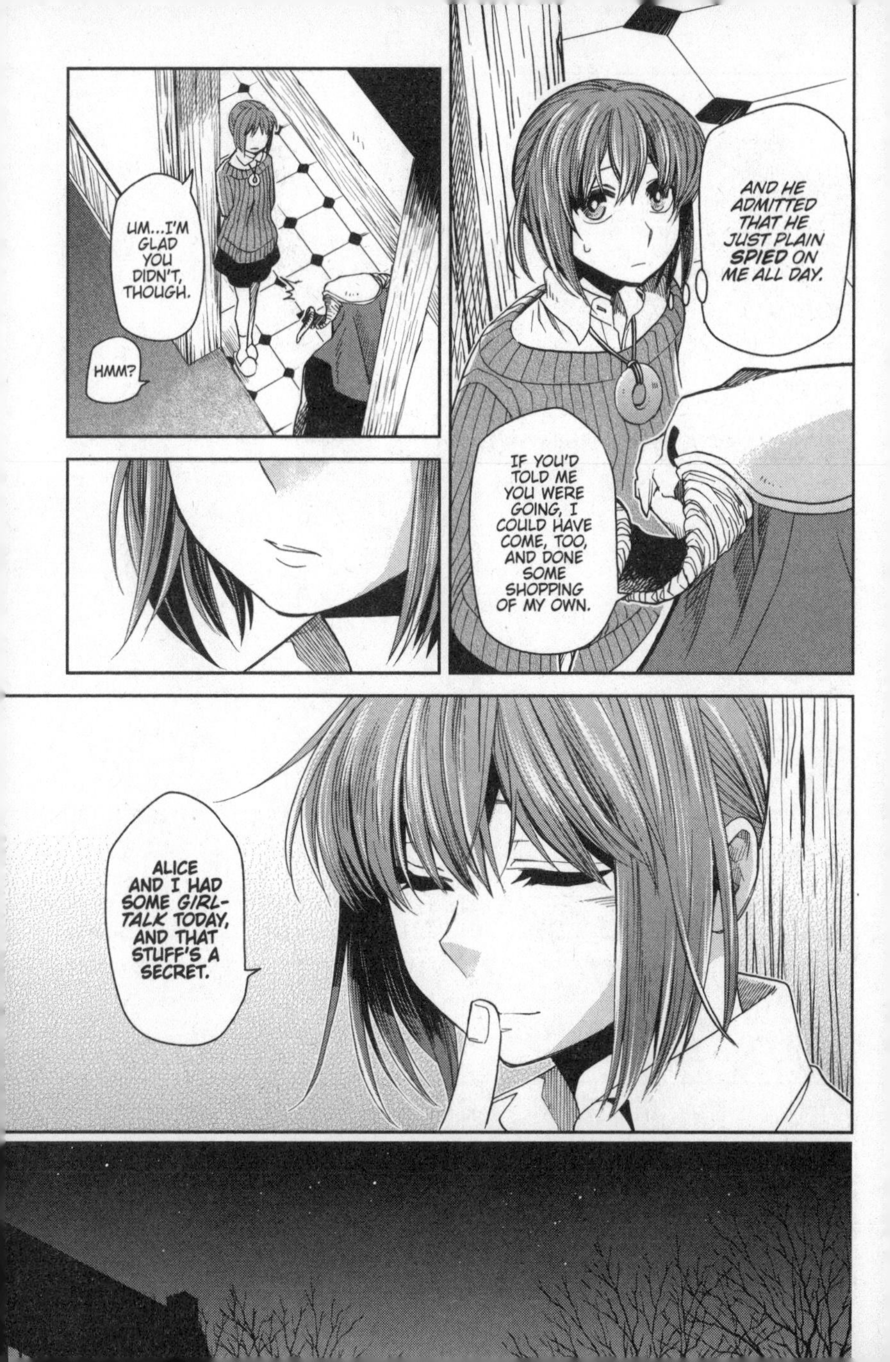
AND HE ADMITTED THAT HE JUST PLAIN SPIED ON ME ALL DAY.
IF YOU'D TOLD ME YOU WERE GOING, I COULD HAVE COME, TOO, AND DONE SOME SHOPPING OF MY OWN.
UM...I'M GLAD YOU DIDN'T, THOUGH.
HMM?
ALICE AND I HAD SOME *GIRL-TALK* TODAY, AND THAT STUFF'S A SECRET.

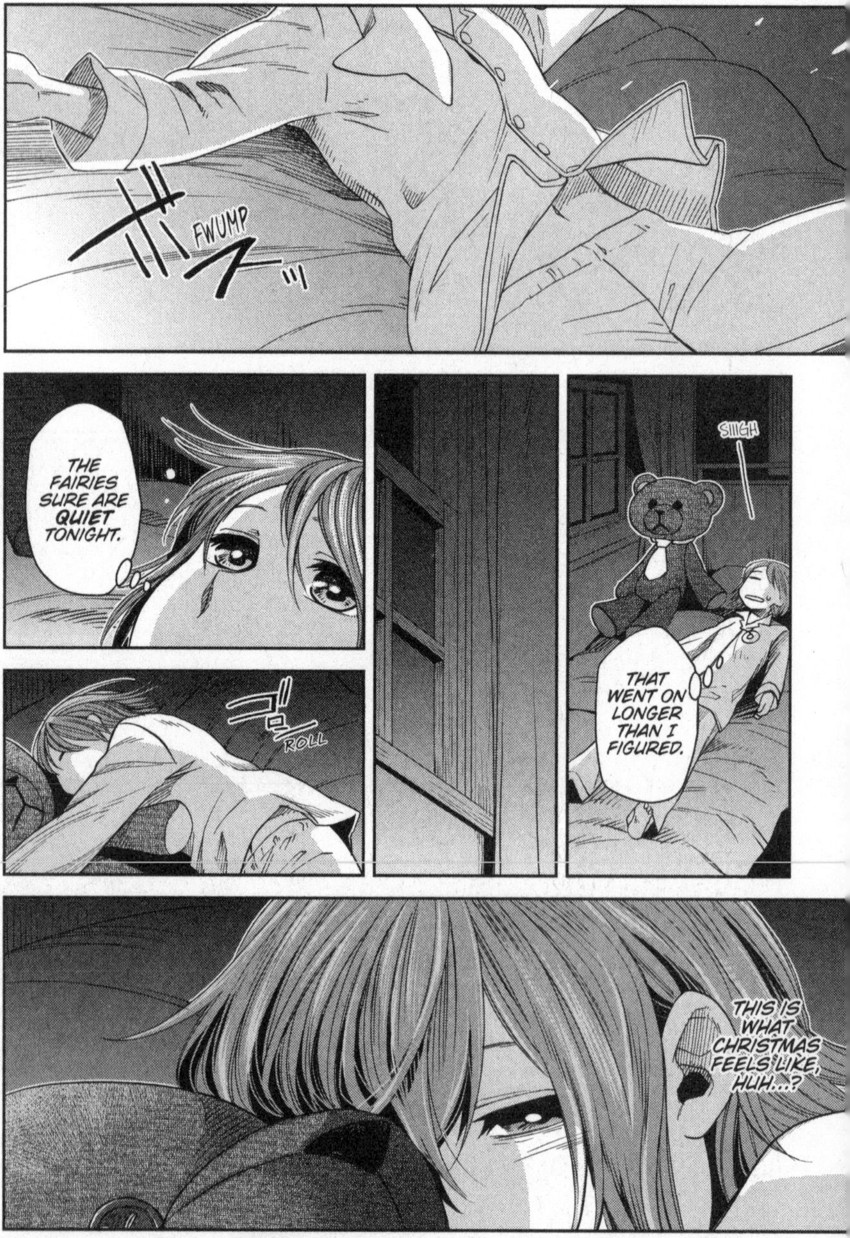
FWUMP
SIIIGH
THAT WENT ON LONGER THAN I FIGURED.
THE FAIRIES SURE ARE QUIET TONIGHT.
ROLL
THIS IS WHAT CHRISTMAS FEELS LIKE, HUH...?

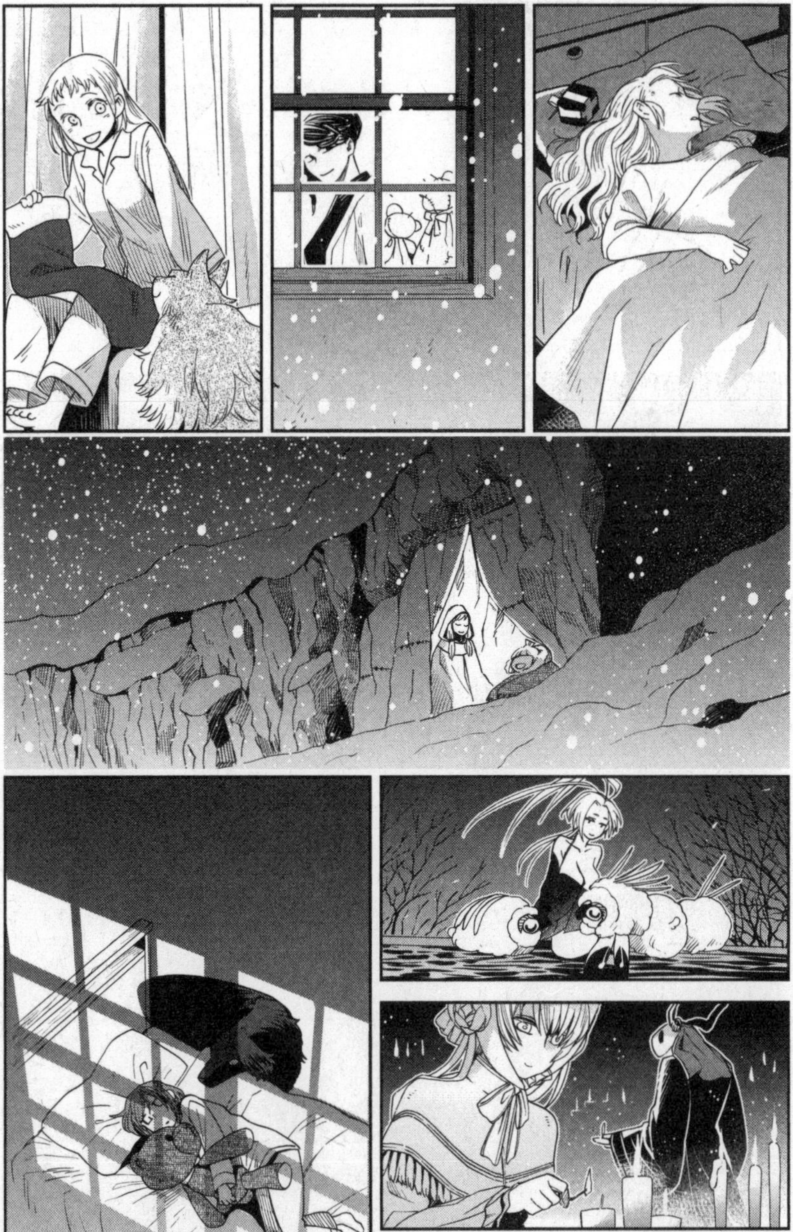

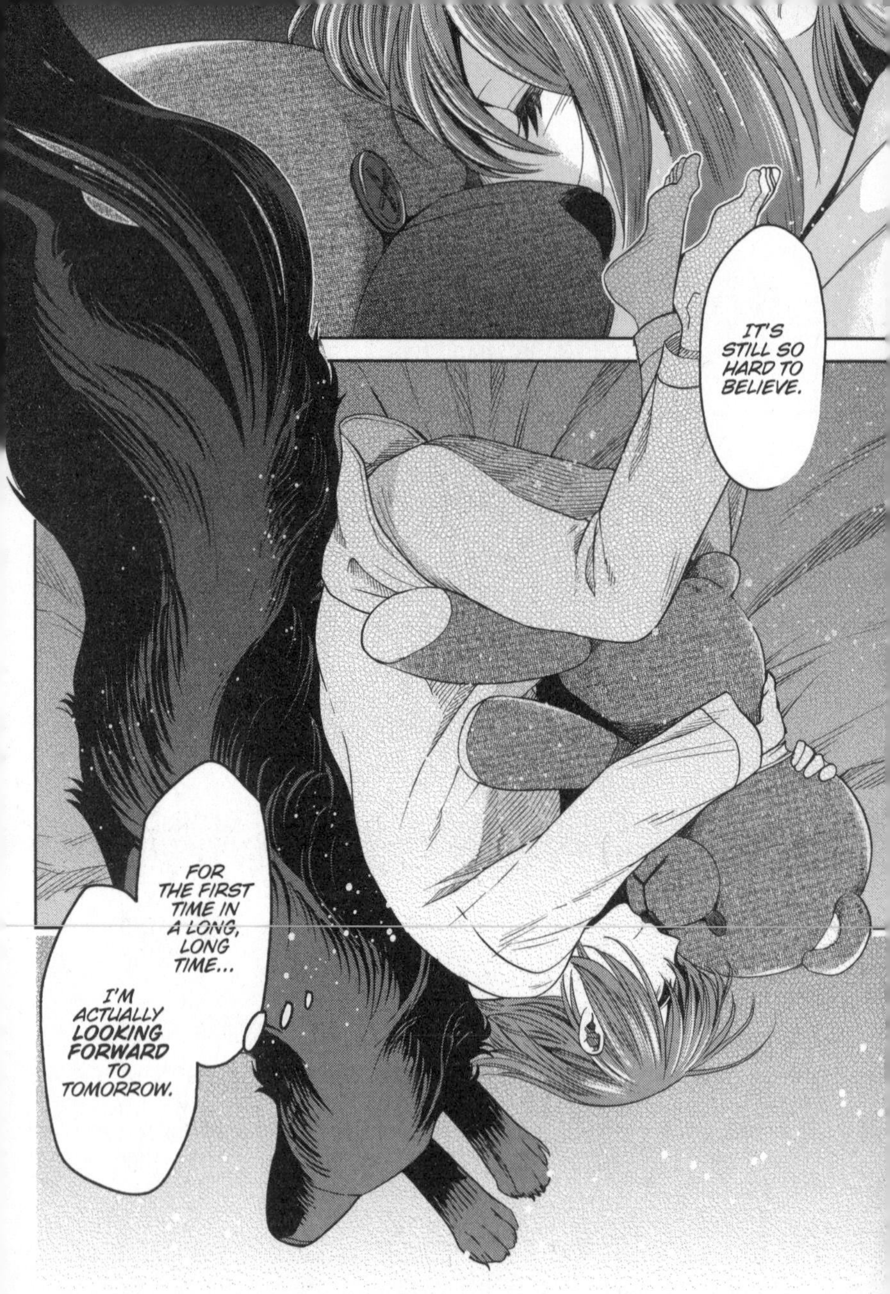
IT'S STILL SO HARD TO BELIEVE.
FOR THE FIRST TIME IN A LONG, LONG TIME...
I'M ACTUALLY LOOKING FORWARD TO TOMORROW.

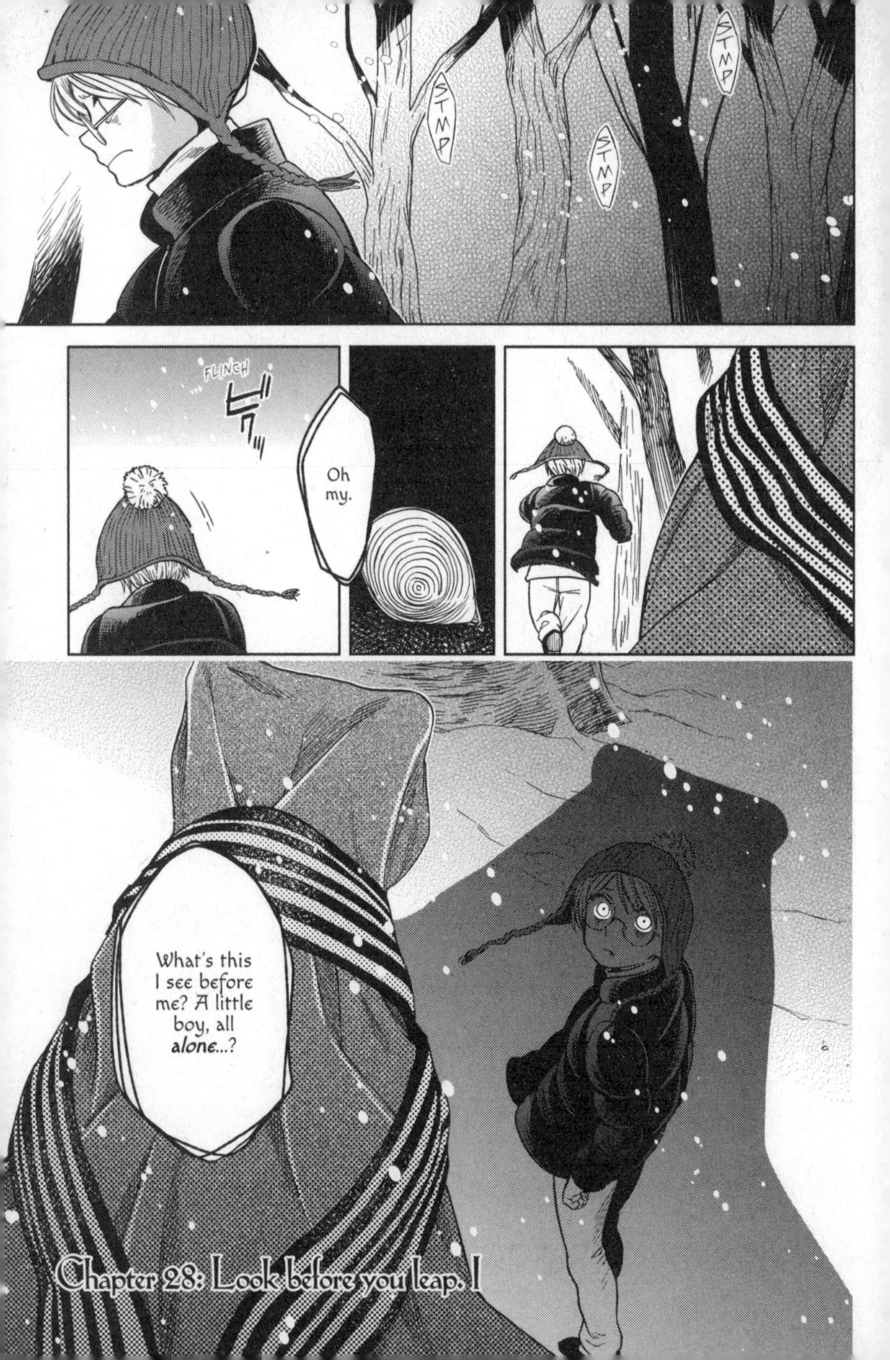
STMP
STMP
STMP
Oh my.
FLINCH
What's this I see before me? A little boy, all **alone**...?
Chapter 28: Look before you leap. I

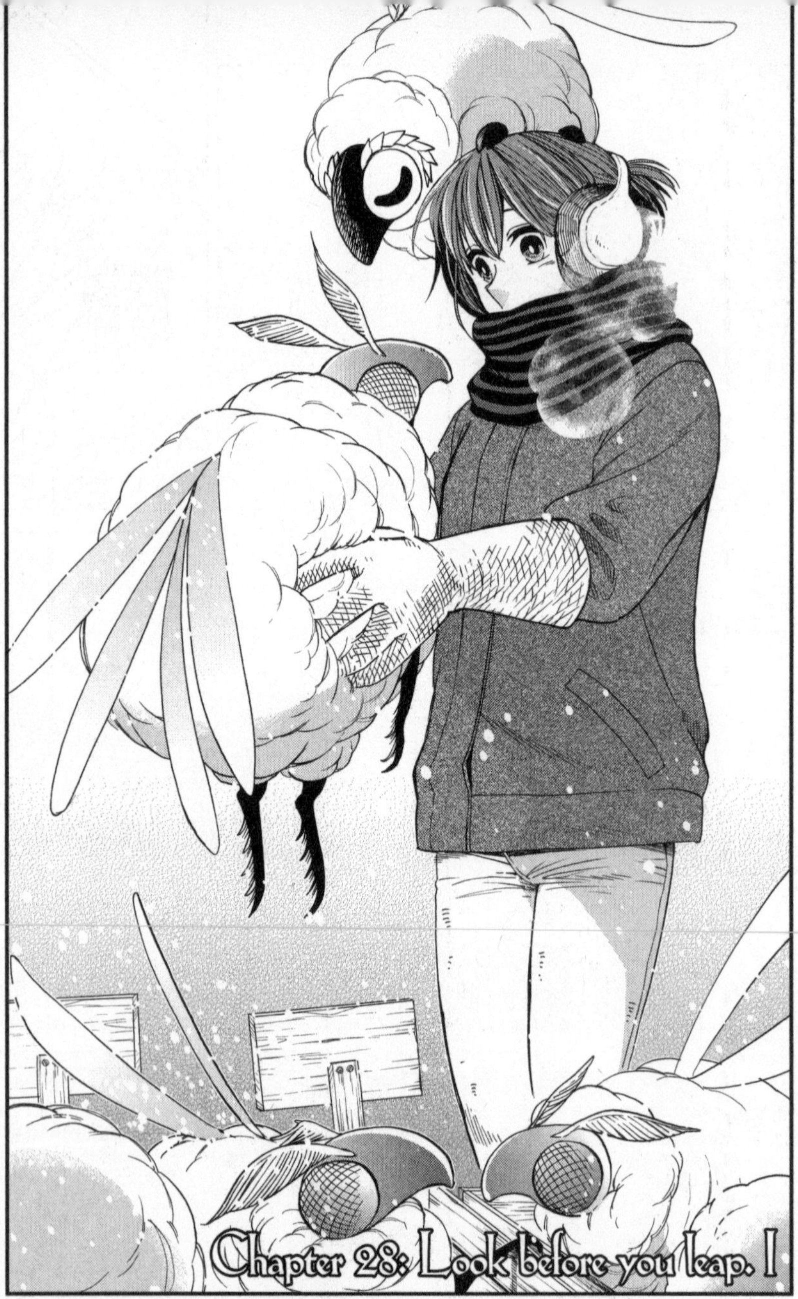
Chapter 28: Look before you leap. 1

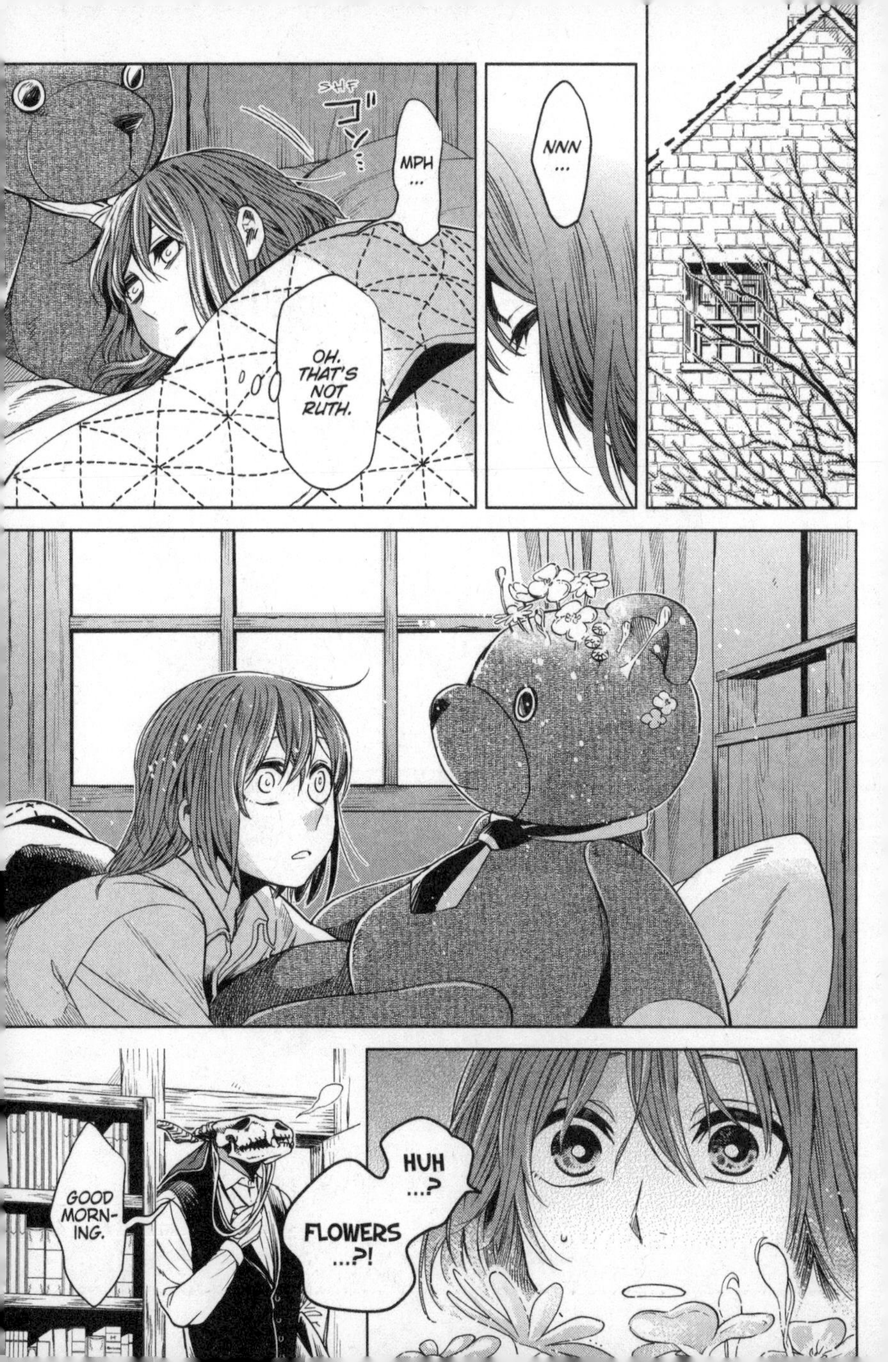
NNN ...
SHF
MPH ...
OH. THAT'S NOT RUTH.
HUH ...?
FLOWERS ...?!
GOOD MORNING.

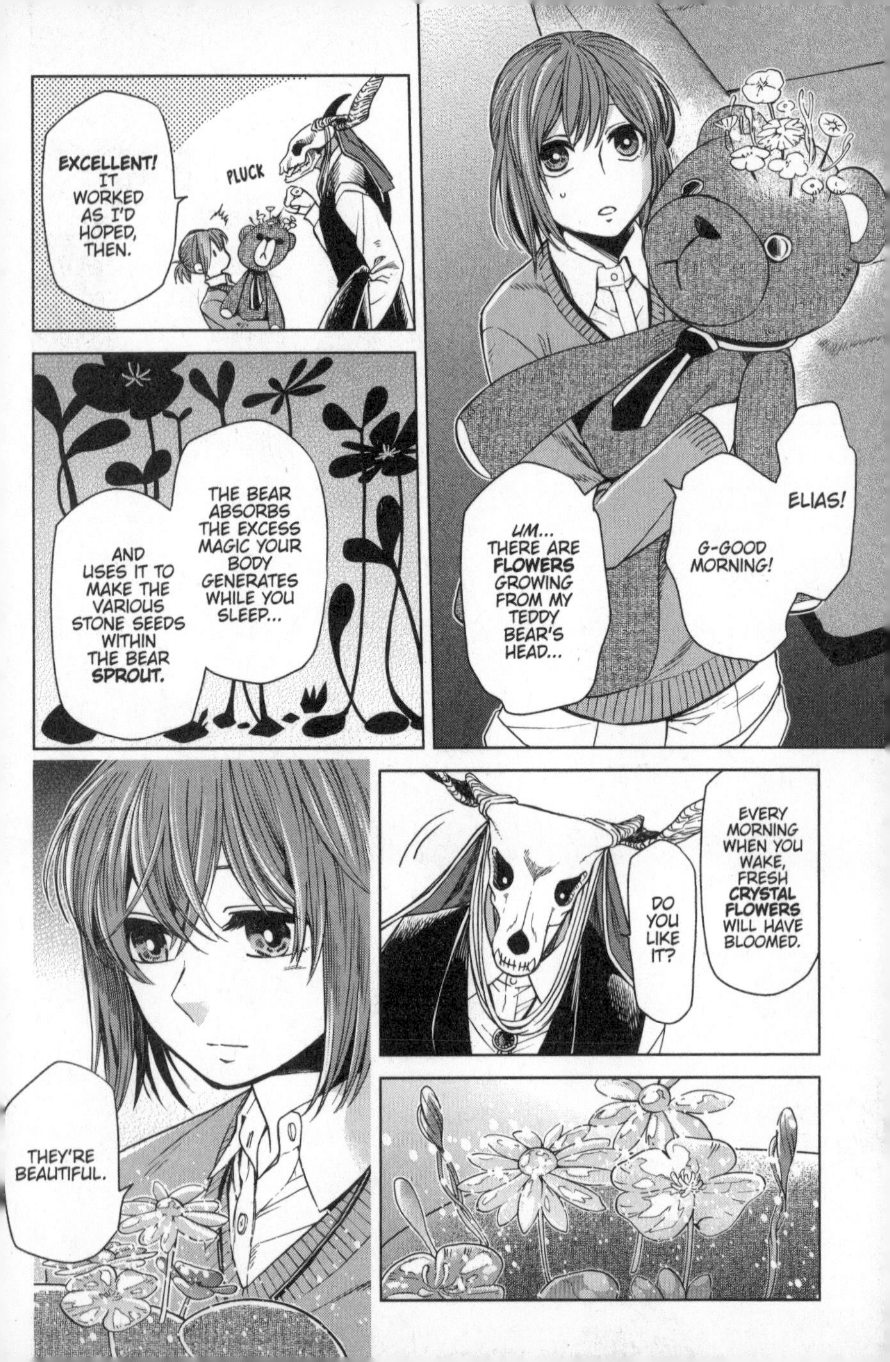
ELIAS!
G-GOOD MORNING!
UM... THERE ARE FLOWERS GROWING FROM MY TEDDY BEAR'S HEAD...
EXCELLENT! IT WORKED AS I'D HOPED, THEN.
PLUCK
THE BEAR ABSORBS THE EXCESS MAGIC YOUR BODY GENERATES WHILE YOU SLEEP...
AND USES IT TO MAKE THE VARIOUS STONE SEEDS WITHIN THE BEAR SPROUT.
EVERY MORNING WHEN YOU WAKE, FRESH CRYSTAL FLOWERS WILL HAVE BLOOMED.
DO YOU LIKE IT?
THEY'RE BEAUTIFUL.

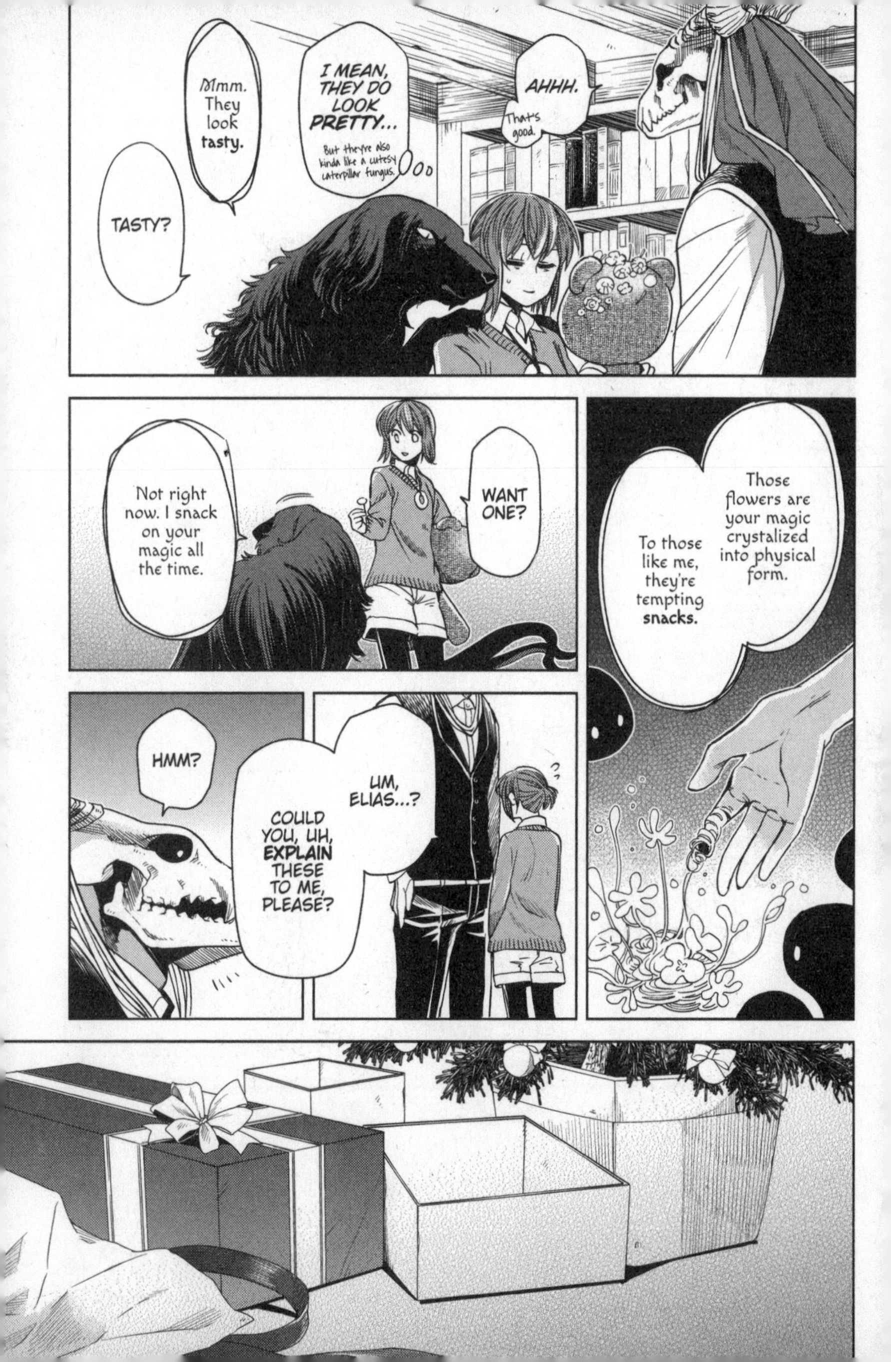
AHHH.
That's good.
I MEAN, THEY DO LOOK PRETTY...
But they're also kinda like a cutesy caterpillar fungus.
Mmm. They look tasty.
TASTY?
Those flowers are your magic crystalized into physical form.
To those like me, they're tempting snacks.
WANT ONE?
Not right now. I snack on your magic all the time.
UM, ELIAS...?
COULD YOU, UH, EXPLAIN THESE TO ME, PLEASE?
HMM?

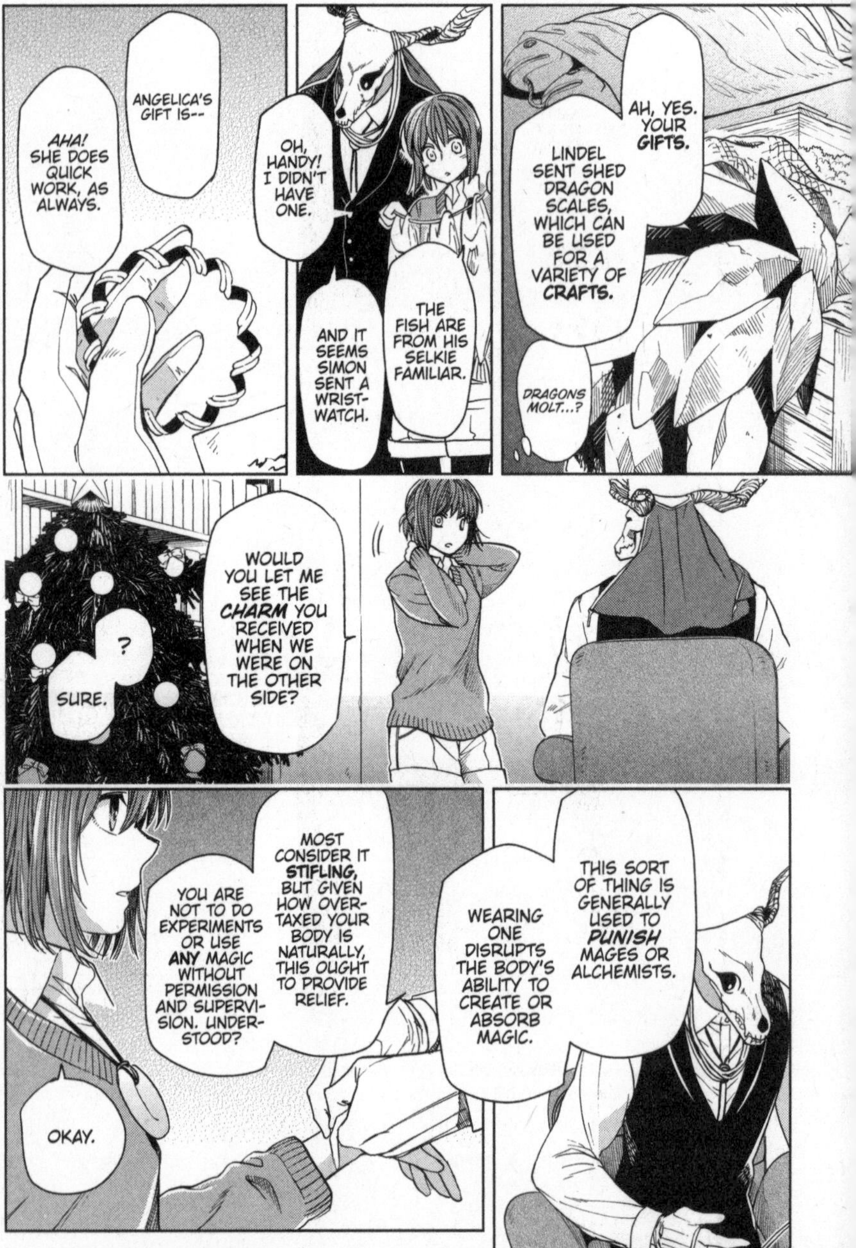
AH, YES. YOUR GIFTS.
LINDEL SENT SHED DRAGON SCALES, WHICH CAN BE USED FOR A VARIETY OF CRAFTS.
DRAGONS MOLT...?
THE FISH ARE FROM HIS SELKIE FAMILIAR.
AND IT SEEMS SIMON SENT A WRIST-WATCH.
OH, HANDY! I DIDN'T HAVE ONE.
ANGELICA'S GIFT IS--
AHA! SHE DOES QUICK WORK, AS ALWAYS.
WOULD YOU LET ME SEE THE CHARM YOU RECEIVED WHEN WE WERE ON THE OTHER SIDE?
?
SURE.
THIS SORT OF THING IS GENERALLY USED TO PUNISH MAGES OR ALCHEMISTS.
WEARING ONE DISRUPTS THE BODY'S ABILITY TO CREATE OR ABSORB MAGIC.
MOST CONSIDER IT STIFLING, BUT GIVEN HOW OVER-TAXED YOUR BODY IS NATURALLY, THIS OUGHT TO PROVIDE RELIEF.
YOU ARE NOT TO DO EXPERIMENTS OR USE ANY MAGIC WITHOUT PERMISSION AND SUPERVI-SION. UNDER-STOOD?
OKAY.

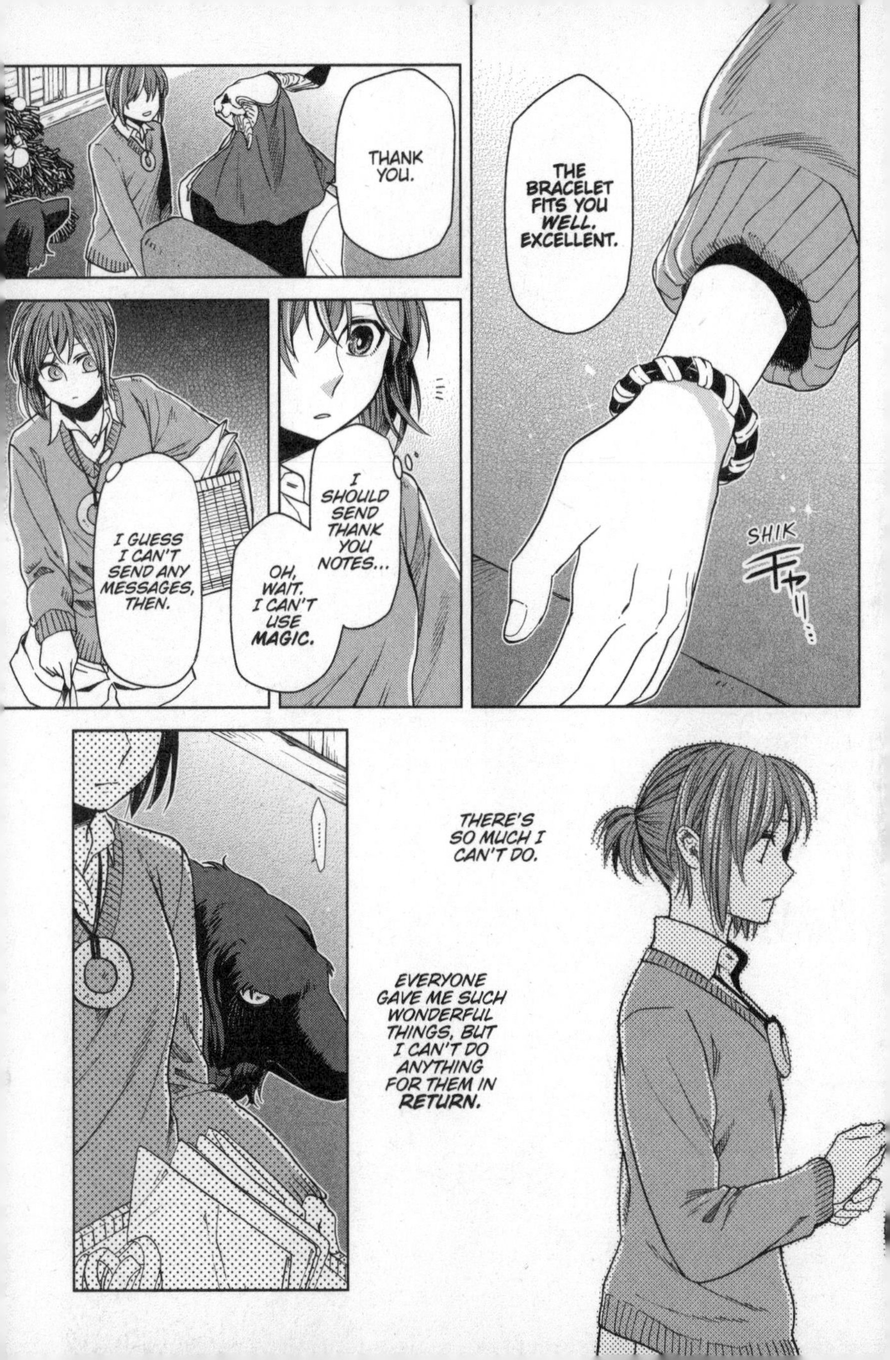
THE BRACELET FITS YOU WELL. EXCELLENT.
SHIK
THANK YOU.
I SHOULD SEND THANK YOU NOTES...
OH, WAIT. I CAN'T USE MAGIC.
I GUESS I CAN'T SEND ANY MESSAGES, THEN.
THERE'S SO MUCH I CAN'T DO.
EVERYONE GAVE ME SUCH WONDERFUL THINGS, BUT I CAN'T DO ANYTHING FOR THEM IN RETURN.

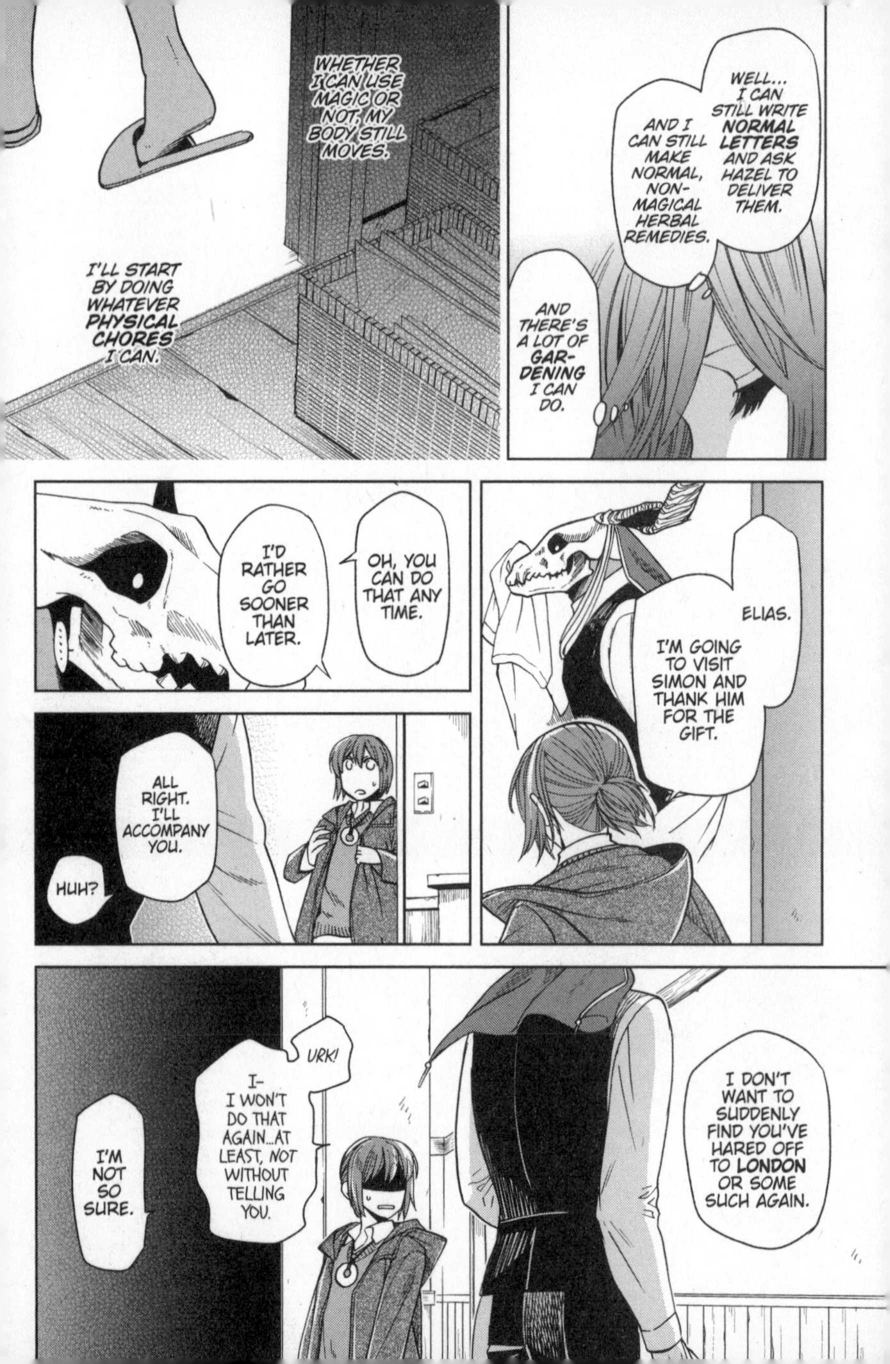
WELL... I CAN STILL WRITE **NORMAL LETTERS** AND ASK HAZEL TO DELIVER THEM.
AND I CAN STILL MAKE NORMAL, NON-MAGICAL HERBAL REMEDIES.
AND THERE'S A LOT OF **GAR-DENING** I CAN DO.
WHETHER I CAN USE MAGIC OR NOT, MY BODY STILL MOVES.
I'LL START BY DOING WHATEVER **PHYSICAL CHORES** I CAN.
ELIAS.
I'M GOING TO VISIT SIMON AND THANK HIM FOR THE GIFT.
OH, YOU CAN DO THAT ANY TIME.
I'D RATHER GO SOONER THAN LATER.
ALL RIGHT. I'LL ACCOMPANY YOU.
HUH?
I DON'T WANT TO SUDDENLY FIND YOU'VE HARED OFF TO **LONDON** OR SOME SUCH AGAIN.
URK!
I- I WON'T DO THAT AGAIN...AT LEAST, *NOT* WITHOUT TELLING YOU.
I'M NOT SO SURE.

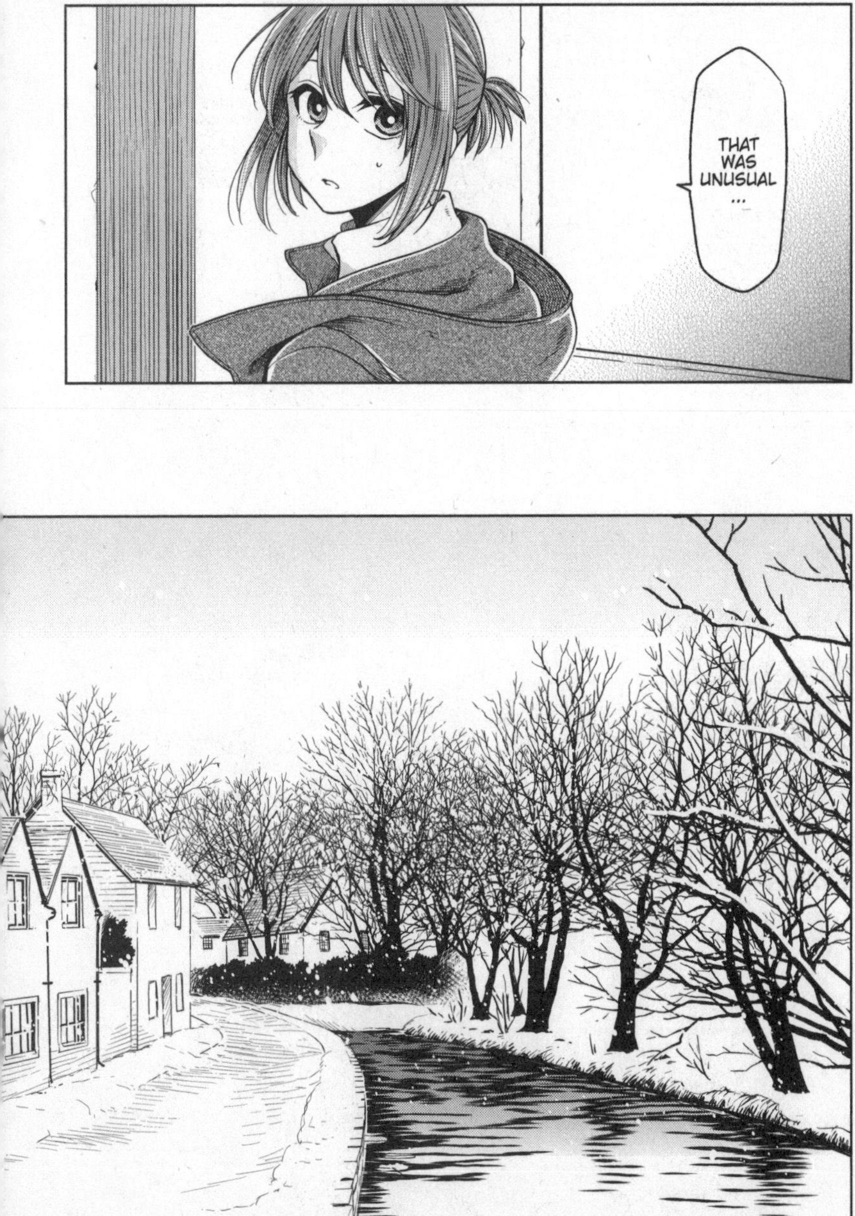
THAT WAS UNUSUAL ...

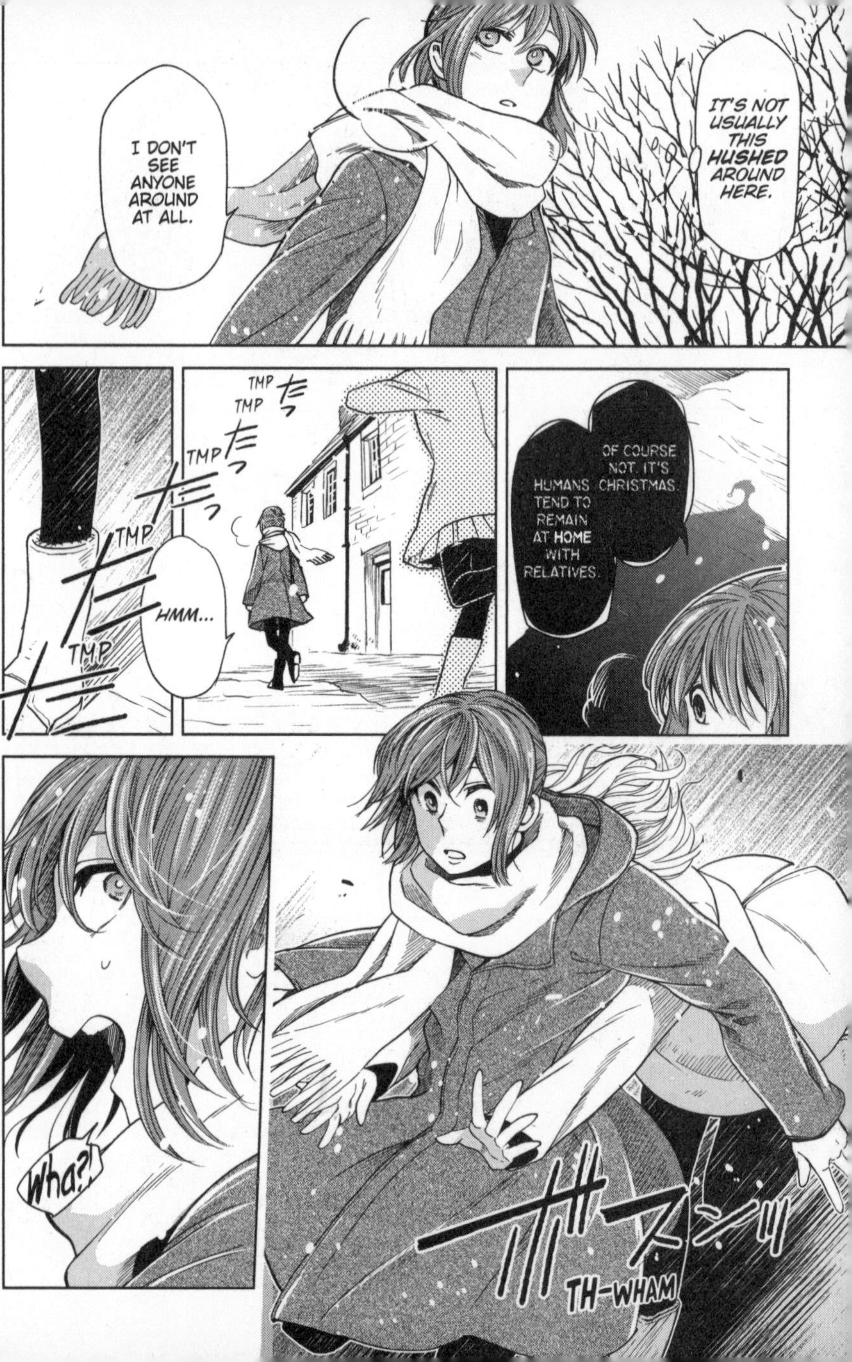
IT'S NOT USUALLY THIS HUSHED AROUND HERE.
I DON'T SEE ANYONE AROUND AT ALL.
OF COURSE NOT. IT'S CHRISTMAS.
HUMANS TEND TO REMAIN AT HOME WITH RELATIVES.
TMP
TMP
TMP
HMM...
TMP
TMP
TH-WHAM
Wha?!

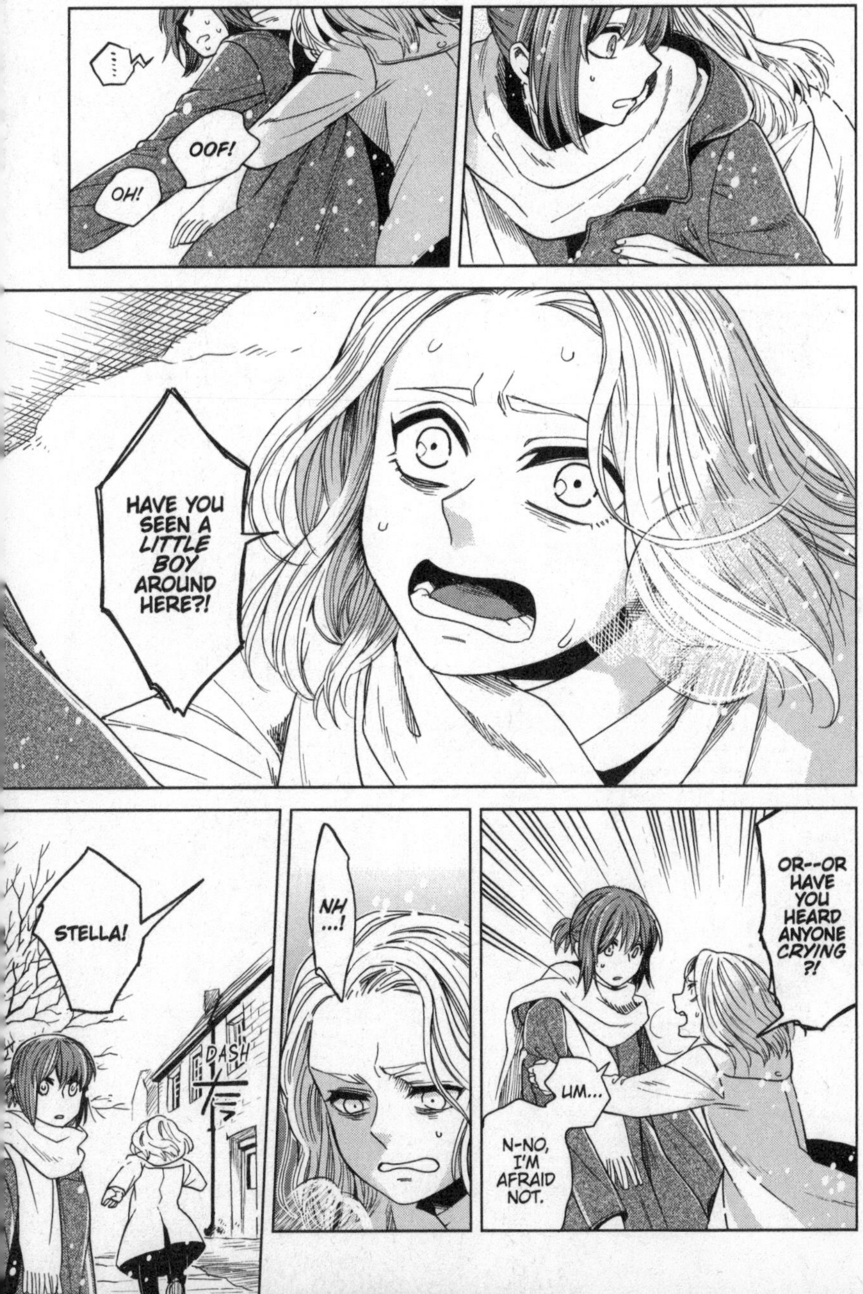

......
OOF!
OH!
HAVE YOU SEEN A LITTLE BOY AROUND HERE?!
OR--OR HAVE YOU HEARD ANYONE CRYING?!
UM...
N-NO, I'M AFRAID NOT.
NH...!
STELLA!
DASH

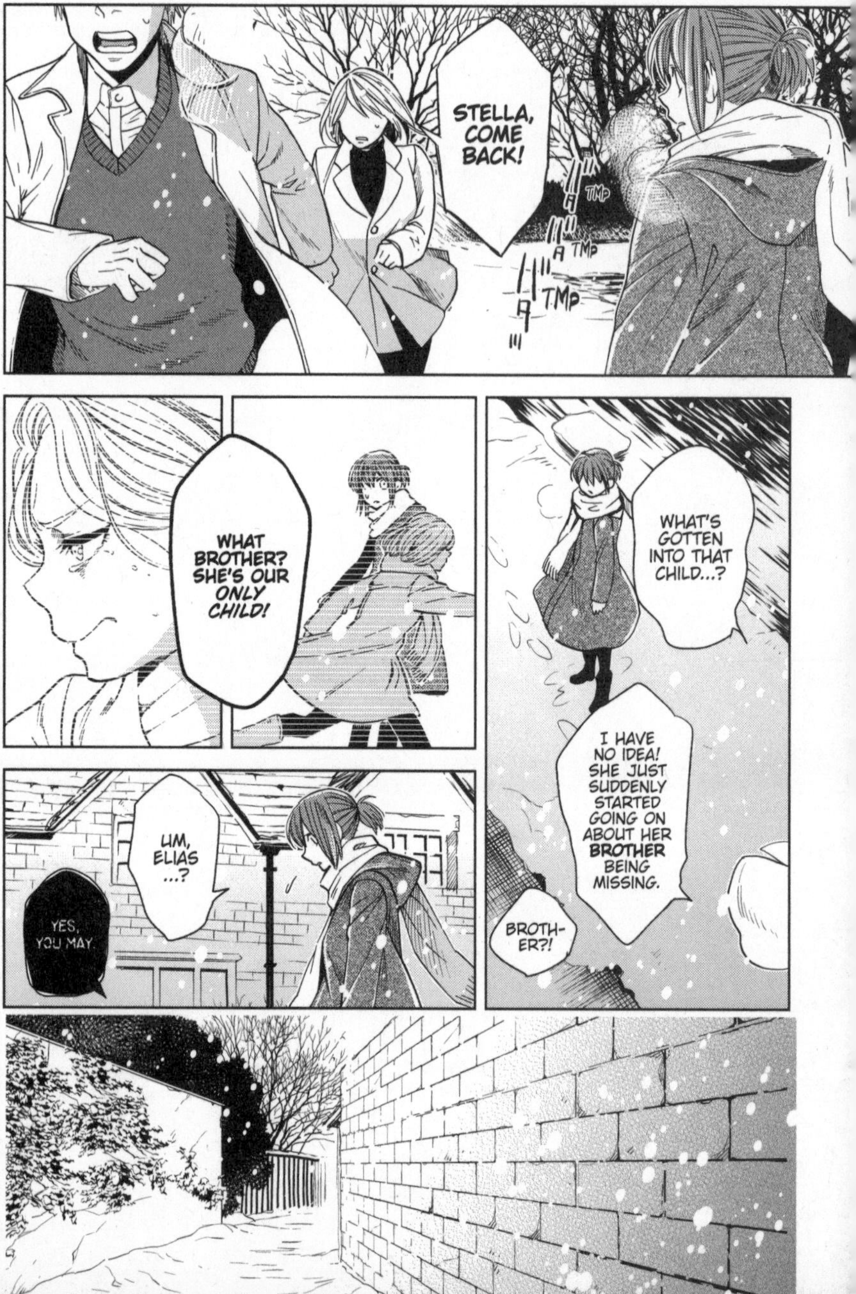
STELLA, COME BACK!
TMP
TMP
TMP
WHAT'S GOTTEN INTO THAT CHILD...?
I HAVE NO IDEA! SHE JUST SUDDENLY STARTED GOING ON ABOUT HER BROTHER BEING MISSING.
BROTHER?!
WHAT BROTHER? SHE'S OUR ONLY CHILD!
UM, ELIAS ...?
YES, YOU MAY.

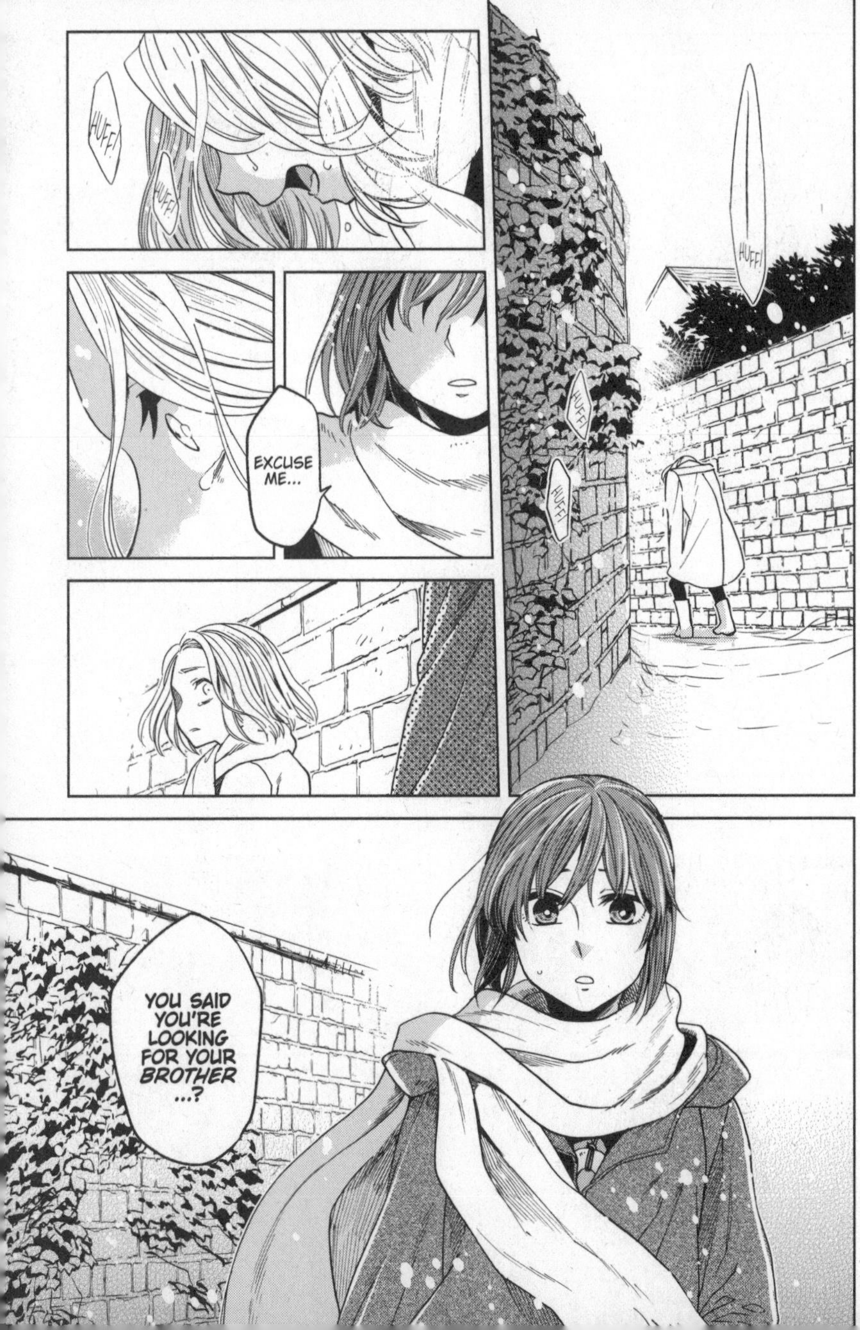
HUFF!
HUFF!
HUFF!
HUFF!
HUFF!
EXCUSE ME...
YOU SAID YOU'RE LOOKING FOR YOUR BROTHER ...?

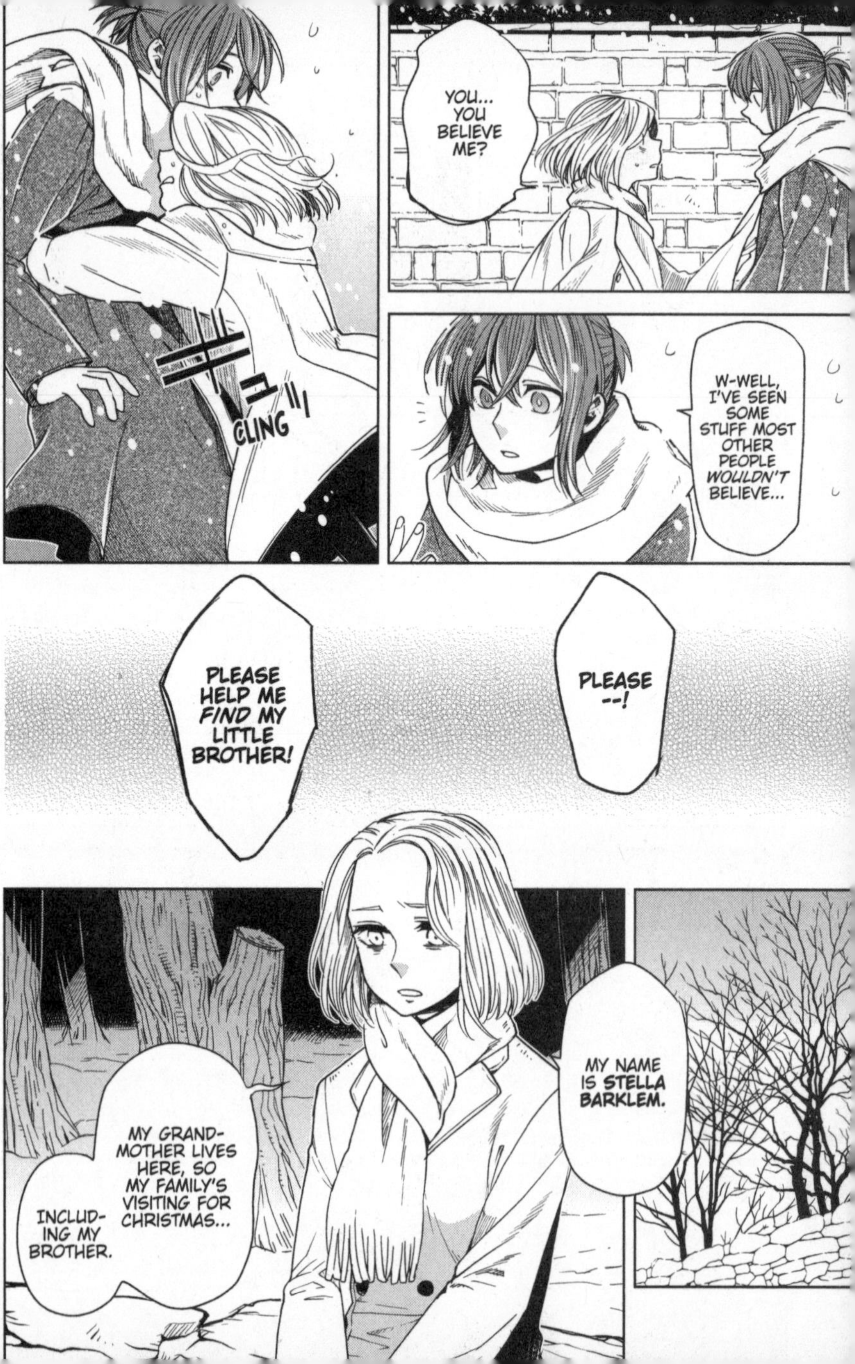
YOU... YOU BELIEVE ME?
W-WELL, I'VE SEEN SOME STUFF MOST OTHER PEOPLE *WOULDN'T* BELIEVE...
CLING
PLEASE --!
PLEASE HELP ME *FIND* MY LITTLE BROTHER!
MY NAME IS STELLA BARKLEM.
MY GRAND-MOTHER LIVES HERE, SO MY FAMILY'S VISITING FOR CHRISTMAS...
INCLUDING MY BROTHER.

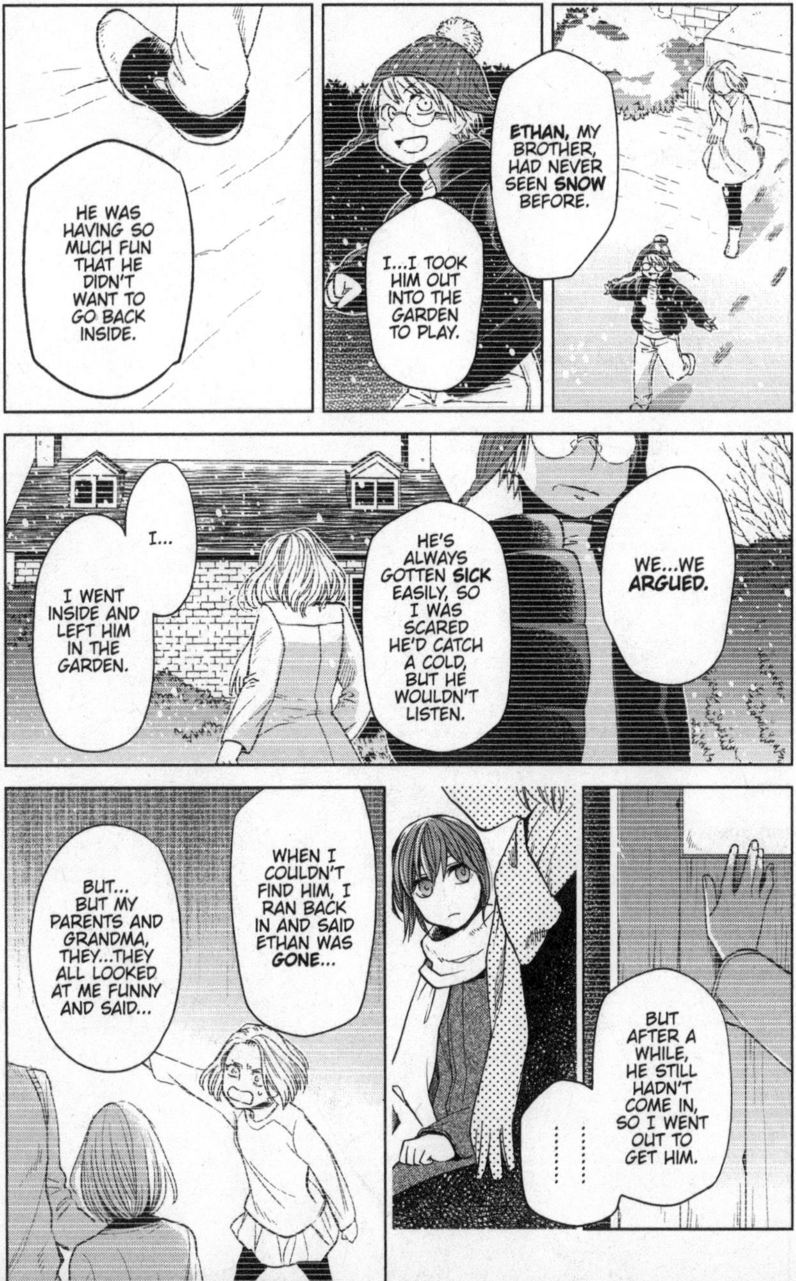
ETHAN, MY BROTHER, HAD NEVER SEEN SNOW BEFORE.
I...I TOOK HIM OUT INTO THE GARDEN TO PLAY.
HE WAS HAVING SO MUCH FUN THAT HE DIDN'T WANT TO GO BACK INSIDE.
WE...WE ARGUED.
HE'S ALWAYS GOTTEN SICK EASILY, SO I WAS SCARED HE'D CATCH A COLD, BUT HE WOULDN'T LISTEN.
I...
I WENT INSIDE AND LEFT HIM IN THE GARDEN.
BUT AFTER A WHILE, HE STILL HADN'T COME IN, SO I WENT OUT TO GET HIM.
......
WHEN I COULDN'T FIND HIM, I RAN BACK IN AND SAID ETHAN WAS GONE...
BUT... BUT MY PARENTS AND GRANDMA, THEY...THEY ALL LOOKED AT ME FUNNY AND SAID...

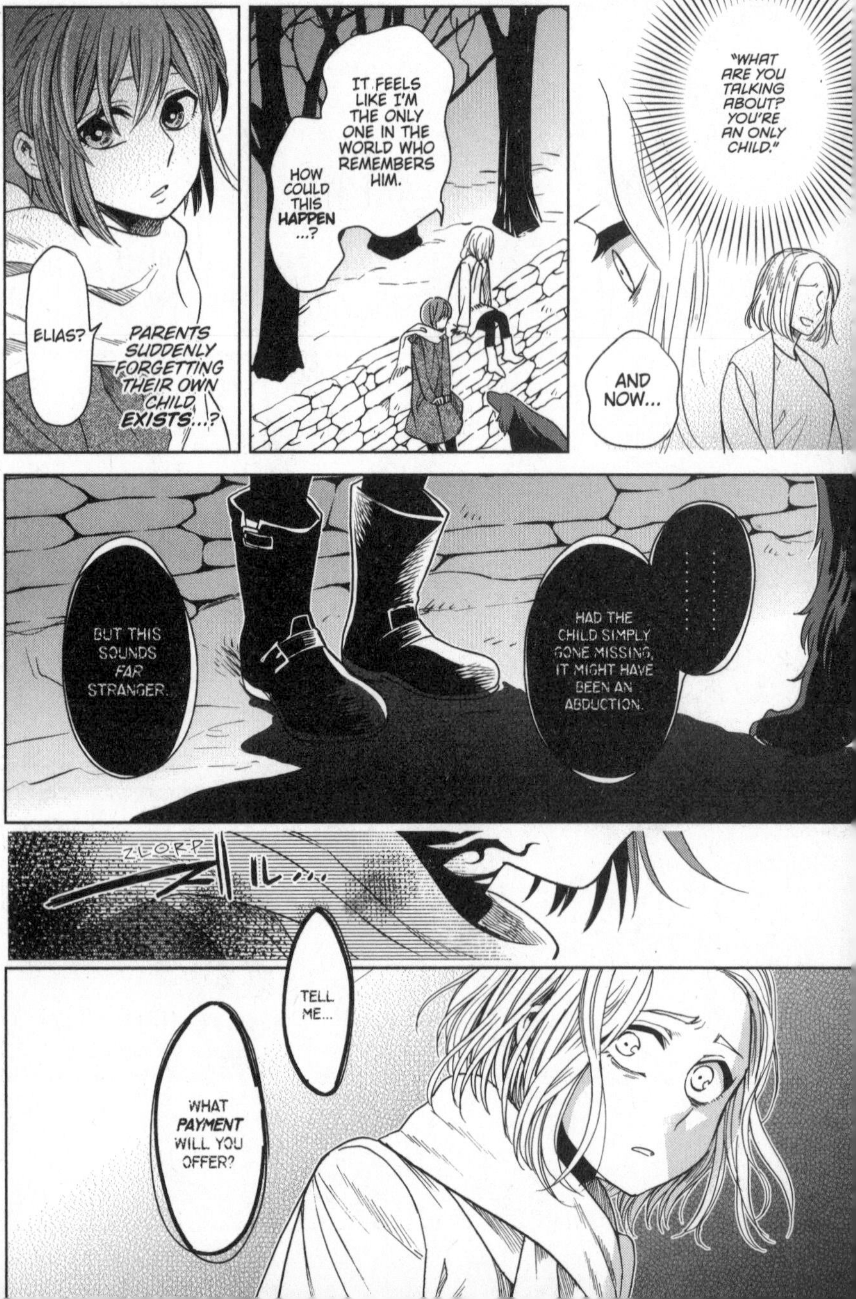
"WHAT ARE YOU TALKING ABOUT? YOU'RE AN ONLY CHILD."
AND NOW...
IT FEELS LIKE I'M THE ONLY ONE IN THE WORLD WHO REMEMBERS HIM.
HOW COULD THIS HAPPEN ...?
PARENTS SUDDENLY FORGETTING THEIR OWN CHILD EXISTS...?
ELIAS?
......
HAD THE CHILD SIMPLY GONE MISSING, IT MIGHT HAVE BEEN AN ABDUCTION.
BUT THIS SOUNDS FAR STRANGER.
ZLORP
TELL ME...
WHAT PAYMENT WILL YOU OFFER?

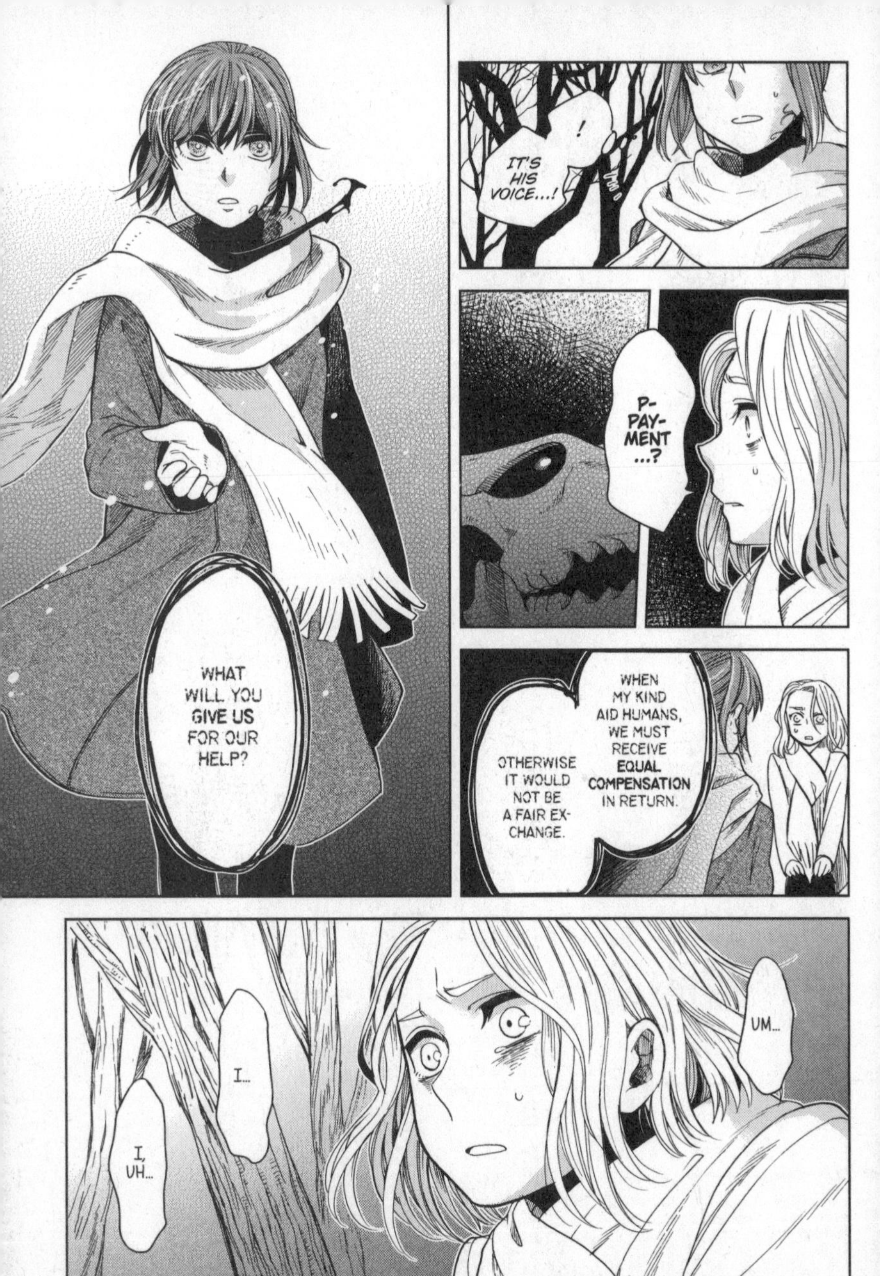
!
IT'S HIS VOICE...!
P-PAYMENT...?
WHEN MY KIND AID HUMANS, WE MUST RECEIVE EQUAL COMPENSATION IN RETURN.
OTHERWISE IT WOULD NOT BE A FAIR EXCHANGE.
WHAT WILL YOU GIVE US FOR OUR HELP?
UM...
I...
I, UH...

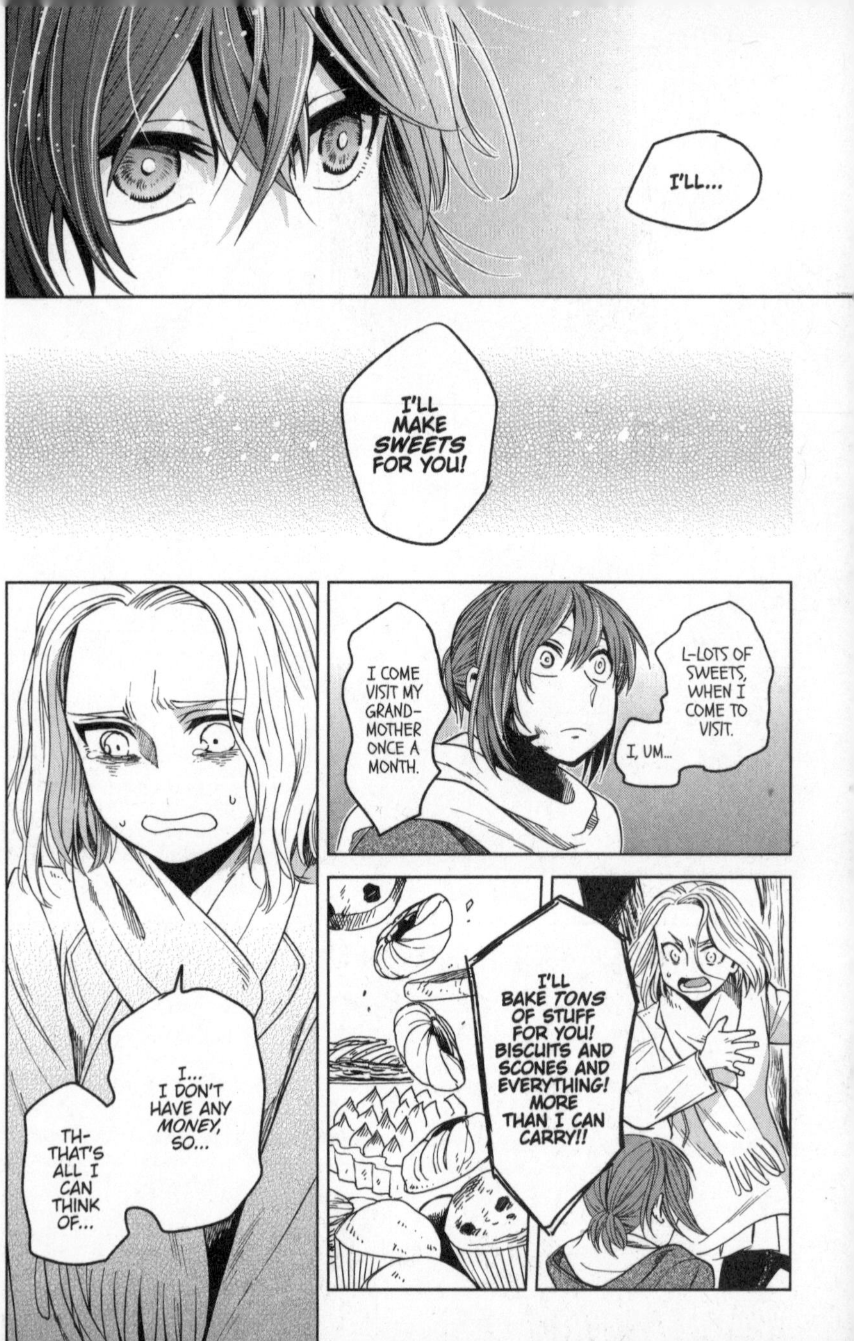
I'LL...
I'LL MAKE *SWEETS* FOR YOU!
L-LOTS OF SWEETS, WHEN I COME TO VISIT.
I, UM...
I COME VISIT MY GRAND-MOTHER ONCE A MONTH.
I'LL BAKE *TONS* OF STUFF FOR YOU! BISCUITS AND SCONES AND EVERYTHING! MORE THAN I CAN CARRY!!
I... I DON'T HAVE ANY *MONEY*, SO...
TH-THAT'S ALL I CAN THINK OF...

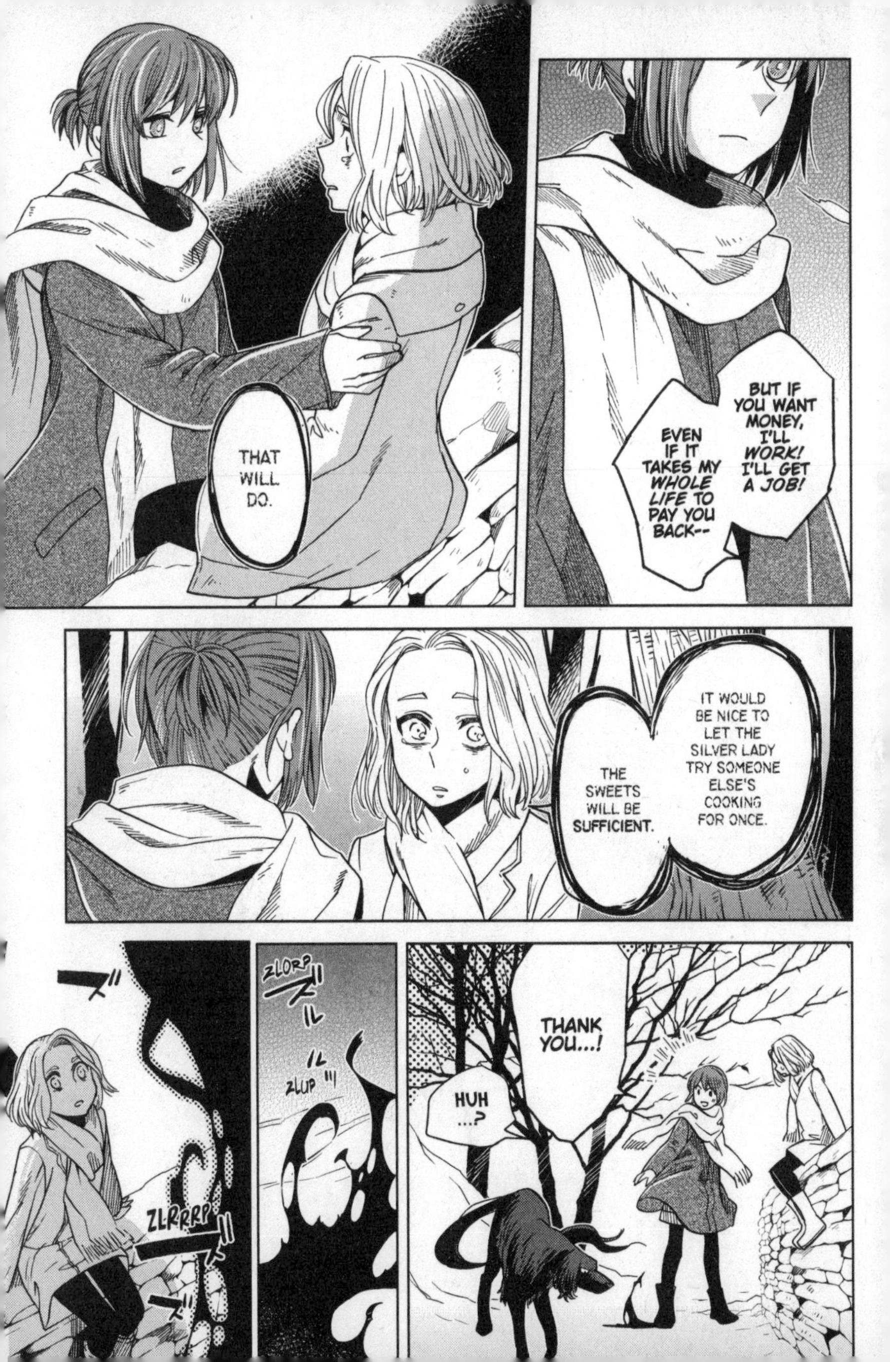
BUT IF YOU WANT MONEY, I'LL WORK! I'LL GET A JOB!
EVEN IF IT TAKES MY WHOLE LIFE TO PAY YOU BACK--
THAT WILL DO.
IT WOULD BE NICE TO LET THE SILVER LADY TRY SOMEONE ELSE'S COOKING FOR ONCE.
THE SWEETS WILL BE SUFFICIENT.
THANK YOU...!
HUH ...?
ZLORP
ZLUP
ZLRRRP

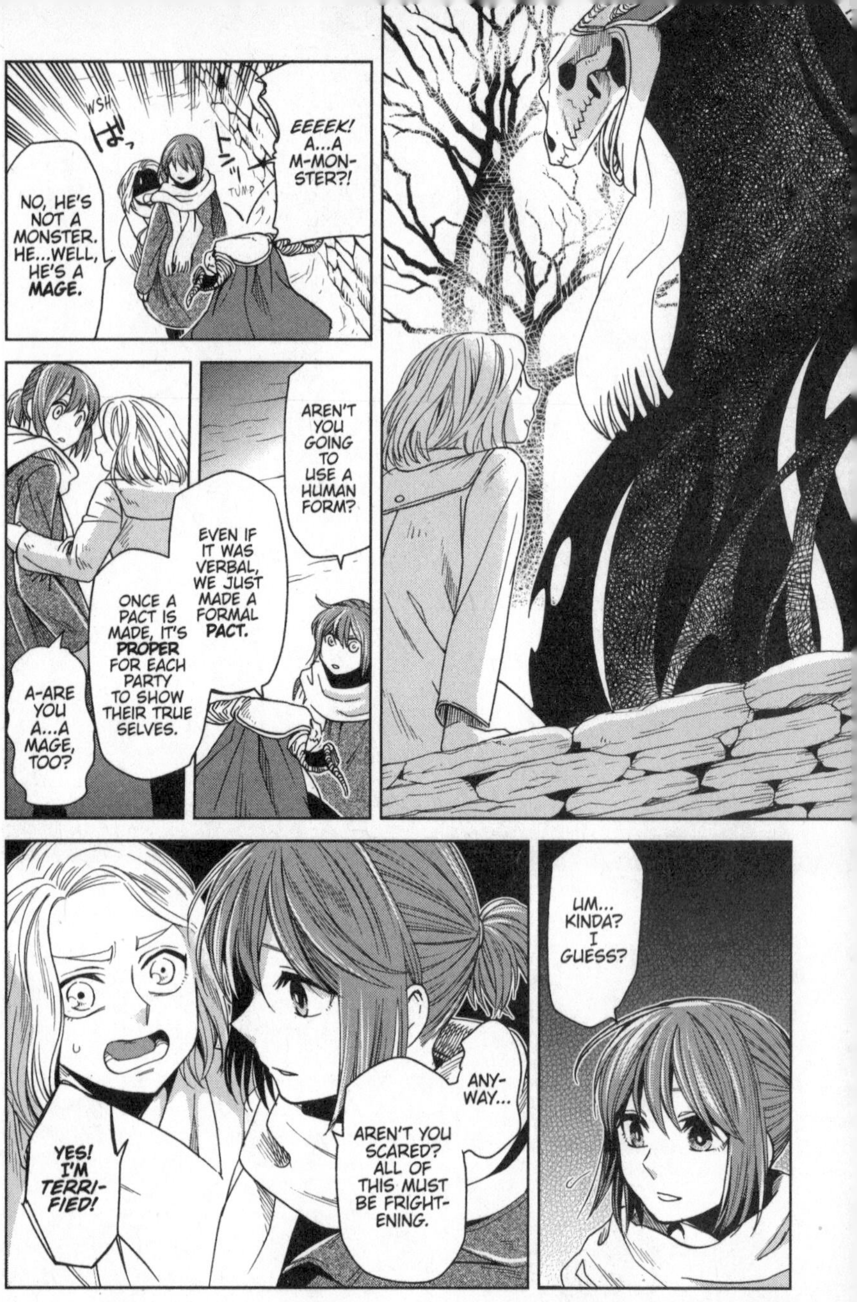
EEEEK! A...A M-MONSTER?!
TUMP
WSH
NO, HE'S NOT A MONSTER. HE...WELL, HE'S A **MAGE.**
AREN'T YOU GOING TO USE A HUMAN FORM?
EVEN IF IT WAS VERBAL, WE JUST MADE A FORMAL **PACT.**
ONCE A PACT IS MADE, IT'S **PROPER** FOR EACH PARTY TO SHOW THEIR TRUE SELVES.
A-ARE YOU A...A MAGE, TOO?
UM... KINDA? I GUESS?
ANY-WAY...
AREN'T YOU SCARED? ALL OF THIS MUST BE FRIGHT-ENING.
YES! I'M TERRI-FIED!

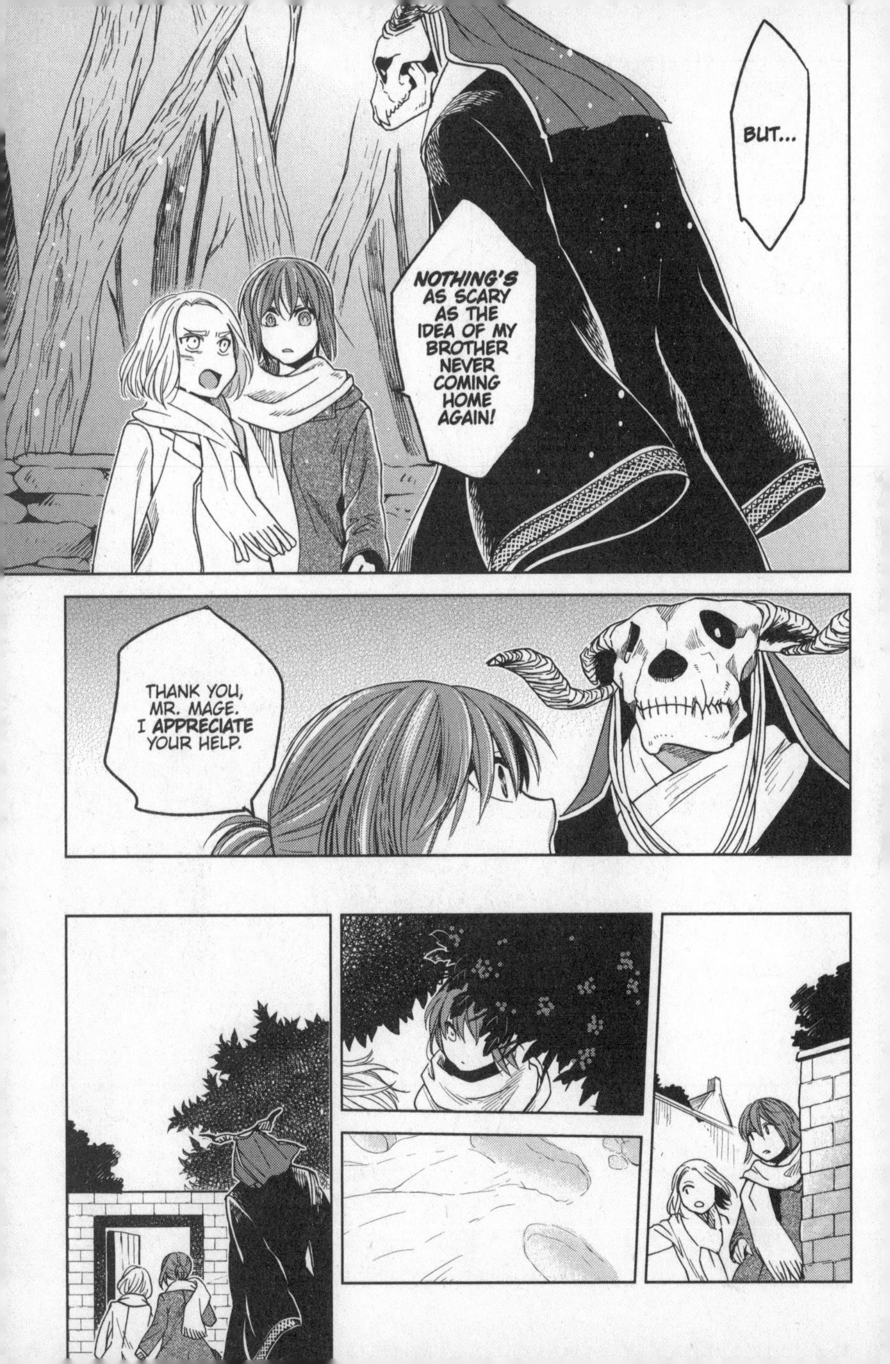
BUT...
NOTHING'S AS SCARY AS THE IDEA OF MY BROTHER NEVER COMING HOME AGAIN!
THANK YOU, MR. MAGE. I APPRECIATE YOUR HELP.

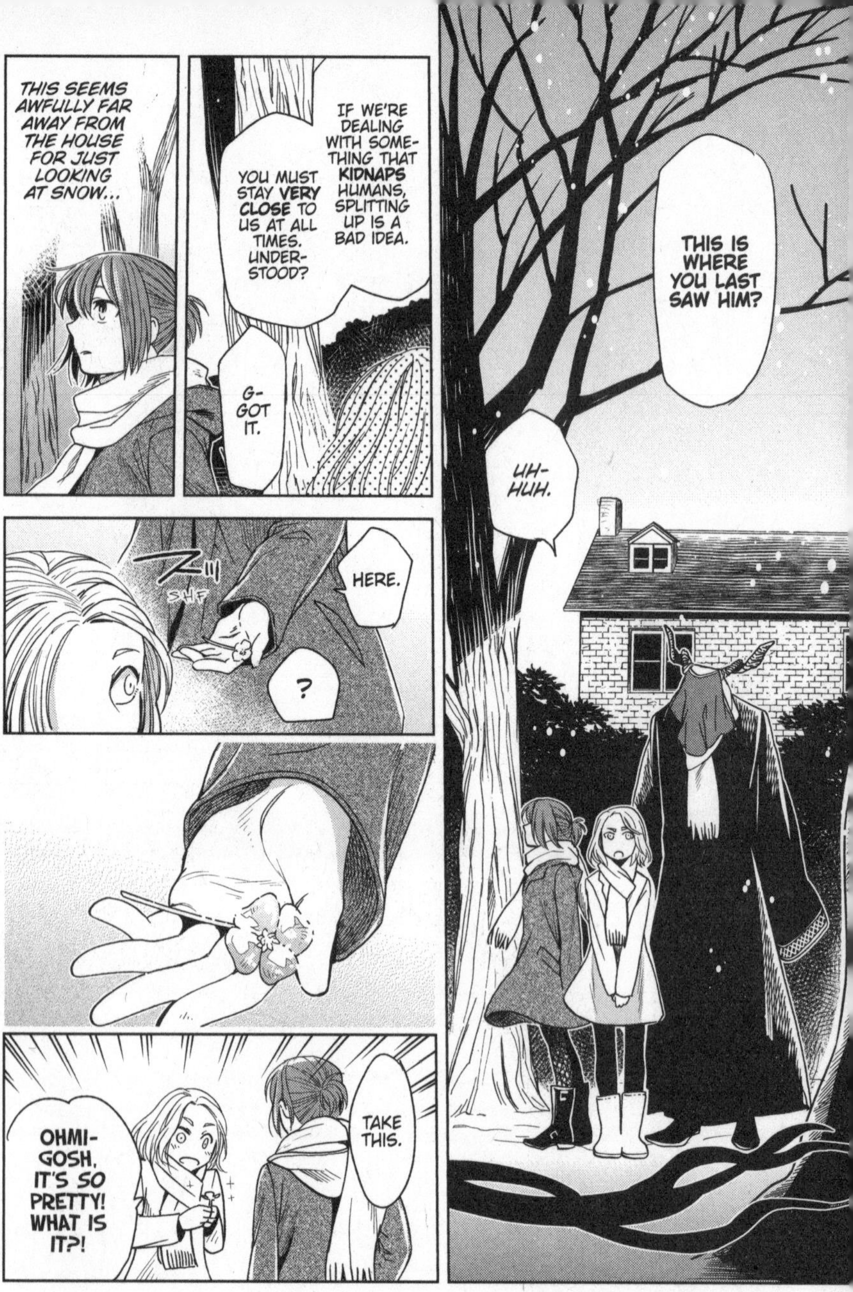
THIS IS WHERE YOU LAST SAW HIM?
UH-HUH.
IF WE'RE DEALING WITH SOMETHING THAT KIDNAPS HUMANS, SPLITTING UP IS A BAD IDEA.
YOU MUST STAY VERY CLOSE TO US AT ALL TIMES. UNDERSTOOD?
G-GOT IT.
THIS SEEMS AWFULLY FAR AWAY FROM THE HOUSE FOR JUST LOOKING AT SNOW...
SHIF
HERE.
?
TAKE THIS.
OHMIGOSH, IT'S SO PRETTY! WHAT IS IT?!

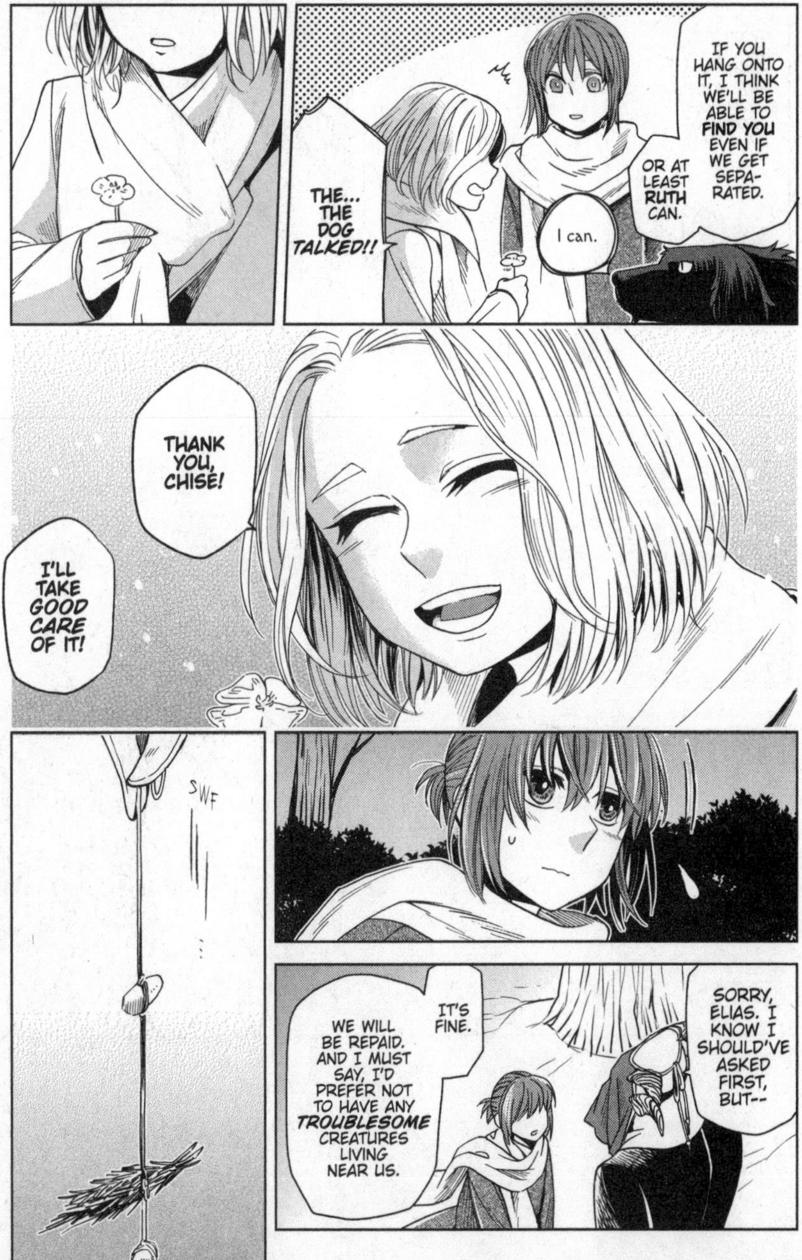
IF YOU HANG ONTO IT, I THINK WE'LL BE ABLE TO FIND YOU EVEN IF WE GET SEPA-RATED.
OR AT LEAST RUTH CAN.
I can.
THE... THE DOG TALKED!!
THANK YOU, CHISE!
I'LL TAKE GOOD CARE OF IT!
SORRY, ELIAS. I KNOW I SHOULD'VE ASKED FIRST, BUT--
IT'S FINE.
WE WILL BE REPAID. AND I MUST SAY, I'D PREFER NOT TO HAVE ANY TROUBLESOME CREATURES LIVING NEAR US.
SWF

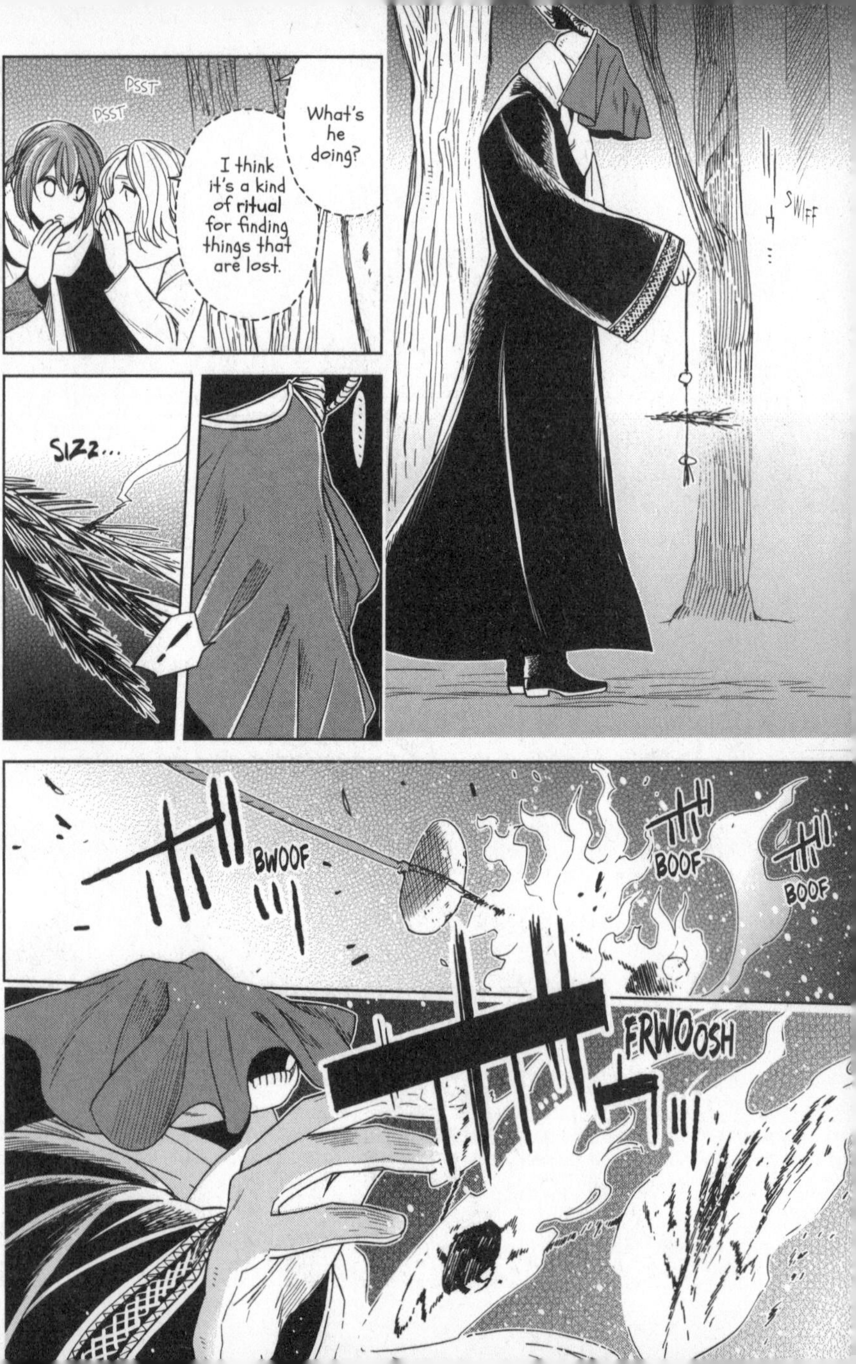
SWIFF
What's he doing?
PSST
PSST
I think it's a kind of ritual for finding things that are lost.
...
SIZZ...
BOOF
BOOF
BWOOF
FRWOOSH

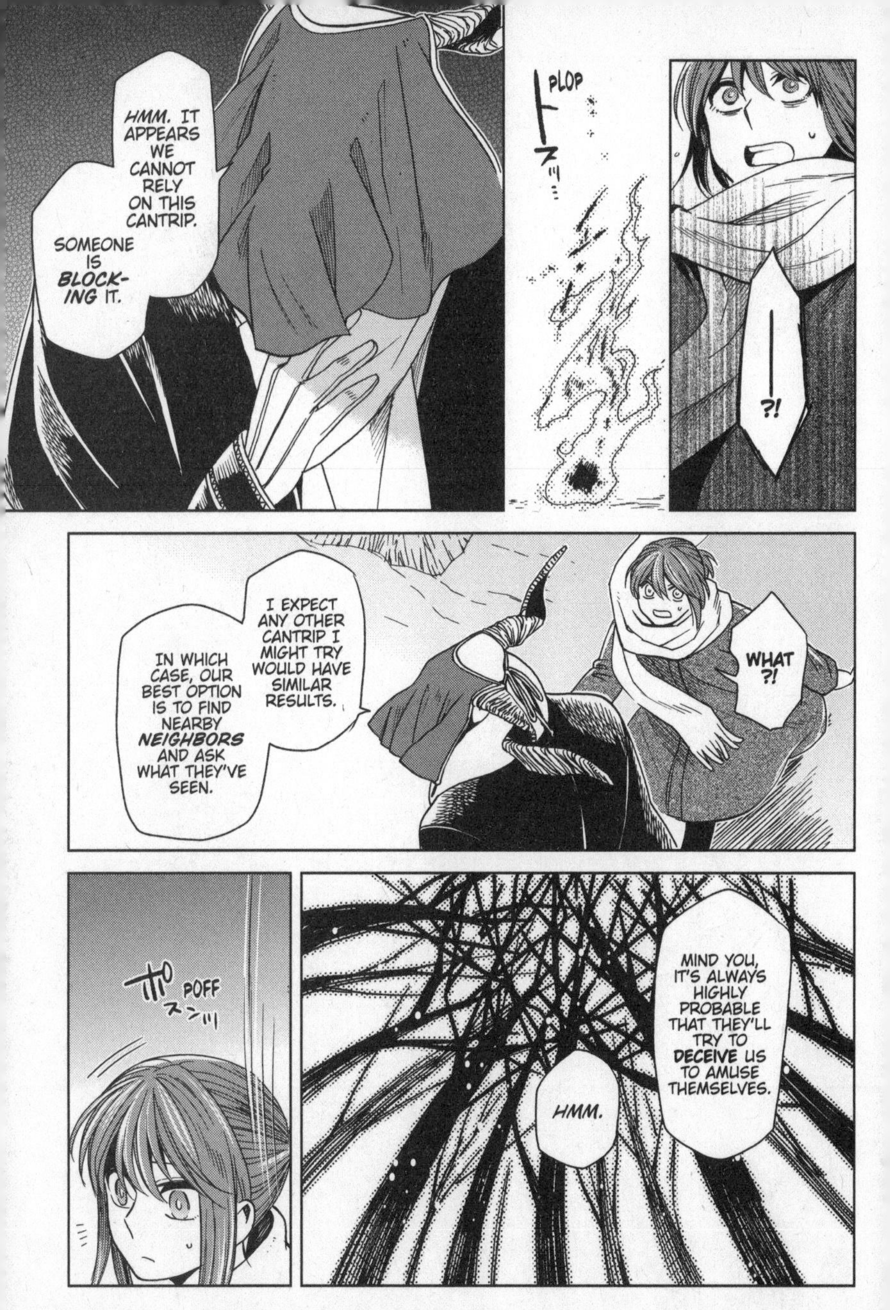

—
?!
PLOP
HMM. IT APPEARS WE CANNOT RELY ON THIS CANTRIP.
SOMEONE IS BLOCKING IT.
WHAT?!
I EXPECT ANY OTHER CANTRIP I MIGHT TRY WOULD HAVE SIMILAR RESULTS.
IN WHICH CASE, OUR BEST OPTION IS TO FIND NEARBY NEIGHBORS AND ASK WHAT THEY'VE SEEN.
MIND YOU, IT'S ALWAYS HIGHLY PROBABLE THAT THEY'LL TRY TO DECEIVE US TO AMUSE THEMSELVES.
HMM.
POFF

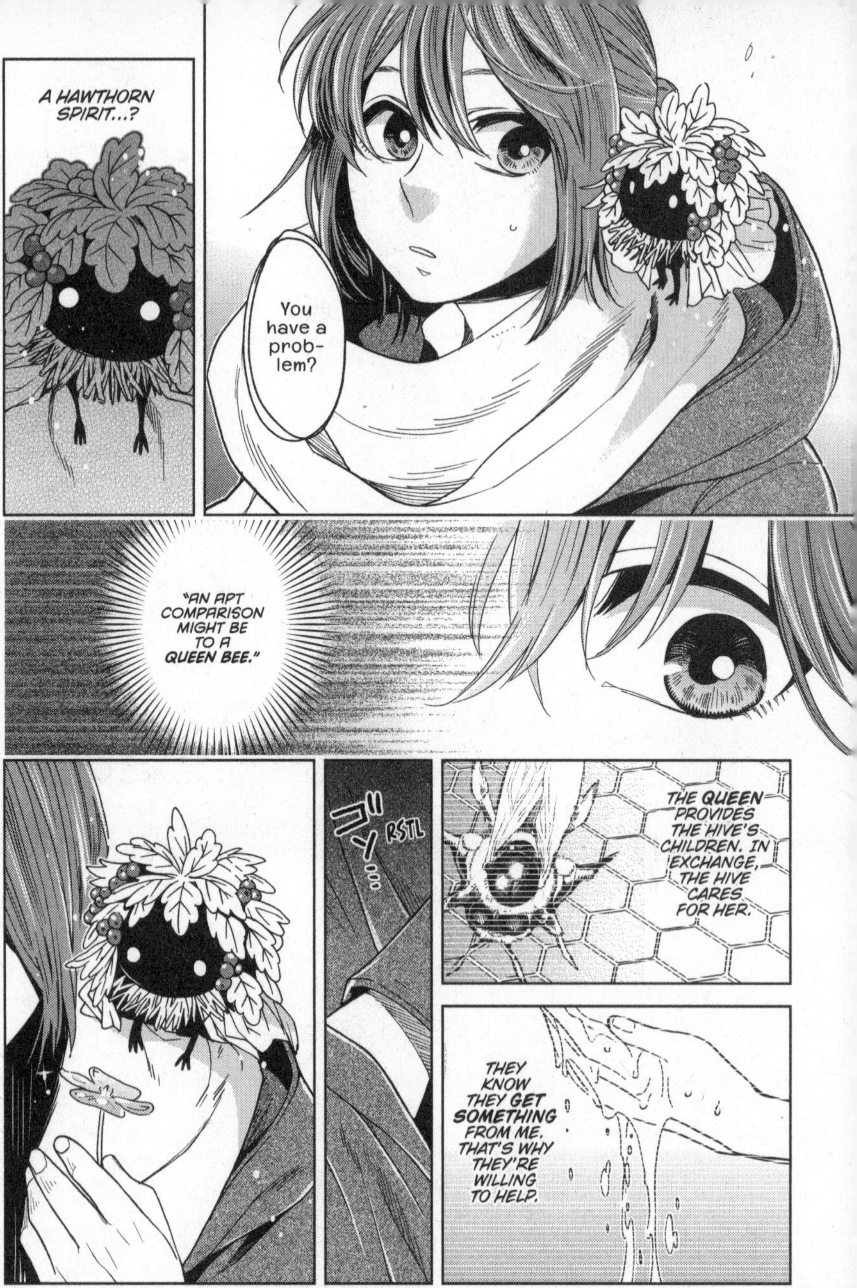
You have a problem?
A HAWTHORN SPIRIT...?
"AN APT COMPARISON MIGHT BE TO A QUEEN BEE."
THE QUEEN PROVIDES THE HIVE'S CHILDREN. IN EXCHANGE, THE HIVE CARES FOR HER.
THEY KNOW THEY GET SOMETHING FROM ME. THAT'S WHY THEY'RE WILLING TO HELP.
RSTL

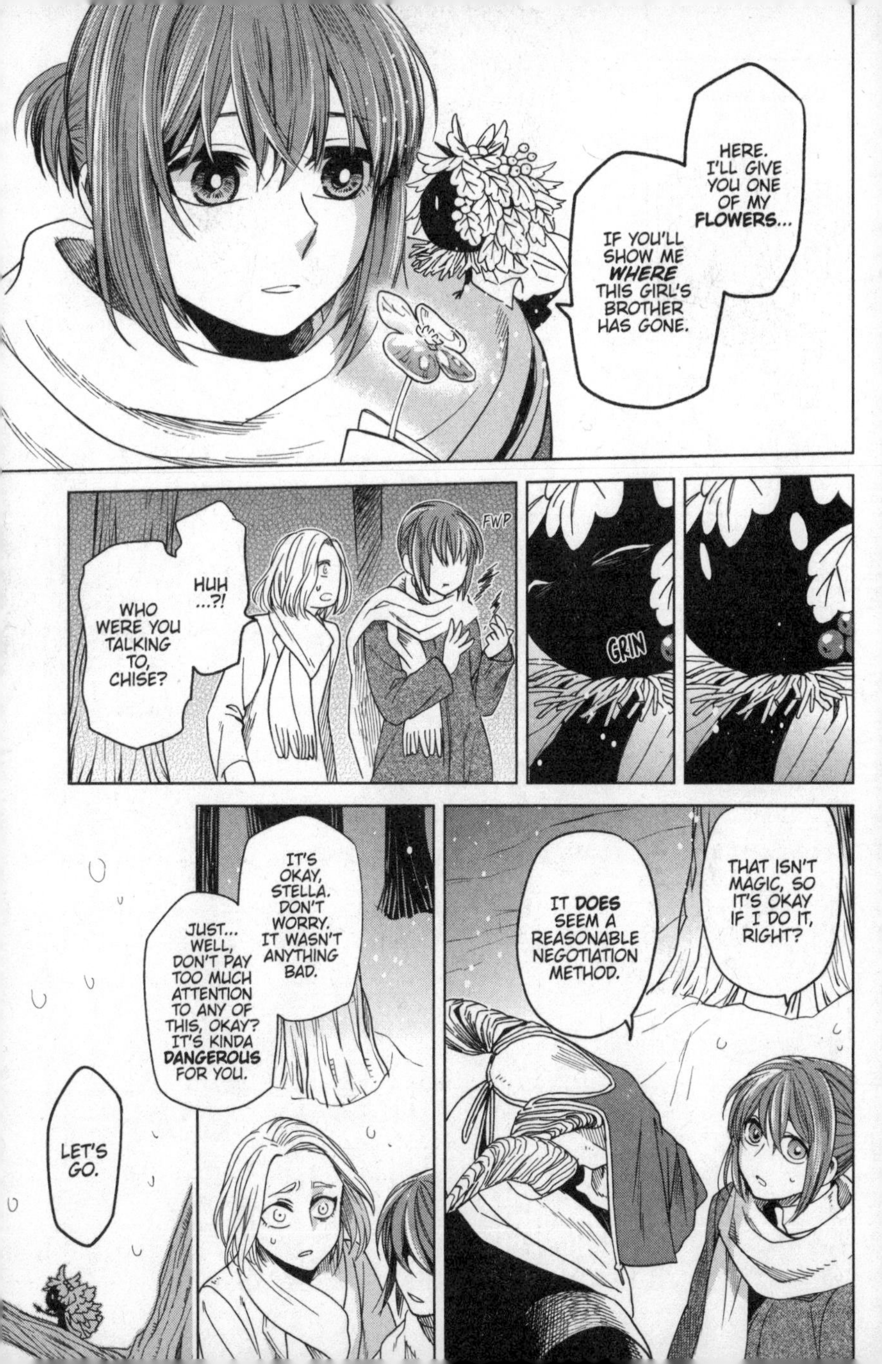
HERE. I'LL GIVE YOU ONE OF MY **FLOWERS...**
IF YOU'LL SHOW ME ***WHERE*** THIS GIRL'S BROTHER HAS GONE.
GRIN
FWP
HUH ...?!
WHO WERE YOU TALKING TO, CHISE?
THAT ISN'T MAGIC, SO IT'S OKAY IF I DO IT, RIGHT?
IT **DOES** SEEM A REASONABLE NEGOTIATION METHOD.
IT'S OKAY, STELLA. DON'T WORRY. IT WASN'T ANYTHING BAD.
JUST... WELL, DON'T PAY TOO MUCH ATTENTION TO ANY OF THIS, OKAY? IT'S KINDA **DANGEROUS** FOR YOU.
LET'S GO.

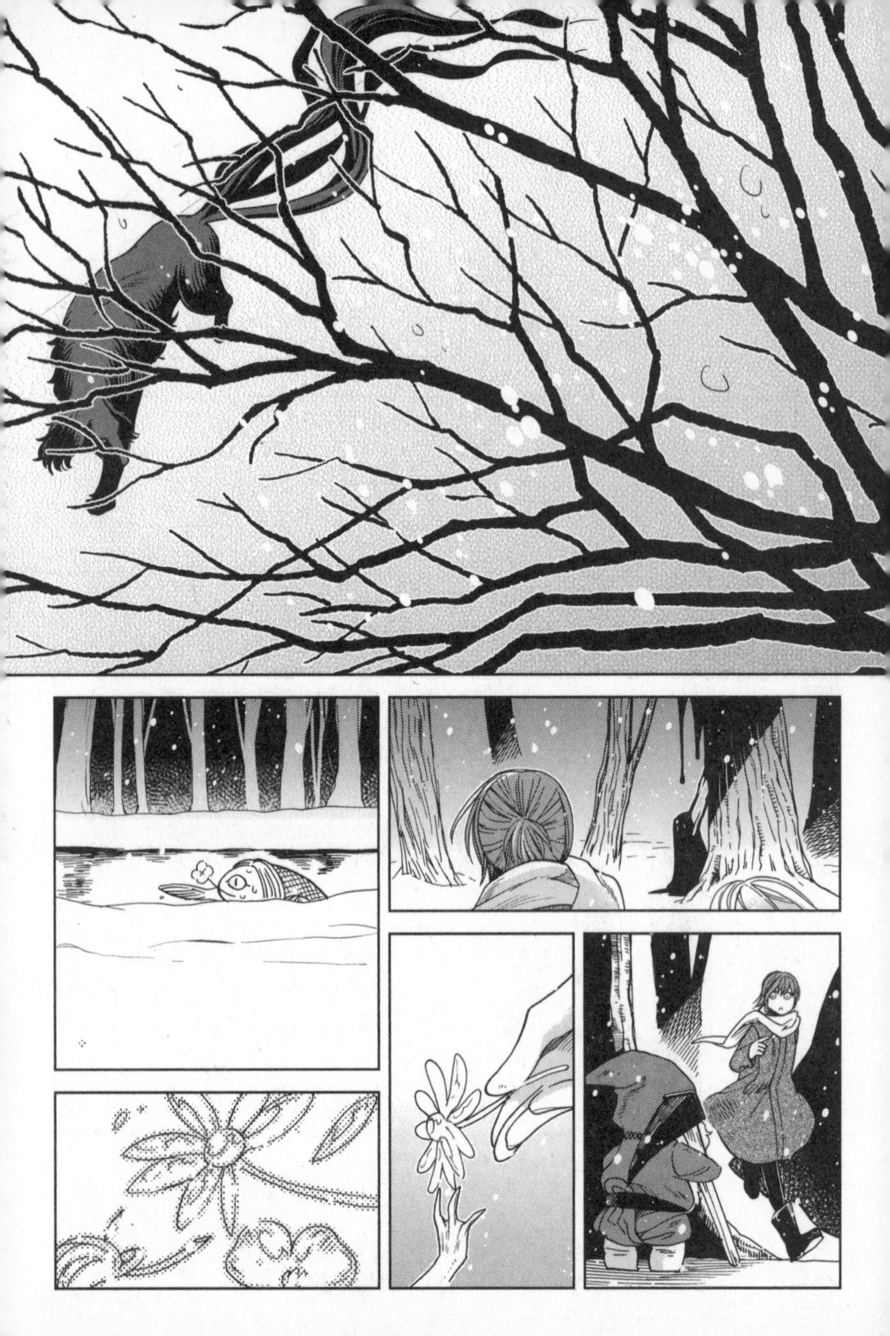

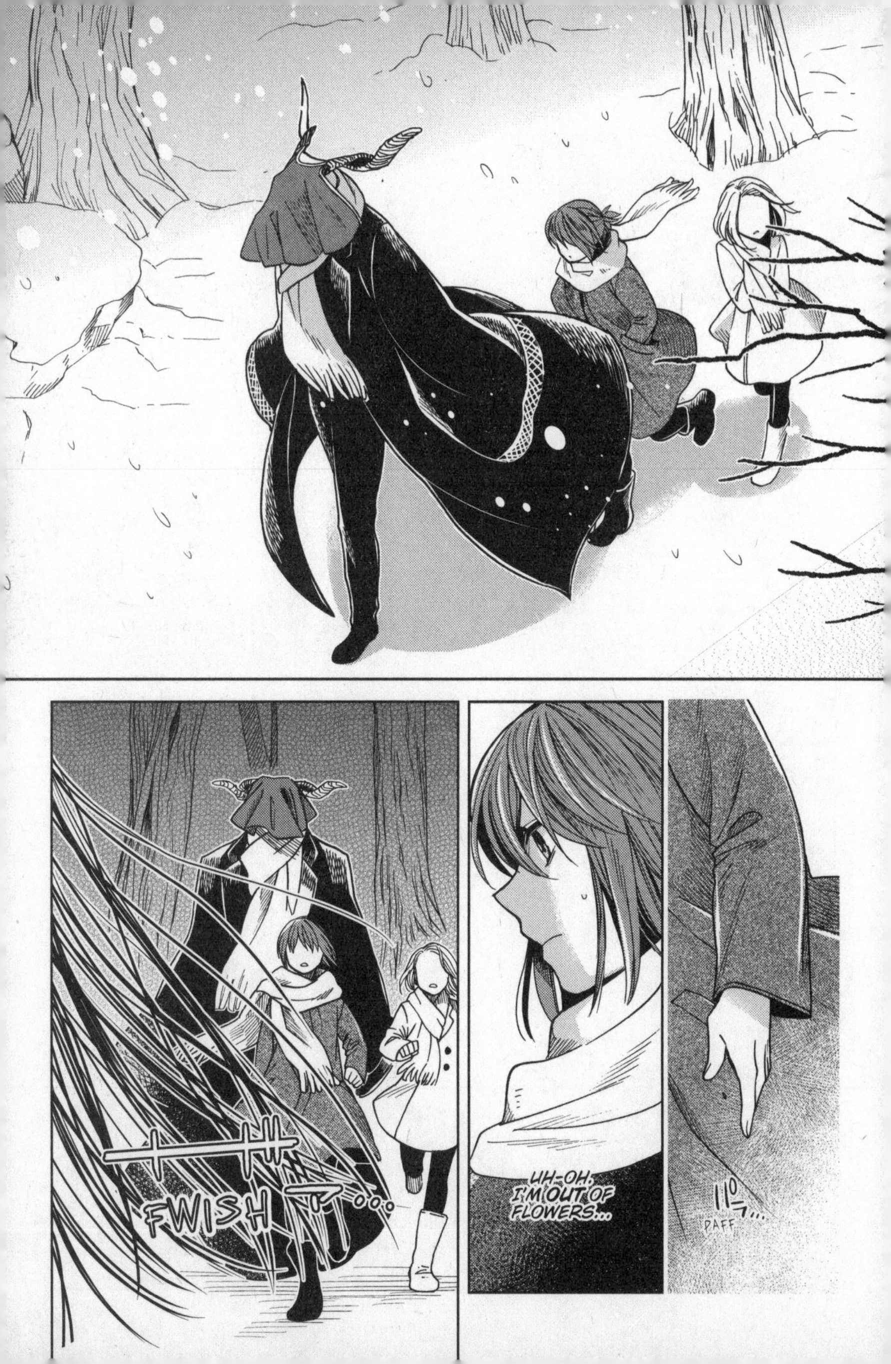
PAFF
UH-OH. I'M OUT OF FLOWERS...
FWISH

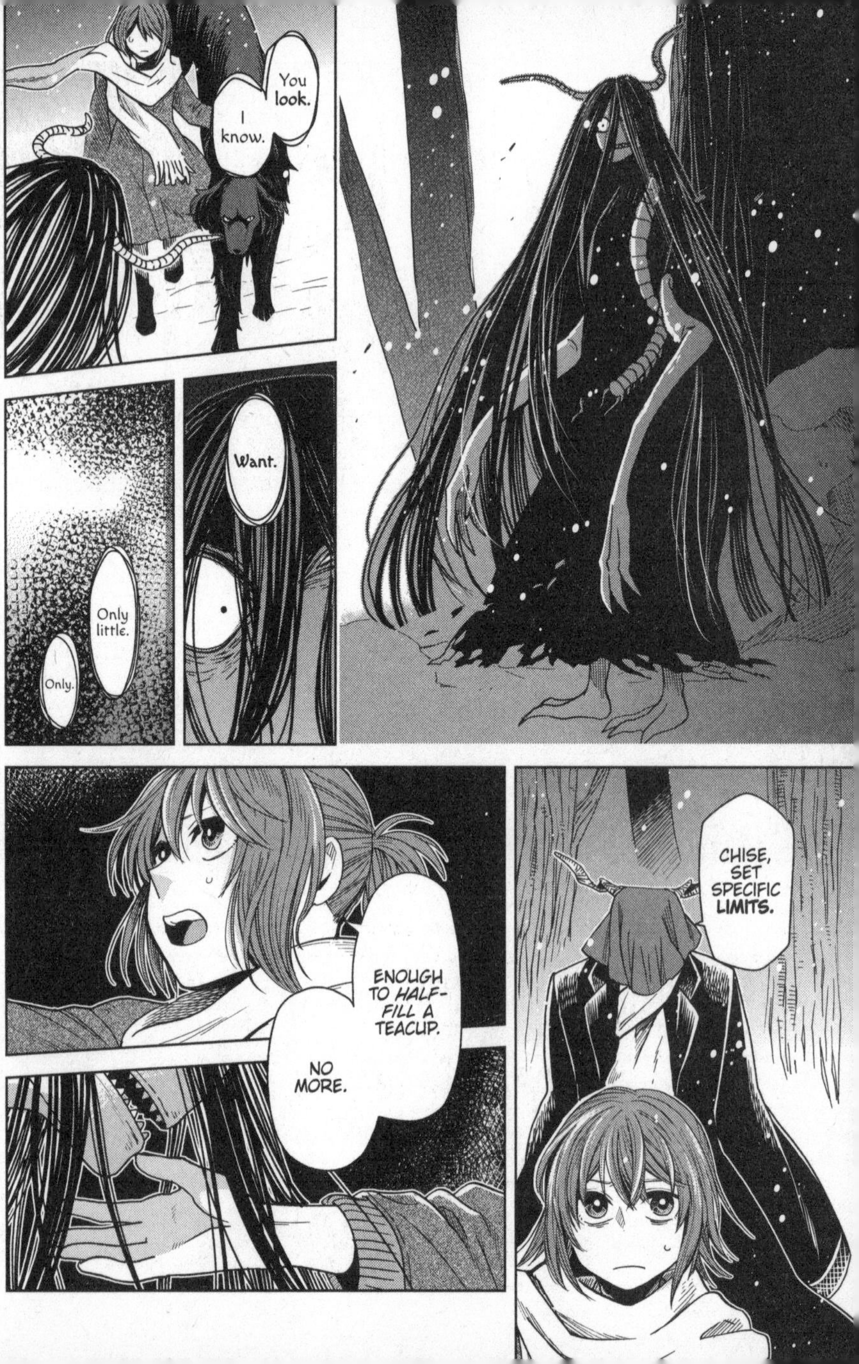
You look.
I know.
Want.
Only little.
Only.
CHISE, SET SPECIFIC LIMITS.
ENOUGH TO HALF-FILL A TEACUP.
NO MORE.

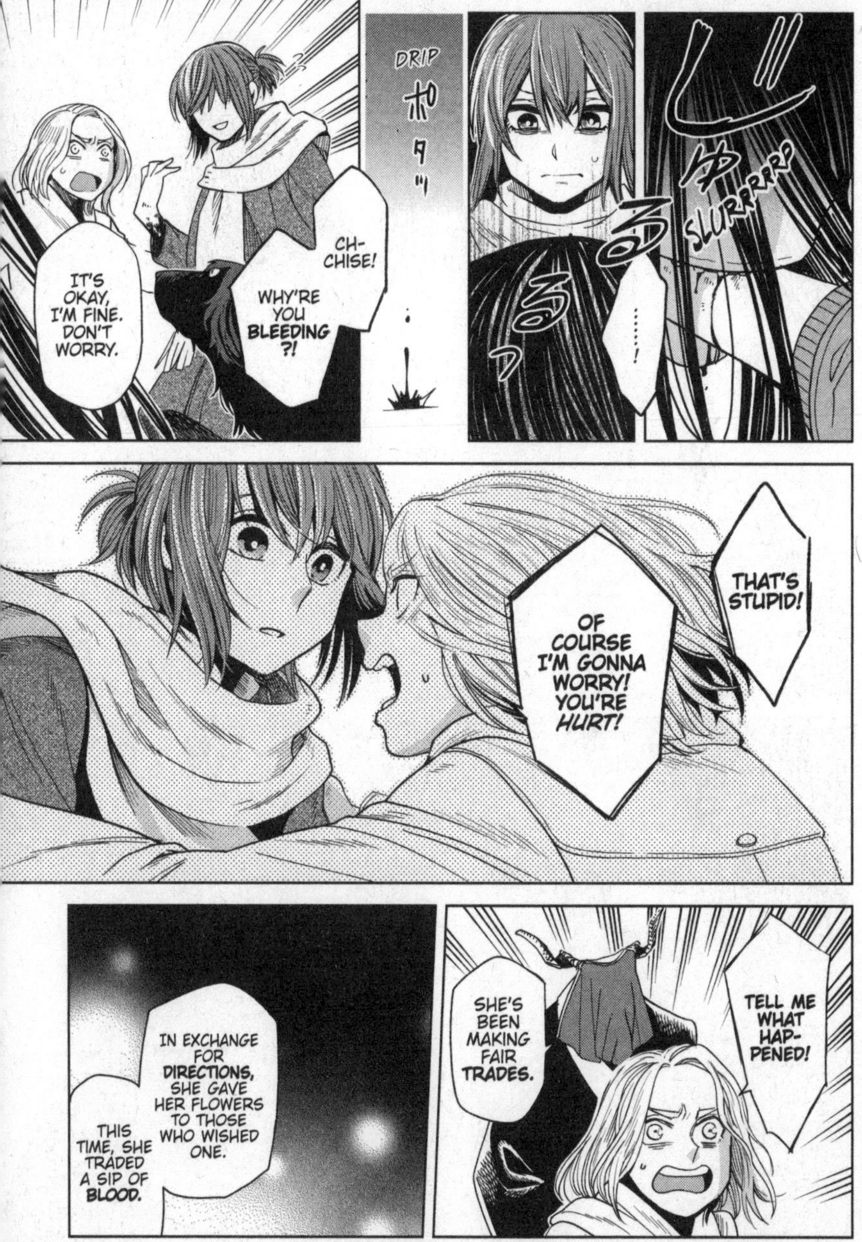

じゅるるっ
SLURRRRP
......!
DRIP
ポタッ
CH-CHISE!
WHY'RE YOU BLEEDING?!
IT'S OKAY, I'M FINE. DON'T WORRY.
THAT'S STUPID!
OF COURSE I'M GONNA WORRY! YOU'RE HURT!
TELL ME WHAT HAP-PENED!
SHE'S BEEN MAKING FAIR TRADES.
IN EXCHANGE FOR DIRECTIONS, SHE GAVE HER FLOWERS TO THOSE WHO WISHED ONE.
THIS TIME, SHE TRADED A SIP OF BLOOD.

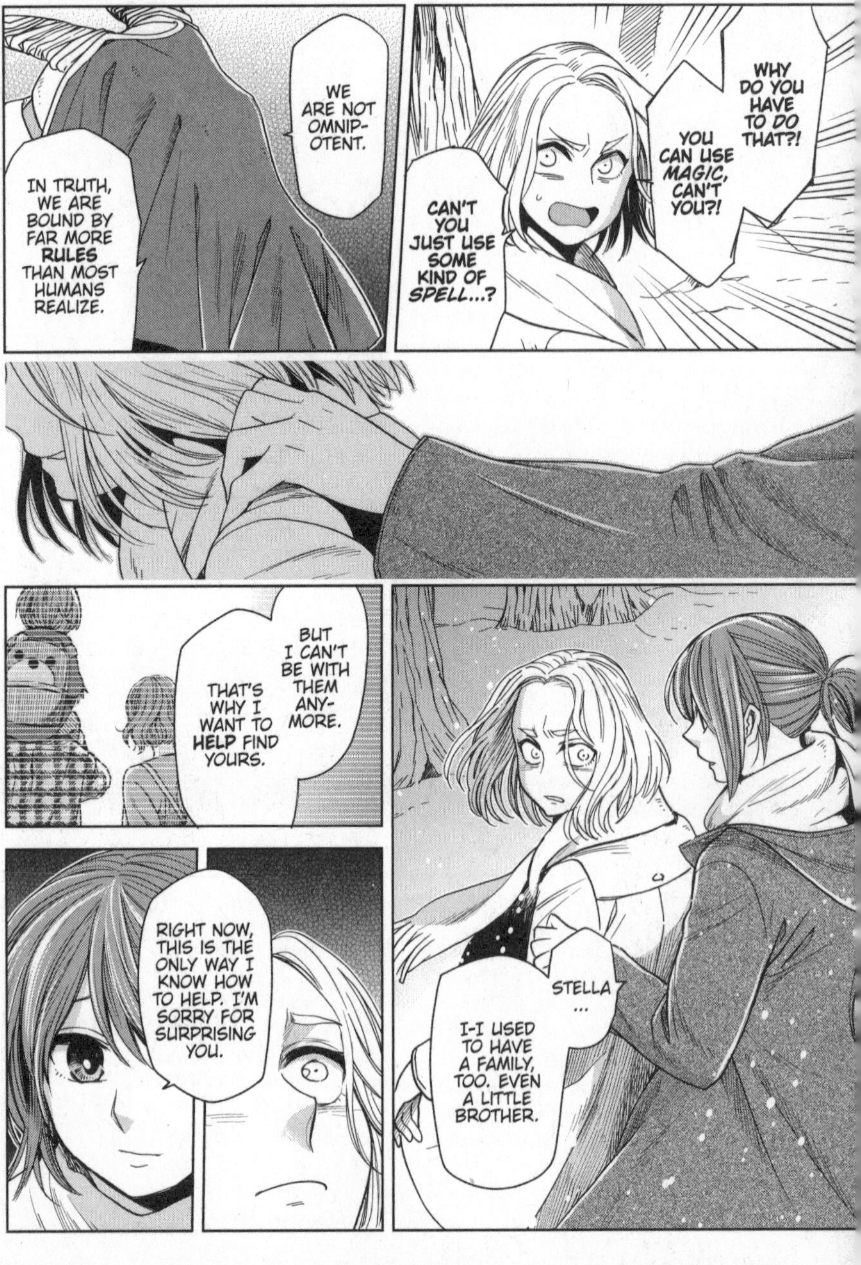
WHY DO YOU HAVE TO DO THAT?!
YOU CAN USE MAGIC, CAN'T YOU?!
CAN'T YOU JUST USE SOME KIND OF SPELL...?
WE ARE NOT OMNIPOTENT.
IN TRUTH, WE ARE BOUND BY FAR MORE RULES THAN MOST HUMANS REALIZE.
STELLA...
I-I USED TO HAVE A FAMILY, TOO. EVEN A LITTLE BROTHER.
BUT I CAN'T BE WITH THEM ANYMORE.
THAT'S WHY I WANT TO HELP FIND YOURS.
RIGHT NOW, THIS IS THE ONLY WAY I KNOW HOW TO HELP. I'M SORRY FOR SURPRISING YOU.

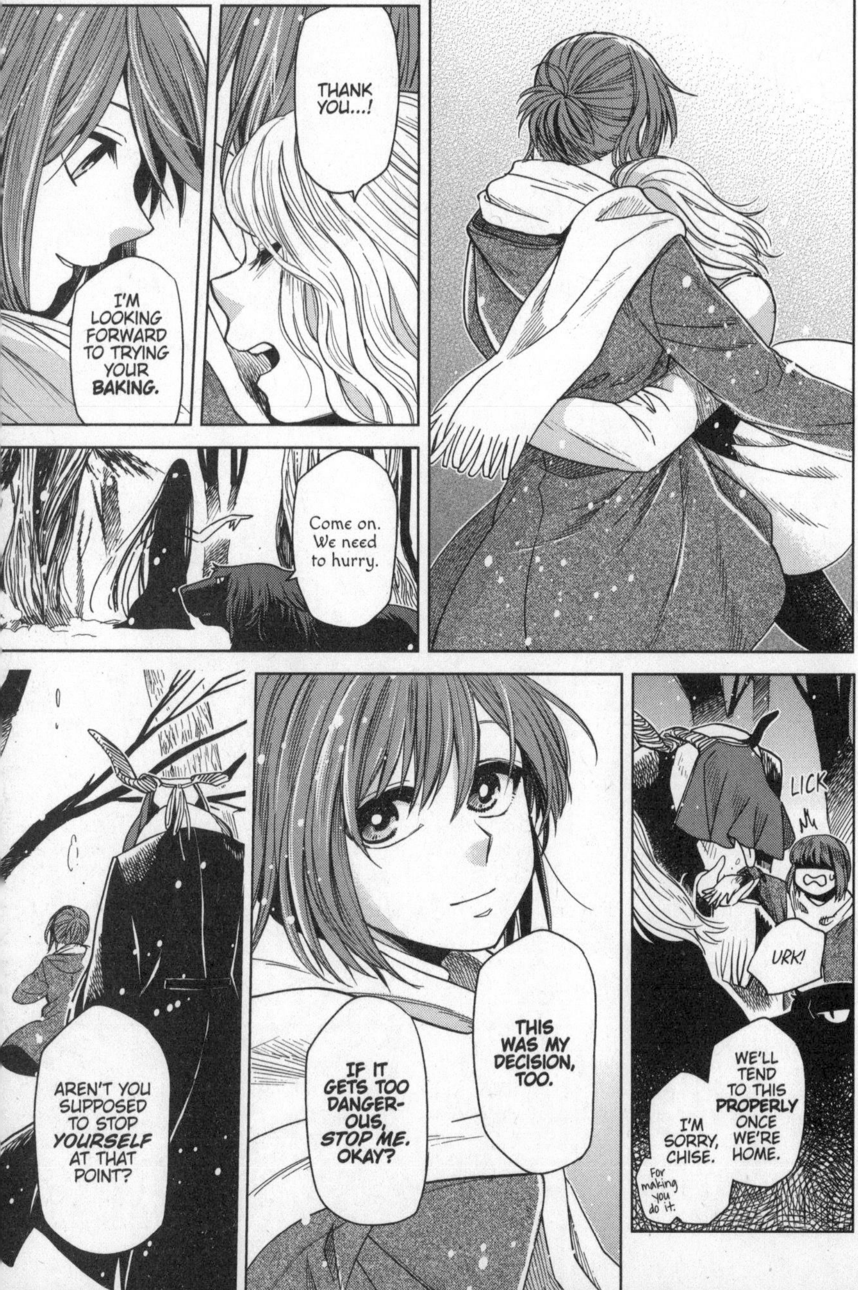
THANK YOU...!
I'M LOOKING FORWARD TO TRYING YOUR BAKING.
Come on. We need to hurry.
LICK
URK!
WE'LL TEND TO THIS PROPERLY ONCE WE'RE HOME.
I'M SORRY, CHISE.
For making you do it.
THIS WAS MY DECISION, TOO.
IF IT GETS TOO DANGER-OUS, STOP ME. OKAY?
AREN'T YOU SUPPOSED TO STOP YOURSELF AT THAT POINT?

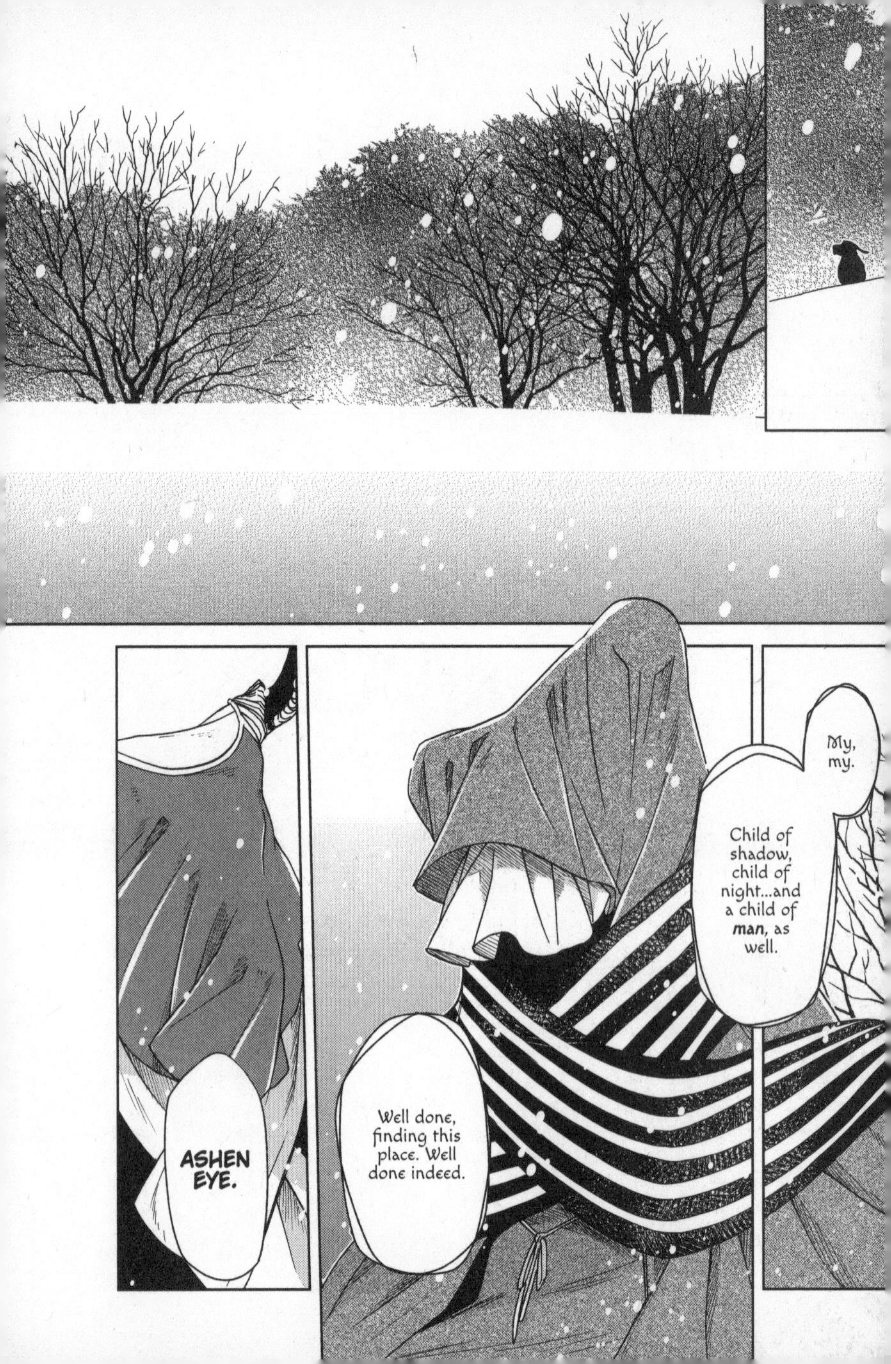
My, my.
Child of shadow, child of night...and a child of ***man***, as well.
Well done, finding this place. Well done indeed.
ASHEN EYE.

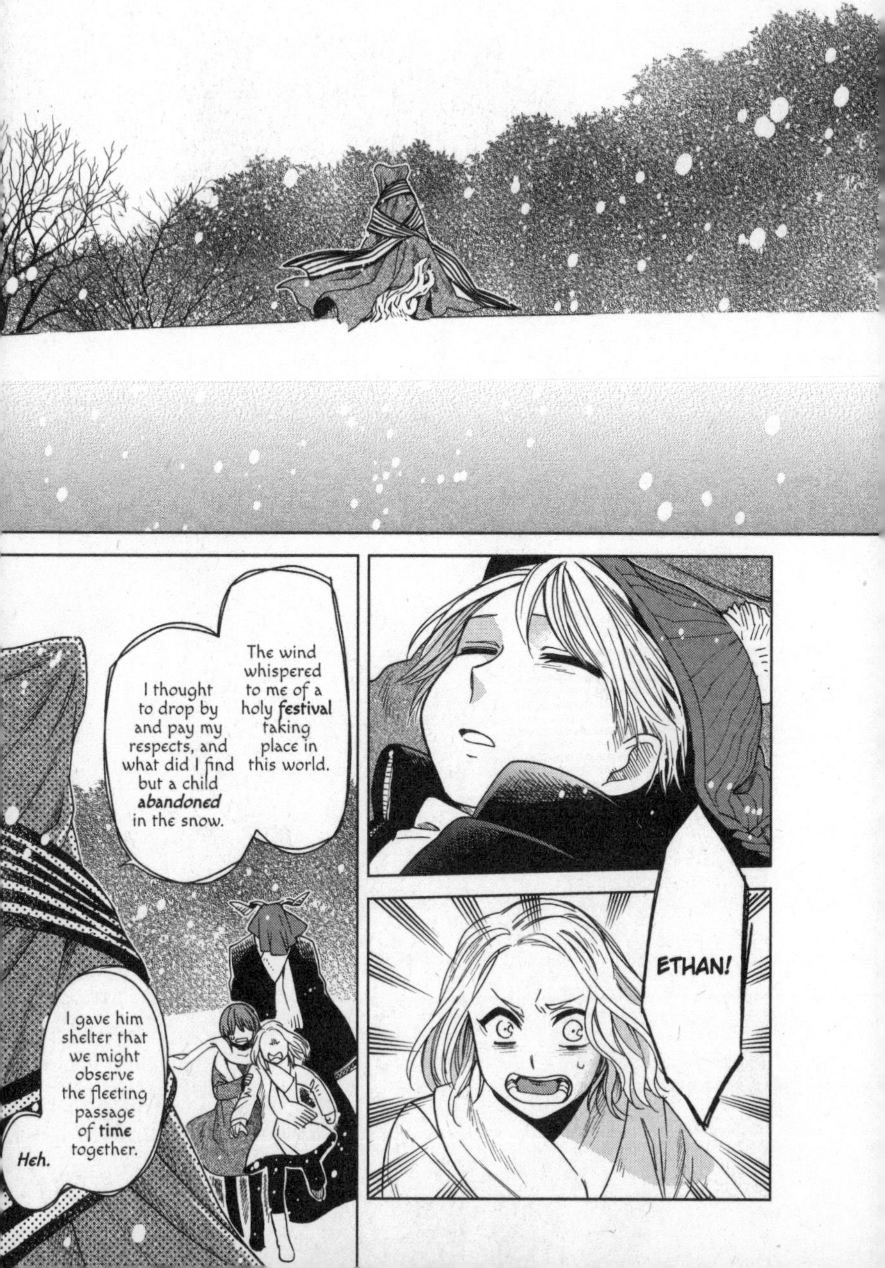
ETHAN!
The wind whispered to me of a holy **festival** taking place in this world.
I thought to drop by and pay my respects, and what did I find but a child ***abandoned*** in the snow.
I gave him shelter that we might observe the fleeting passage of **time** together.
Heh.

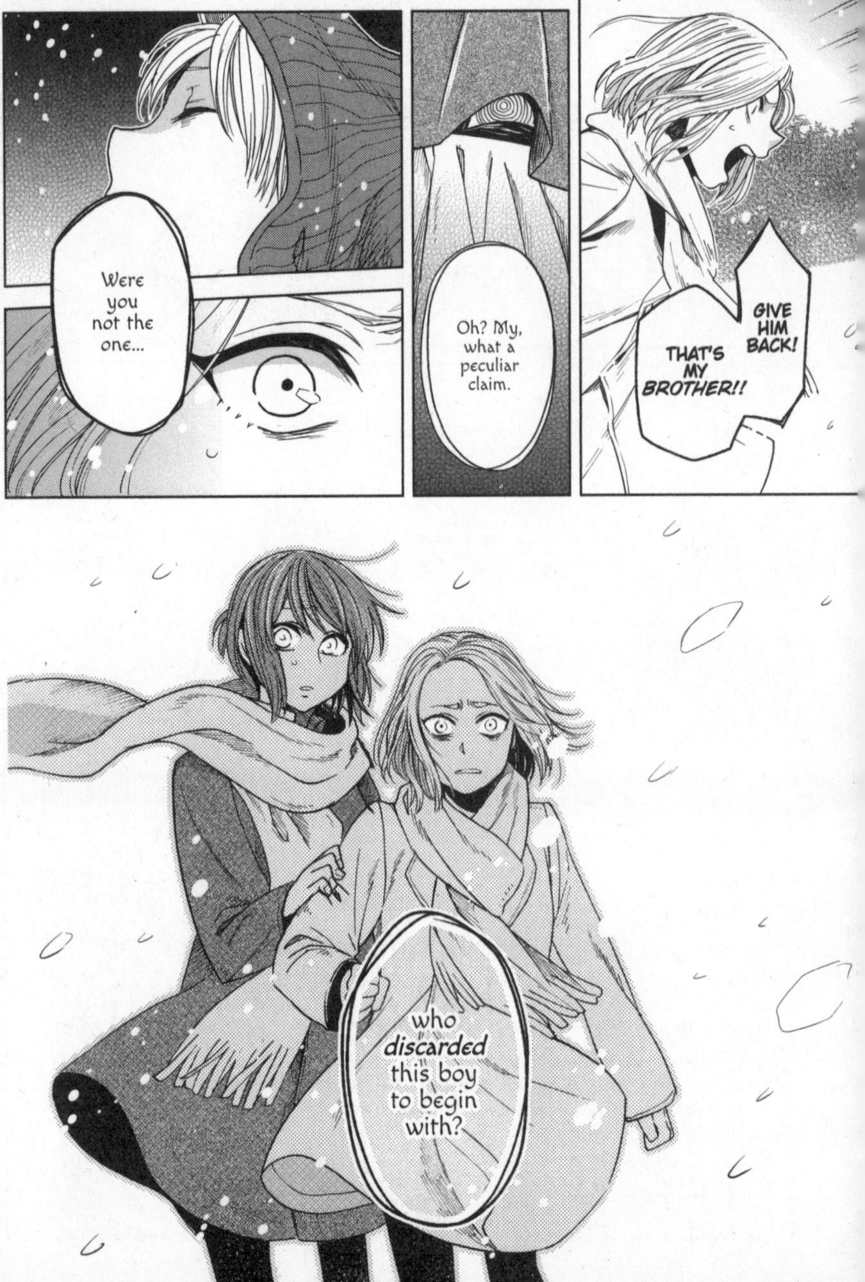
GIVE HIM BACK!
THAT'S MY BROTHER!!
Oh? My, what a peculiar claim.
Were you not the one...
who discarded this boy to begin with?

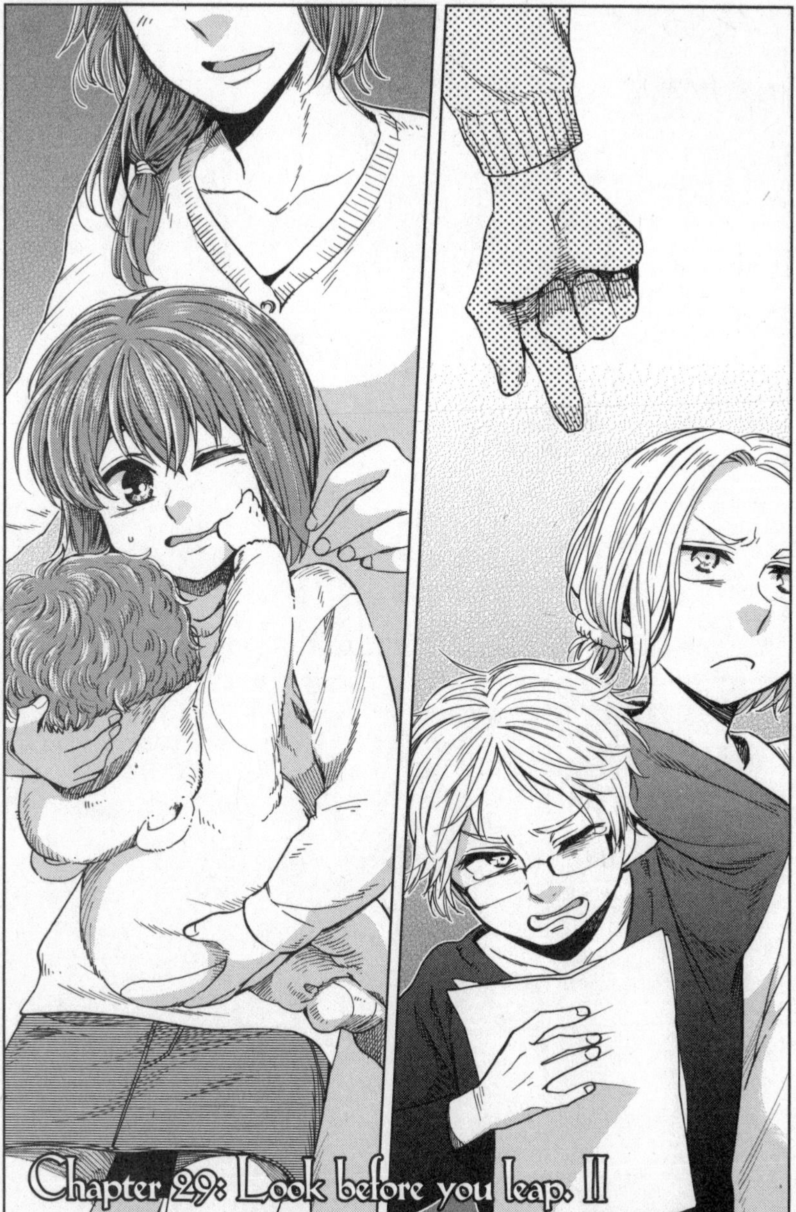
Chapter 29: Look before you leap. II

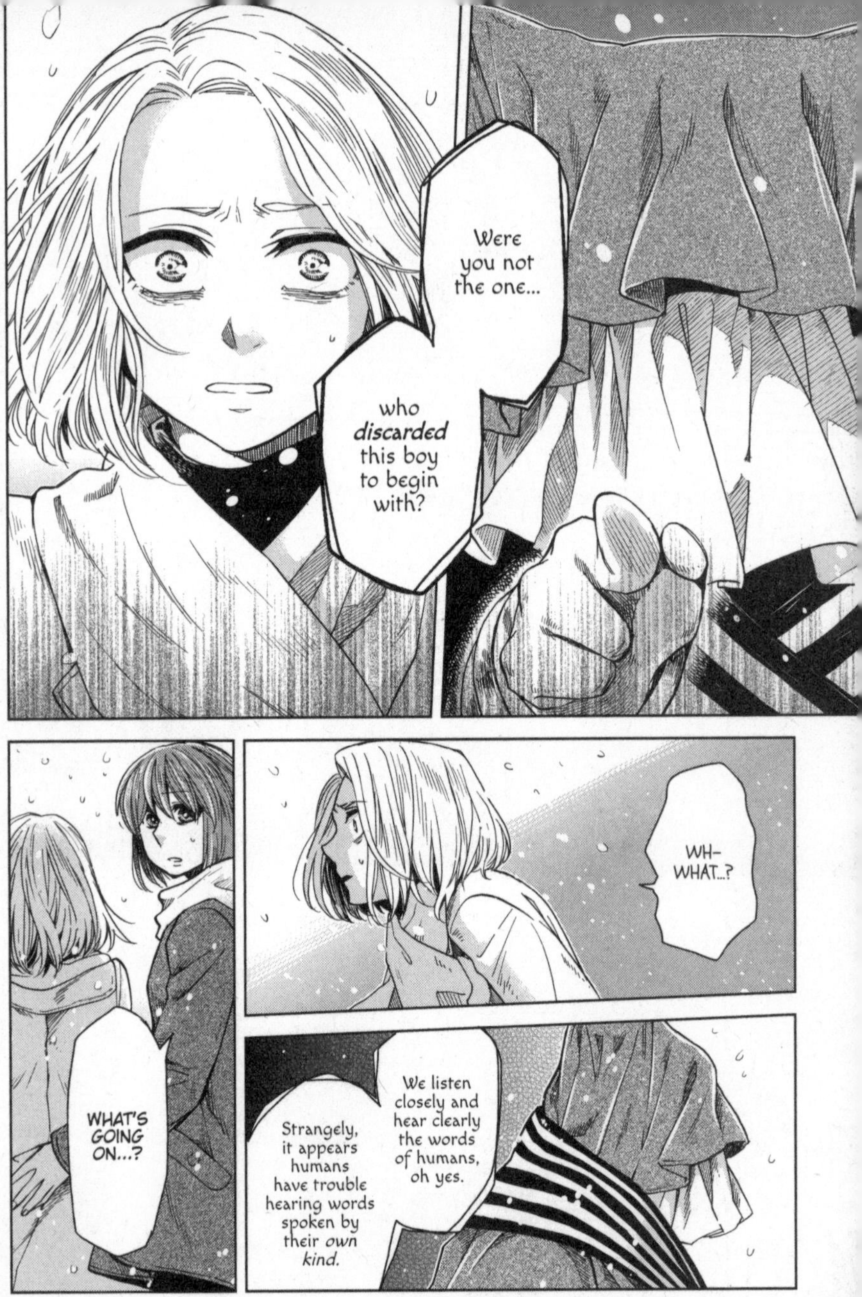

Were you not the one...
who *discarded* this boy to begin with?
WH-WHAT...?
We listen closely and hear clearly the words of humans, oh yes.
Strangely, it appears humans have trouble hearing words spoken by their *own* kind.
WHAT'S GOING ON...?

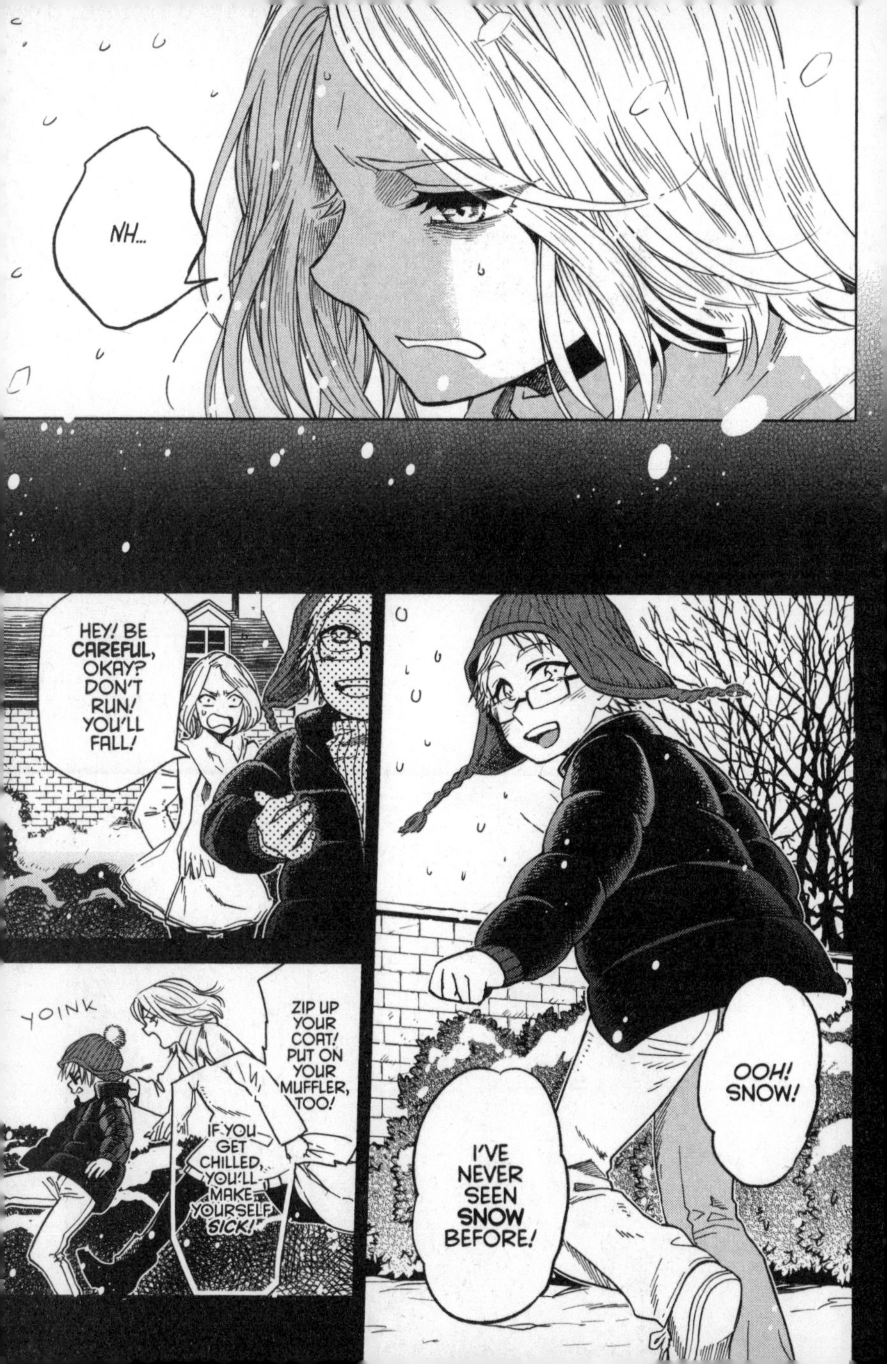
NH...
OOH! SNOW!
I'VE NEVER SEEN SNOW BEFORE!
HEY! BE CAREFUL, OKAY? DON'T RUN! YOU'LL FALL!
YOINK
ZIP UP YOUR COAT! PUT ON YOUR MUFFLER, TOO!
IF YOU GET CHILLED, YOU'LL MAKE YOURSELF SICK!

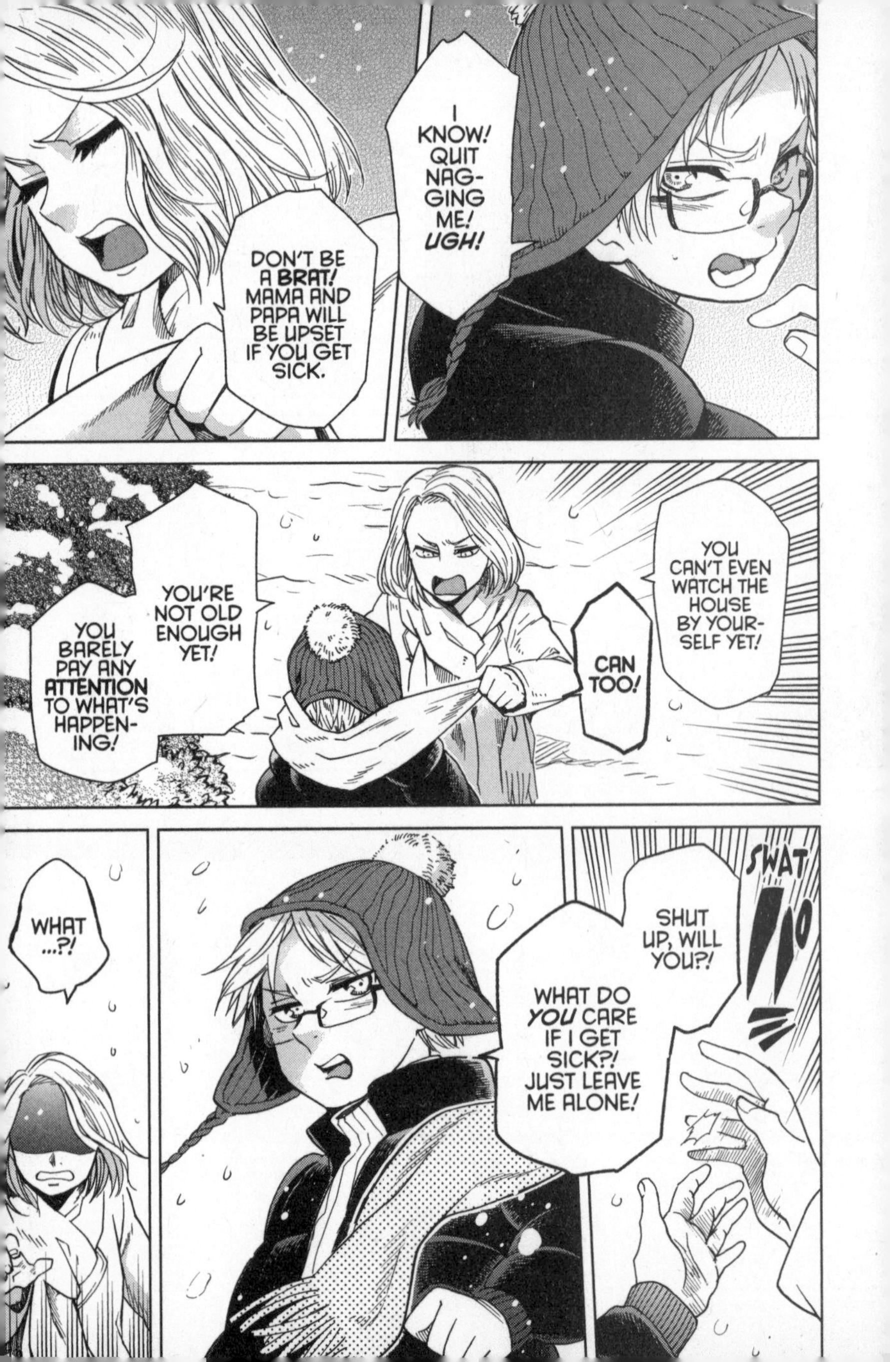
I KNOW! QUIT NAGGING ME! UGH!
DON'T BE A BRAT! MAMA AND PAPA WILL BE UPSET IF YOU GET SICK.
YOU CAN'T EVEN WATCH THE HOUSE BY YOURSELF YET!
CAN TOO!
YOU'RE NOT OLD ENOUGH YET!
YOU BARELY PAY ANY ATTENTION TO WHAT'S HAPPENING!
SWAT
SHUT UP, WILL YOU?!
WHAT DO YOU CARE IF I GET SICK?! JUST LEAVE ME ALONE!
WHAT ...?!

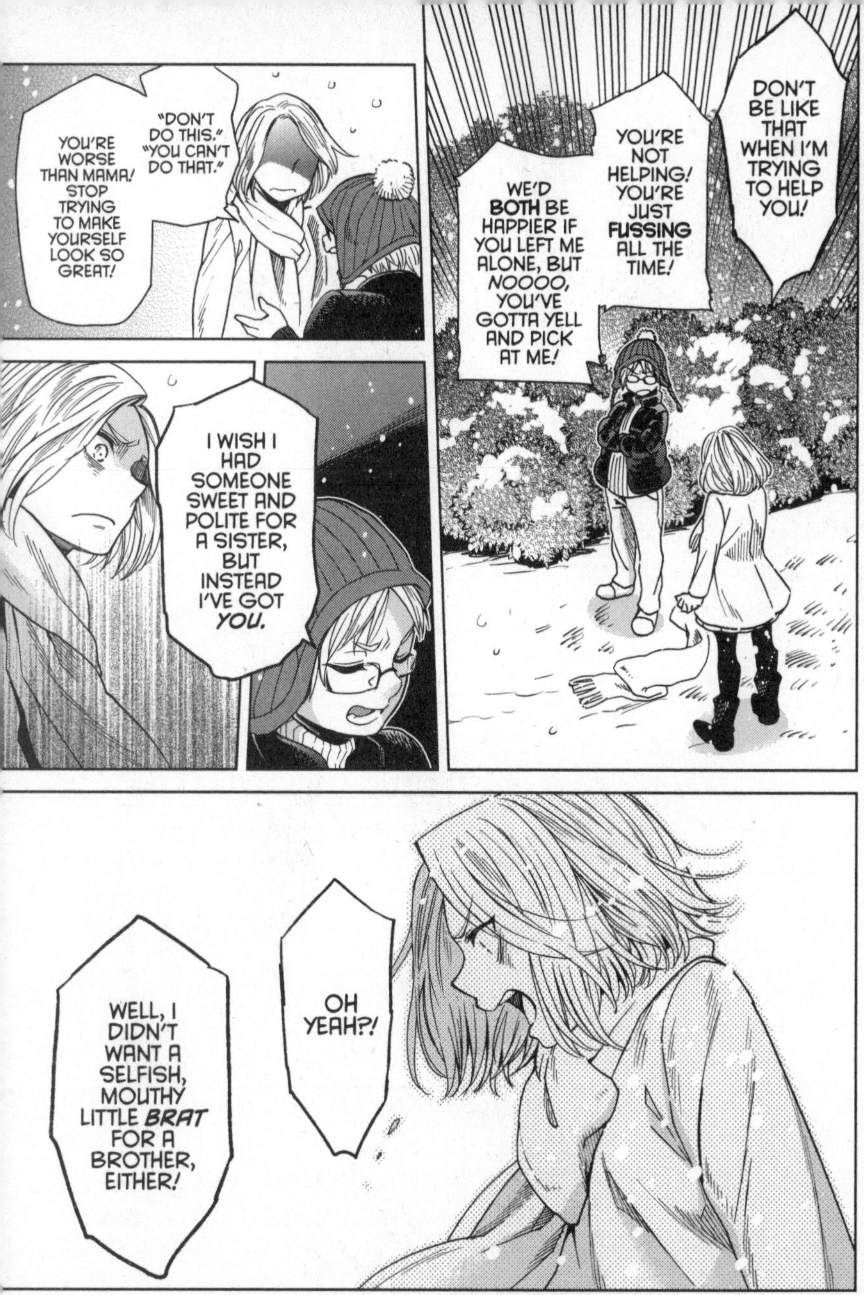
DON'T BE LIKE THAT WHEN I'M TRYING TO HELP YOU!
YOU'RE NOT HELPING! YOU'RE JUST **FUSSING** ALL THE TIME!
WE'D **BOTH** BE HAPPIER IF YOU LEFT ME ALONE, BUT *NOOOO*, YOU'VE GOTTA YELL AND PICK AT ME!
"DON'T DO THIS." "YOU CAN'T DO THAT."
YOU'RE WORSE THAN MAMA! STOP TRYING TO MAKE YOURSELF LOOK SO GREAT!
I WISH I HAD SOMEONE SWEET AND POLITE FOR A SISTER, BUT INSTEAD I'VE GOT ***YOU***.
OH YEAH?!
WELL, I DIDN'T WANT A SELFISH, MOUTHY LITTLE ***BRAT*** FOR A BROTHER, EITHER!

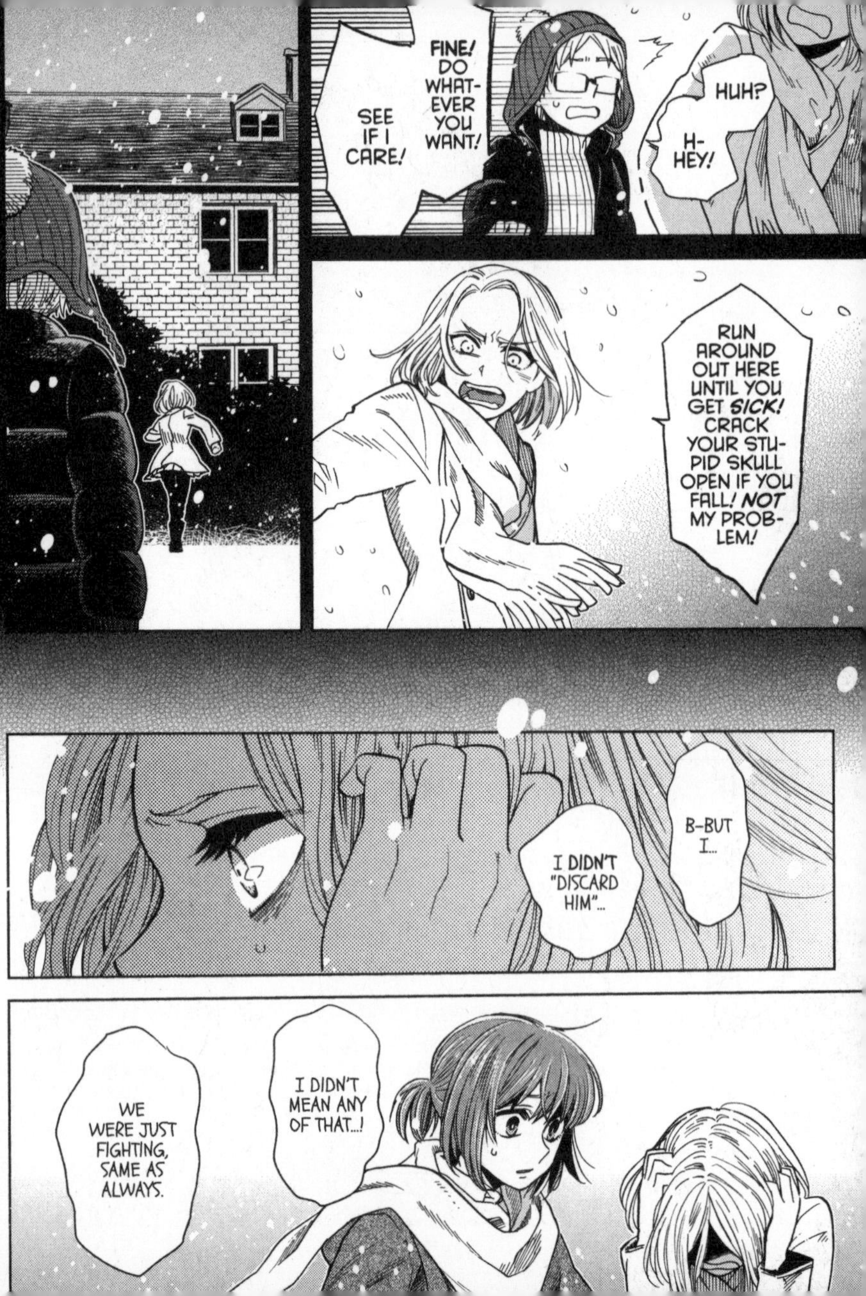
HUH?
H-HEY!
FINE! DO WHATEVER YOU WANT!
SEE IF I CARE!
RUN AROUND OUT HERE UNTIL YOU GET **SICK!** CRACK YOUR STUPID SKULL OPEN IF YOU FALL! **NOT** MY PROBLEM!
B-BUT I...
I DIDN'T "DISCARD HIM"...
I DIDN'T MEAN ANY OF THAT...!
WE WERE JUST FIGHTING, SAME AS ALWAYS.

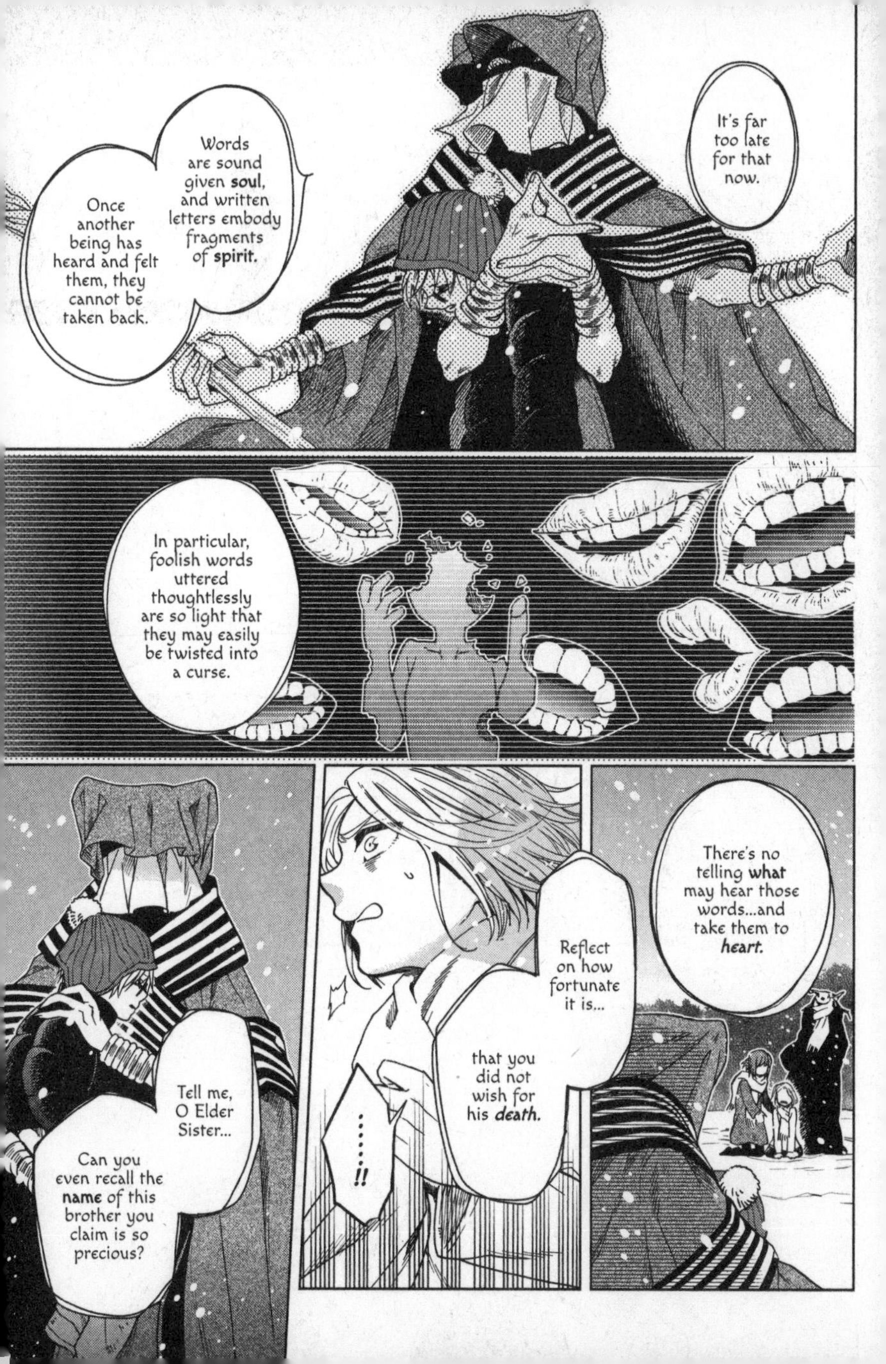
It's far too late for that now.
Words are sound given soul, and written letters embody fragments of spirit.
Once another being has heard and felt them, they cannot be taken back.
In particular, foolish words uttered thoughtlessly are so light that they may easily be twisted into a curse.
There's no telling what may hear those words...and take them to heart.
Reflect on how fortunate it is...
that you did not wish for his death.
......!!
Tell me, O Elder Sister...
Can you even recall the name of this brother you claim is so precious?

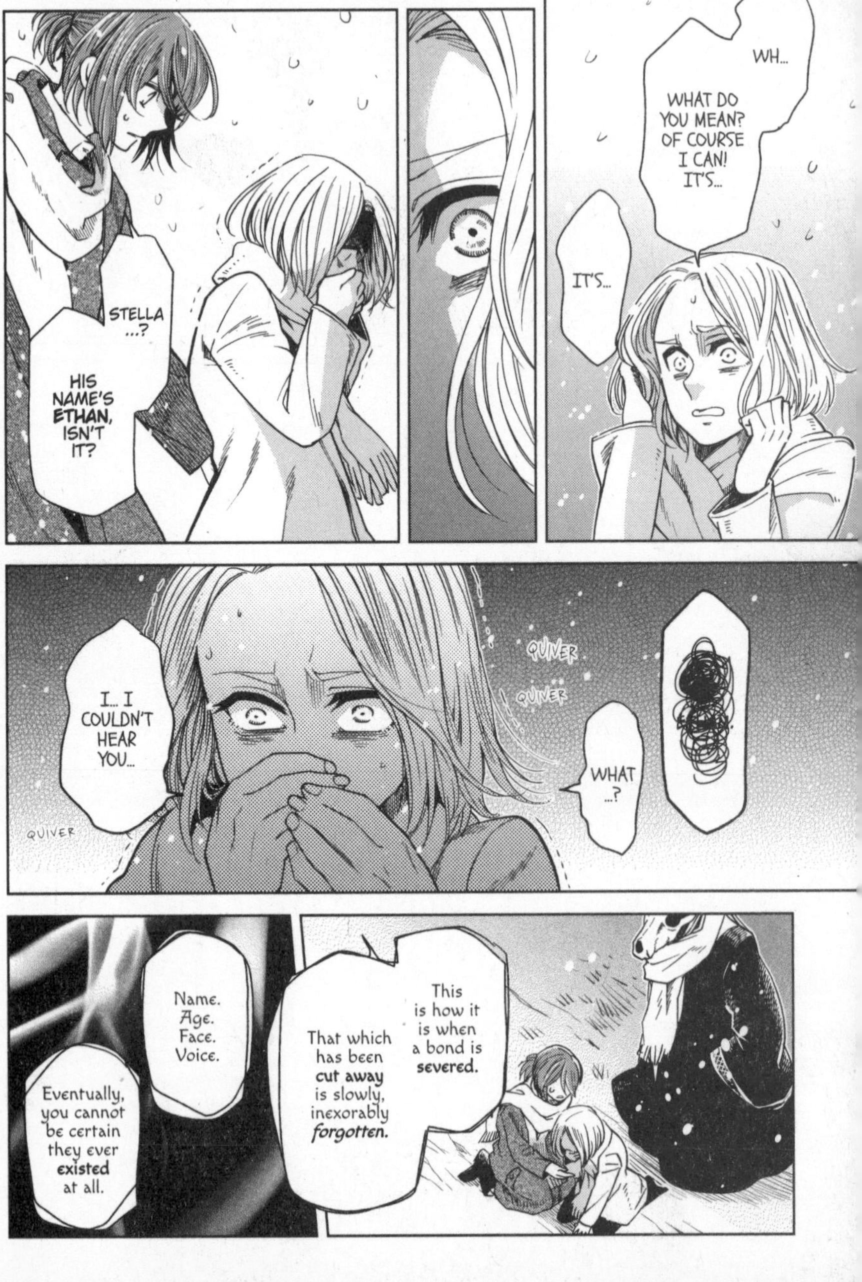
WH...
WHAT DO YOU MEAN? OF COURSE I CAN! IT'S...
IT'S...
STELLA ...?
HIS NAME'S ETHAN, ISN'T IT?
QUIVER
QUIVER
WHAT ...?
I... I COULDN'T HEAR YOU...
QUIVER
This is how it is when a bond is severed.
That which has been cut away is slowly, inexorably forgotten.
Name. Age. Face. Voice.
Eventually, you cannot be certain they ever existed at all.

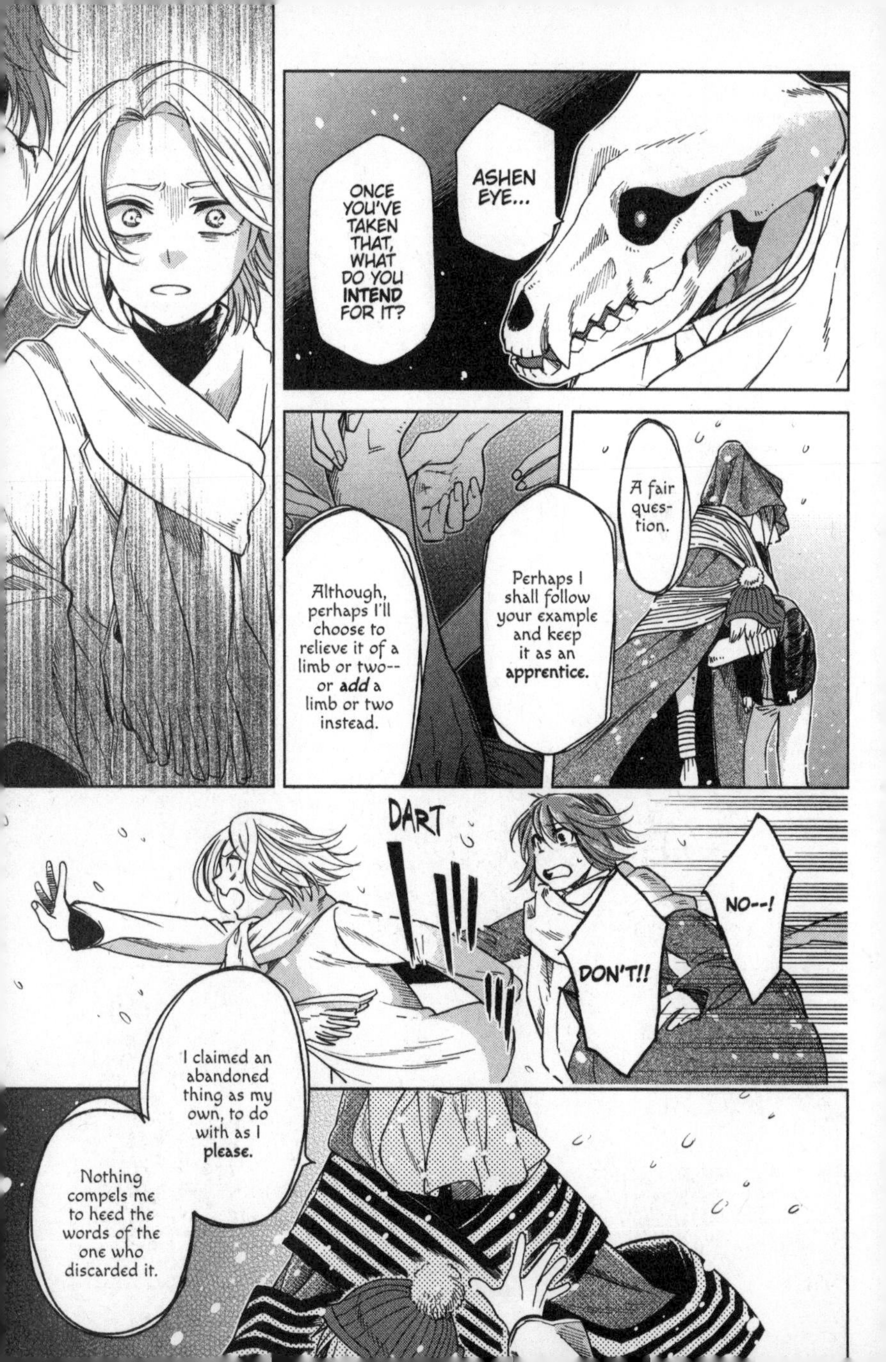
ASHEN EYE...
ONCE YOU'VE TAKEN THAT, WHAT DO YOU INTEND FOR IT?
A fair question.
Perhaps I shall follow your example and keep it as an **apprentice.**
Although, perhaps I'll choose to relieve it of a limb or two-- or ***add*** a limb or two instead.
NO--!
DON'T!!
DART
I claimed an abandoned thing as my own, to do with as I **please.**
Nothing compels me to heed the words of the one who discarded it.

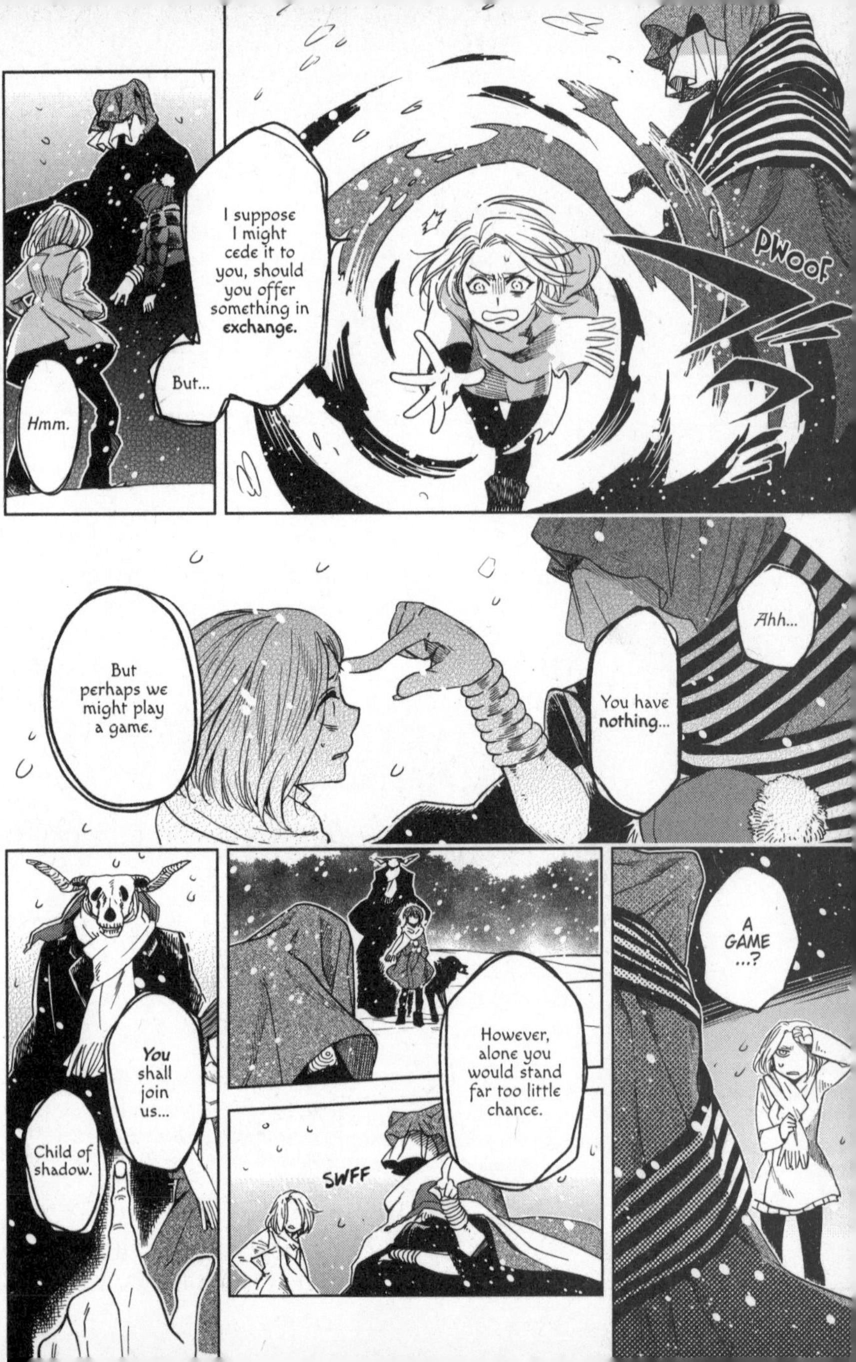
PWOOF
I suppose I might cede it to you, should you offer something in **exchange.**
But...
Hmm.
Ahh...
You have **nothing...**
But perhaps we might play a game.
A GAME ...?
However, alone you would stand far too little chance.
SWFF
You shall join us...
Child of shadow.

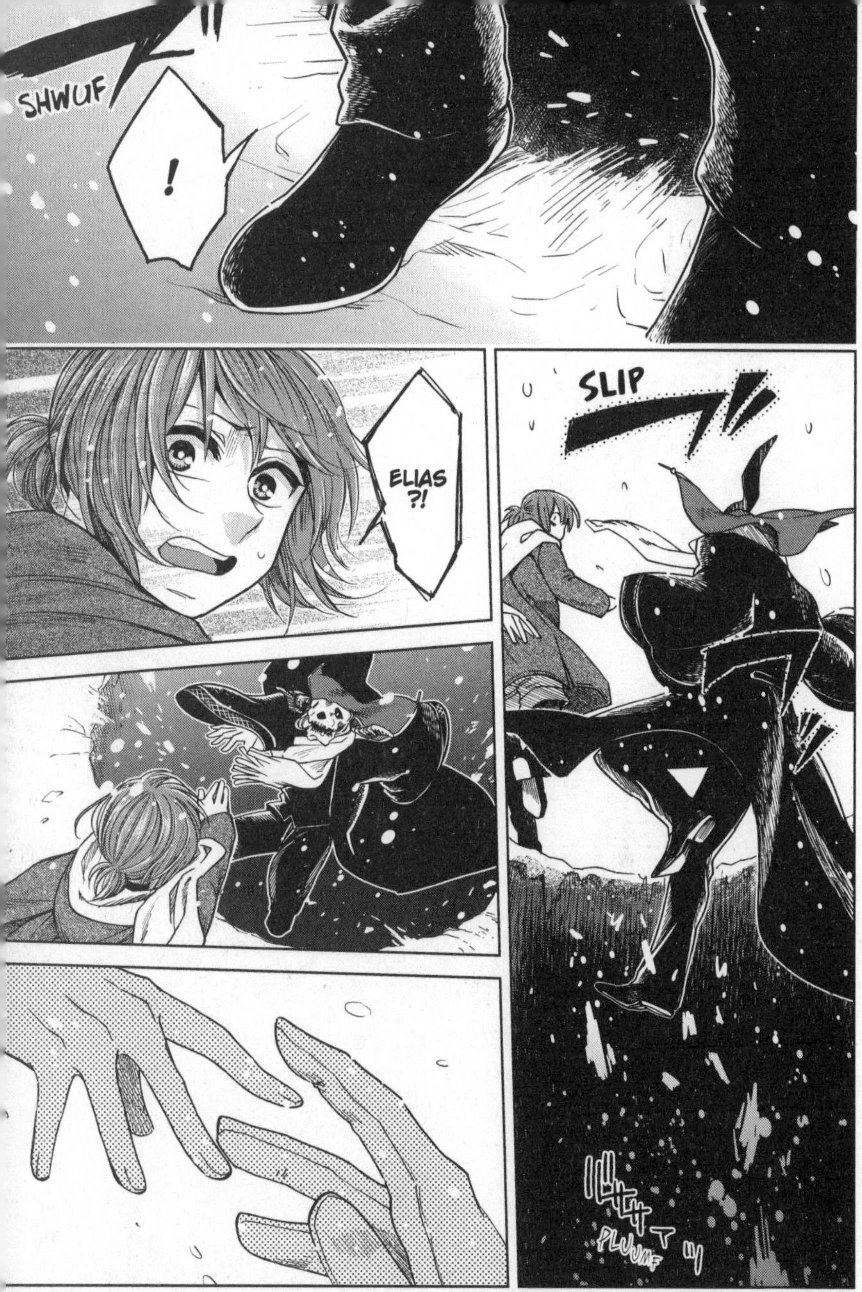
SHWUF
!
SLIP
PLUUMF
ELIAS ?!

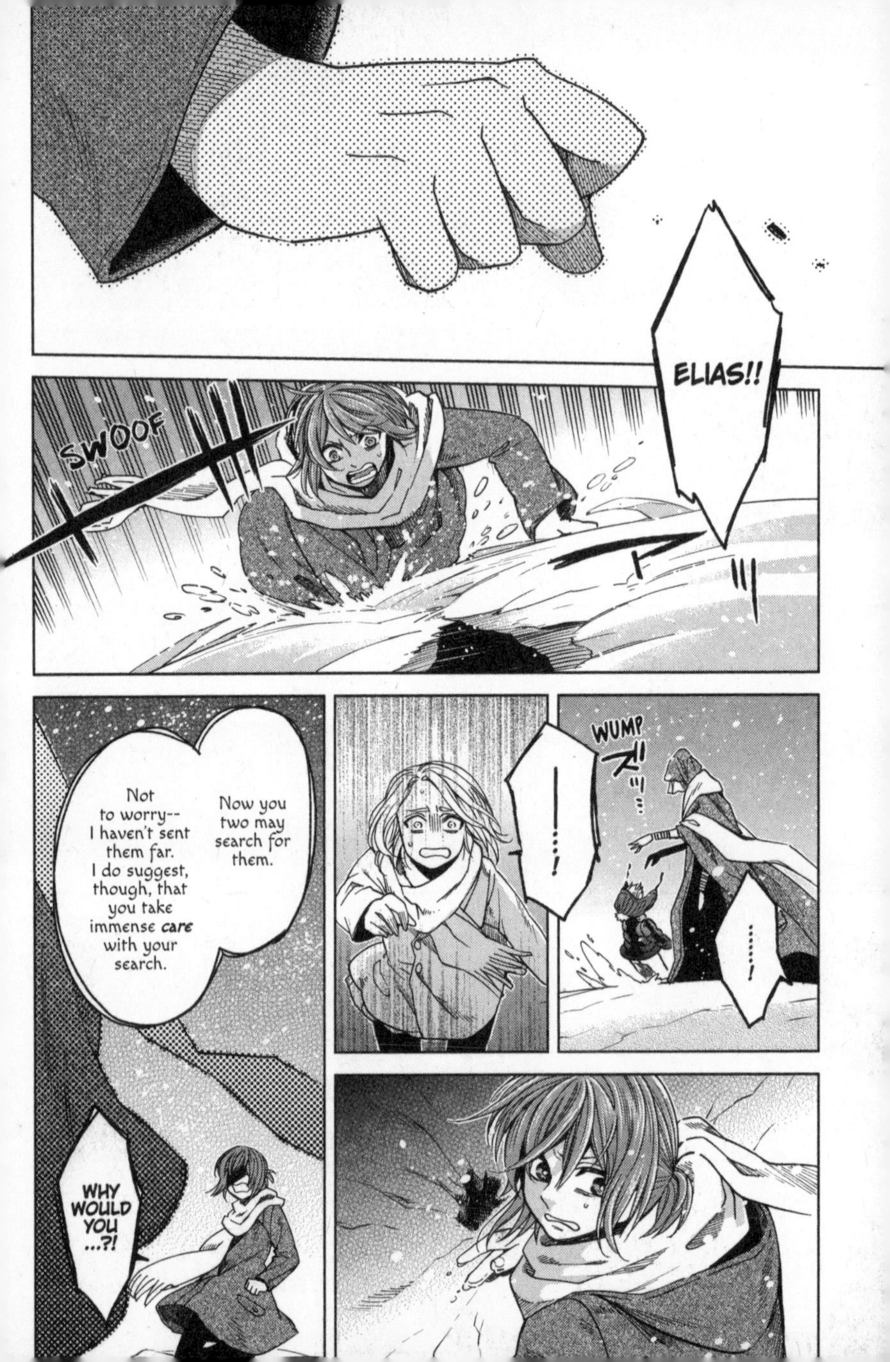

ELIAS!!
SWOOF
WUMP
......!
......!
Not to worry-- I haven't sent them far. I do suggest, though, that you take immense care with your search.
Now you two may search for them.
WHY WOULD YOU ...?!

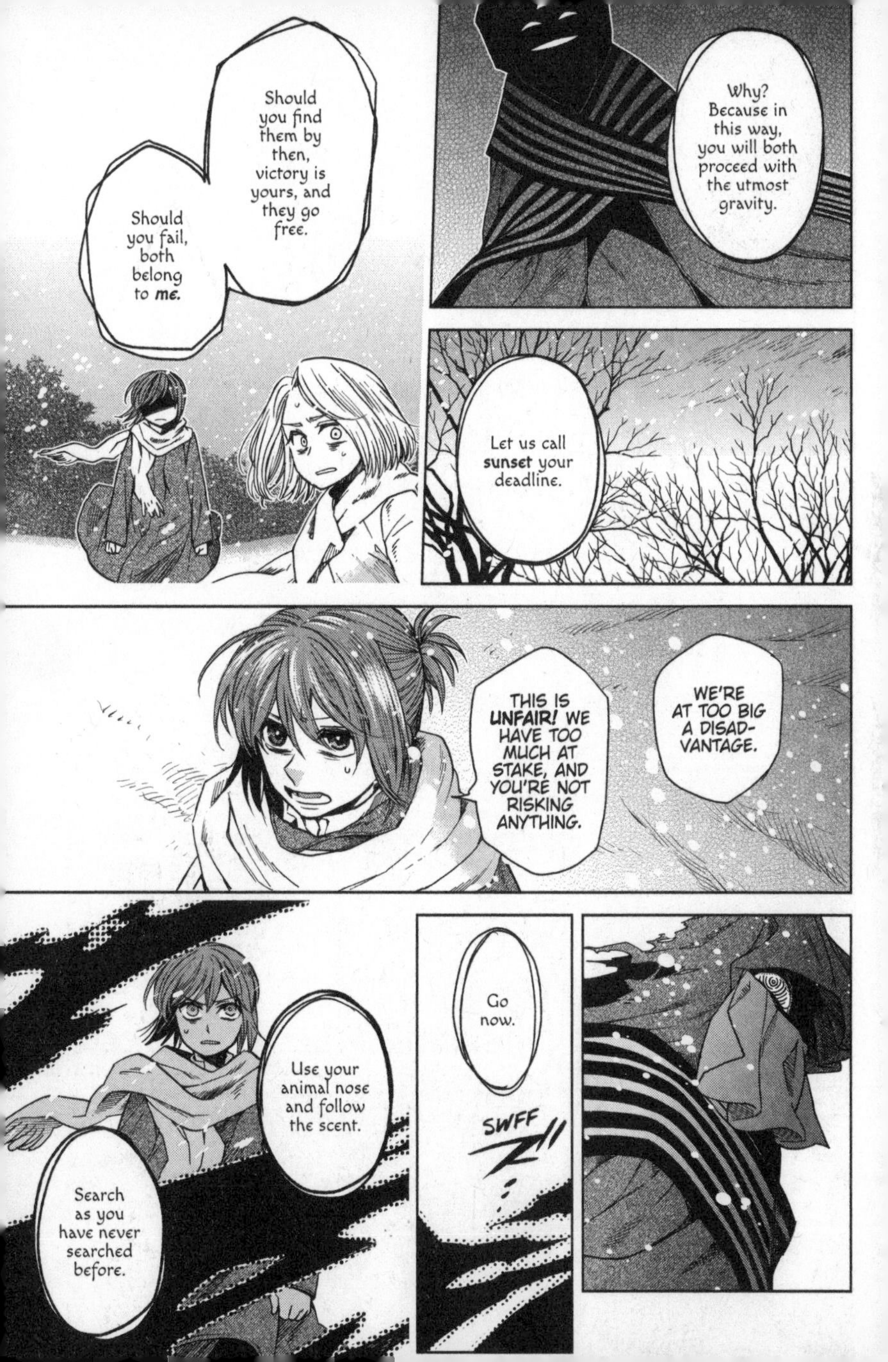
Why? Because in this way, you will both proceed with the utmost gravity.
Let us call **sunset** your deadline.
Should you find them by then, victory is yours, and they go free.
Should you fail, both belong to *me.*
WE'RE AT TOO BIG A DISADVANTAGE.
THIS IS **UNFAIR!** WE HAVE TOO MUCH AT STAKE, AND YOU'RE NOT RISKING ANYTHING.
SWFF
Go now.
Use your animal nose and follow the scent.
Search as you have never searched before.

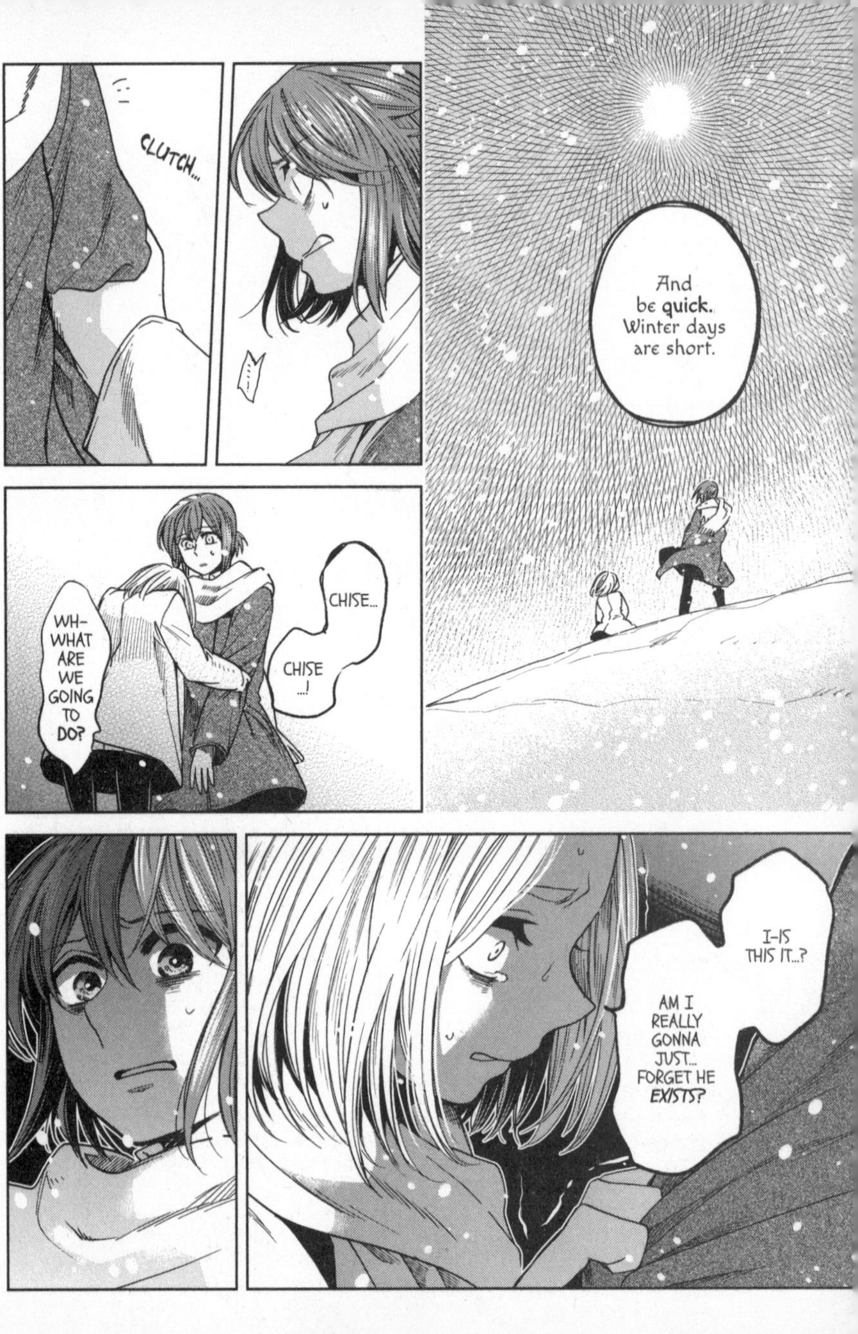
And be **quick.** Winter days are short.
...!
CLUTCH...
CHISE...
CHISE ...!
WH-WHAT ARE WE GOING TO DO?
I-IS THIS IT...?
AM I REALLY GONNA JUST... FORGET HE *EXISTS?*

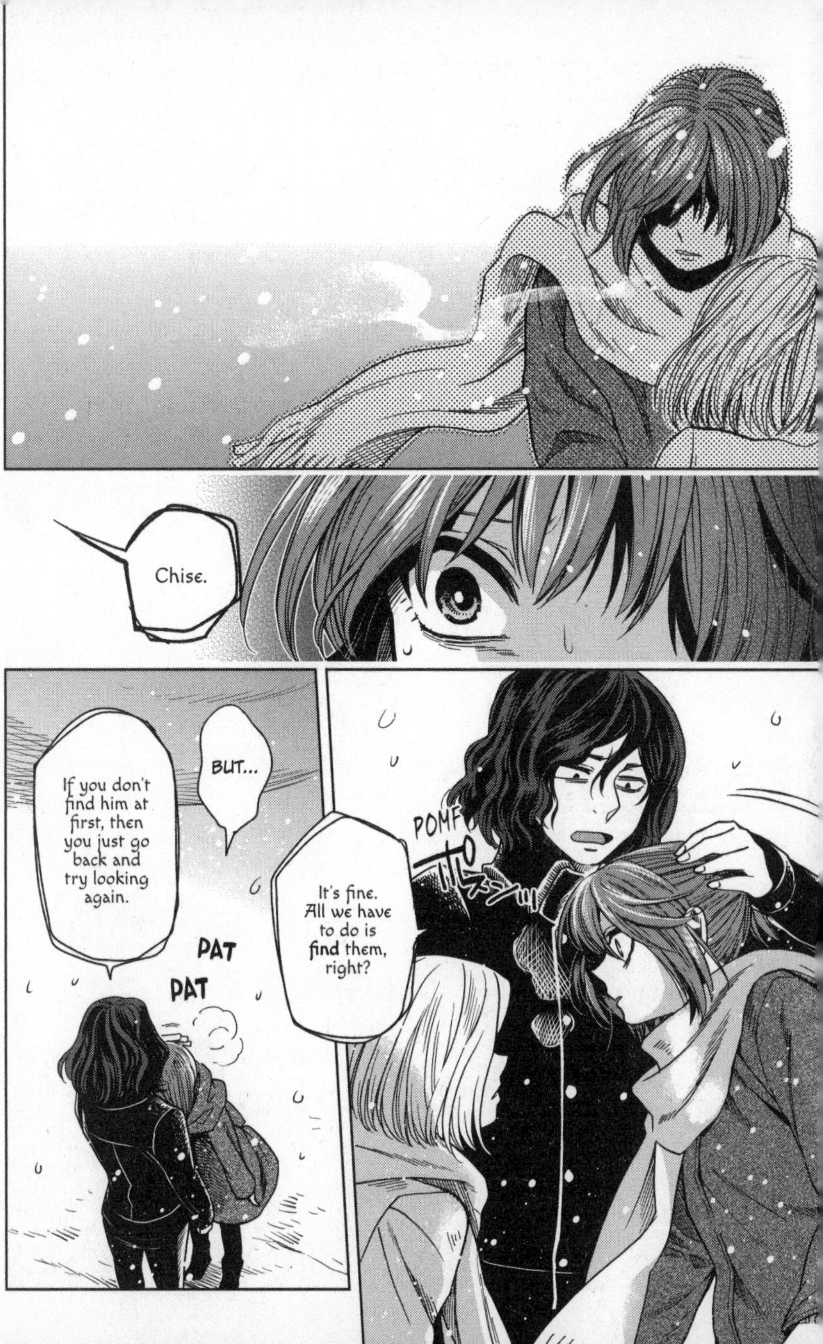
Chise.
POMF
It's fine. All we have to do is find them, right?
BUT...
If you don't find him at first, then you just go back and try looking again.
PAT
PAT

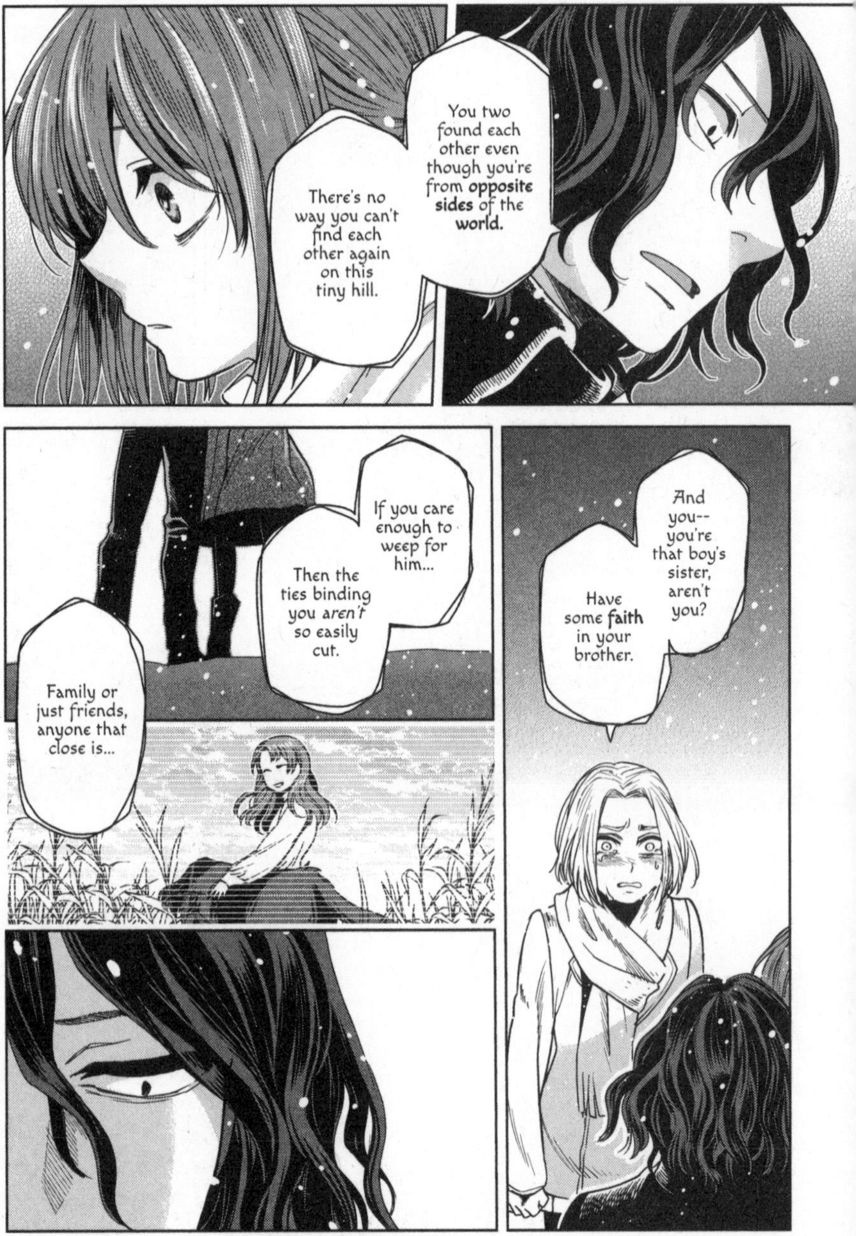
You two found each other even though you're from **opposite sides** of the **world.**
There's no way you can't find each other again on this tiny hill.
And you-- you're that boy's sister, aren't you?
Have some **faith** in your brother.
If you care enough to weep for him...
Then the ties binding you *aren't* so easily cut.
Family or just friends, anyone that close is...

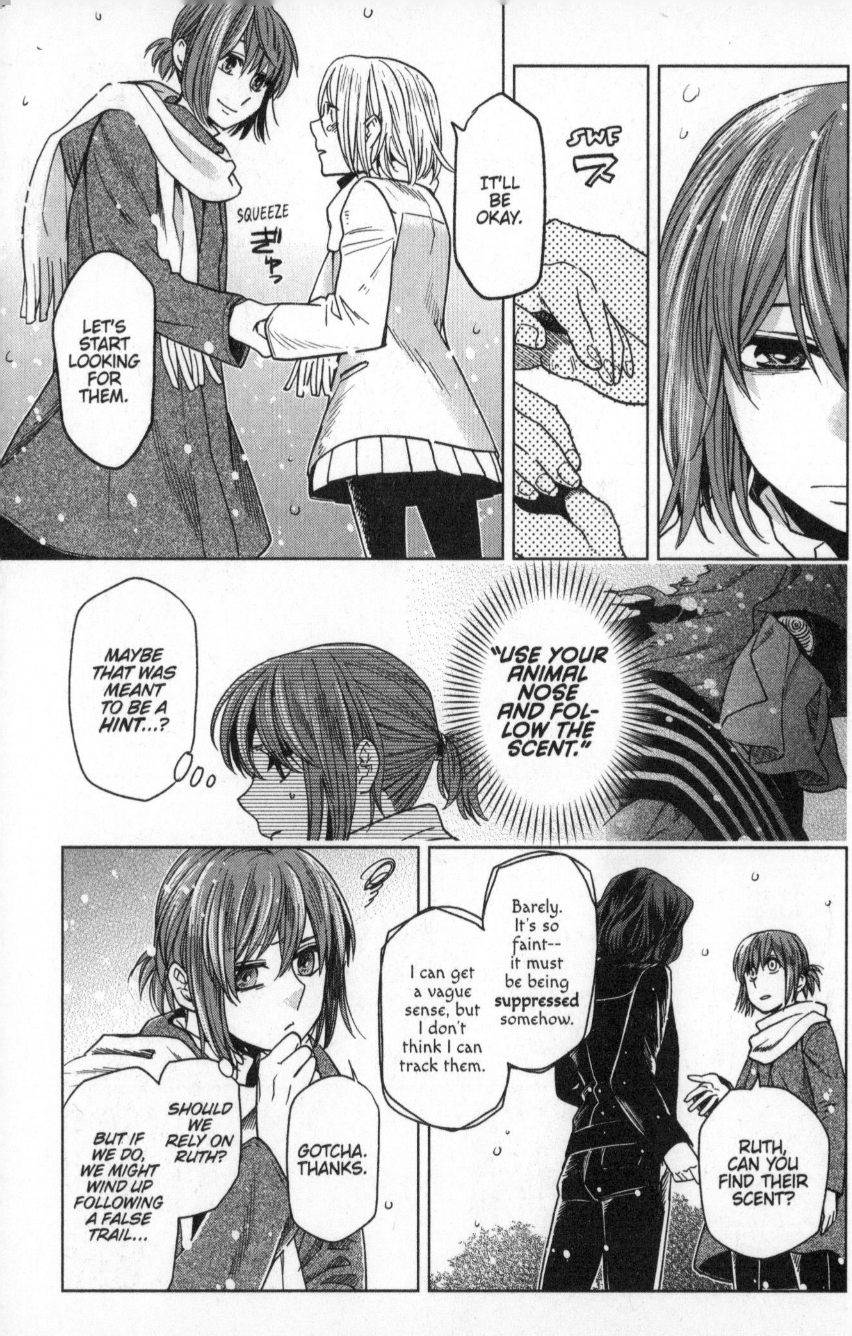
SWF
IT'LL BE OKAY.
SQUEEZE
LET'S START LOOKING FOR THEM.
"USE YOUR ANIMAL NOSE AND FOL-LOW THE SCENT."
MAYBE THAT WAS MEANT TO BE A HINT...?
RUTH, CAN YOU FIND THEIR SCENT?
Barely. It's so faint-- it must be being **suppressed** somehow.
I can get a vague sense, but I don't think I can track them.
GOTCHA. THANKS.
SHOULD WE RELY ON RUTH?
BUT IF WE DO, WE MIGHT WIND UP FOLLOWING A FALSE TRAIL...

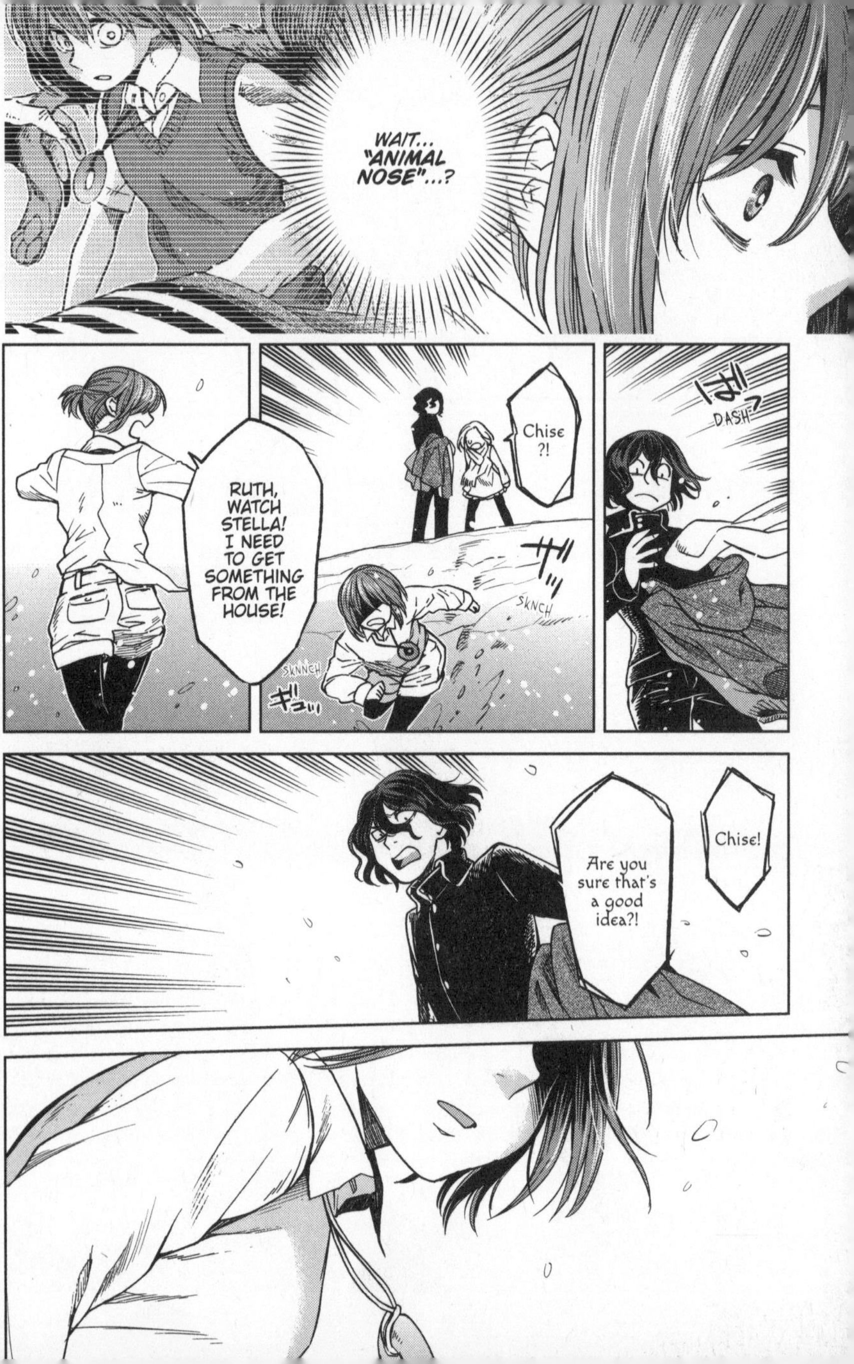
WAIT... "ANIMAL NOSE"...?
DASH
Chise ?!
SKNCH
SKNNCH
RUTH, WATCH STELLA! I NEED TO GET SOMETHING FROM THE HOUSE!
Chise!
Are you sure that's a good idea?!

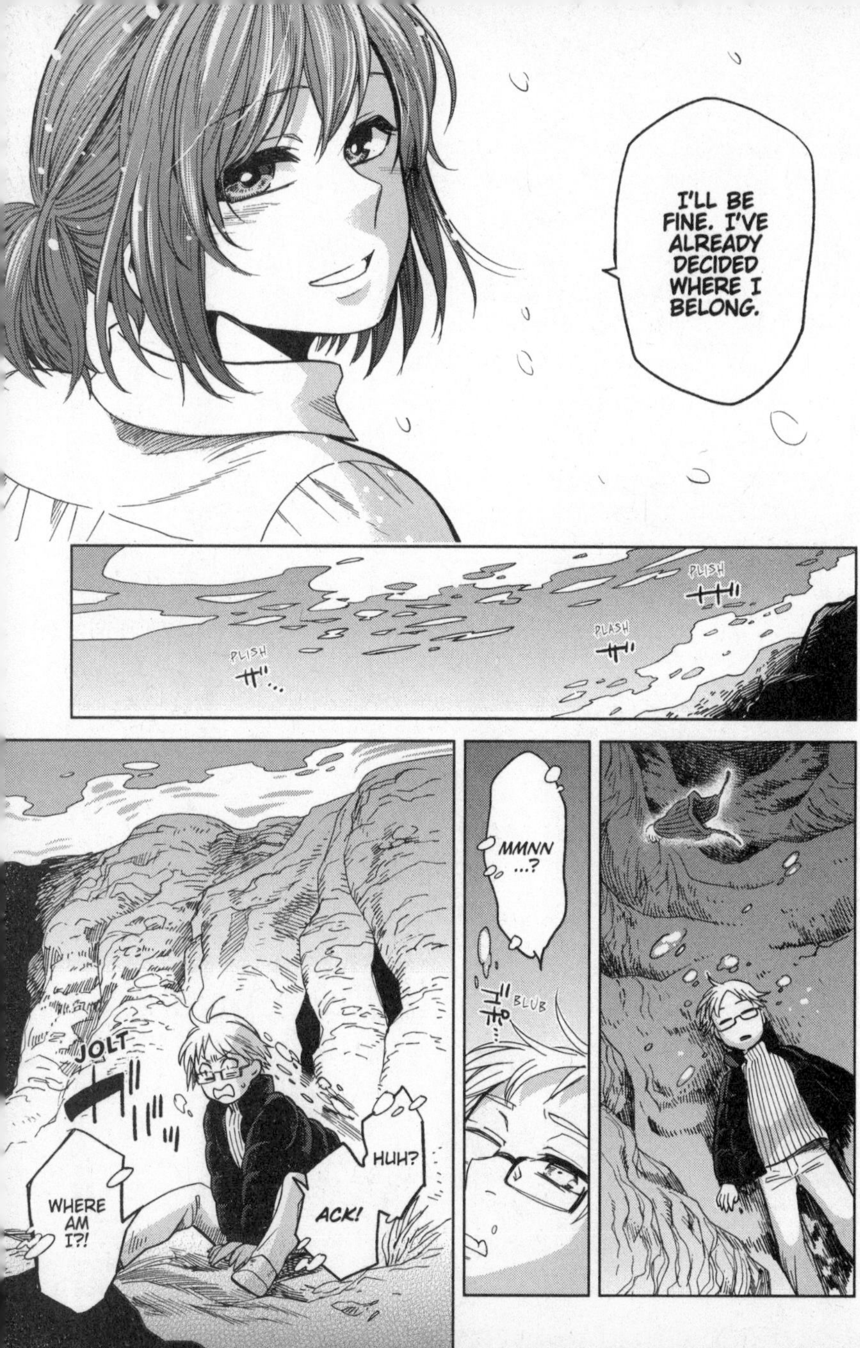

I'LL BE FINE. I'VE ALREADY DECIDED WHERE I BELONG.
PLISH
PLASH
PLISH
MMNN ...?
BLUB
JOLT
HUH?
ACK!
WHERE AM I?!

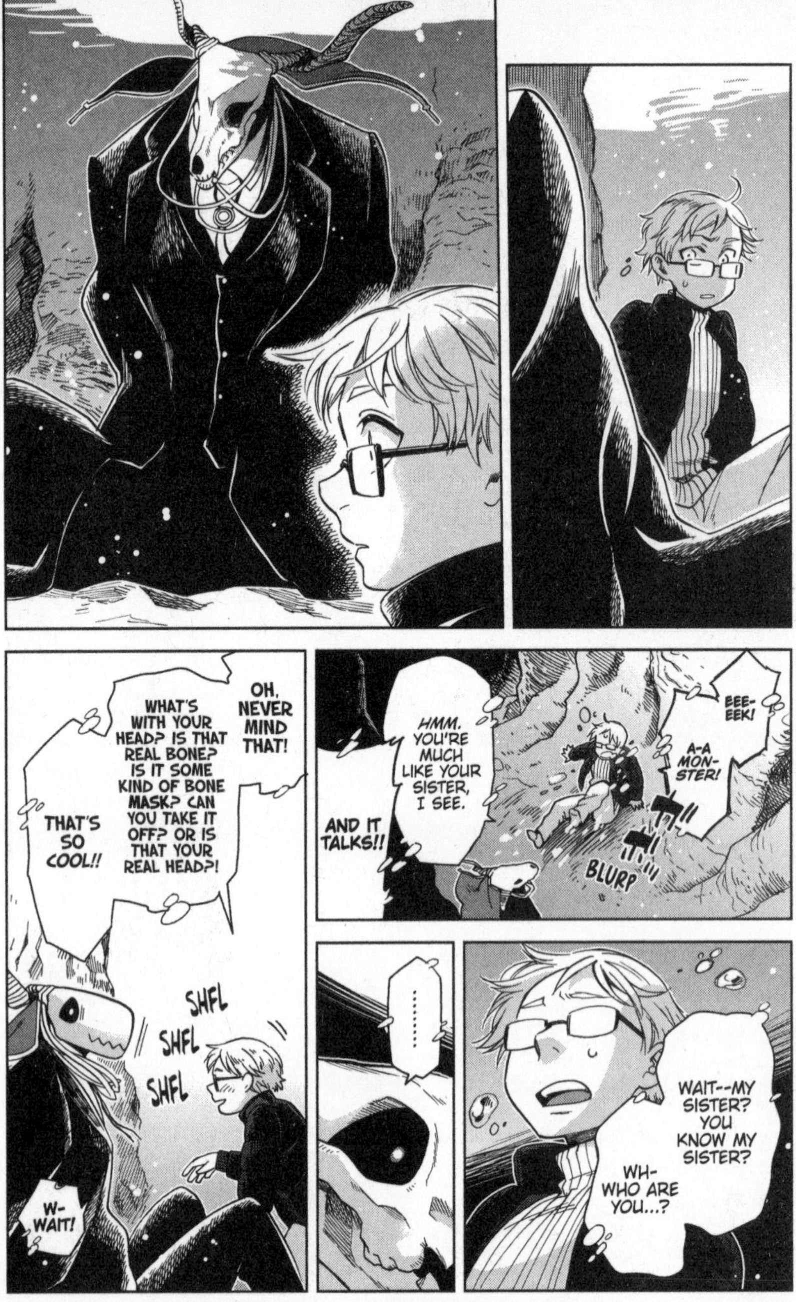
BEEE-EEK!
A-A MON-STER!
BLURP
HMM. YOU'RE MUCH LIKE YOUR SISTER, I SEE.
AND IT TALKS!!
WAIT--MY SISTER? YOU KNOW MY SISTER?
WH-WHO ARE YOU...?
......
OH, NEVER MIND THAT!
WHAT'S WITH YOUR HEAD? IS THAT REAL BONE? IS IT SOME KIND OF BONE MASK? CAN YOU TAKE IT OFF? OR IS THAT YOUR REAL HEAD?!
THAT'S SO COOL!!
SHFL
SHFL
SHFL
W-WAIT!

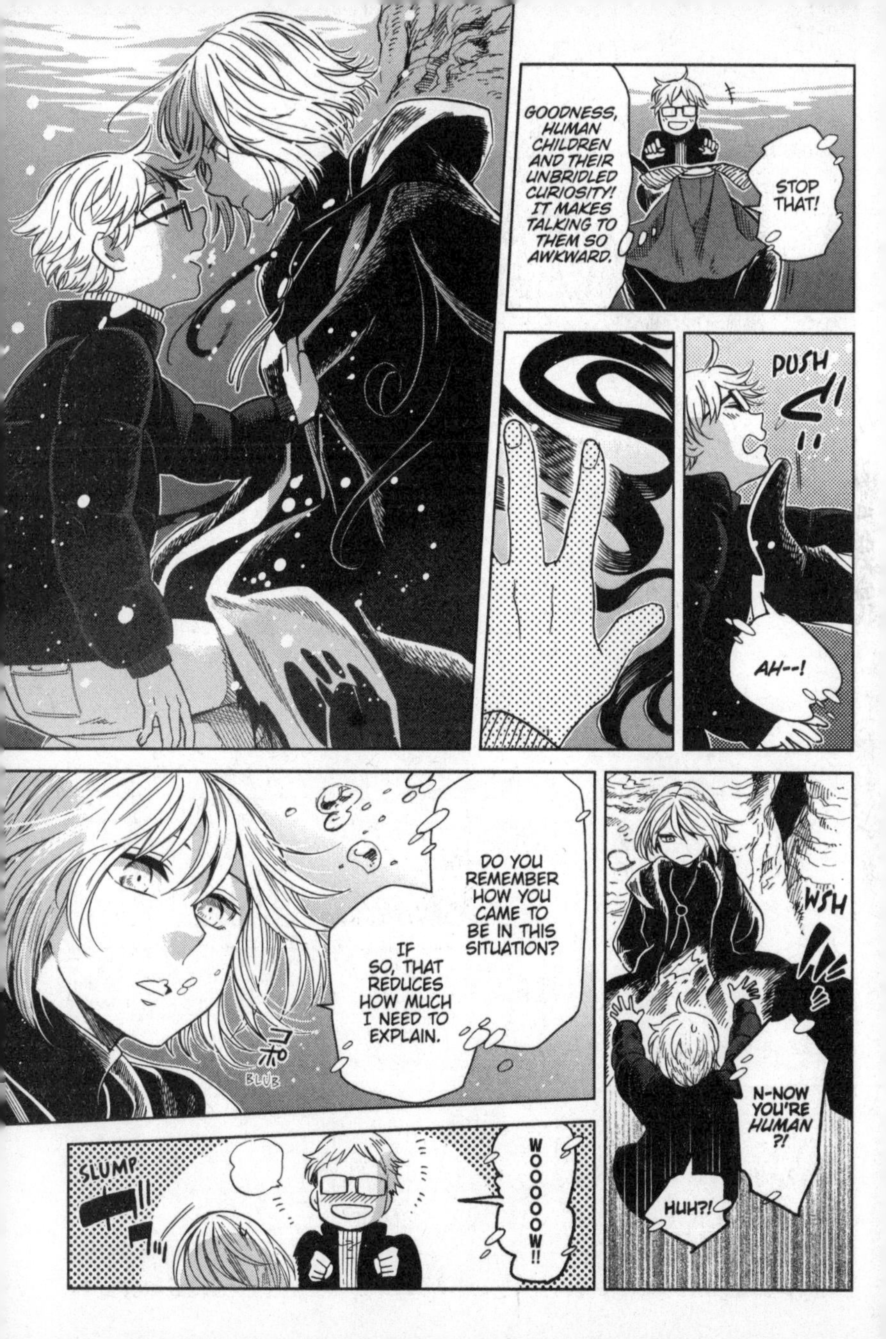
STOP THAT!
GOODNESS, HUMAN CHILDREN AND THEIR UNBRIDLED CURIOSITY! IT MAKES TALKING TO THEM SO AWKWARD.
PUSH
AH--!
WSH
N-NOW YOU'RE HUMAN?!
HUH?!
DO YOU REMEMBER HOW YOU CAME TO BE IN THIS SITUATION?
IF SO, THAT REDUCES HOW MUCH I NEED TO EXPLAIN.
BLUB
WOOOOOOW!!
SLUMP

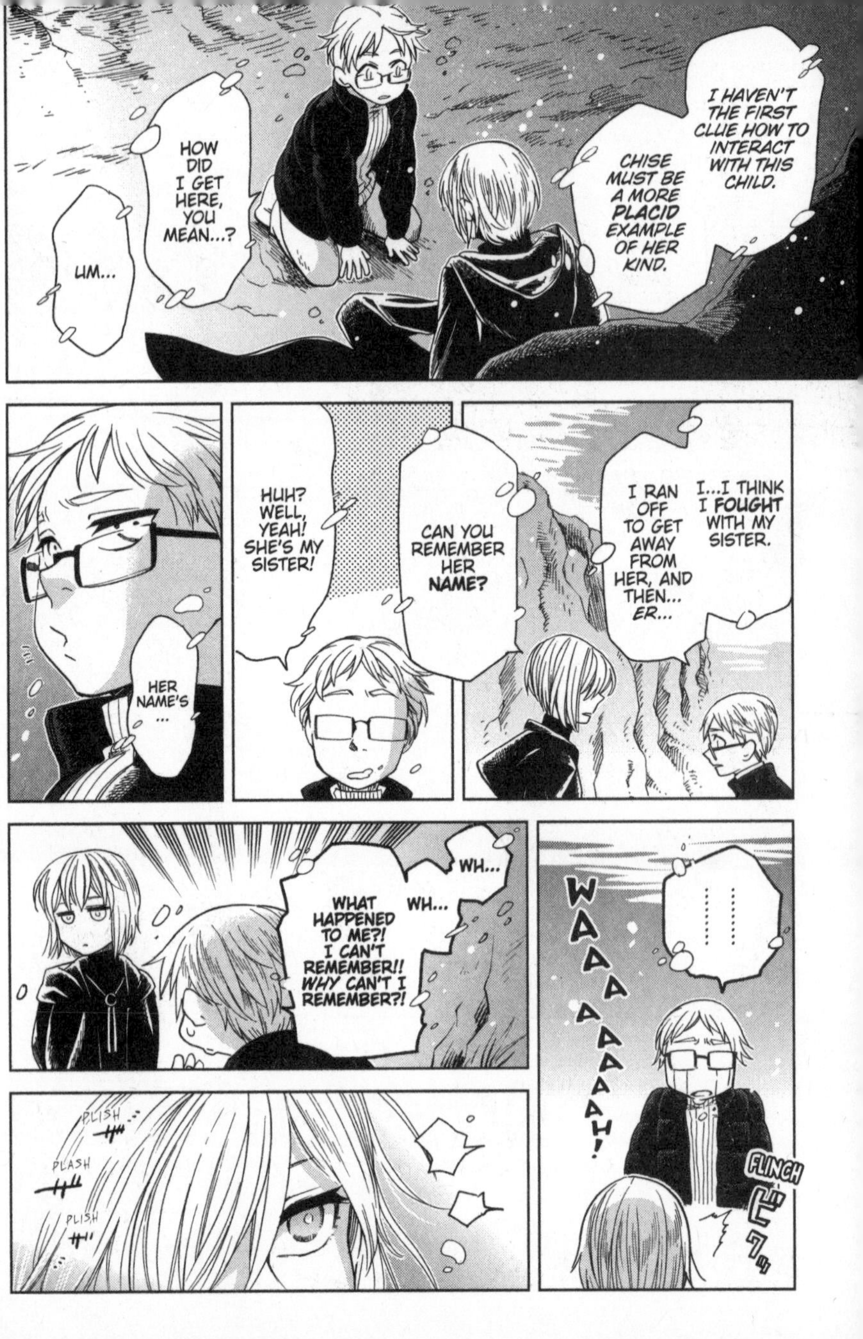
I HAVEN'T THE FIRST CLUE HOW TO INTERACT WITH THIS CHILD.
CHISE MUST BE A MORE **PLACID** EXAMPLE OF HER KIND.
HOW DID I GET HERE, YOU MEAN...?
UM...
I...I THINK I **FOUGHT** WITH MY SISTER.
I RAN OFF TO GET AWAY FROM HER, AND THEN... *ER*...
CAN YOU REMEMBER HER **NAME?**
HUH? WELL, YEAH! SHE'S MY SISTER!
HER NAME'S ...
......
WAAAAAAAAAAH!
FLINCH
WH...
WH...
WHAT HAPPENED TO ME?! I CAN'T REMEMBER!! *WHY* CAN'T I REMEMBER?!
PLISH
PLASH
PLISH

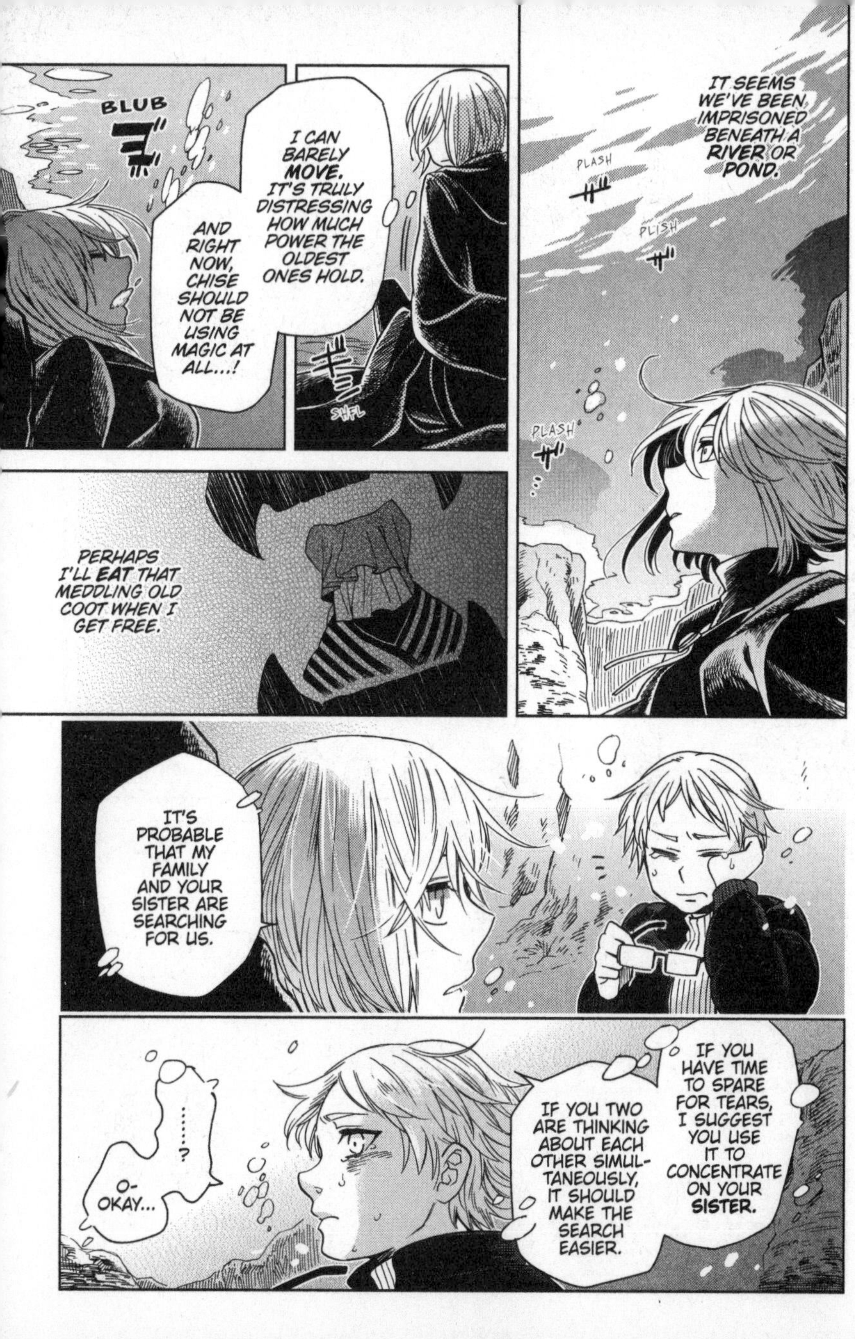
IT SEEMS WE'VE BEEN IMPRISONED BENEATH A RIVER OR POND.
PLASH
PLISH
PLASH
I CAN BARELY MOVE. IT'S TRULY DISTRESSING HOW MUCH POWER THE OLDEST ONES HOLD.
SHFL
BLUB
AND RIGHT NOW, CHISE SHOULD NOT BE USING MAGIC AT ALL...!
PERHAPS I'LL EAT THAT MEDDLING OLD COOT WHEN I GET FREE.
IT'S PROBABLE THAT MY FAMILY AND YOUR SISTER ARE SEARCHING FOR US.
IF YOU HAVE TIME TO SPARE FOR TEARS, I SUGGEST YOU USE IT TO CONCENTRATE ON YOUR SISTER.
IF YOU TWO ARE THINKING ABOUT EACH OTHER SIMUL-TANEOUSLY, IT SHOULD MAKE THE SEARCH EASIER.
......?
O-OKAY...

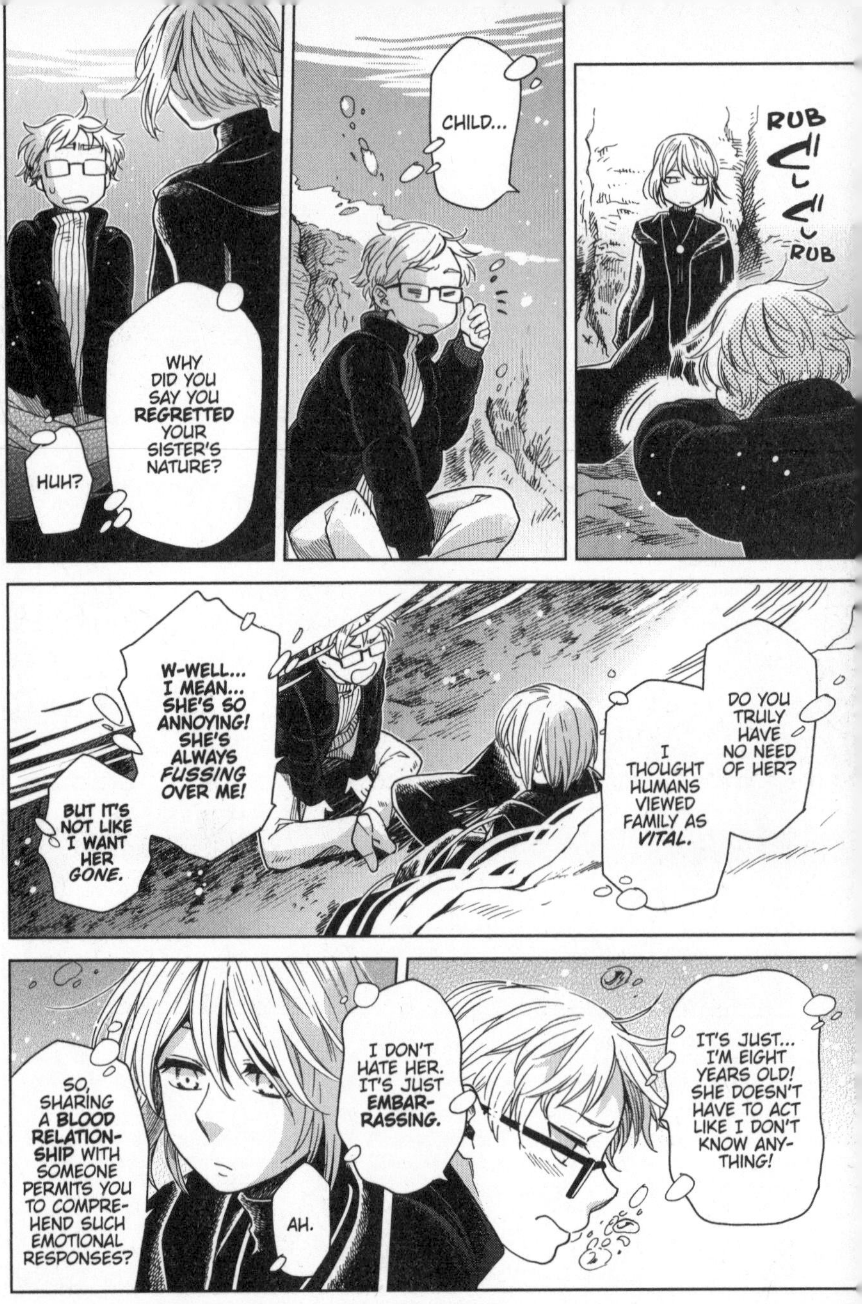
RUB RUB
CHILD...
WHY DID YOU SAY YOU REGRETTED YOUR SISTER'S NATURE?
HUH?
DO YOU TRULY HAVE NO NEED OF HER?
I THOUGHT HUMANS VIEWED FAMILY AS VITAL.
W-WELL... I MEAN... SHE'S SO ANNOYING! SHE'S ALWAYS FUSSING OVER ME!
BUT IT'S NOT LIKE I WANT HER GONE.
IT'S JUST... I'M EIGHT YEARS OLD! SHE DOESN'T HAVE TO ACT LIKE I DON'T KNOW ANYTHING!
I DON'T HATE HER. IT'S JUST EMBARRASSING.
SO, SHARING A BLOOD RELATIONSHIP WITH SOMEONE PERMITS YOU TO COMPREHEND SUCH EMOTIONAL RESPONSES?
AH.

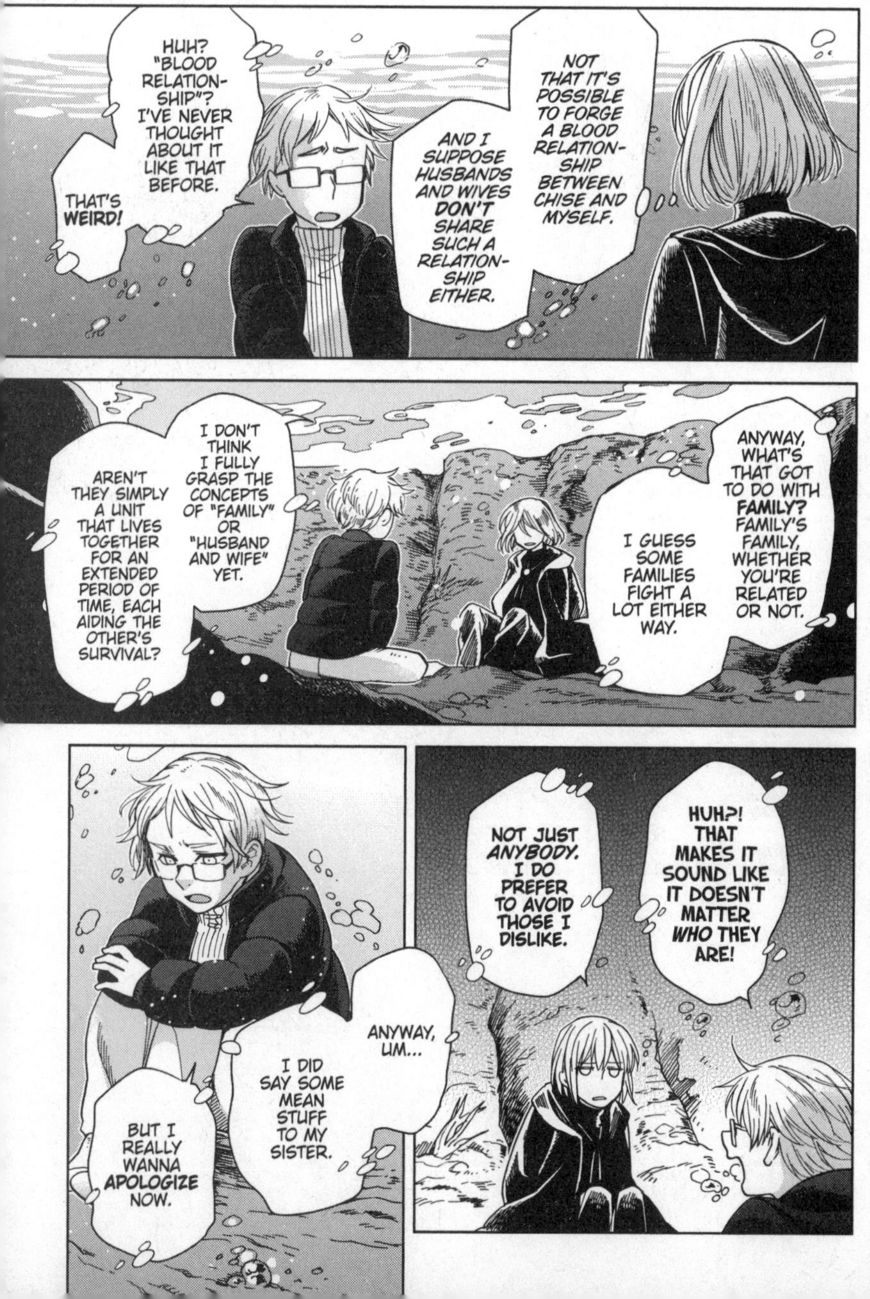
NOT THAT IT'S POSSIBLE TO FORGE A BLOOD RELATIONSHIP BETWEEN CHISE AND MYSELF.
AND I SUPPOSE HUSBANDS AND WIVES **DON'T** SHARE SUCH A RELATIONSHIP EITHER.
HUH? "BLOOD RELATIONSHIP"? I'VE NEVER THOUGHT ABOUT IT LIKE THAT BEFORE.
THAT'S **WEIRD!**
ANYWAY, WHAT'S THAT GOT TO DO WITH **FAMILY?** FAMILY'S FAMILY, WHETHER YOU'RE RELATED OR NOT.
I GUESS SOME FAMILIES FIGHT A LOT EITHER WAY.
I DON'T THINK I FULLY GRASP THE CONCEPTS OF "FAMILY" OR "HUSBAND AND WIFE" YET.
AREN'T THEY SIMPLY A UNIT THAT LIVES TOGETHER FOR AN EXTENDED PERIOD OF TIME, EACH AIDING THE OTHER'S SURVIVAL?
HUH?! THAT MAKES IT SOUND LIKE IT DOESN'T MATTER *WHO* THEY ARE!
NOT JUST *ANYBODY.* I DO PREFER TO AVOID THOSE I DISLIKE.
ANYWAY, UM...
I DID SAY SOME MEAN STUFF TO MY SISTER.
BUT I REALLY WANNA **APOLOGIZE** NOW.

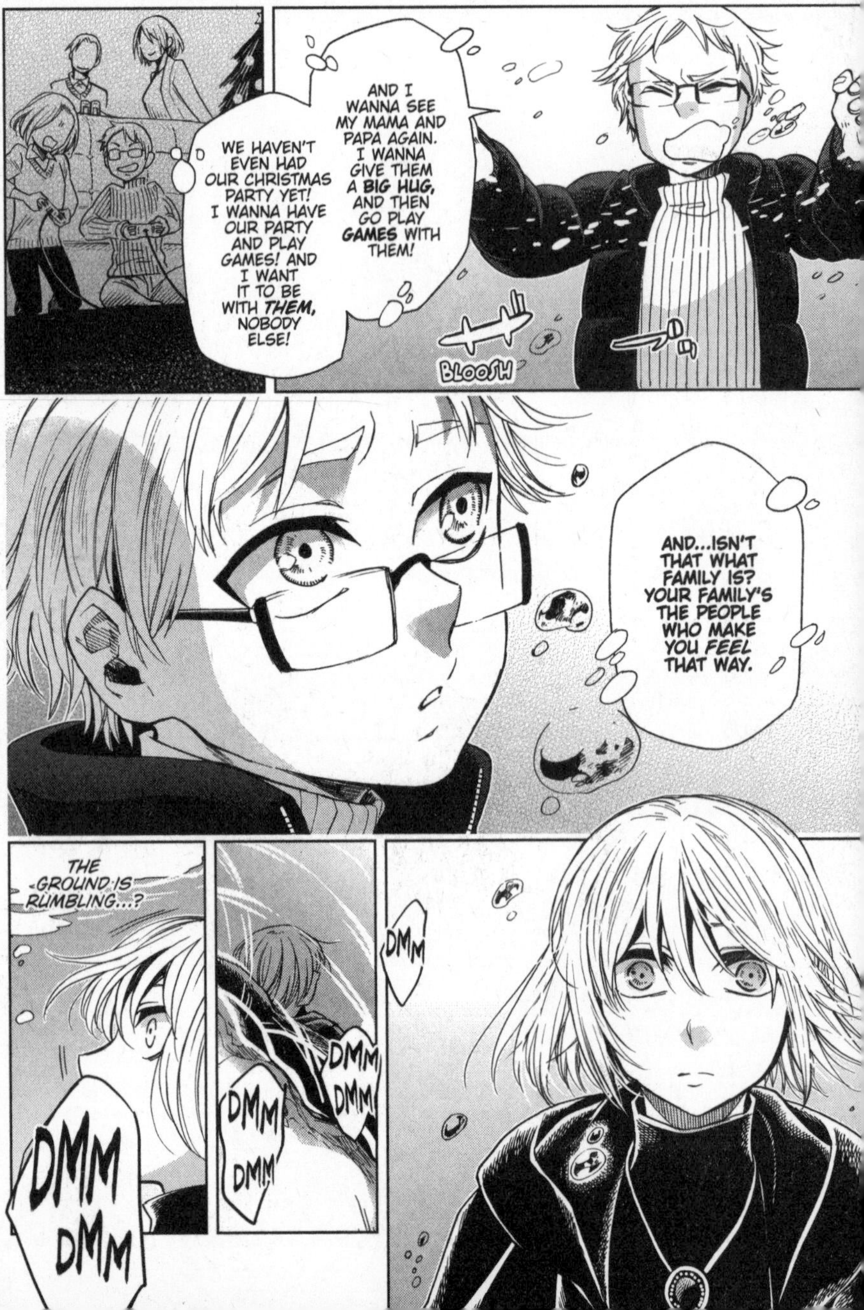
WE HAVEN'T EVEN HAD OUR CHRISTMAS PARTY YET! I WANNA HAVE OUR PARTY AND PLAY GAMES! AND I WANT IT TO BE WITH *THEM*, NOBODY ELSE!
AND I WANNA SEE MY MAMA AND PAPA AGAIN. I WANNA GIVE THEM A **BIG HUG**, AND THEN GO PLAY **GAMES** WITH THEM!
BLOOSH
AND...ISN'T THAT WHAT FAMILY IS? YOUR FAMILY'S THE PEOPLE WHO MAKE YOU *FEEL* THAT WAY.
DMM
DMM DMM
DMM
DMM
THE GROUND IS RUMBLING...?
DMM DMM

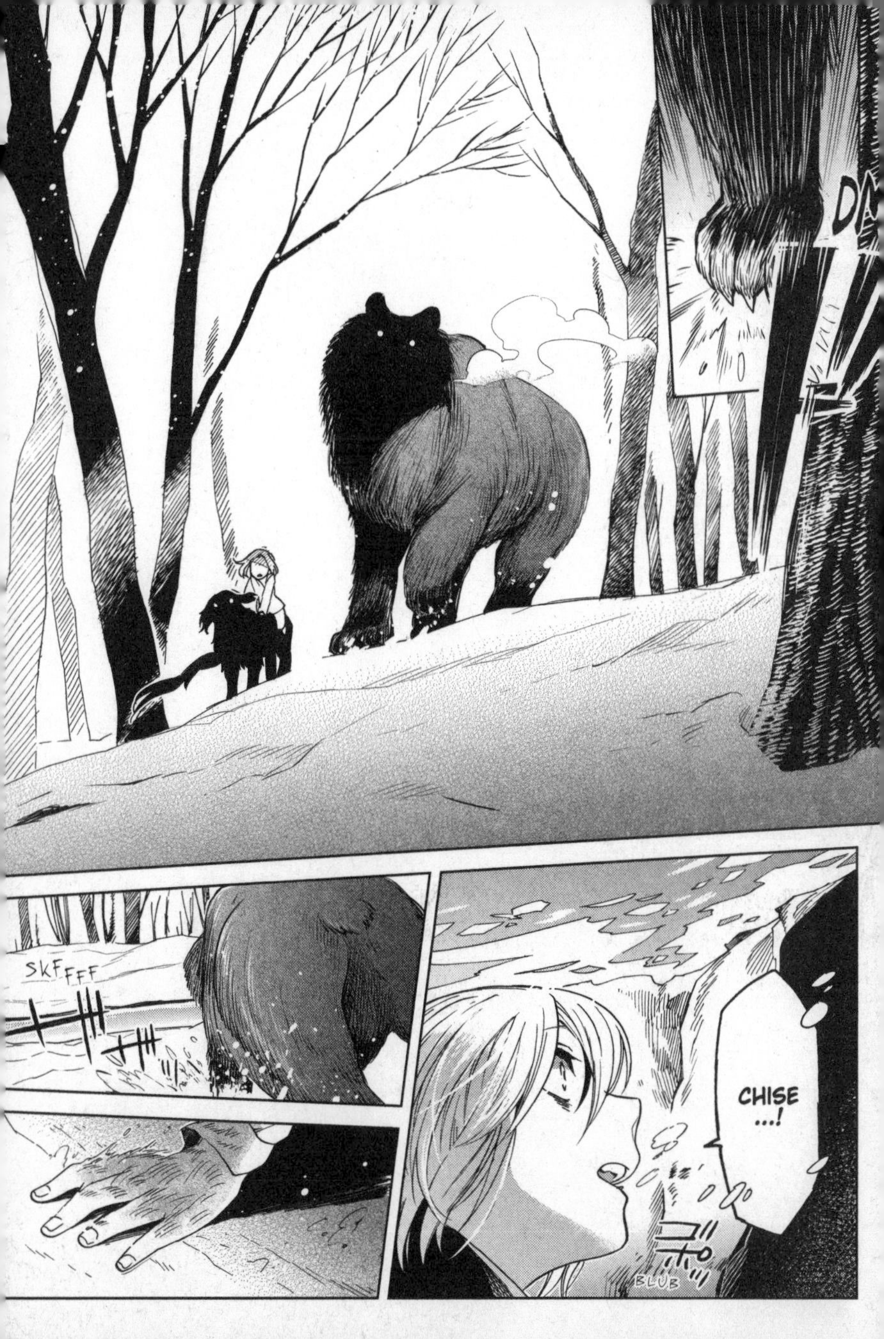
DA
CHISE ...!
BLUB
SKFFFF

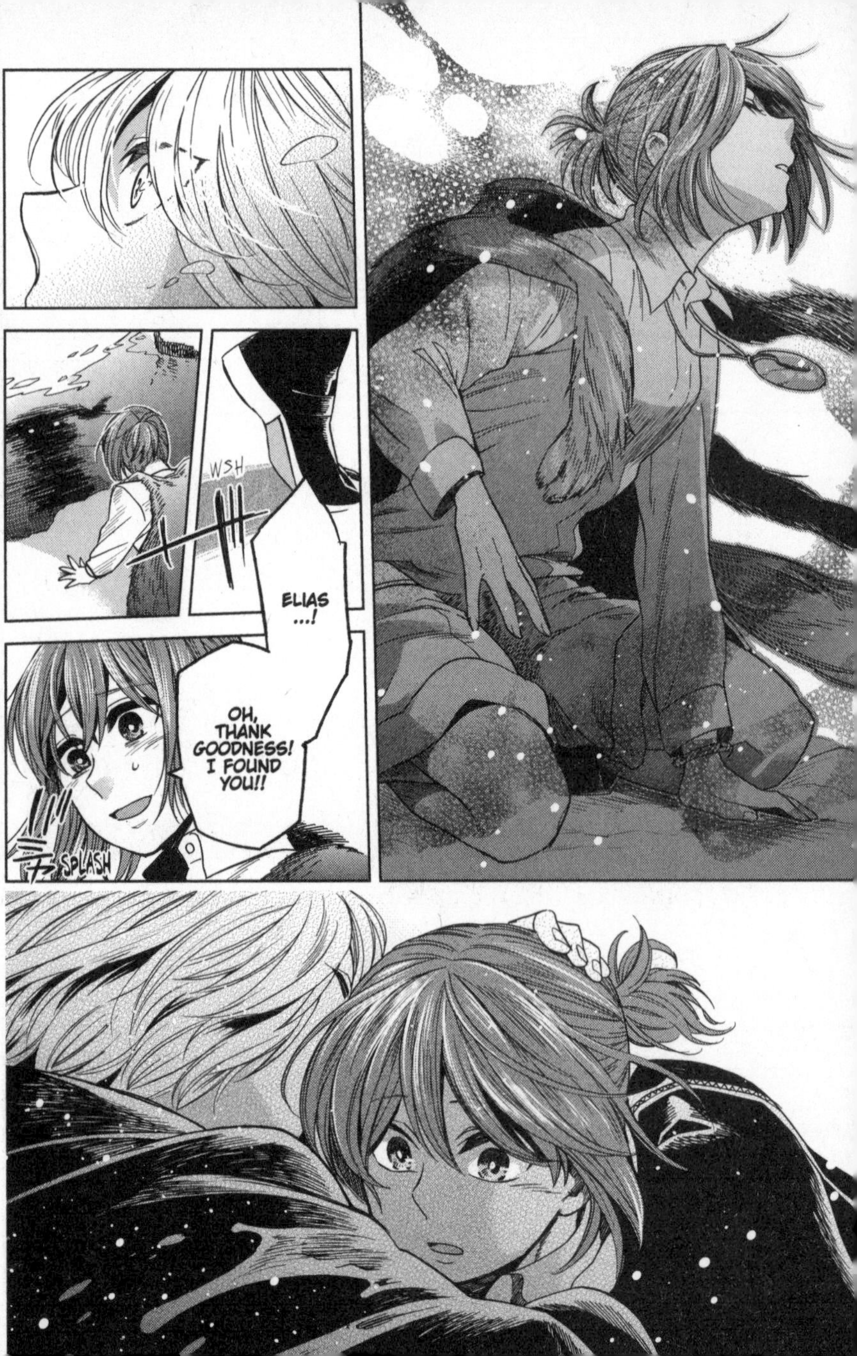
WSH
ELIAS ...!
OH, THANK GOODNESS! I FOUND YOU!!
SPLASH

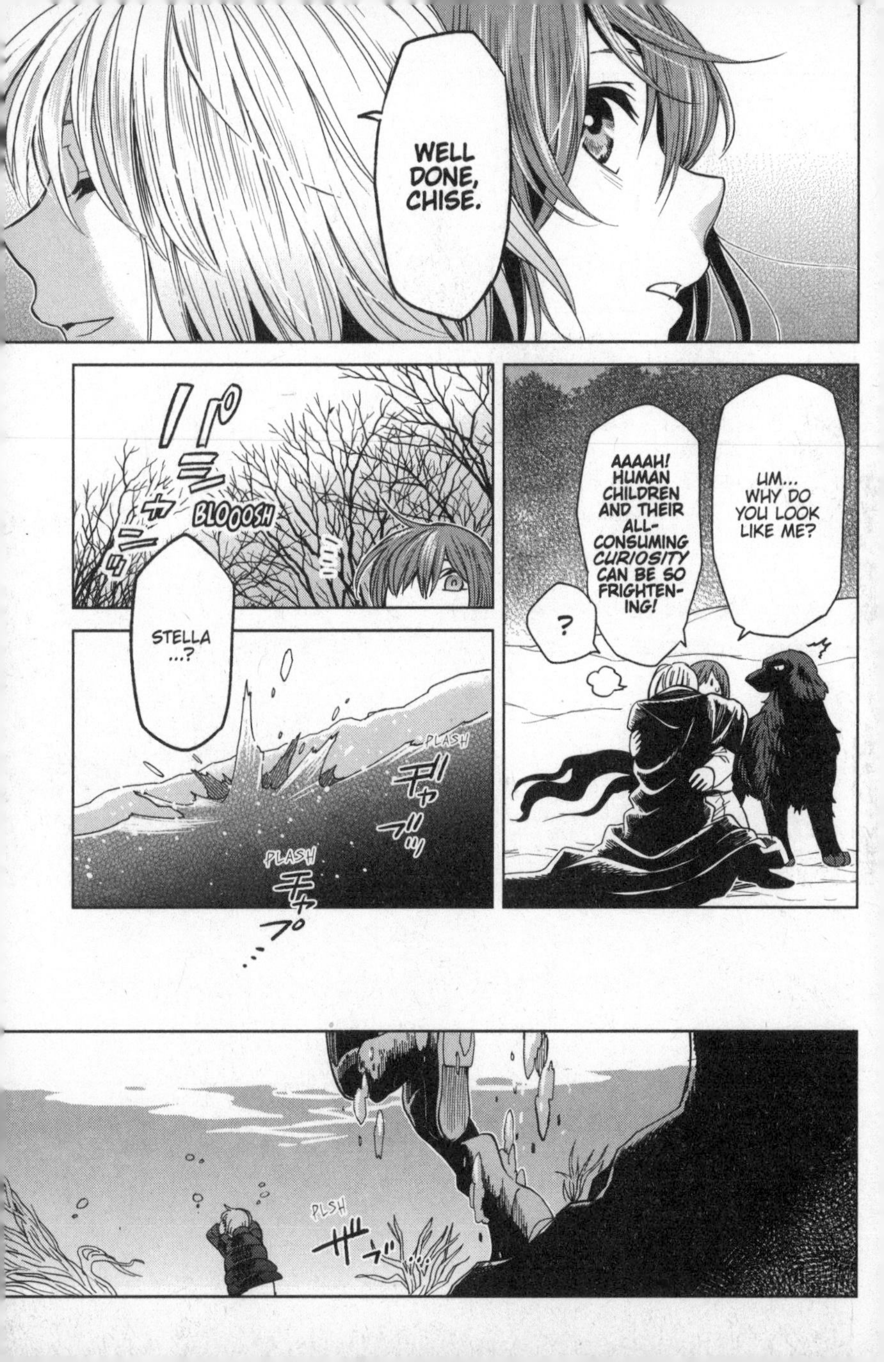
WELL DONE, CHISE.
UM... WHY DO YOU LOOK LIKE ME?
AAAAH! HUMAN CHILDREN AND THEIR ALL-CONSUMING CURIOSITY CAN BE SO FRIGHTENING!
?
BLOOOSH
STELLA ...?
PLASH
PLASH
PLSH

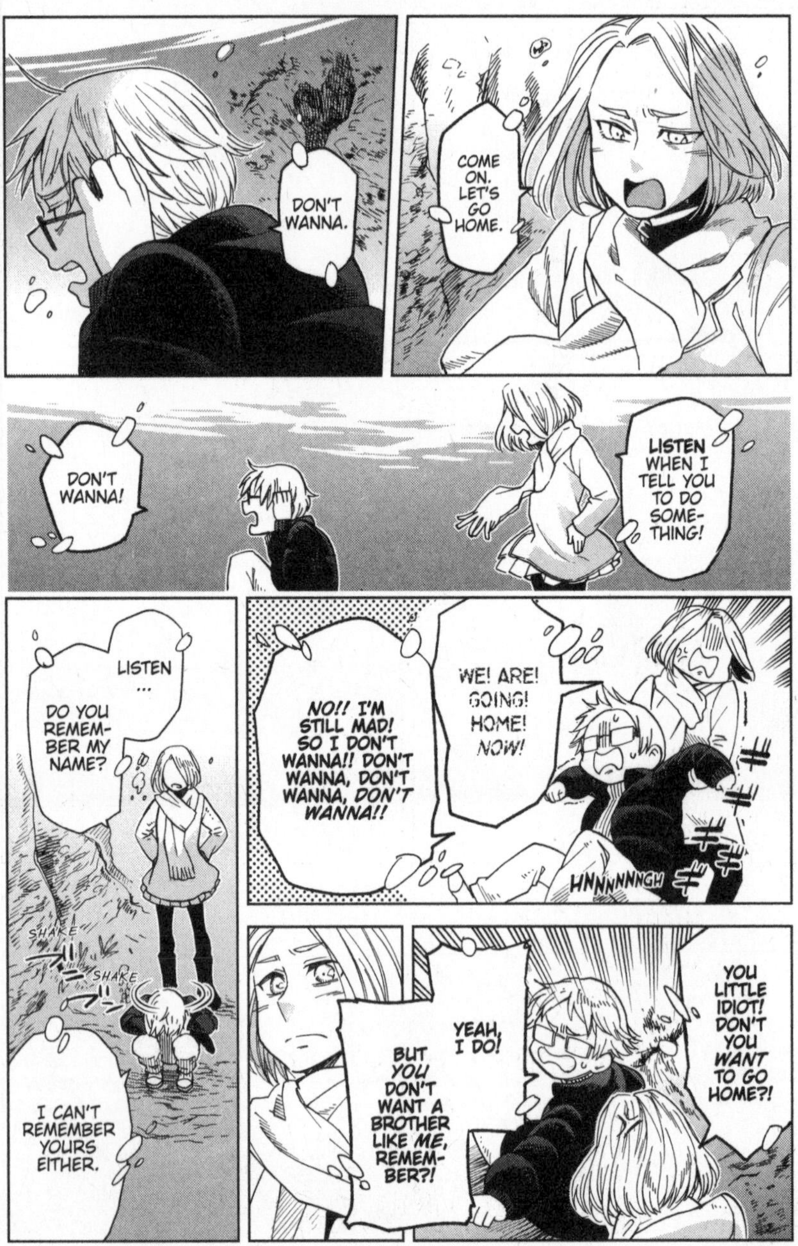

COME ON. LET'S GO HOME.
DON'T WANNA.
LISTEN WHEN I TELL YOU TO DO SOME-THING!
DON'T WANNA!
WE! ARE! GOING! HOME! NOW!
NO!! I'M STILL MAD! SO I DON'T WANNA!! DON'T WANNA, DON'T WANNA, DON'T WANNA!!
HNNNNNNGH
YOU LITTLE IDIOT! DON'T YOU WANT TO GO HOME?!
YEAH, I DO!
BUT YOU DON'T WANT A BROTHER LIKE ME, REMEMBER?!
LISTEN ...
DO YOU REMEMBER MY NAME?
SHAKE
SHAKE
I CAN'T REMEMBER YOURS EITHER.

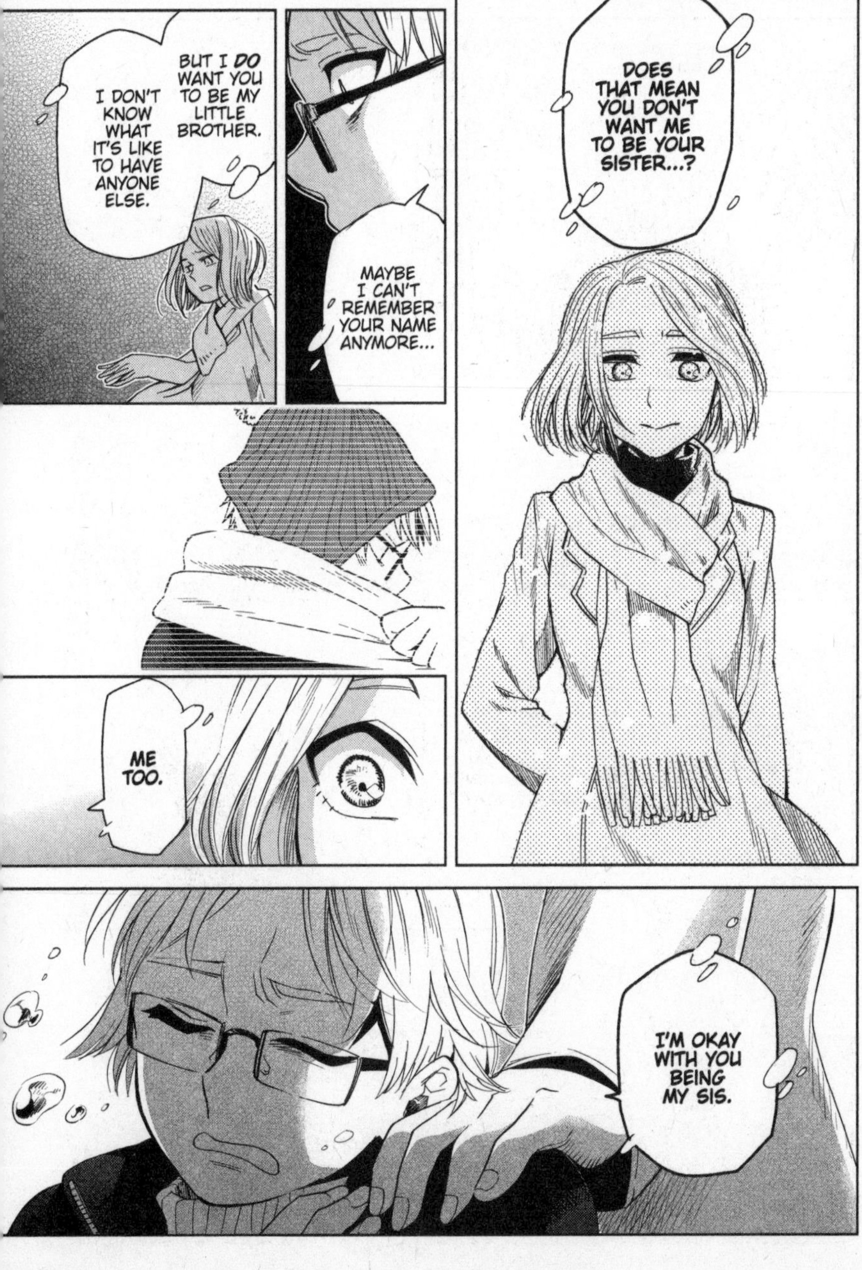
DOES THAT MEAN YOU DON'T WANT ME TO BE YOUR SISTER...?
MAYBE I CAN'T REMEMBER YOUR NAME ANYMORE...
BUT I *DO* WANT YOU TO BE MY LITTLE BROTHER.
I DON'T KNOW WHAT IT'S LIKE TO HAVE ANYONE ELSE.
ME TOO.
I'M OKAY WITH YOU BEING MY SIS.

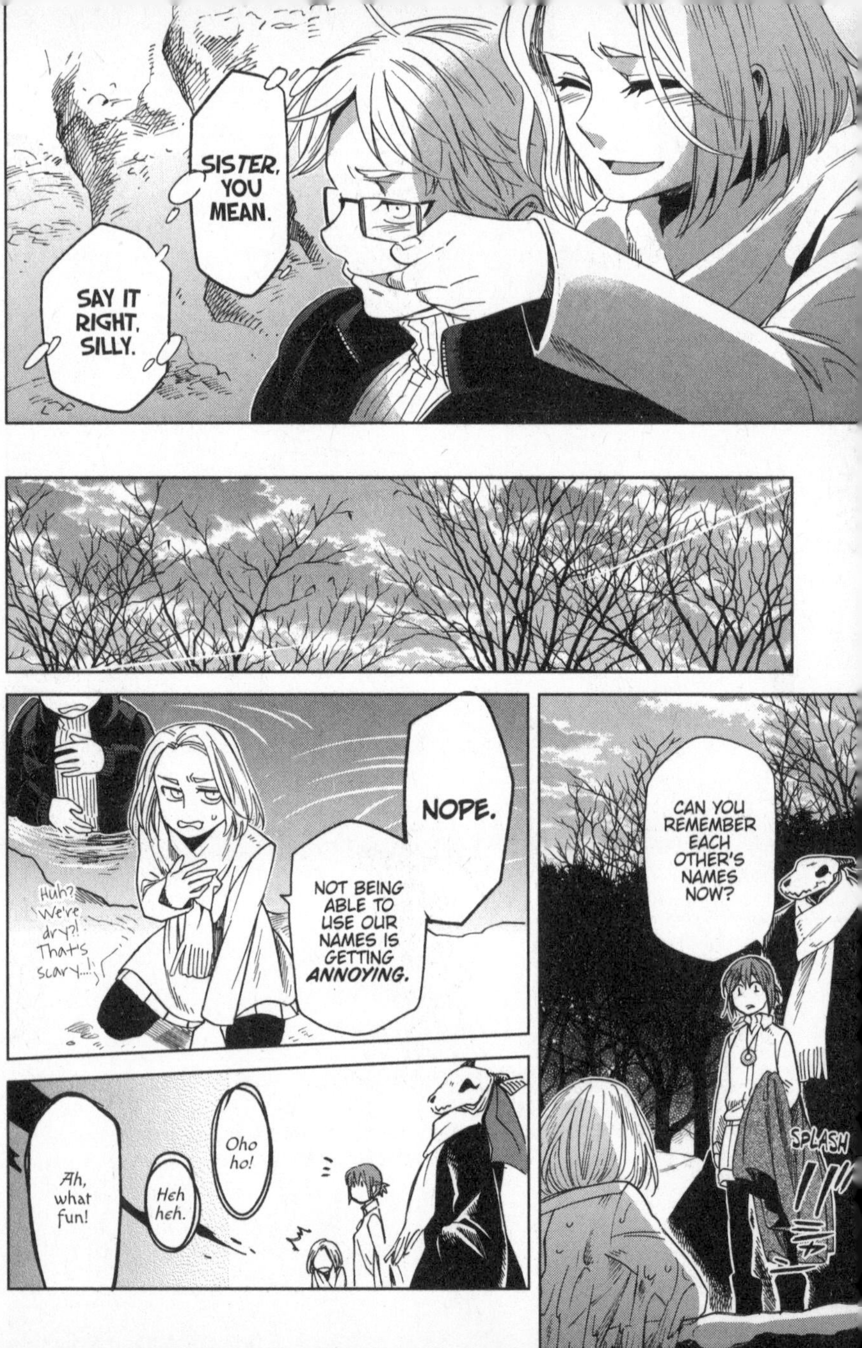
SISTER, YOU MEAN.
SAY IT RIGHT, SILLY.
CAN YOU REMEMBER EACH OTHER'S NAMES NOW?
SPLASH
NOPE.
NOT BEING ABLE TO USE OUR NAMES IS GETTING ANNOYING.
Huh? We're dry?! That's scary...!
Oho ho!
Heh heh.
Ah, what fun!

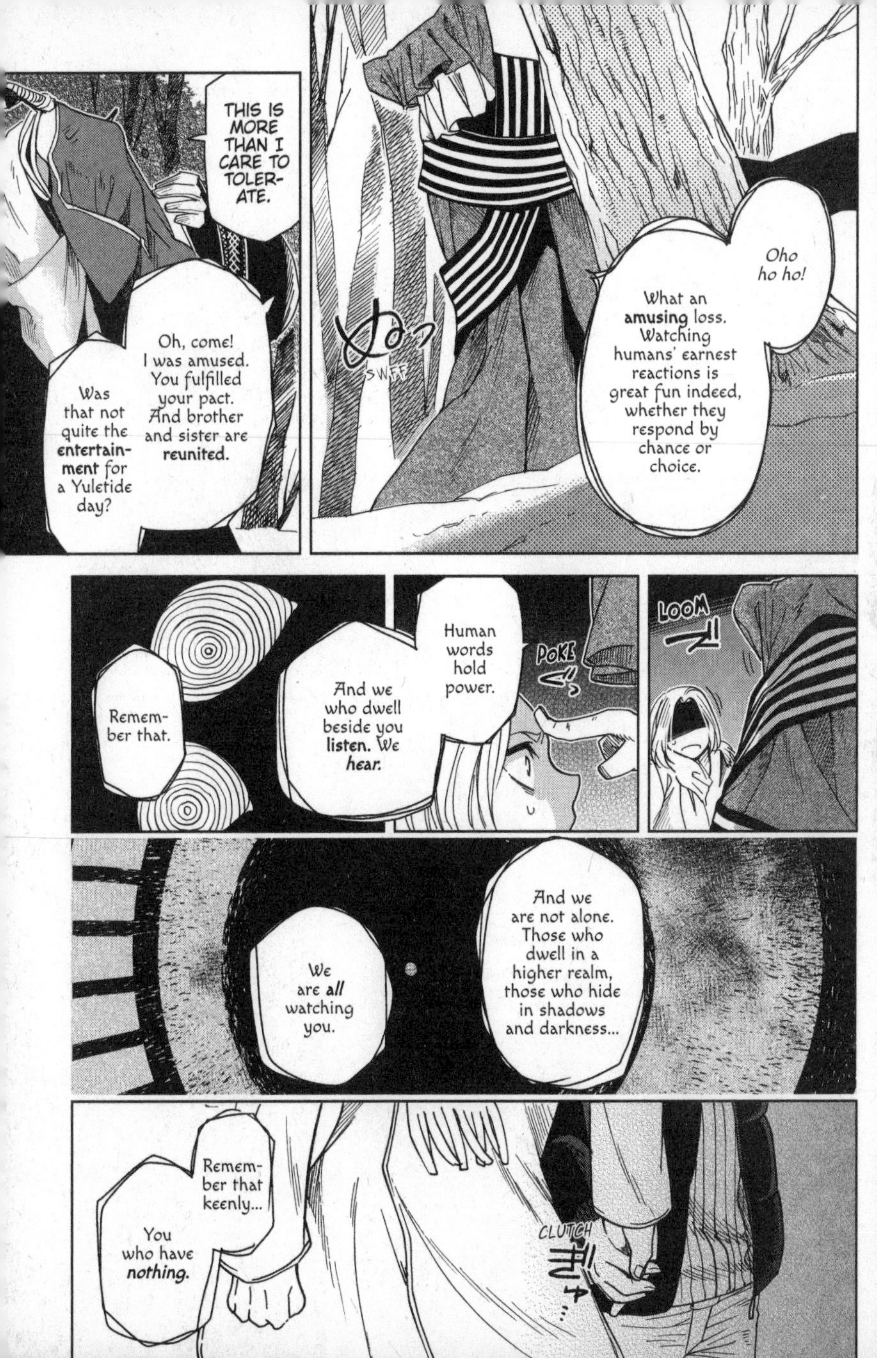
Oho ho ho!
What an amusing loss. Watching humans' earnest reactions is great fun indeed, whether they respond by chance or choice.
SWFF
THIS IS MORE THAN I CARE TO TOLERATE.
Oh, come! I was amused. You fulfilled your pact. And brother and sister are reunited.
Was that not quite the entertainment for a Yuletide day?
LOOM
POKE
Human words hold power.
And we who dwell beside you listen. We hear.
Remember that.
And we are not alone. Those who dwell in a higher realm, those who hide in shadows and darkness...
We are all watching you.
Remember that keenly...
You who have nothing.
CLUTCH

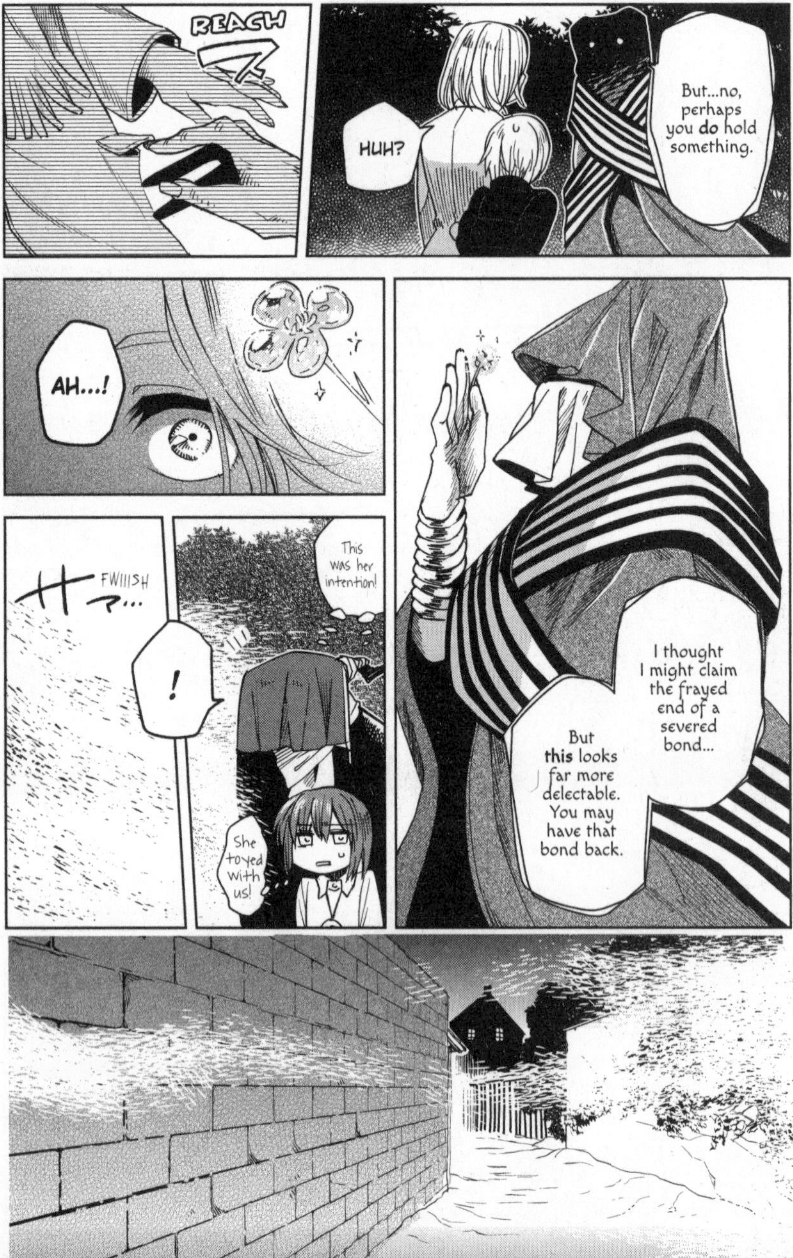
But...no, perhaps you do hold something.
HUH?
REACH
I thought I might claim the frayed end of a severed bond...
But this looks far more delectable. You may have that bond back.
AH...!
This was her intention!
She toyed with us!
FWIIISH
!

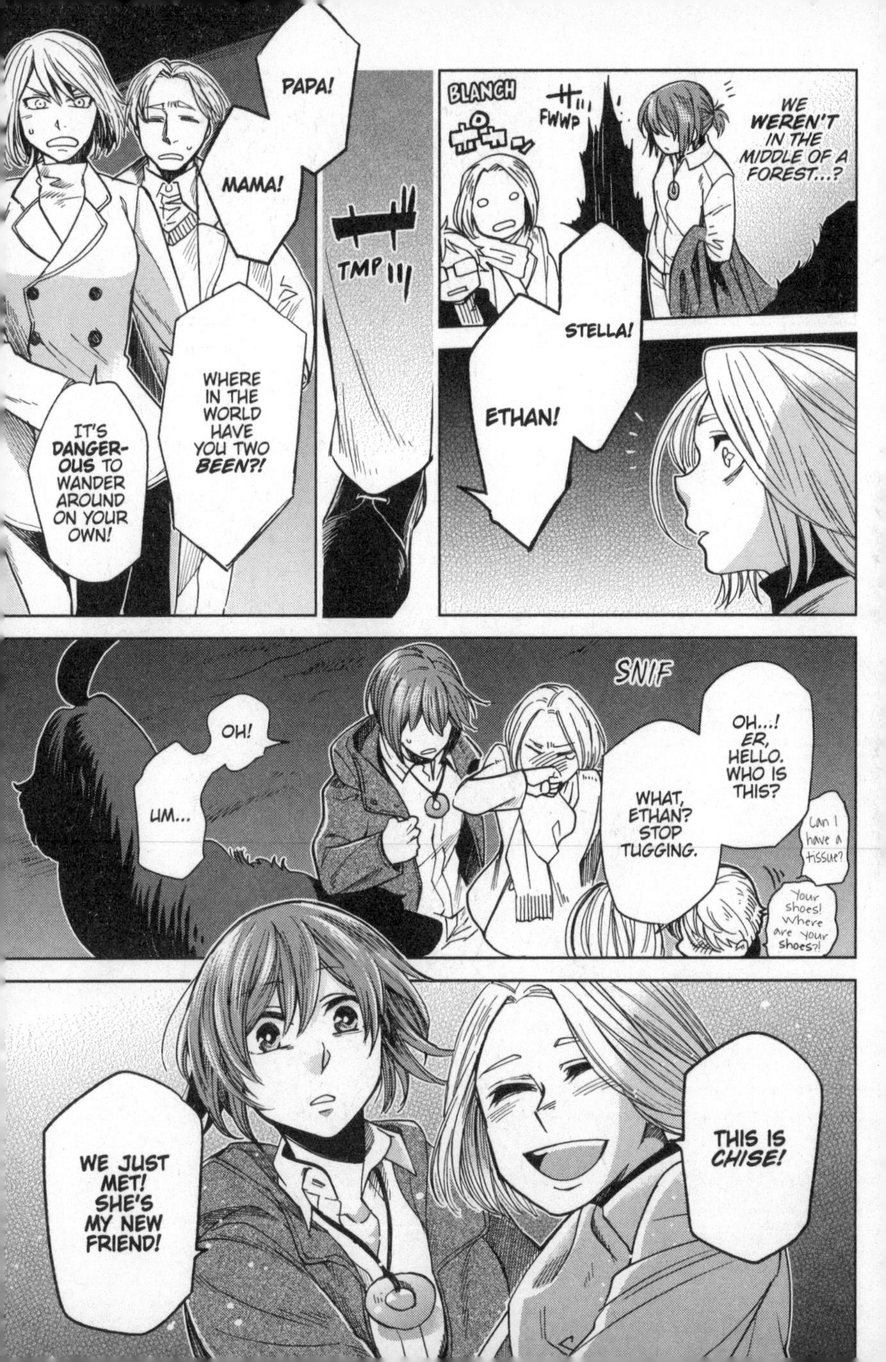
WE WEREN'T IN THE MIDDLE OF A FOREST...?
FWWP
BLANCH
STELLA!
ETHAN!
TMP
PAPA!
MAMA!
WHERE IN THE WORLD HAVE YOU TWO BEEN?!
IT'S DANGEROUS TO WANDER AROUND ON YOUR OWN!
SNIF
OH...! ER, HELLO. WHO IS THIS?
Can I have a tissue?
Your shoes! Where are your shoes?!
WHAT, ETHAN? STOP TUGGING.
OH!
UM...
THIS IS CHISE!
WE JUST MET! SHE'S MY NEW FRIEND!

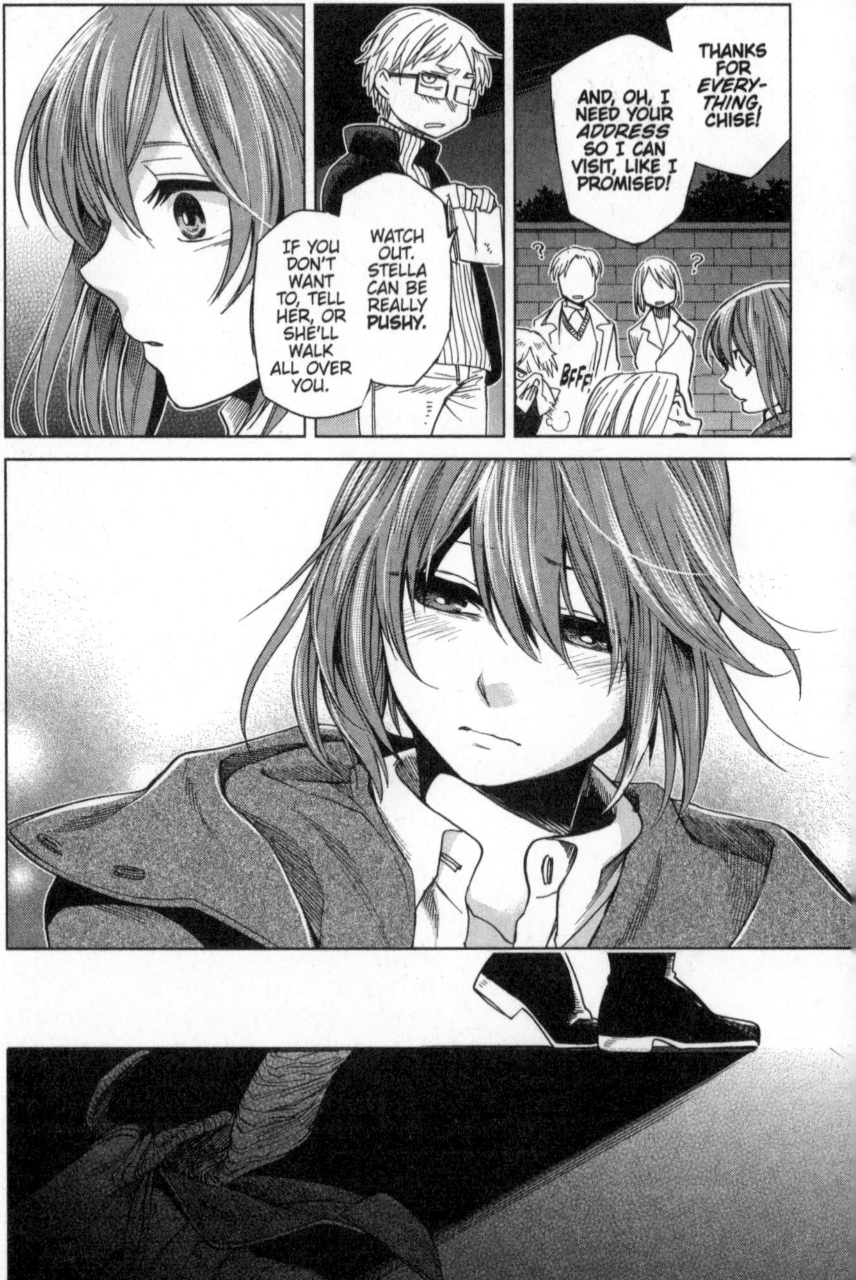

THANKS FOR EVERY-THING, CHISE!
AND, OH, I NEED YOUR ADDRESS SO I CAN VISIT, LIKE I PROMISED!
?
?
BFFF
WATCH OUT. STELLA CAN BE REALLY PUSHY.
IF YOU DON'T WANT TO, TELL HER, OR SHE'LL WALK ALL OVER YOU.

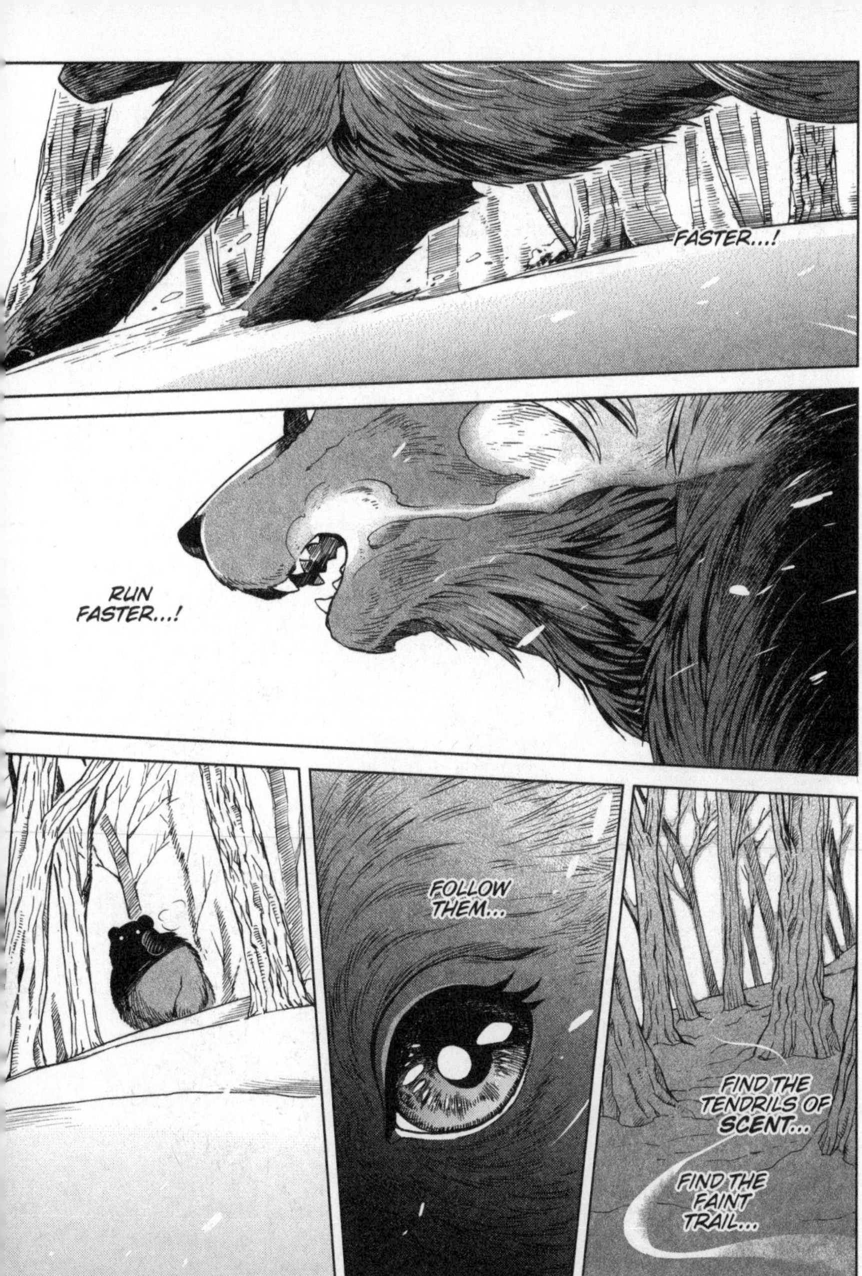
FASTER...!
RUN FASTER...!
FIND THE TENDRILS OF SCENT...
FIND THE FAINT TRAIL...
FOLLOW THEM...

Chapter 30: Zeal without knowledge is a runaway horse.

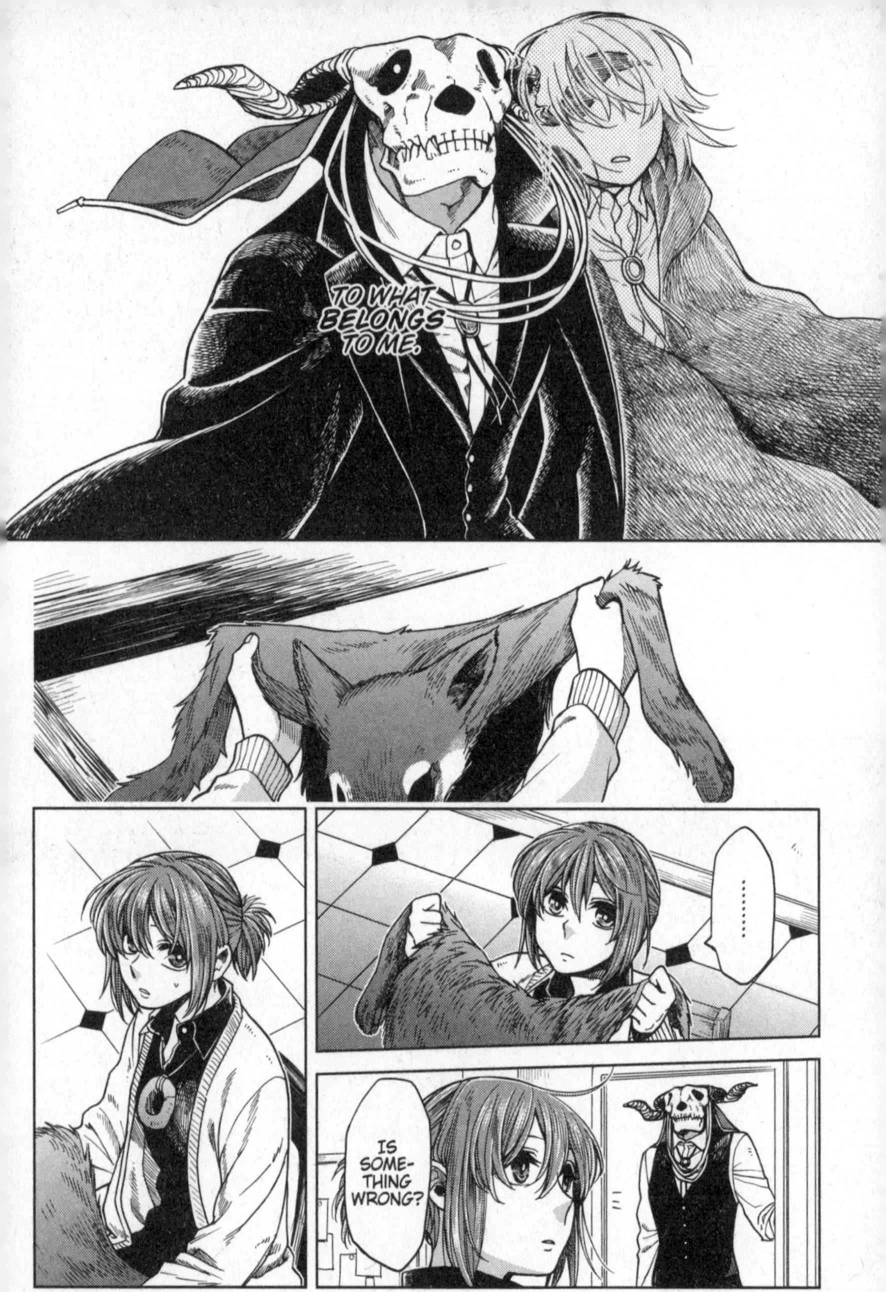
TO WHAT BELONGS TO ME.
......
IS SOME-THING WRONG?

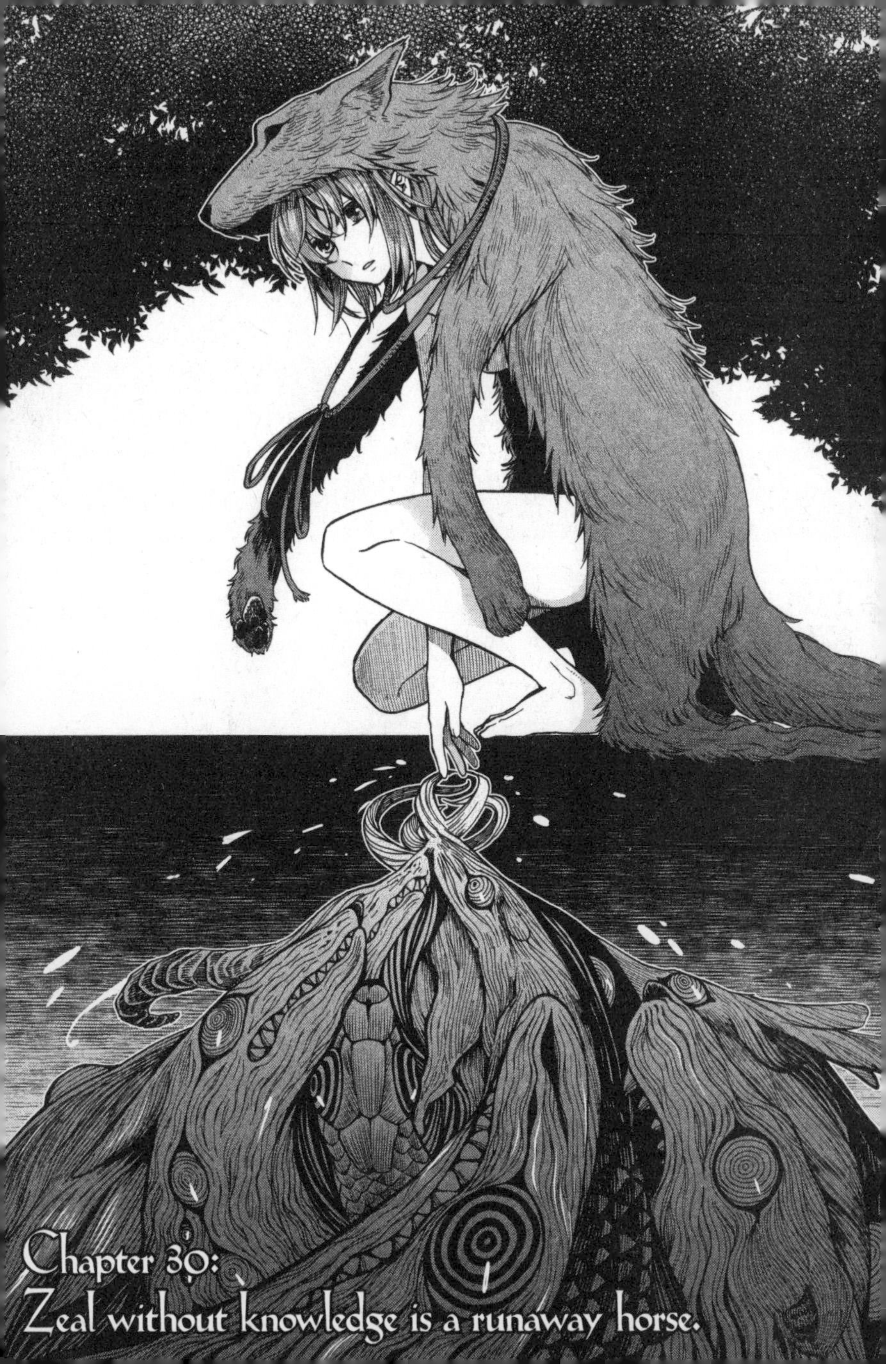
Chapter 30:
Zeal without knowledge is a runaway horse.

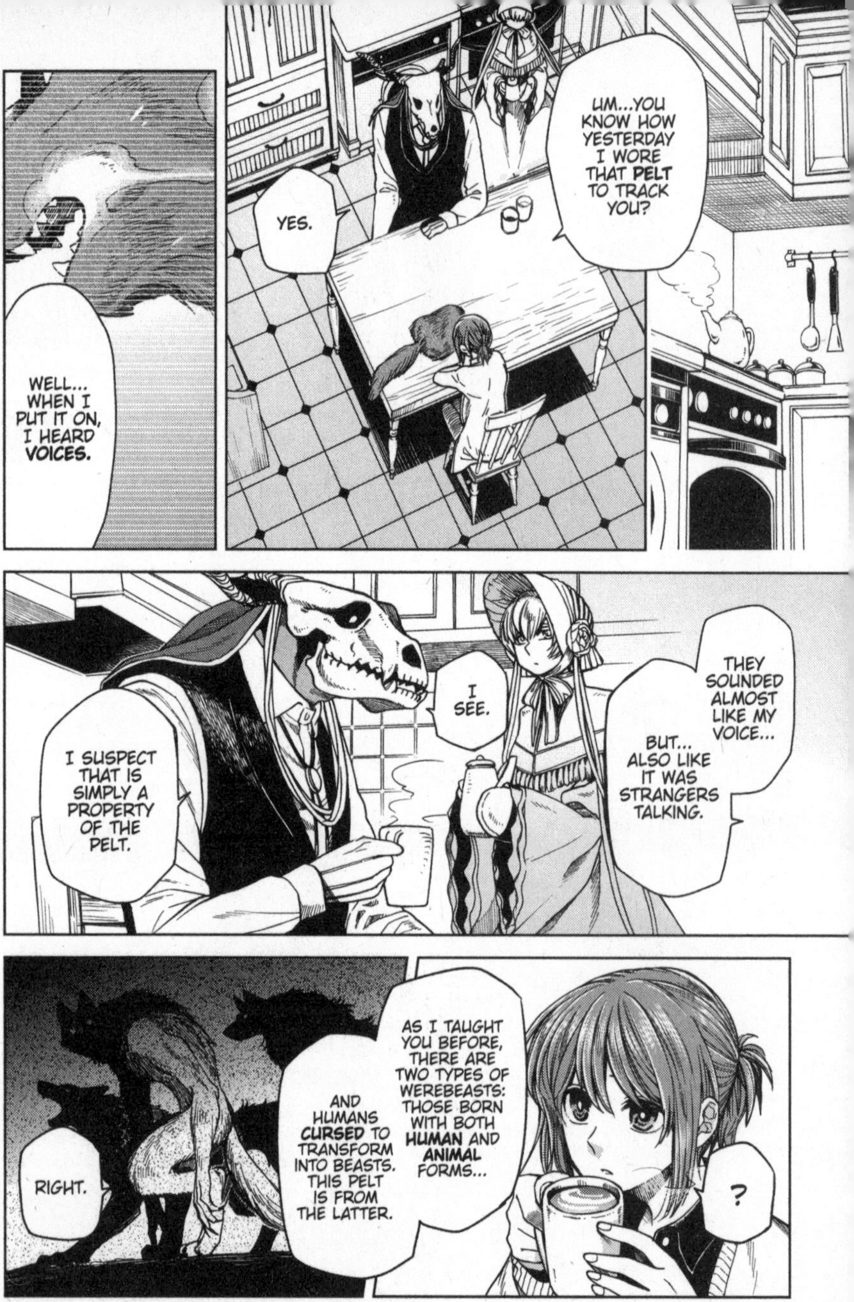
UM...YOU KNOW HOW YESTERDAY I WORE THAT **PELT** TO TRACK YOU?
YES.
WELL... WHEN I PUT IT ON, I HEARD **VOICES.**
THEY SOUNDED ALMOST LIKE MY VOICE...
BUT... ALSO LIKE IT WAS STRANGERS TALKING.
I SEE.
I SUSPECT THAT IS SIMPLY A PROPERTY OF THE PELT.
?
AS I TAUGHT YOU BEFORE, THERE ARE TWO TYPES OF WEREBEASTS: THOSE BORN WITH BOTH **HUMAN** AND **ANIMAL** FORMS...
AND HUMANS **CURSED** TO TRANSFORM INTO BEASTS. THIS PELT IS FROM THE LATTER.
RIGHT.

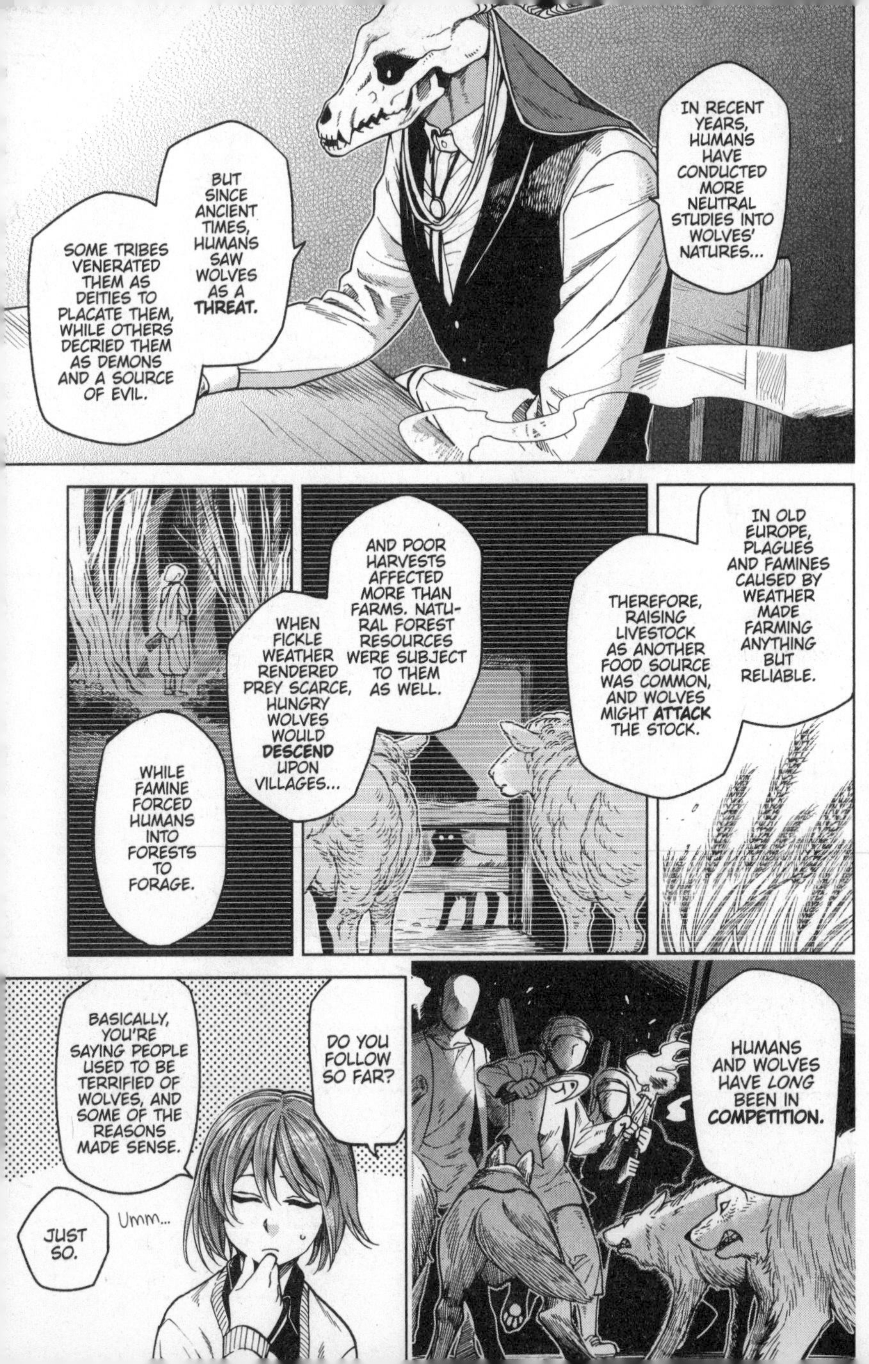
IN RECENT YEARS, HUMANS HAVE CONDUCTED MORE NEUTRAL STUDIES INTO WOLVES' NATURES...
BUT SINCE ANCIENT TIMES, HUMANS SAW WOLVES AS A **THREAT.**
SOME TRIBES VENERATED THEM AS DEITIES TO PLACATE THEM, WHILE OTHERS DECRIED THEM AS DEMONS AND A SOURCE OF EVIL.
IN OLD EUROPE, PLAGUES AND FAMINES CAUSED BY WEATHER MADE FARMING ANYTHING BUT RELIABLE.
THEREFORE, RAISING LIVESTOCK AS ANOTHER FOOD SOURCE WAS COMMON, AND WOLVES MIGHT **ATTACK** THE STOCK.
AND POOR HARVESTS AFFECTED MORE THAN FARMS. NATURAL FOREST RESOURCES WERE SUBJECT TO THEM AS WELL.
WHEN FICKLE WEATHER RENDERED PREY SCARCE, HUNGRY WOLVES WOULD **DESCEND** UPON VILLAGES...
WHILE FAMINE FORCED HUMANS INTO FORESTS TO FORAGE.
HUMANS AND WOLVES HAVE *LONG* BEEN IN **COMPETITION.**
DO YOU FOLLOW SO FAR?
BASICALLY, YOU'RE SAYING PEOPLE USED TO BE TERRIFIED OF WOLVES, AND SOME OF THE REASONS MADE SENSE.
Umm...
JUST SO.

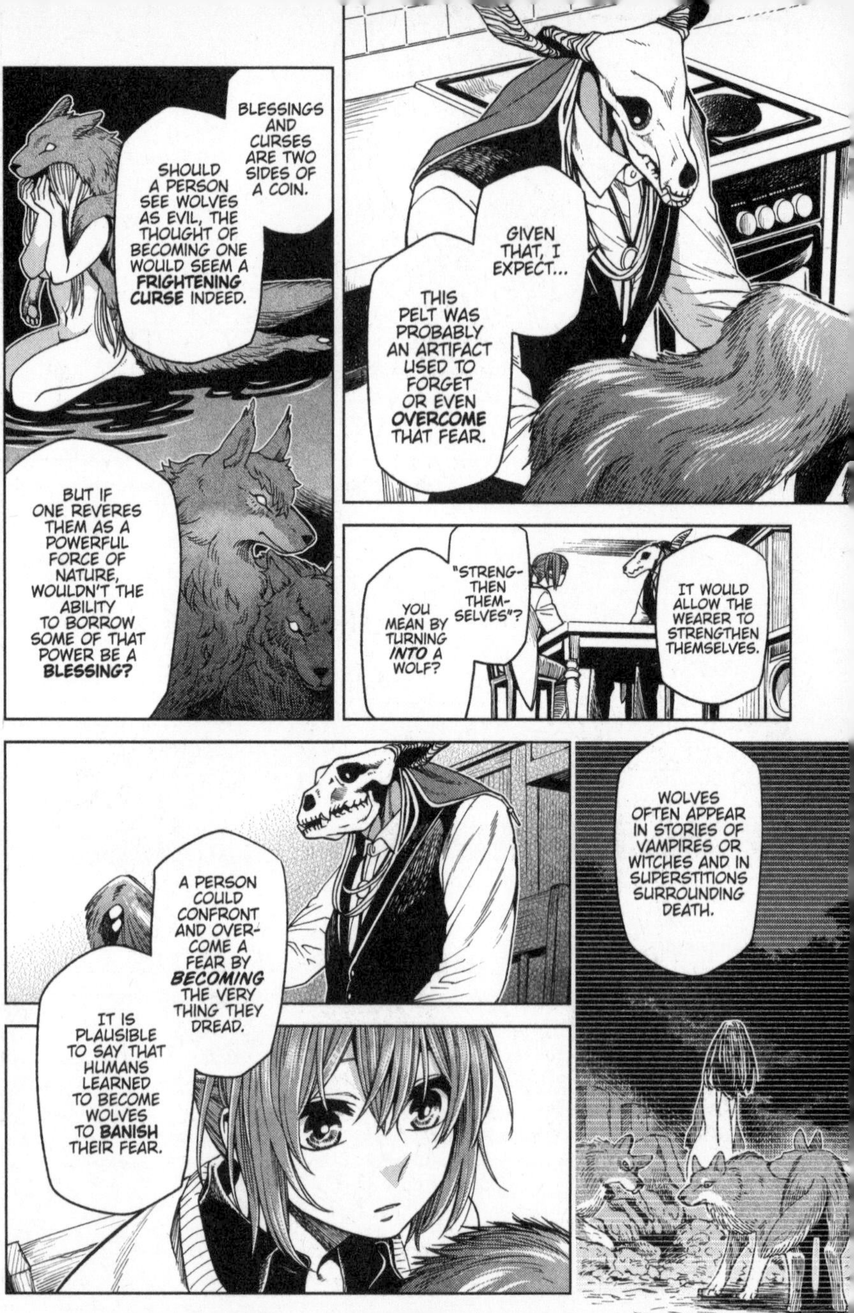
GIVEN THAT, I EXPECT...
THIS PELT WAS PROBABLY AN ARTIFACT USED TO FORGET OR EVEN **OVERCOME** THAT FEAR.
IT WOULD ALLOW THE WEARER TO STRENGTHEN THEMSELVES.
"STRENGTHEN THEMSELVES"?
YOU MEAN BY TURNING *INTO* A WOLF?
BLESSINGS AND CURSES ARE TWO SIDES OF A COIN.
SHOULD A PERSON SEE WOLVES AS EVIL, THE THOUGHT OF BECOMING ONE WOULD SEEM A **FRIGHTENING CURSE** INDEED.
BUT IF ONE REVERES THEM AS A POWERFUL FORCE OF NATURE, WOULDN'T THE ABILITY TO BORROW SOME OF THAT POWER BE A **BLESSING?**
WOLVES OFTEN APPEAR IN STORIES OF VAMPIRES OR WITCHES AND IN SUPERSTITIONS SURROUNDING DEATH.
A PERSON COULD CONFRONT AND OVERCOME A FEAR BY ***BECOMING*** THE VERY THING THEY DREAD.
IT IS PLAUSIBLE TO SAY THAT HUMANS LEARNED TO BECOME WOLVES TO **BANISH** THEIR FEAR.

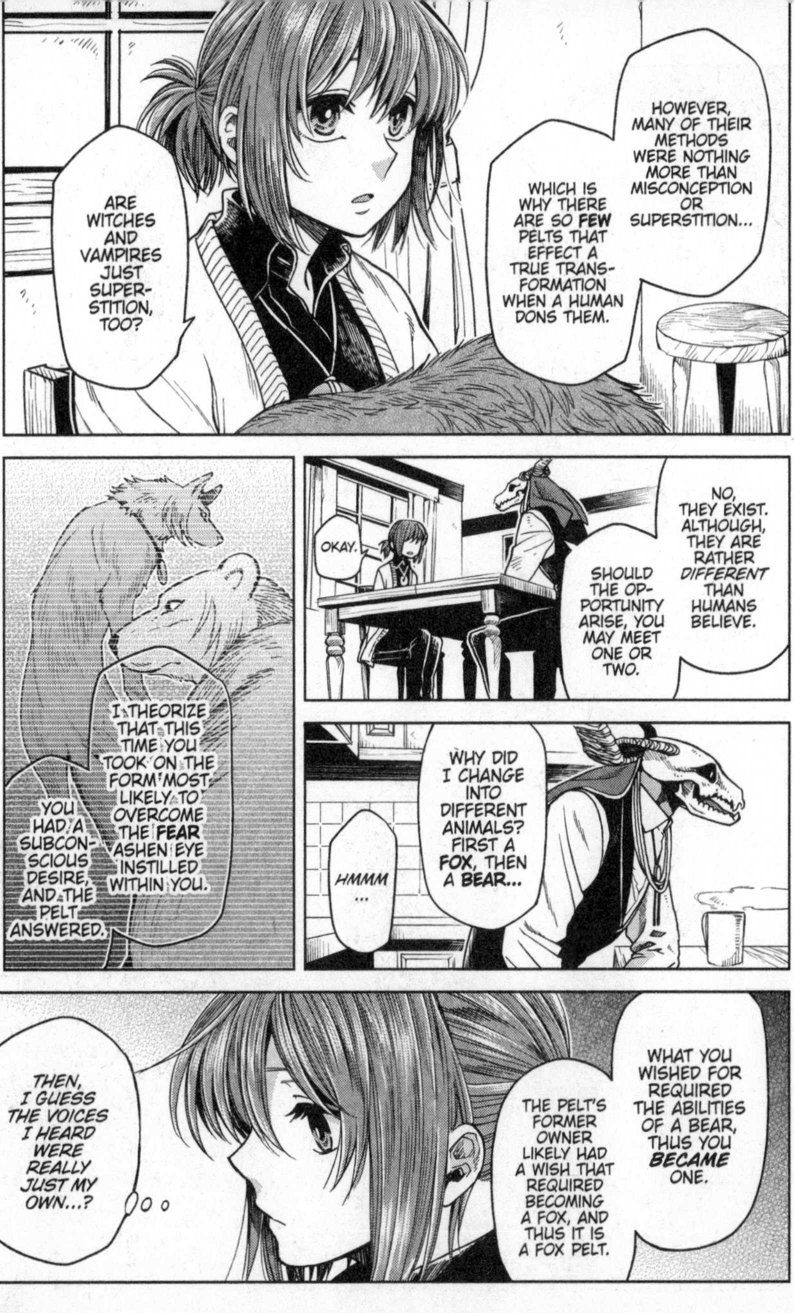

HOWEVER, MANY OF THEIR METHODS WERE NOTHING MORE THAN MISCONCEPTION OR SUPERSTITION...
WHICH IS WHY THERE ARE SO **FEW** PELTS THAT EFFECT A TRUE TRANSFORMATION WHEN A HUMAN DONS THEM.
ARE WITCHES AND VAMPIRES JUST SUPERSTITION, TOO?
NO, THEY EXIST. ALTHOUGH, THEY ARE RATHER *DIFFERENT* THAN HUMANS BELIEVE.
SHOULD THE OPPORTUNITY ARISE, YOU MAY MEET ONE OR TWO.
OKAY.
WHY DID I CHANGE INTO DIFFERENT ANIMALS? FIRST A **FOX**, THEN A **BEAR**...
HMMM...
I THEORIZE THAT THIS TIME YOU TOOK ON THE FORM MOST LIKELY TO OVERCOME THE **FEAR** ASHEN EYE INSTILLED WITHIN YOU.
YOU HAD A SUBCONSCIOUS DESIRE, AND THE PELT ANSWERED.
WHAT YOU WISHED FOR REQUIRED THE ABILITIES OF A BEAR, THUS YOU ***BECAME*** ONE.
THE PELT'S FORMER OWNER LIKELY HAD A WISH THAT REQUIRED BECOMING A FOX, AND THUS IT IS A FOX PELT.
THEN, I GUESS THE VOICES I HEARD WERE REALLY JUST MY OWN...?

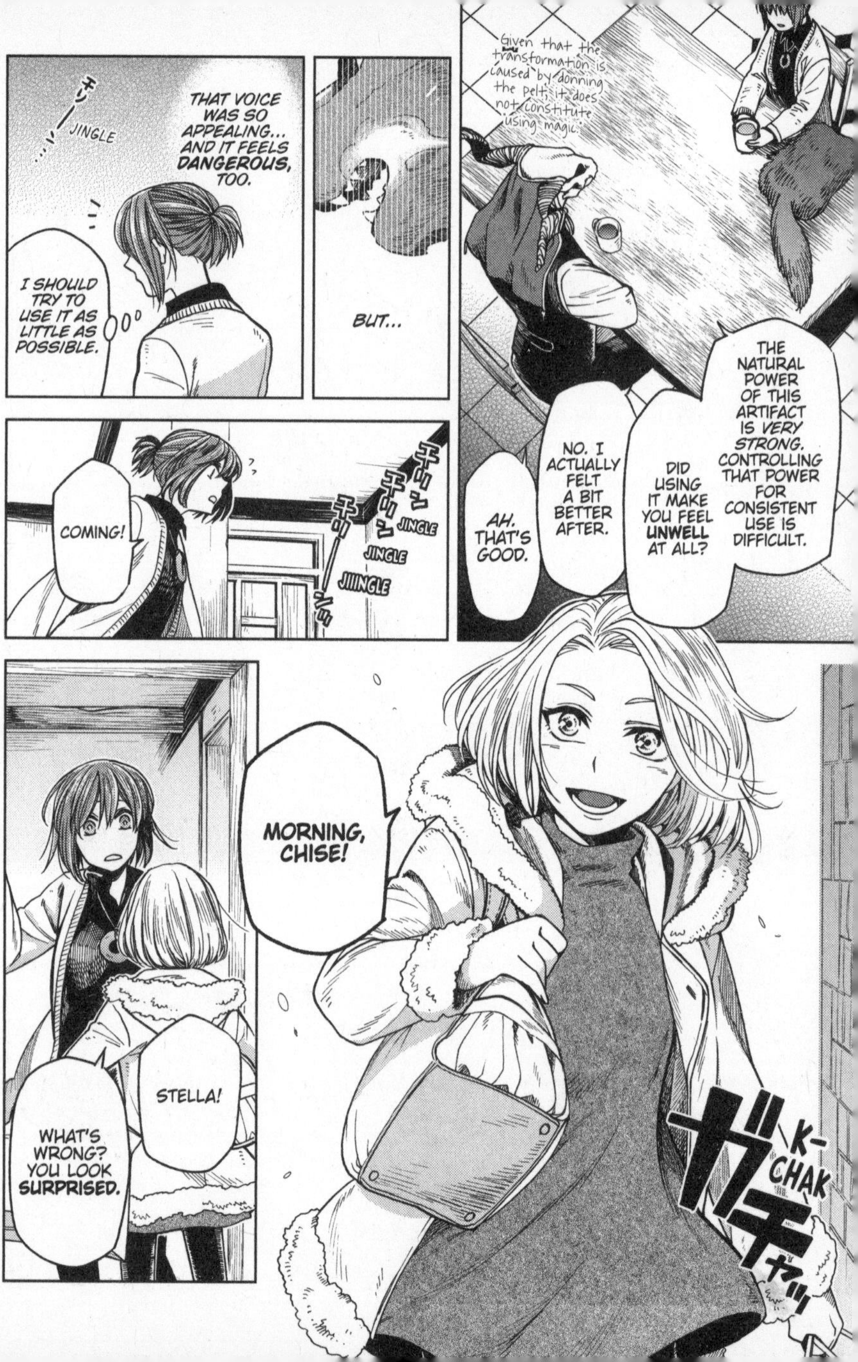

Given that the transformation is caused by donning the pelt, it does not constitute using magic.
THE NATURAL POWER OF THIS ARTIFACT IS *VERY STRONG*. CONTROLLING THAT POWER FOR CONSISTENT USE IS DIFFICULT.
DID USING IT MAKE YOU FEEL **UNWELL** AT ALL?
NO. I ACTUALLY FELT A BIT BETTER AFTER.
AH. THAT'S GOOD.
BUT...
JINGLE
THAT VOICE WAS SO APPEALING... AND IT FEELS **DANGEROUS,** TOO.
I SHOULD TRY TO USE IT AS LITTLE AS POSSIBLE.
JINGLE
JINGLE
JIIINGLE
COMING!
K-CHAK
MORNING, CHISE!
STELLA!
WHAT'S WRONG? YOU LOOK **SURPRISED.**

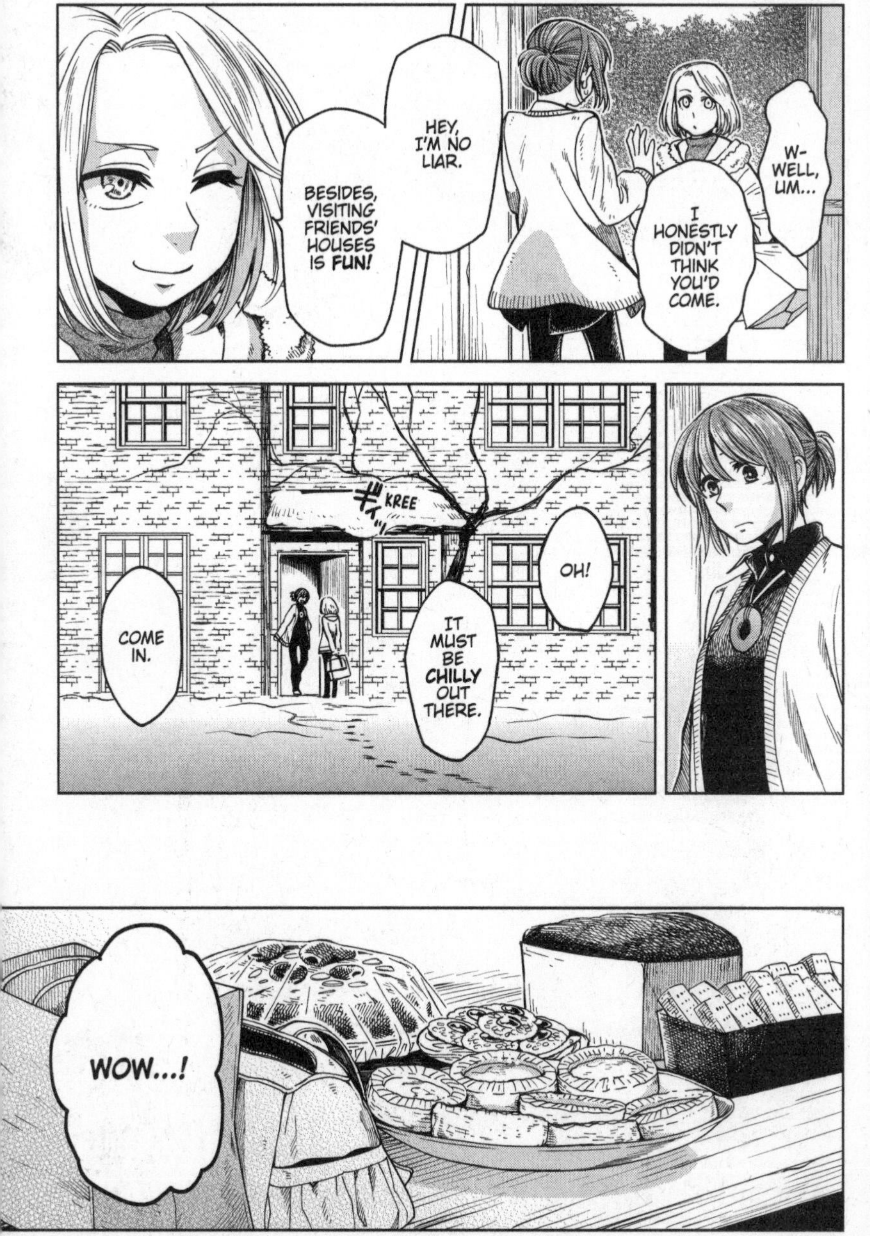
W-WELL, UM...
I HONESTLY DIDN'T THINK YOU'D COME.
HEY, I'M NO LIAR.
BESIDES, VISITING FRIENDS' HOUSES IS **FUN!**
KREE
OH!
IT MUST BE **CHILLY** OUT THERE.
COME IN.
WOW...!

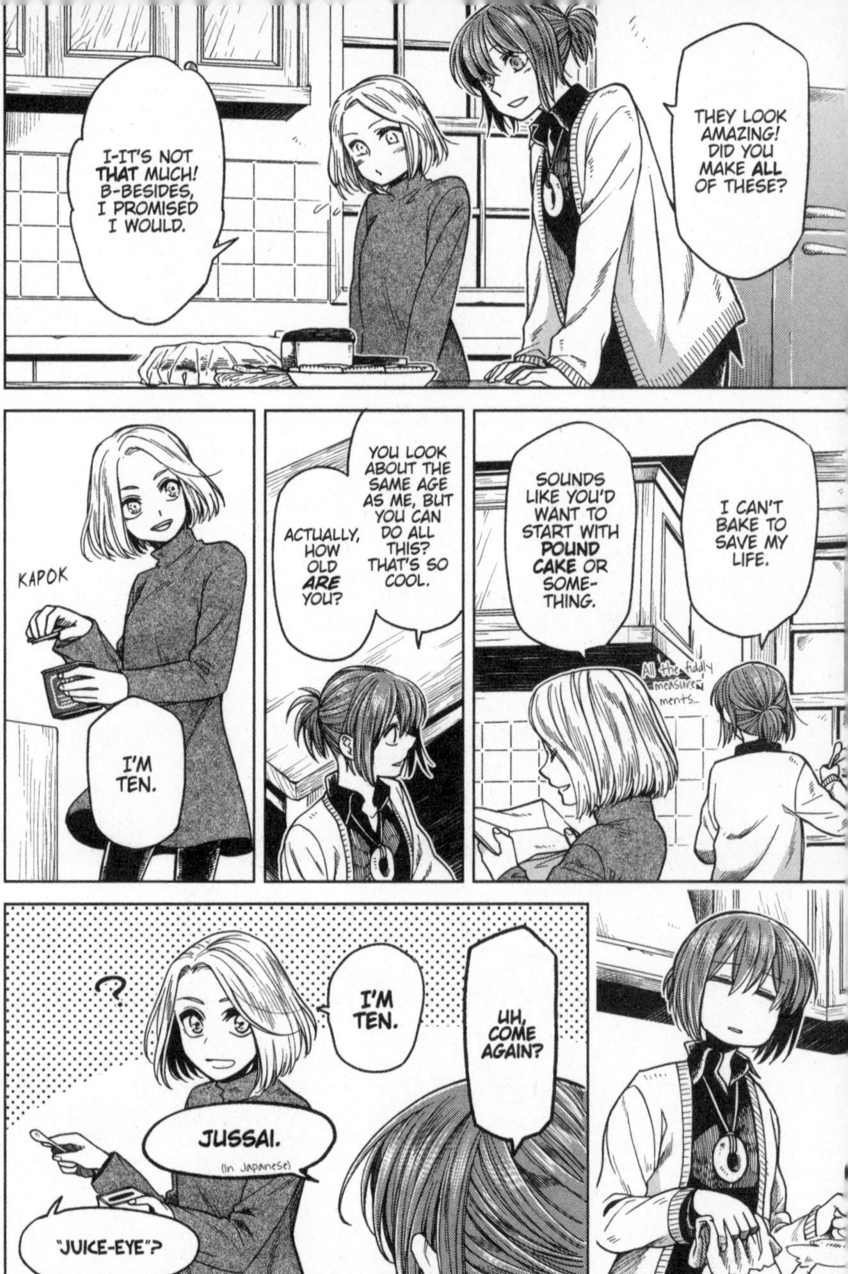
THEY LOOK AMAZING! DID YOU MAKE **ALL** OF THESE?
I-IT'S NOT **THAT** MUCH! B-BESIDES, I PROMISED I WOULD.
I CAN'T BAKE TO SAVE MY LIFE.
All the fiddly measurements...
SOUNDS LIKE YOU'D WANT TO START WITH **POUND CAKE** OR SOME-THING.
YOU LOOK ABOUT THE SAME AGE AS ME, BUT YOU CAN DO ALL THIS? THAT'S SO COOL.
ACTUALLY, HOW OLD ***ARE*** YOU?
KAPOK
I'M TEN.
?
I'M TEN.
UH, COME AGAIN?
JUSSAI.
(In Japanese)
"JUICE-EYE"?

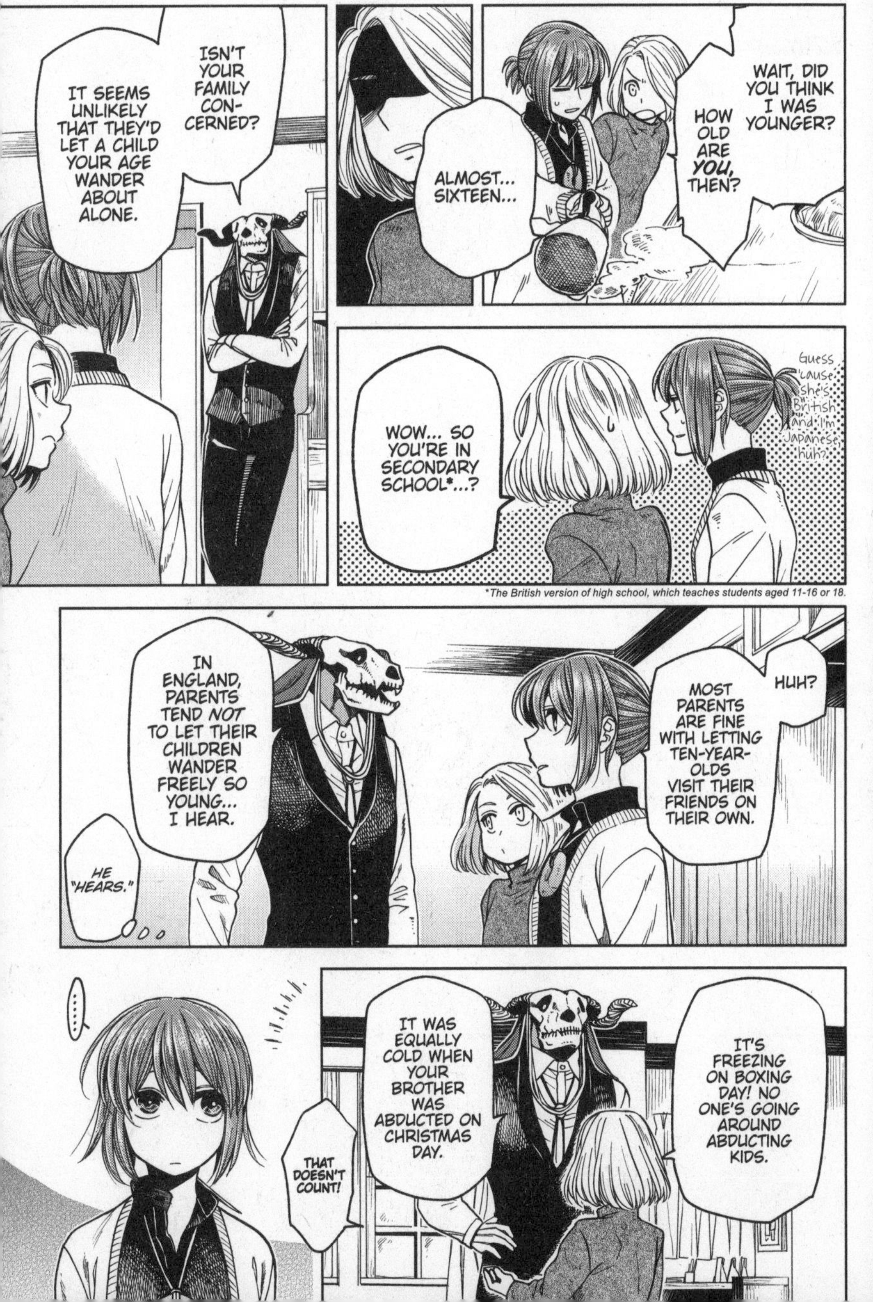
WAIT, DID YOU THINK I WAS YOUNGER?
HOW OLD ARE *YOU*, THEN?
ALMOST... SIXTEEN...
Guess 'cause she's British and I'm Japanese, huh?
WOW... SO YOU'RE IN SECONDARY SCHOOL*...?
ISN'T YOUR FAMILY CON-CERNED?
IT SEEMS UNLIKELY THAT THEY'D LET A CHILD YOUR AGE WANDER ABOUT ALONE.
HUH?
MOST PARENTS ARE FINE WITH LETTING TEN-YEAR-OLDS VISIT THEIR FRIENDS ON THEIR OWN.
IN ENGLAND, PARENTS TEND *NOT* TO LET THEIR CHILDREN WANDER FREELY SO YOUNG... I HEAR.
HE "HEARS."
IT'S FREEZING ON BOXING DAY! NO ONE'S GOING AROUND ABDUCTING KIDS.
IT WAS EQUALLY COLD WHEN YOUR BROTHER WAS ABDUCTED ON CHRISTMAS DAY.
THAT DOESN'T COUNT!
......

*The British version of high school, which teaches students aged 11-16 or 18.

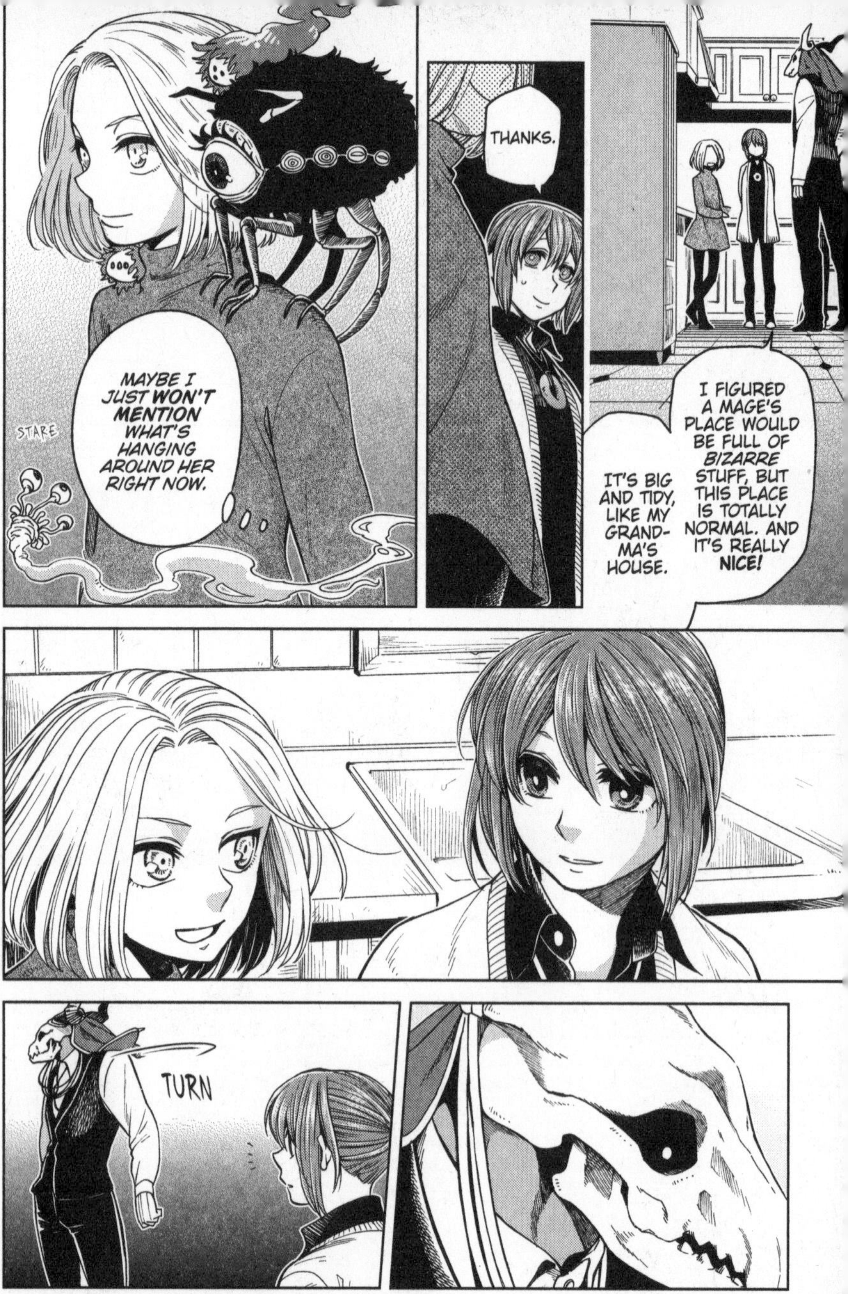
I FIGURED A MAGE'S PLACE WOULD BE FULL OF BIZARRE STUFF, BUT THIS PLACE IS TOTALLY NORMAL. AND IT'S REALLY NICE!
IT'S BIG AND TIDY, LIKE MY GRAND-MA'S HOUSE.
THANKS.
MAYBE I JUST WON'T MENTION WHAT'S HANGING AROUND HER RIGHT NOW.
STARE
TURN

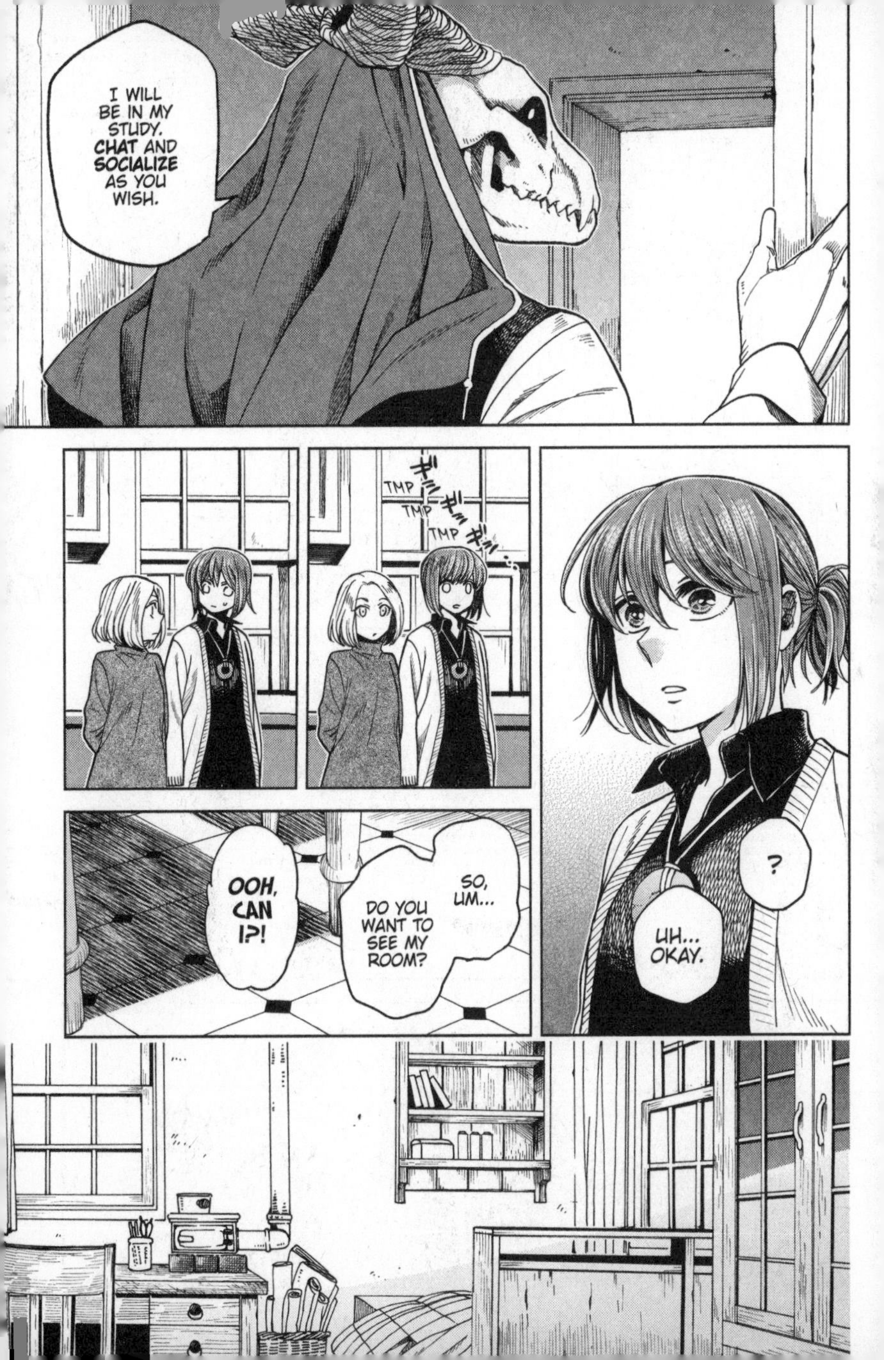
I WILL BE IN MY STUDY. CHAT AND SOCIALIZE AS YOU WISH.
?
UH... OKAY.
TMP
TMP
TMP
SO, UM...
DO YOU WANT TO SEE MY ROOM?
OOH, CAN I?!
...

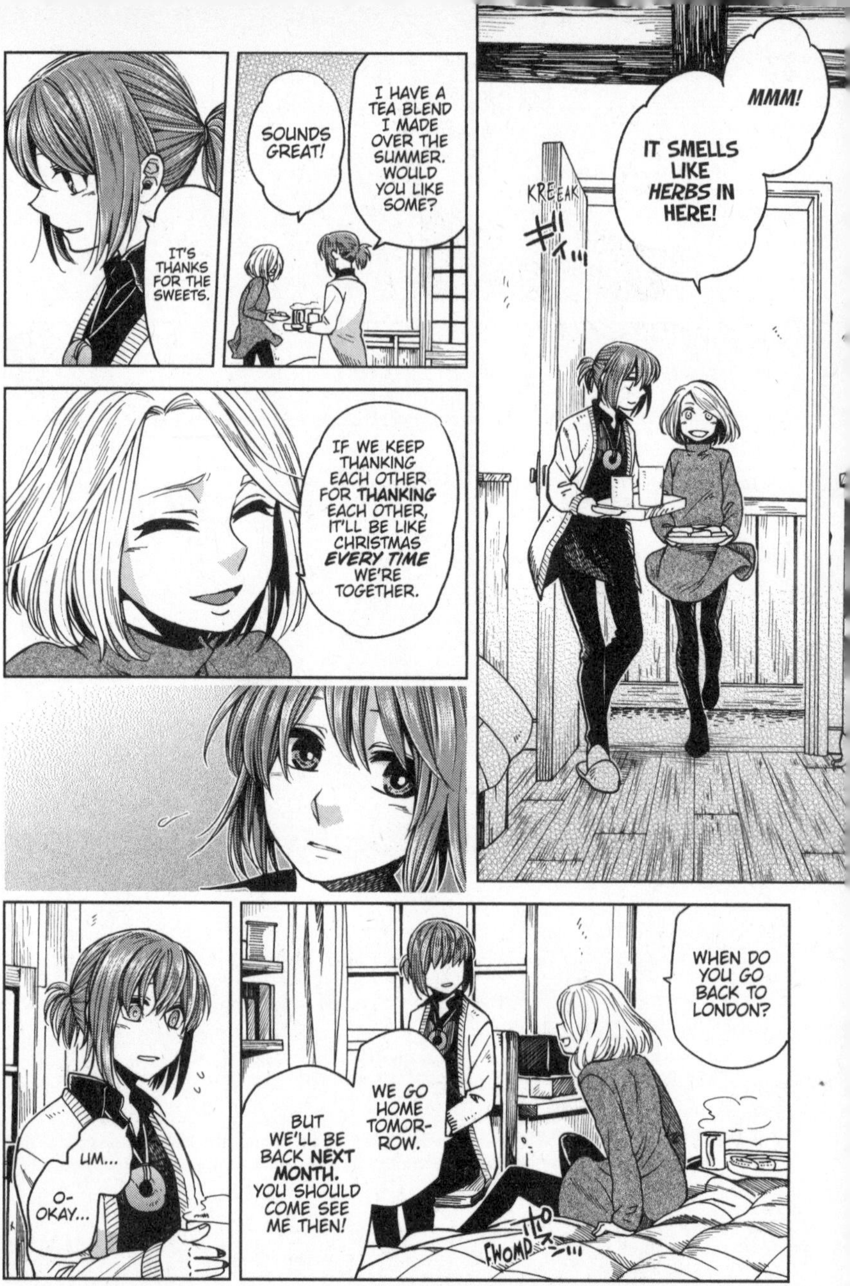
MMM!
IT SMELLS LIKE HERBS IN HERE!
KREEAK
I HAVE A TEA BLEND I MADE OVER THE SUMMER. WOULD YOU LIKE SOME?
SOUNDS GREAT!
IT'S THANKS FOR THE SWEETS.
IF WE KEEP THANKING EACH OTHER FOR THANKING EACH OTHER, IT'LL BE LIKE CHRISTMAS EVERY TIME WE'RE TOGETHER.
WHEN DO YOU GO BACK TO LONDON?
WE GO HOME TOMORROW.
BUT WE'LL BE BACK NEXT MONTH. YOU SHOULD COME SEE ME THEN!
FWOMP
UM...
O-OKAY...

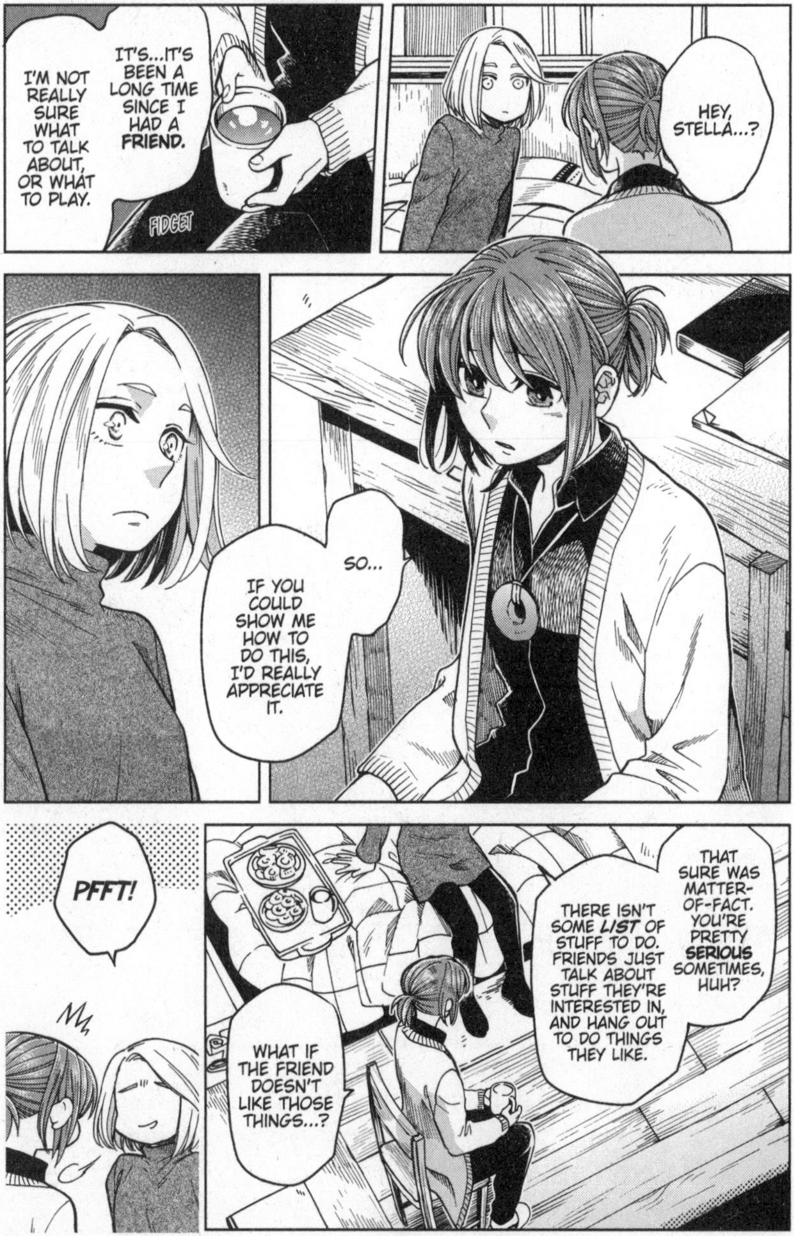
HEY, STELLA...?
IT'S...IT'S BEEN A LONG TIME SINCE I HAD A FRIEND.
I'M NOT REALLY SURE WHAT TO TALK ABOUT, OR WHAT TO PLAY.
FIDGET
SO...
IF YOU COULD SHOW ME HOW TO DO THIS, I'D REALLY APPRECIATE IT.
THAT SURE WAS MATTER-OF-FACT. YOU'RE PRETTY SERIOUS SOMETIMES, HUH?
THERE ISN'T SOME LIST OF STUFF TO DO. FRIENDS JUST TALK ABOUT STUFF THEY'RE INTERESTED IN, AND HANG OUT TO DO THINGS THEY LIKE.
WHAT IF THE FRIEND DOESN'T LIKE THOSE THINGS...?
PFFT!

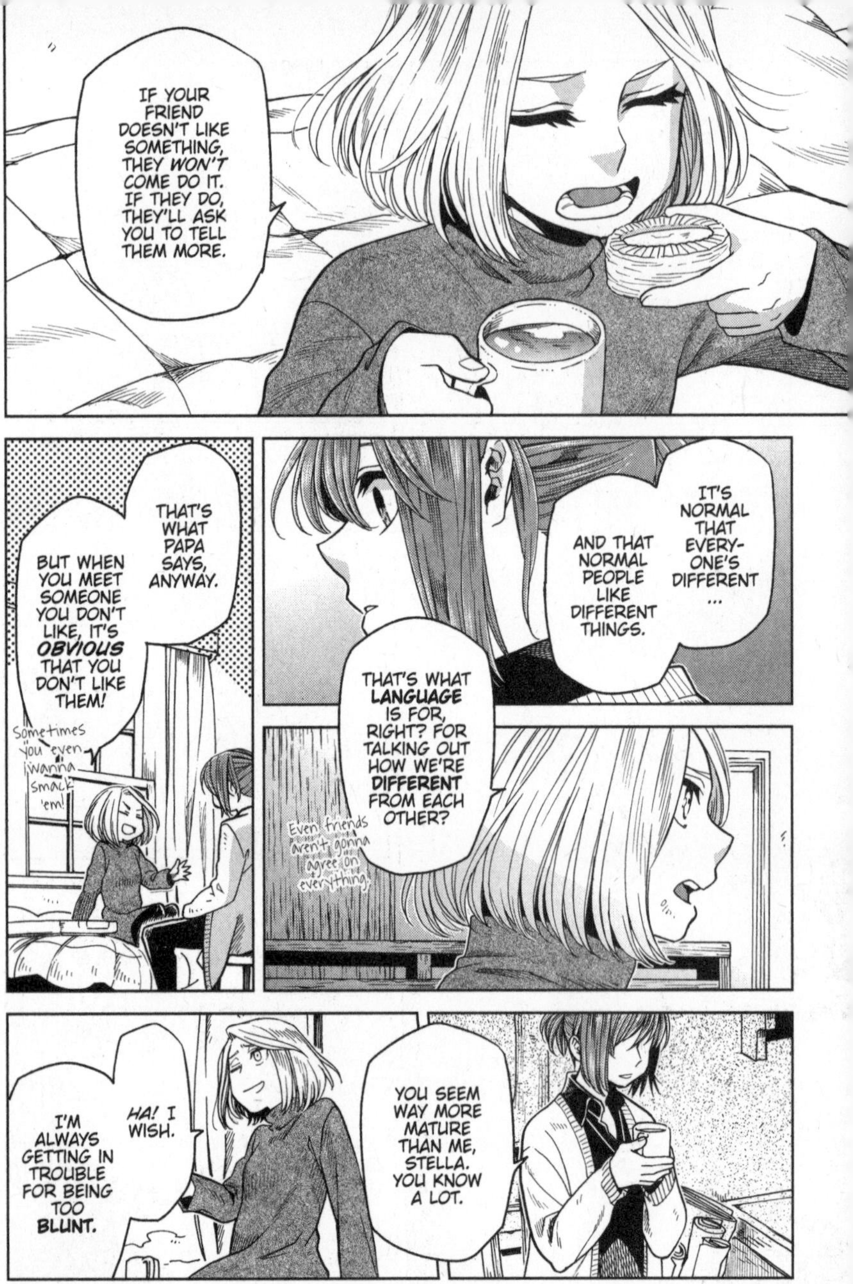
IF YOUR FRIEND DOESN'T LIKE SOMETHING, THEY *WON'T* COME DO IT. IF THEY DO, THEY'LL ASK YOU TO TELL THEM MORE.
IT'S NORMAL THAT EVERYONE'S DIFFERENT ...
AND THAT NORMAL PEOPLE LIKE DIFFERENT THINGS.
THAT'S WHAT **LANGUAGE** IS FOR, RIGHT? FOR TALKING OUT HOW WE'RE **DIFFERENT** FROM EACH OTHER?
Even friends aren't gonna agree on everything.
THAT'S WHAT PAPA SAYS, ANYWAY.
BUT WHEN YOU MEET SOMEONE YOU DON'T LIKE, IT'S ***OBVIOUS*** THAT YOU DON'T LIKE THEM!
Sometimes you even wanna smack 'em!
YOU SEEM WAY MORE MATURE THAN ME, STELLA. YOU KNOW A LOT.
HA! I WISH.
I'M ALWAYS GETTING IN TROUBLE FOR BEING TOO **BLUNT.**

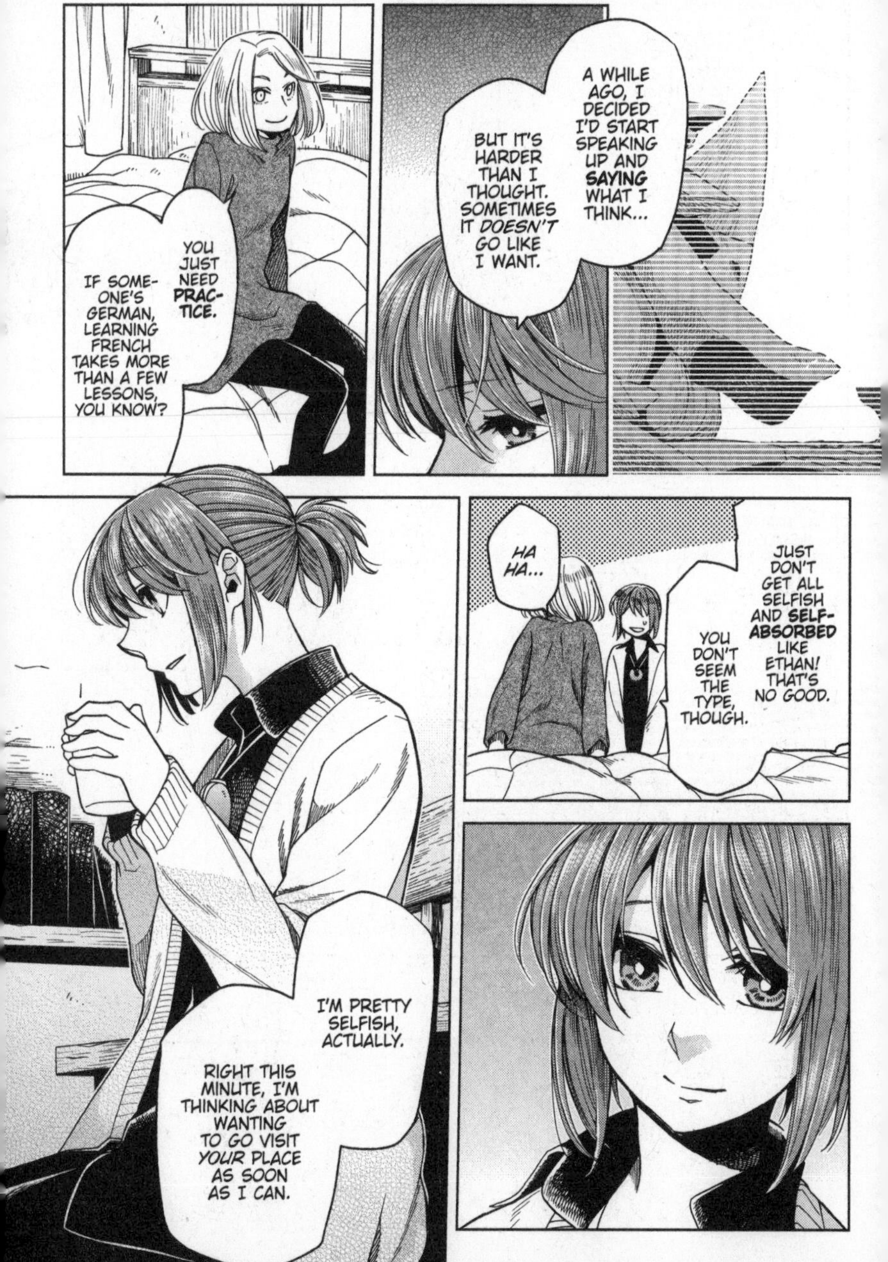
A WHILE AGO, I DECIDED I'D START SPEAKING UP AND SAYING WHAT I THINK...
BUT IT'S HARDER THAN I THOUGHT. SOMETIMES IT DOESN'T GO LIKE I WANT.
YOU JUST NEED PRACTICE.
IF SOMEONE'S GERMAN, LEARNING FRENCH TAKES MORE THAN A FEW LESSONS, YOU KNOW?
JUST DON'T GET ALL SELFISH AND SELF-ABSORBED LIKE ETHAN! THAT'S NO GOOD.
YOU DON'T SEEM THE TYPE, THOUGH.
HA HA...
I'M PRETTY SELFISH, ACTUALLY.
RIGHT THIS MINUTE, I'M THINKING ABOUT WANTING TO GO VISIT YOUR PLACE AS SOON AS I CAN.

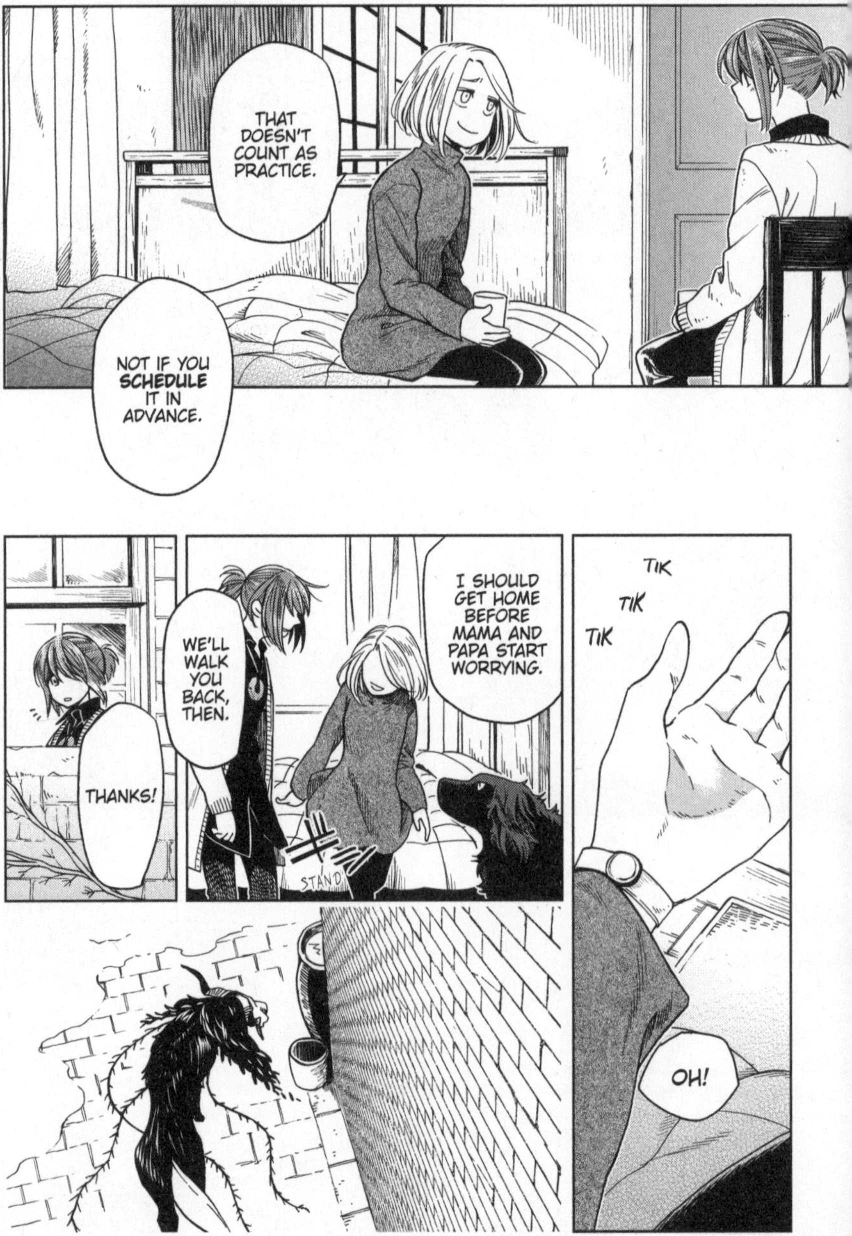
THAT DOESN'T COUNT AS PRACTICE.
NOT IF YOU **SCHEDULE** IT IN ADVANCE.
TIK
TIK
TIK
OH!
I SHOULD GET HOME BEFORE MAMA AND PAPA START WORRYING.
WE'LL WALK YOU BACK, THEN.
STAND
THANKS!

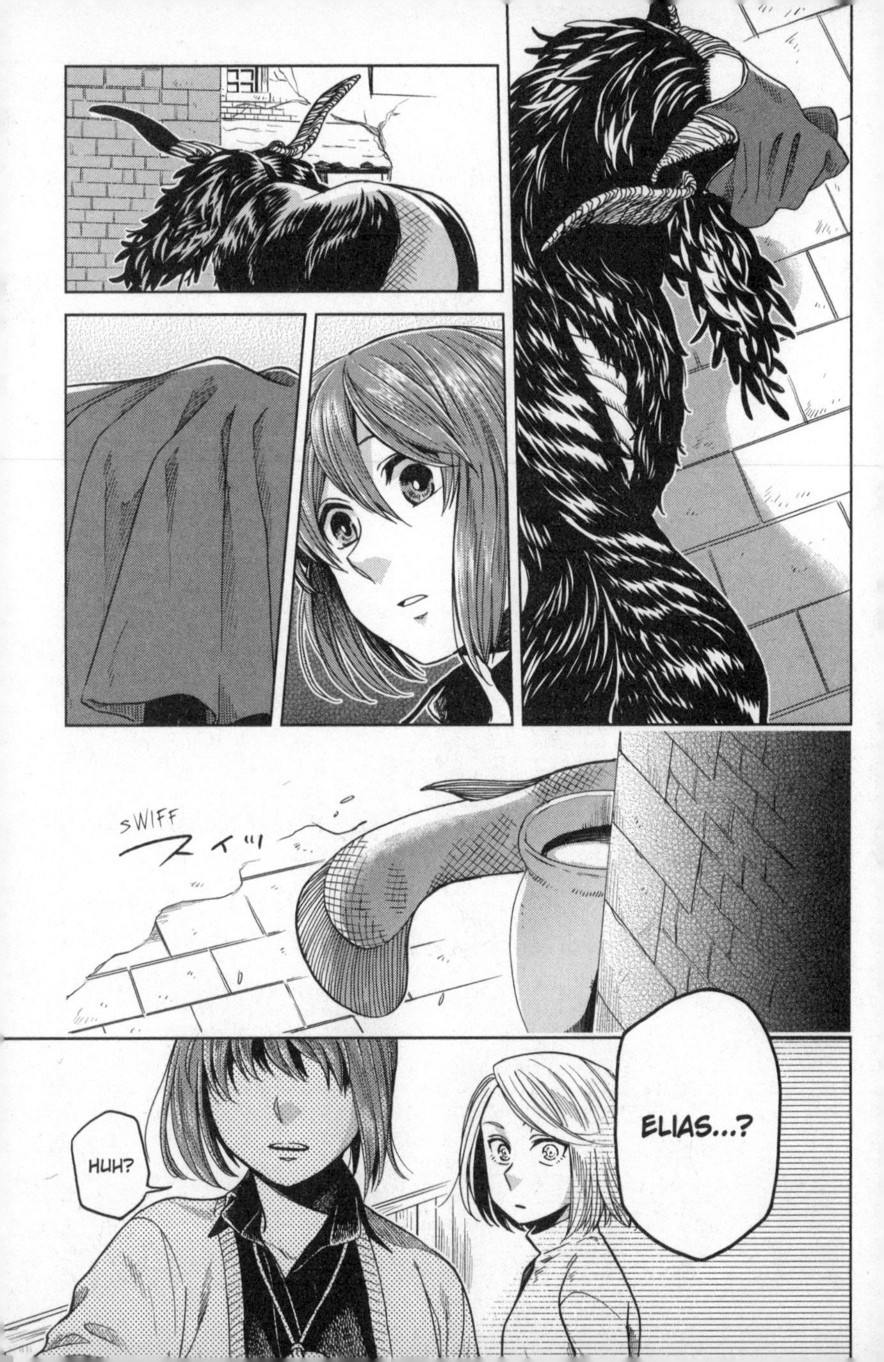
SWIFF
スイッ
ELIAS...?
HUH?

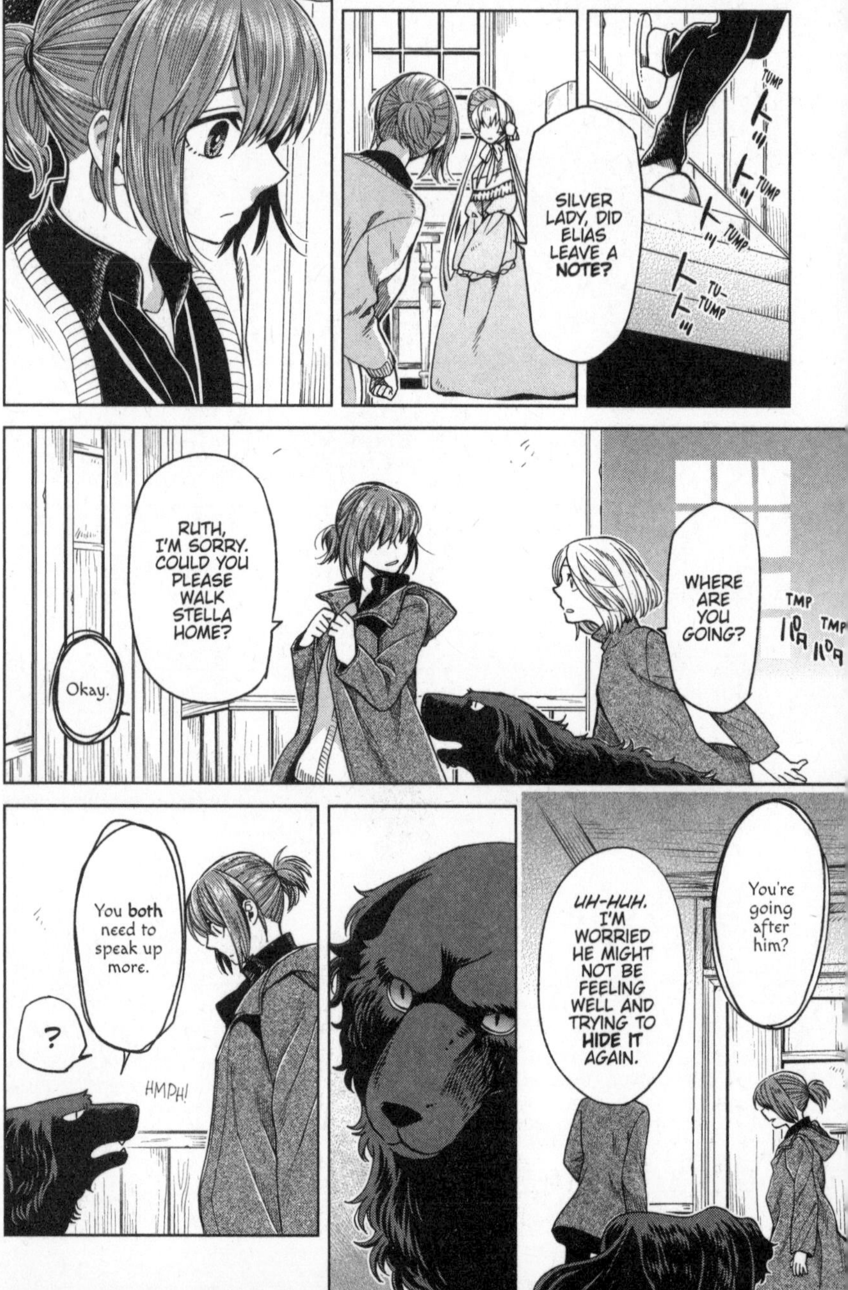

TUMP
TUMP
TUMP
TU-TUMP
SILVER LADY, DID ELIAS LEAVE A **NOTE?**
TMP TMP
WHERE ARE YOU GOING?
RUTH, I'M SORRY. COULD YOU PLEASE WALK STELLA HOME?
Okay.
You're going after him?
UH-HUH. I'M WORRIED HE MIGHT NOT BE FEELING WELL AND TRYING TO **HIDE IT** AGAIN.
You **both** need to speak up more.
?
HMPH!

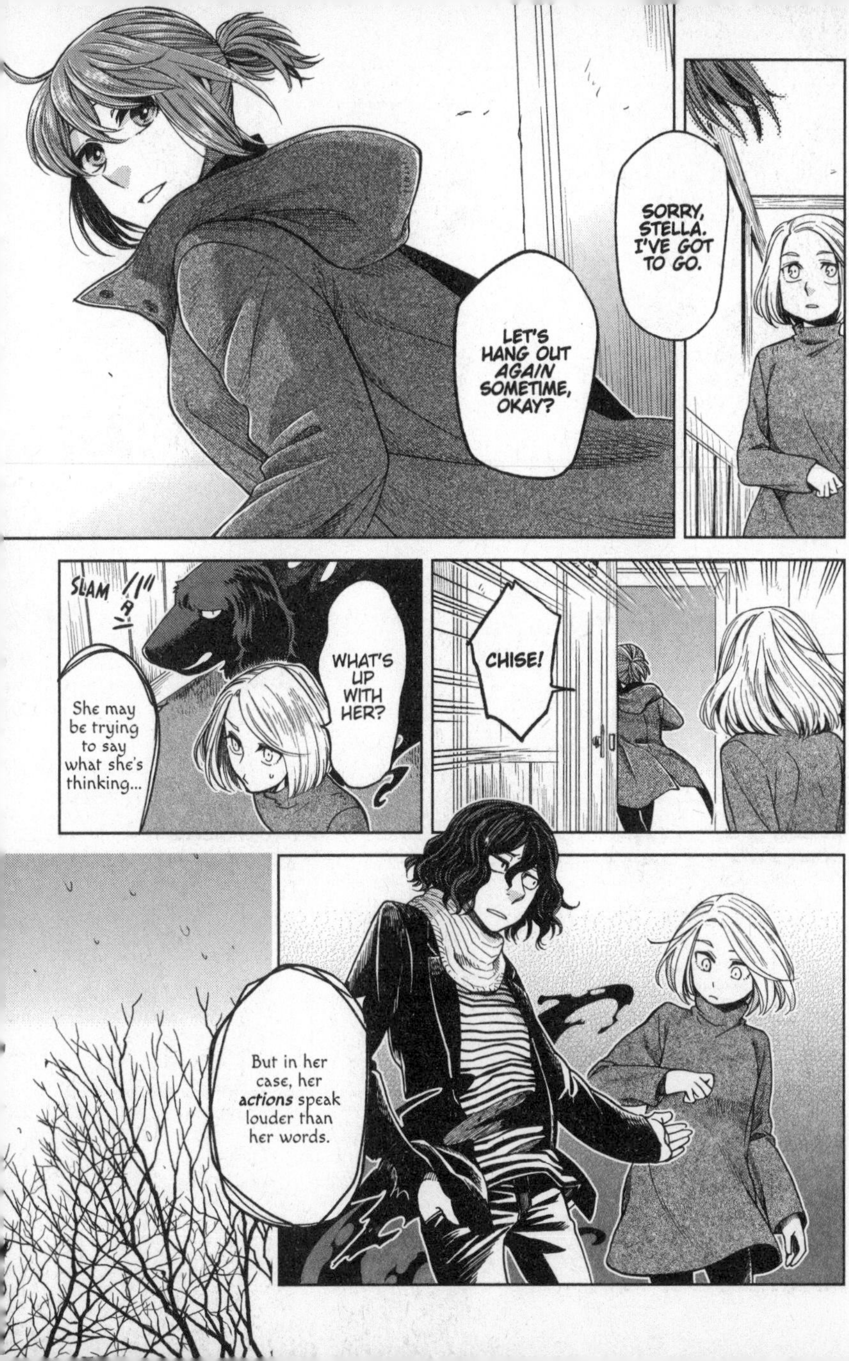
SORRY, STELLA. I'VE GOT TO GO.
LET'S HANG OUT AGAIN SOMETIME, OKAY?
CHISE!
WHAT'S UP WITH HER?
SLAM
She may be trying to say what she's thinking...
But in her case, her actions speak louder than her words.

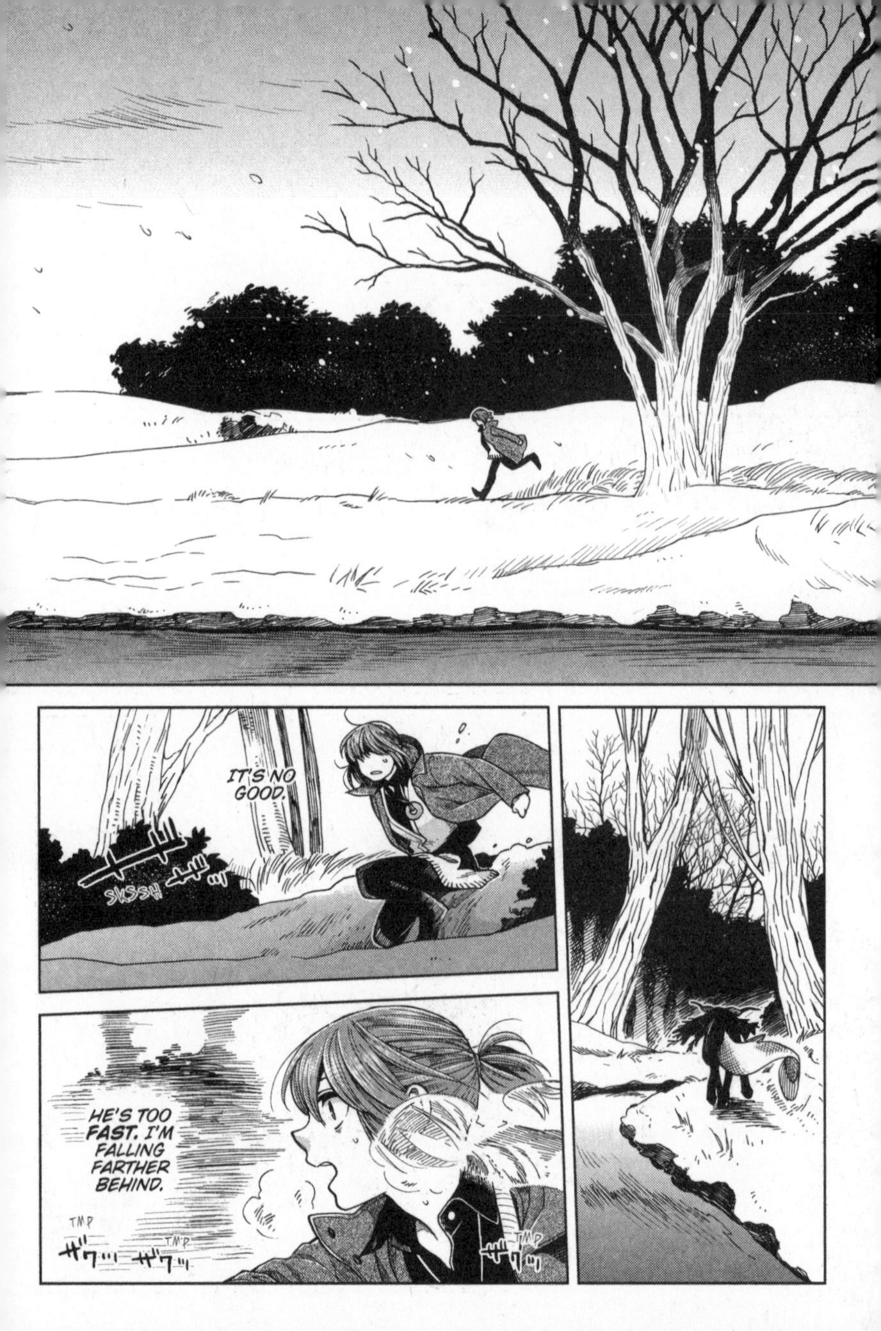
IT'S NO GOOD.
SKSSH
HE'S TOO FAST. I'M FALLING FARTHER BEHIND.
TMP
TMP
TMP

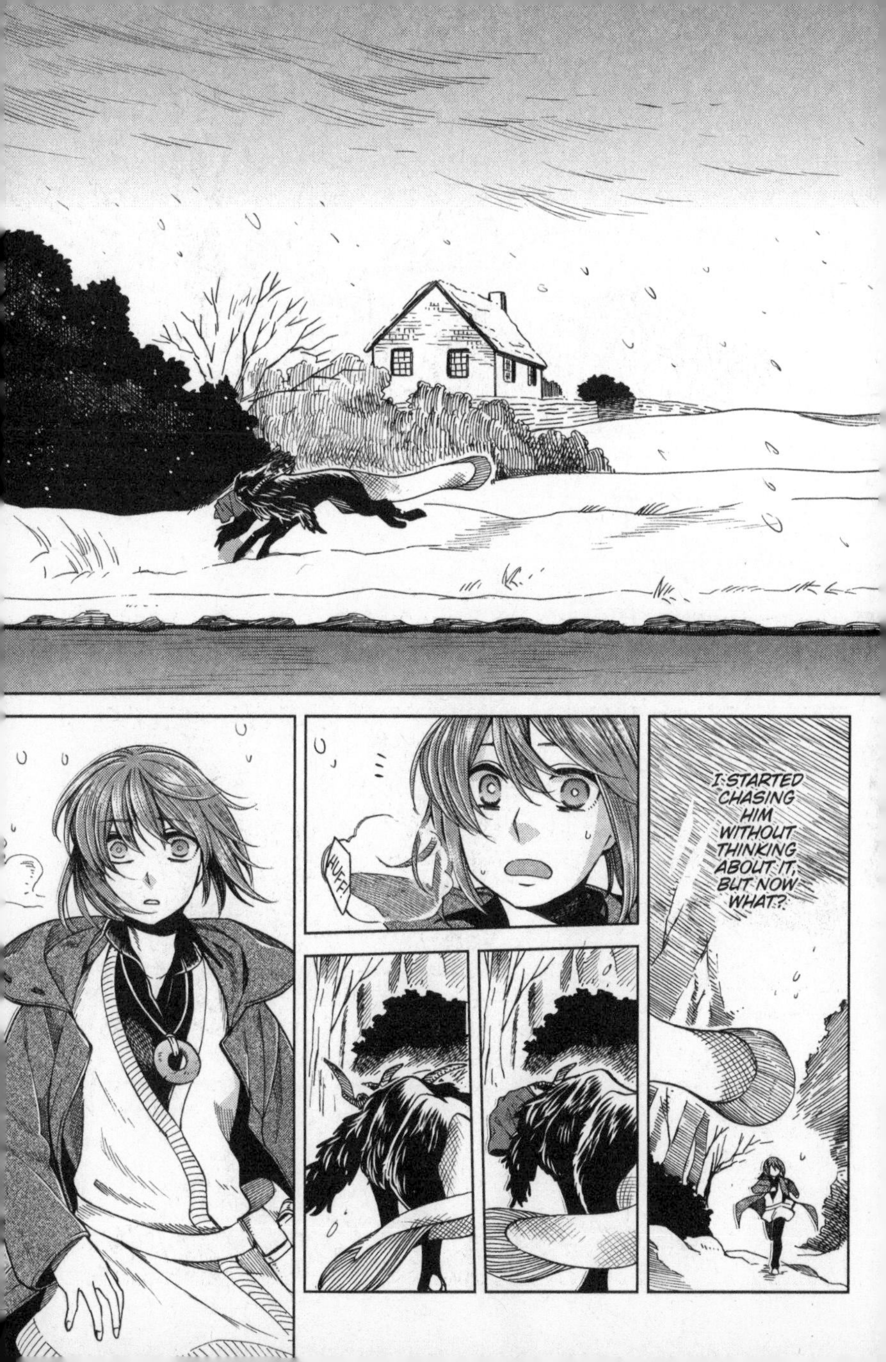
HUFF!
I STARTED CHASING HIM WITHOUT THINKING ABOUT IT, BUT NOW WHAT?

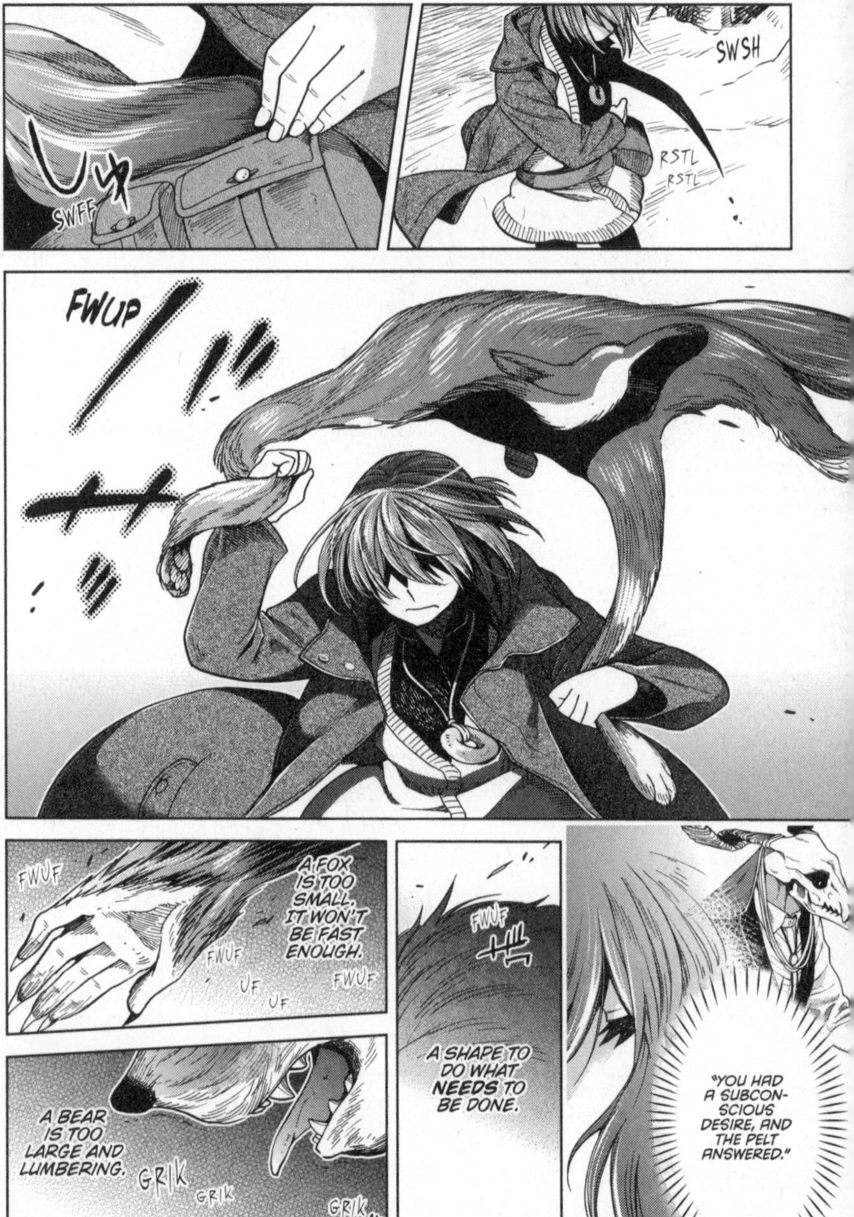
SWSH
RSTL
RSTL
SWFF
FWUP
"YOU HAD A SUBCONSCIOUS DESIRE, AND THE PELT ANSWERED."
FWUF
A SHAPE TO DO WHAT NEEDS TO BE DONE.
A FOX IS TOO SMALL. IT WON'T BE FAST ENOUGH.
FWUF
FWUF
UF
UF
FWUF
A BEAR IS TOO LARGE AND LUMBERING.
GRIK
GRIK
GRIK...

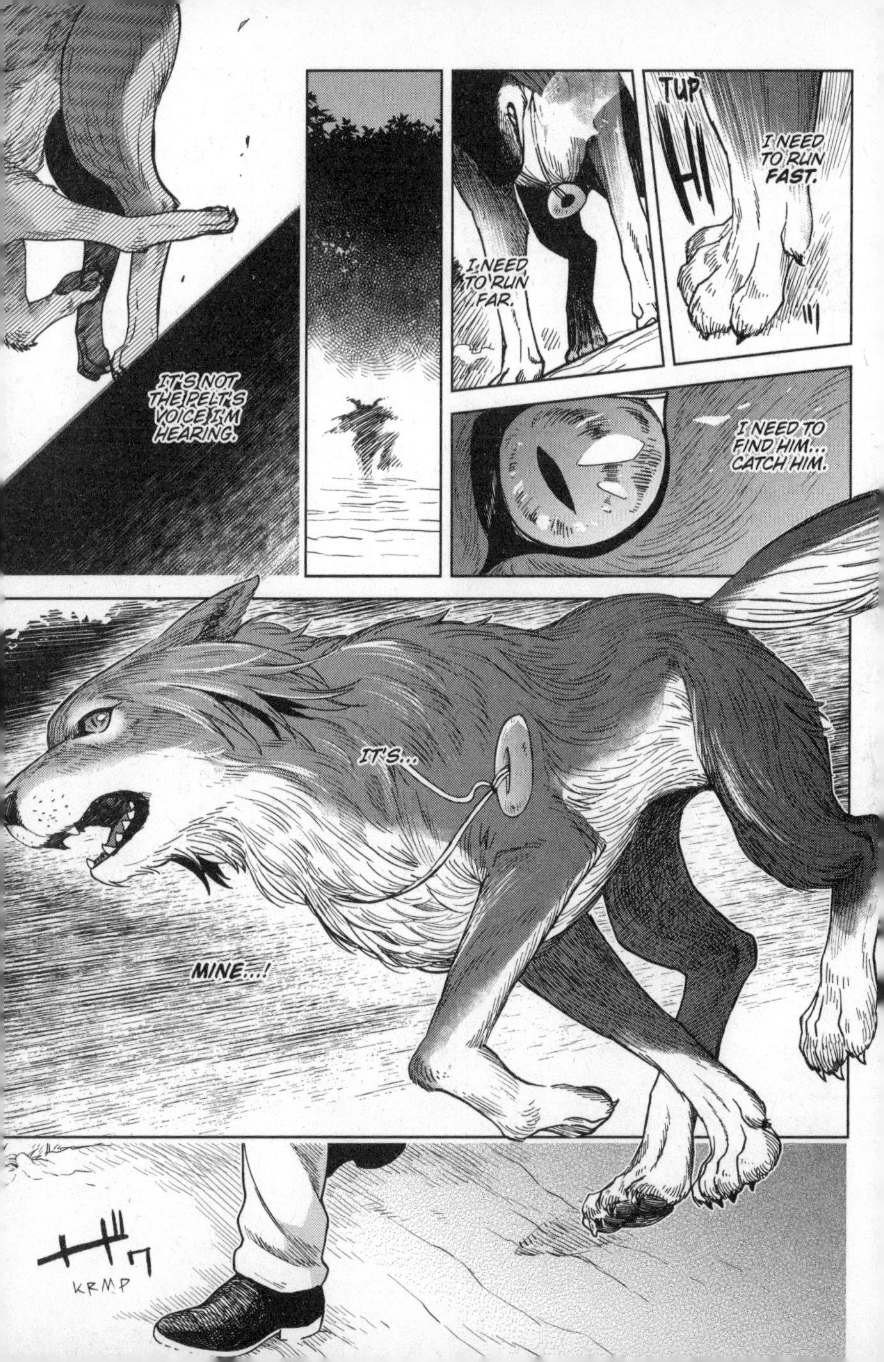
TUP
I NEED TO RUN FAST.
I NEED TO RUN FAR.
I NEED TO FIND HIM... CATCH HIM.
IT'S NOT THE PELT'S VOICE I'M HEARING.
IT'S...
MINE...!
KRMP

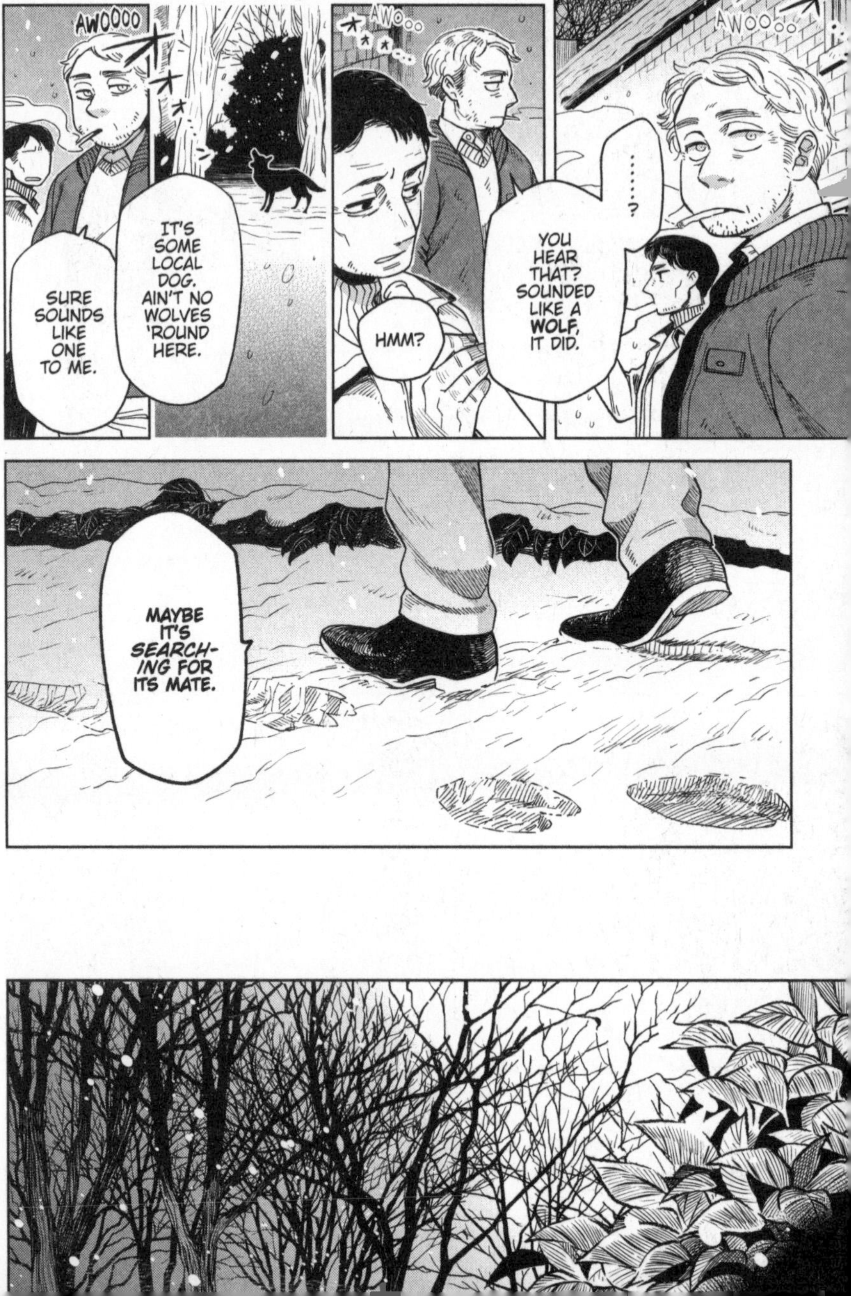
AWOO..
......?
YOU HEAR THAT? SOUNDED LIKE A WOLF, IT DID.
AWO..
HMM?
AWOOOO
IT'S SOME LOCAL DOG. AIN'T NO WOLVES 'ROUND HERE.
SURE SOUNDS LIKE ONE TO ME.
MAYBE IT'S SEARCHING FOR ITS MATE.

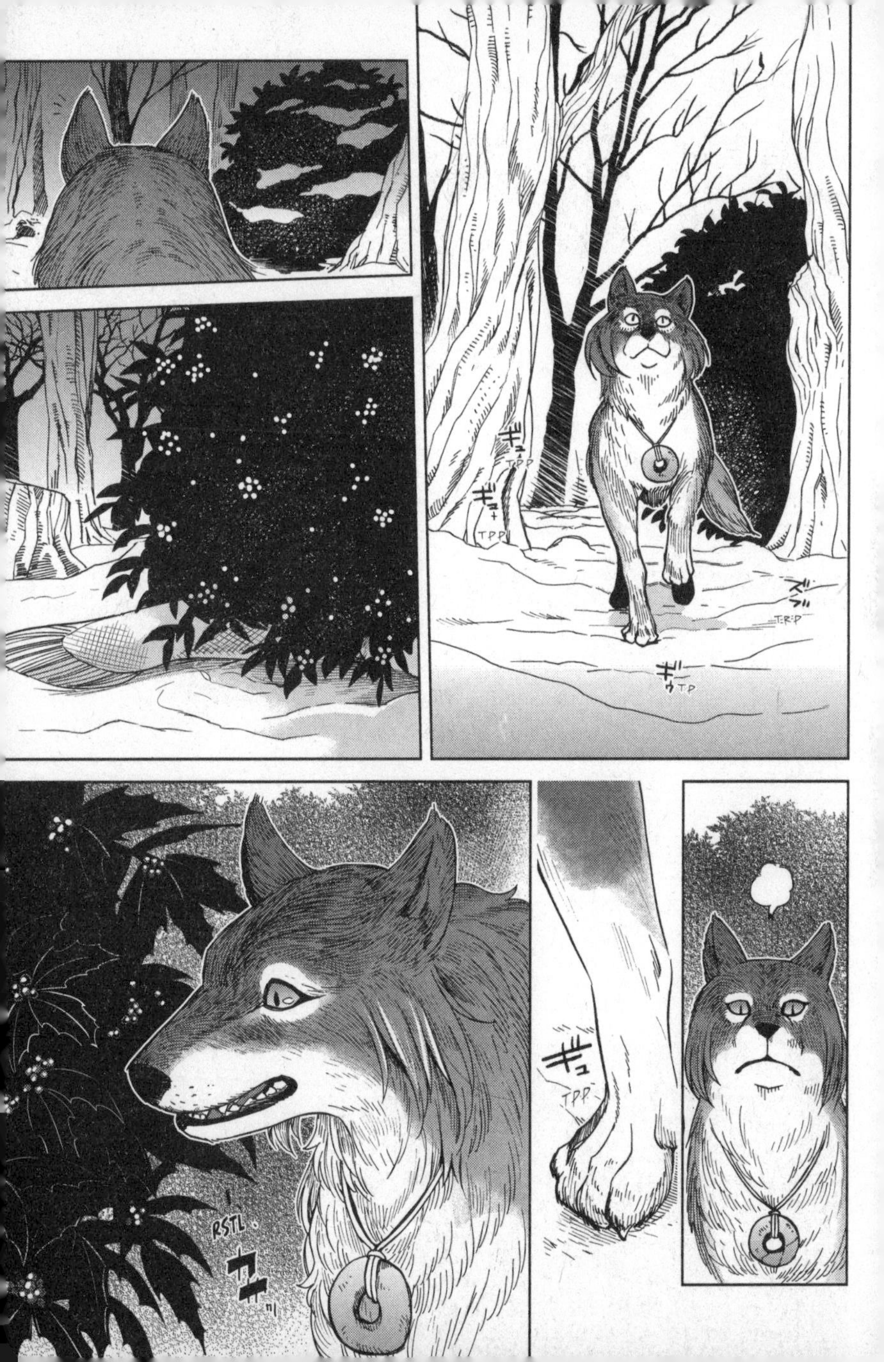

ギュ
TPP
ギュ
TPP
ズブ
T:R:P
ギュ
TP
ギュ
TPP
RSTL
ガサッ

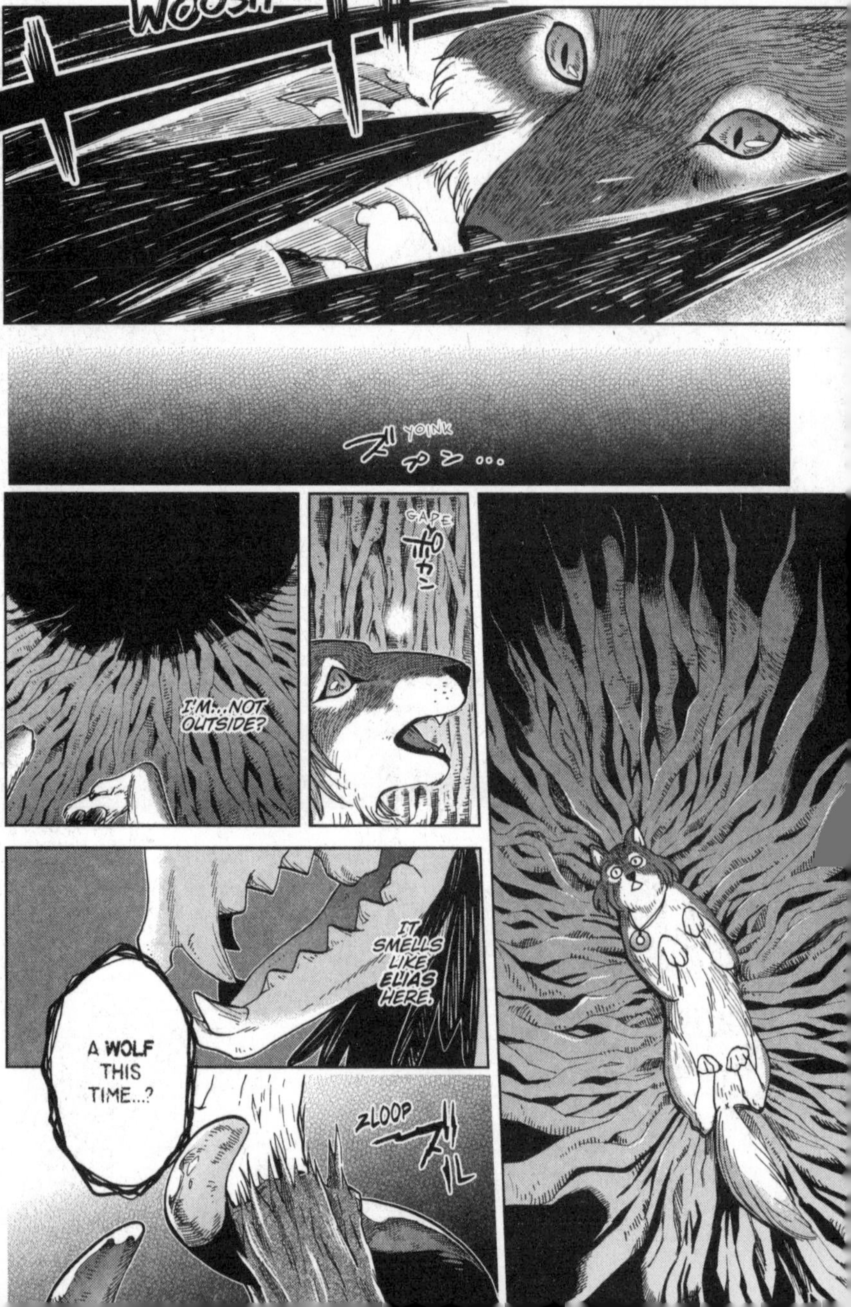
WOOSH
YOINK
ズポン...
GAPE
ポカン
I'M...NOT OUTSIDE?
IT SMELLS LIKE ELIAS HERE.
A WOLF THIS TIME...?
ZLOOP
ズル

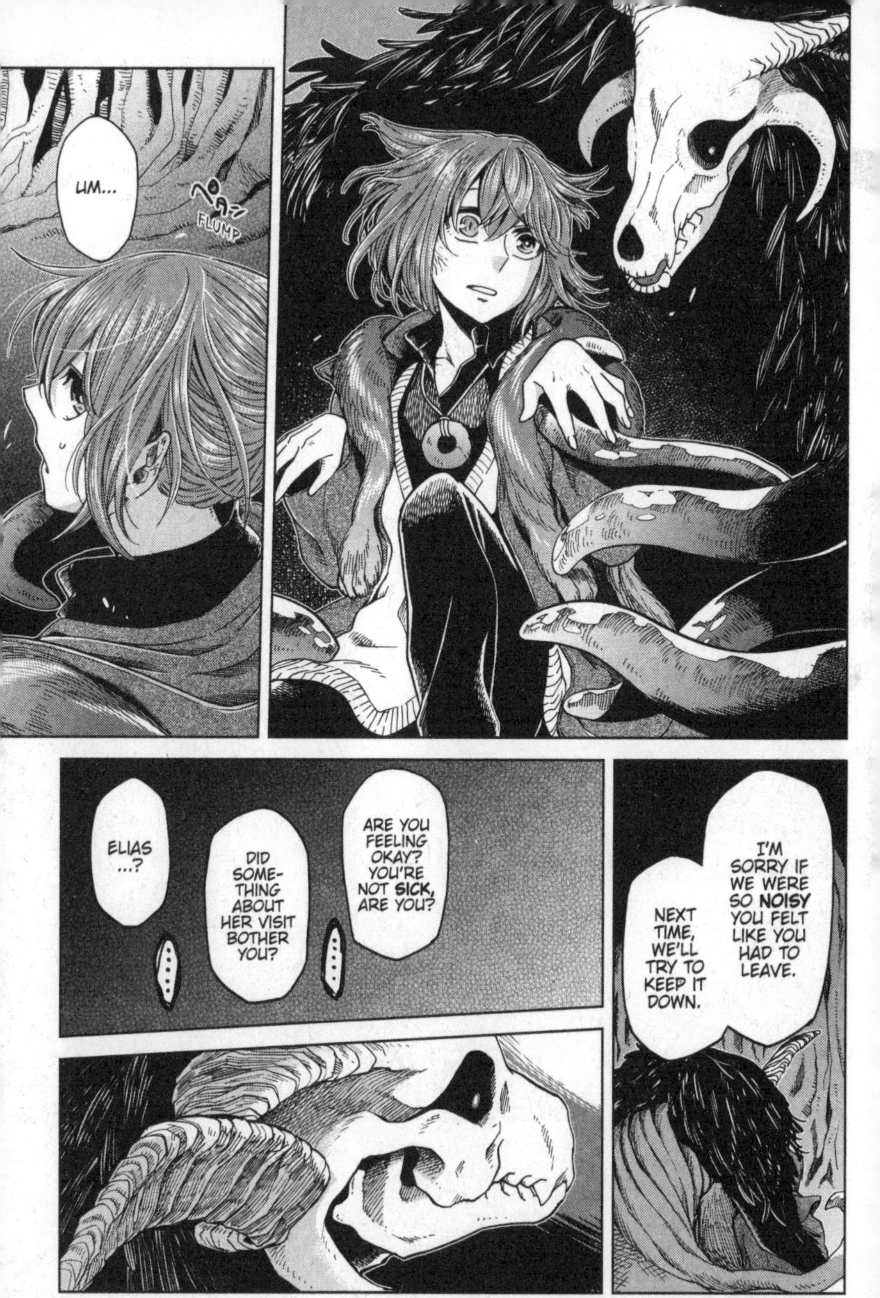
UM...
FLUMP
I'M SORRY IF WE WERE SO **NOISY** YOU FELT LIKE YOU HAD TO LEAVE.
NEXT TIME, WE'LL TRY TO KEEP IT DOWN.
ARE YOU FEELING OKAY? YOU'RE NOT **SICK**, ARE YOU?
......
DID SOME-THING ABOUT HER VISIT BOTHER YOU?
......
ELIAS ...?

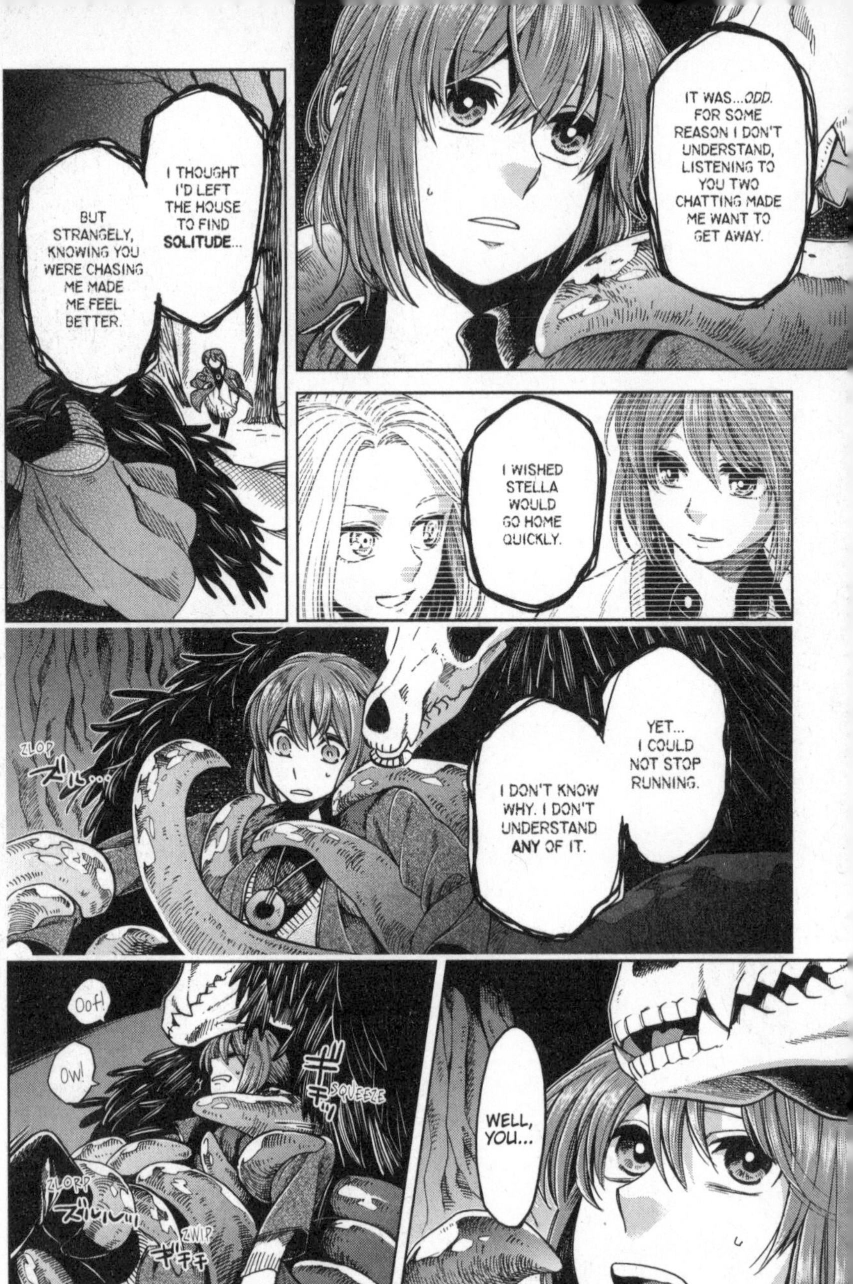
IT WAS...*ODD.* FOR SOME REASON I DON'T UNDERSTAND, LISTENING TO YOU TWO CHATTING MADE ME WANT TO GET AWAY.
I WISHED STELLA WOULD GO HOME QUICKLY.
I THOUGHT I'D LEFT THE HOUSE TO FIND **SOLITUDE**...
BUT STRANGELY, KNOWING YOU WERE CHASING ME MADE ME FEEL BETTER.
YET... I COULD NOT STOP RUNNING.
I DON'T KNOW WHY. I DON'T UNDERSTAND **ANY** OF IT.
ZLOP
WELL, YOU...
Oof!
Ow!
SQUEEZE
ZLORP
ZWIP

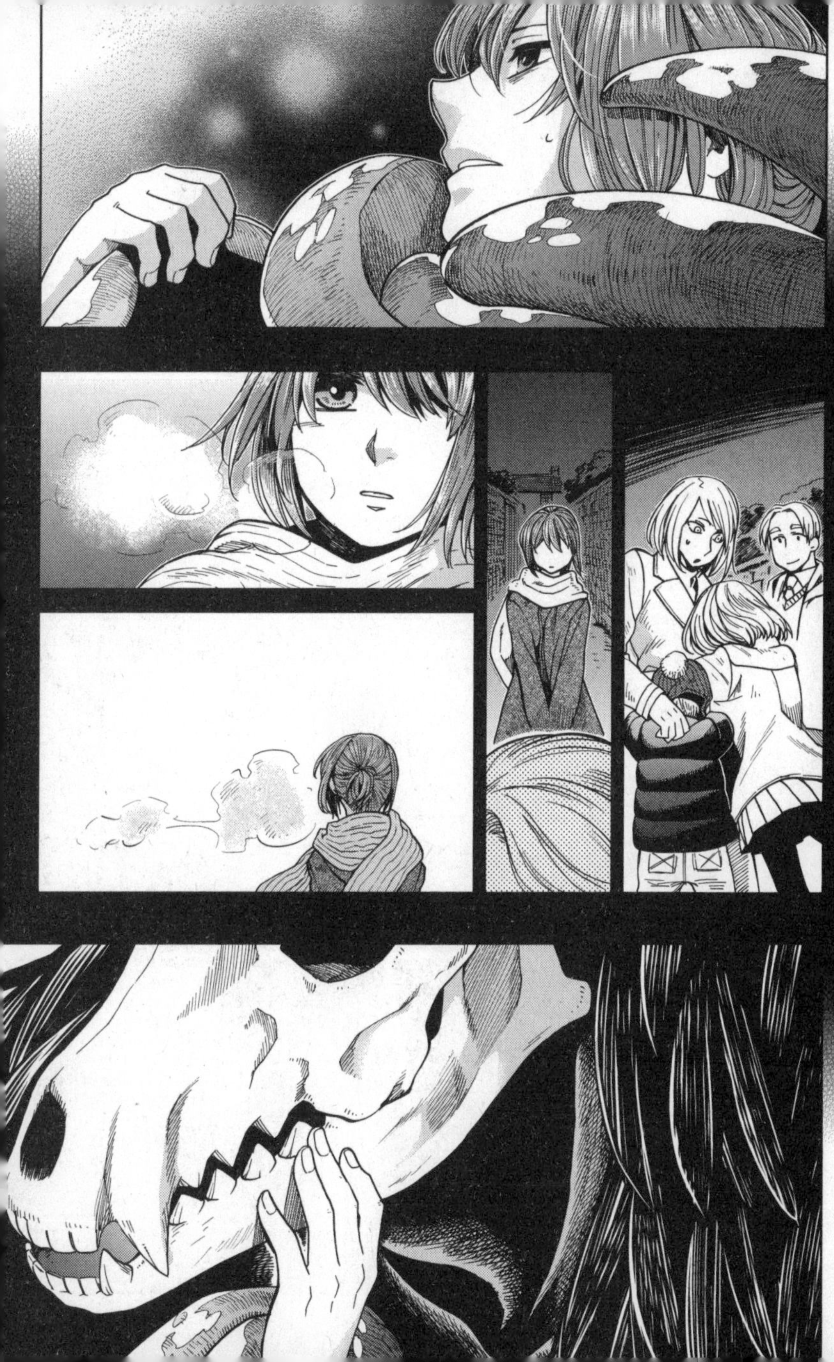

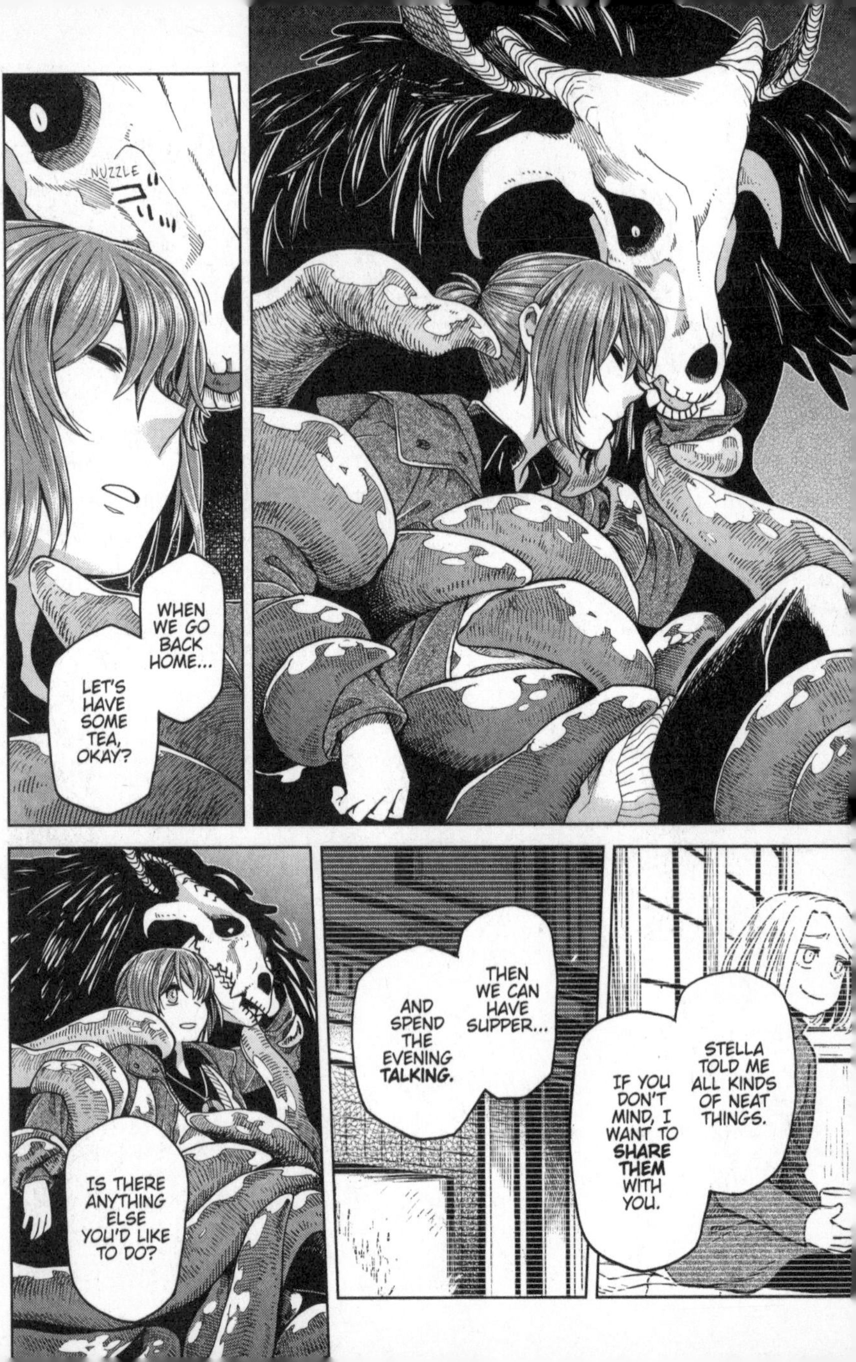
NUZZLE
WHEN WE GO BACK HOME...
LET'S HAVE SOME TEA, OKAY?
STELLA TOLD ME ALL KINDS OF NEAT THINGS.
IF YOU DON'T MIND, I WANT TO **SHARE THEM** WITH YOU.
THEN WE CAN HAVE SUPPER...
AND SPEND THE EVENING **TALKING.**
IS THERE ANYTHING ELSE YOU'D LIKE TO DO?

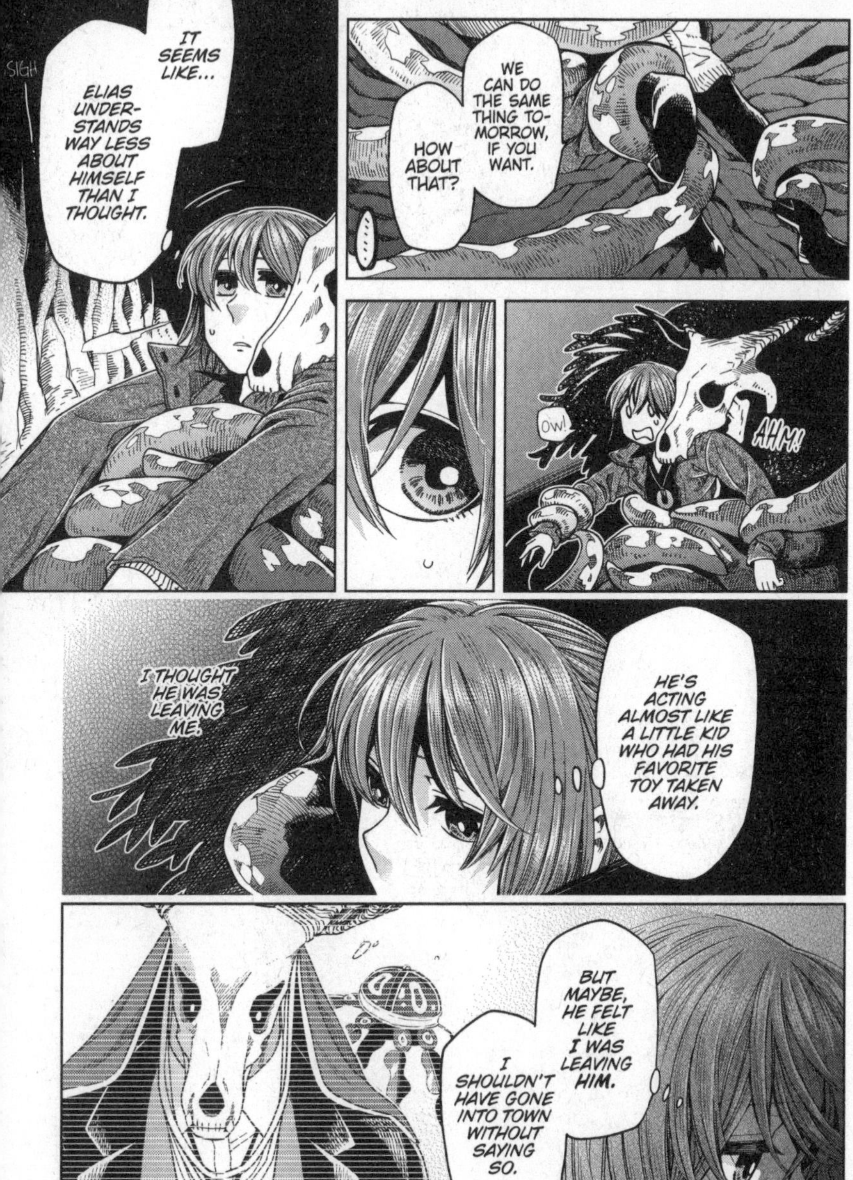
WE CAN DO THE SAME THING TOMORROW, IF YOU WANT.
HOW ABOUT THAT?
...
AHM!
OW!
SIGH
IT SEEMS LIKE... ELIAS UNDERSTANDS WAY LESS ABOUT HIMSELF THAN I THOUGHT.
HE'S ACTING ALMOST LIKE A LITTLE KID WHO HAD HIS FAVORITE TOY TAKEN AWAY.
I THOUGHT HE WAS LEAVING ME.
BUT MAYBE, HE FELT LIKE I WAS LEAVING HIM.
I SHOULDN'T HAVE GONE INTO TOWN WITHOUT SAYING SO.

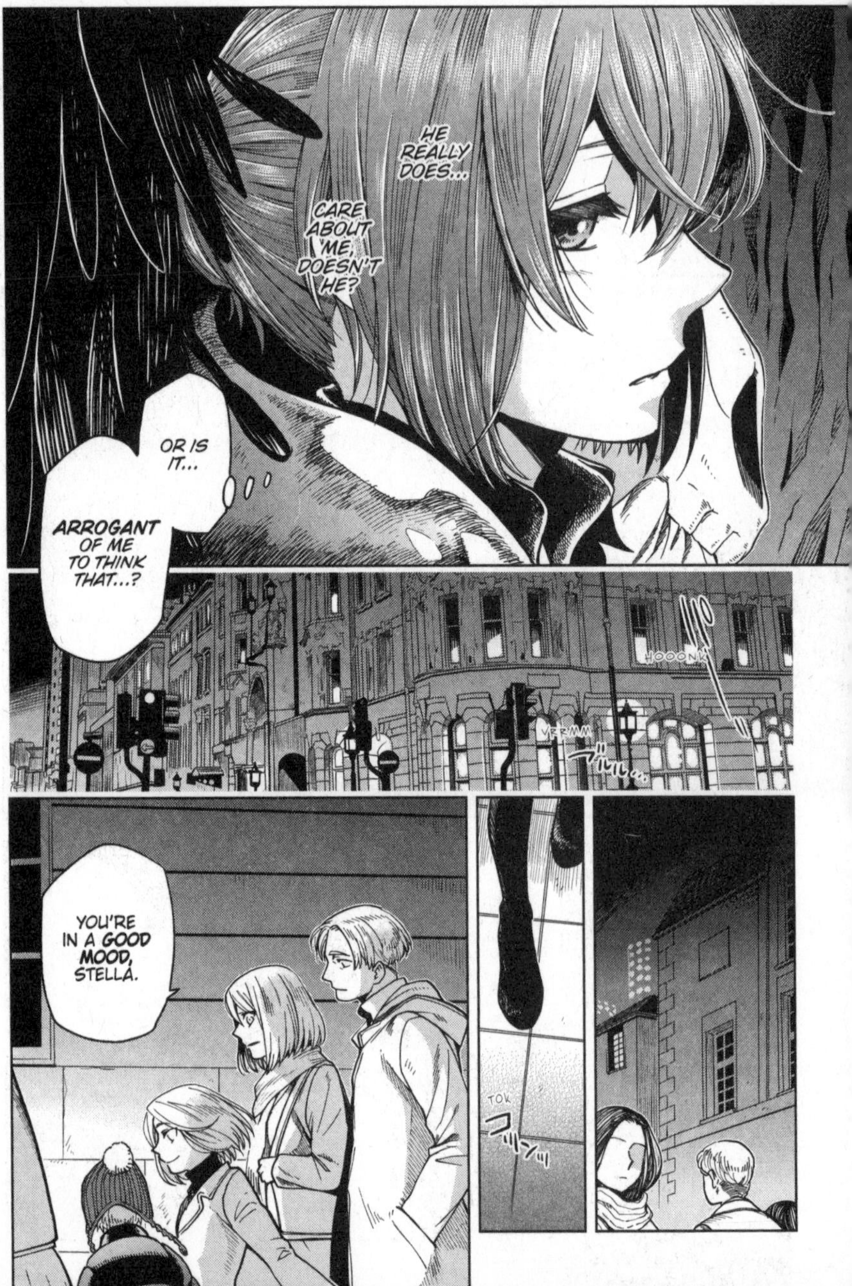
HE REALLY DOES...
CARE ABOUT ME, DOESN'T HE?
OR IS IT...
ARROGANT OF ME TO THINK THAT...?
HOOONK
VRRMM
TOK
YOU'RE IN A GOOD MOOD, STELLA.

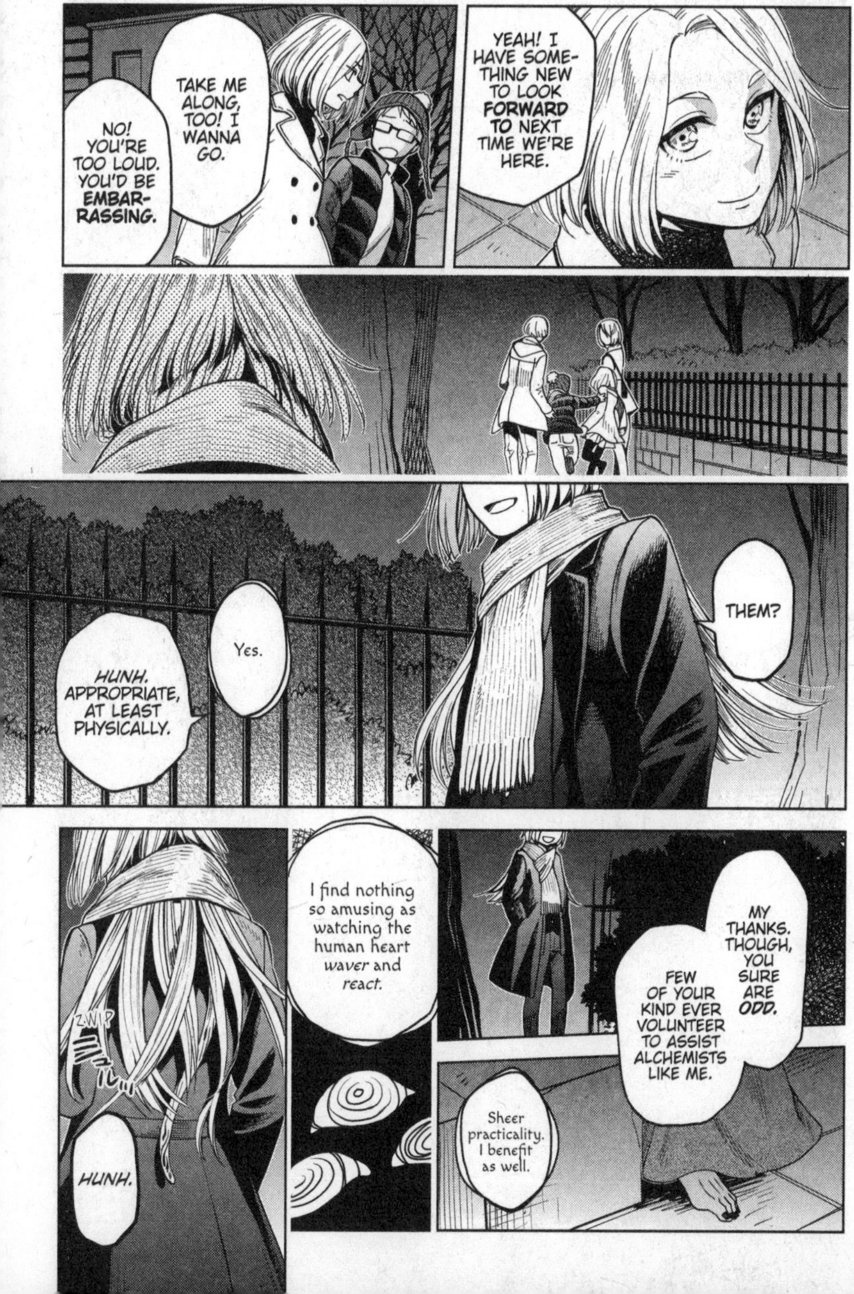
YEAH! I HAVE SOME-THING NEW TO LOOK **FORWARD** TO NEXT TIME WE'RE HERE.
TAKE ME ALONG, TOO! I WANNA GO.
NO! YOU'RE TOO LOUD. YOU'D BE **EMBAR-RASSING.**
THEM?
Yes.
HUNH. APPROPRIATE, AT LEAST PHYSICALLY.
MY THANKS. THOUGH, YOU SURE ARE ***ODD.***
FEW OF YOUR KIND EVER VOLUNTEER TO ASSIST ALCHEMISTS LIKE ME.
Sheer practicality. I benefit as well.
I find nothing so amusing as watching the human heart *waver* and *react.*
ZWIP
HUNH.

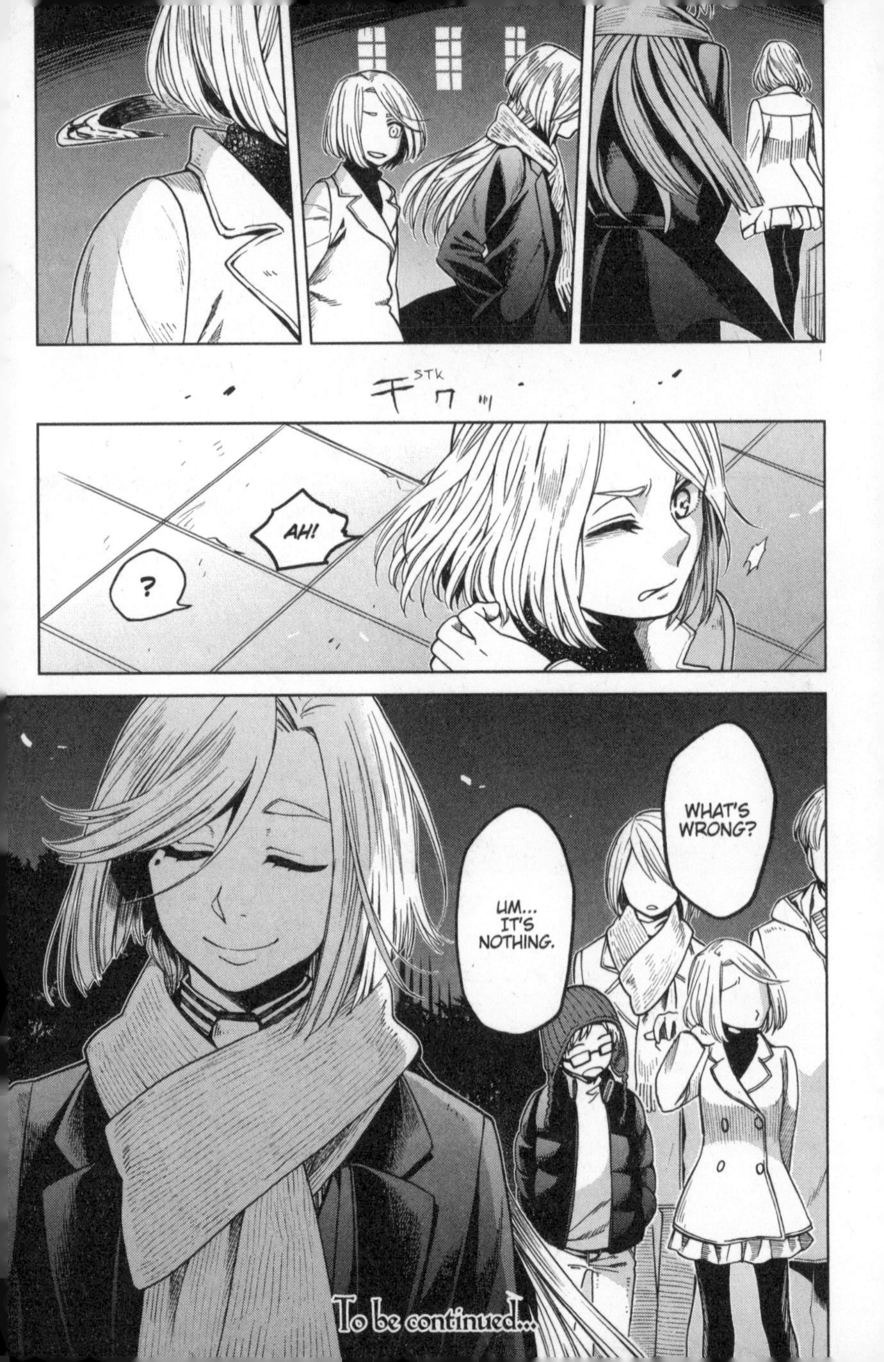
STK
AH!
?
WHAT'S WRONG?
UM... IT'S NOTHING.
To be continued...

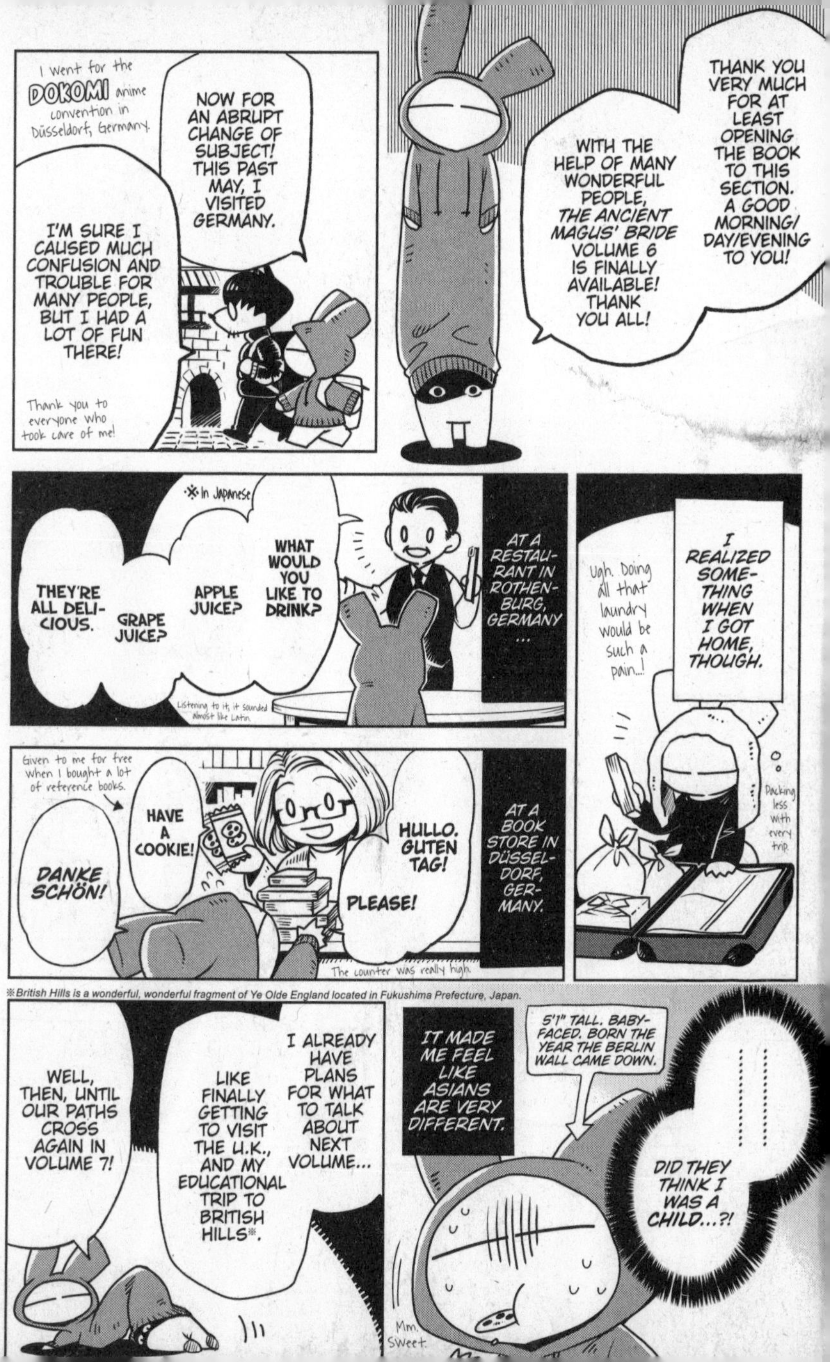
THANK YOU VERY MUCH FOR AT LEAST OPENING THE BOOK TO THIS SECTION. A GOOD MORNING/DAY/EVENING TO YOU!
WITH THE HELP OF MANY WONDERFUL PEOPLE, THE ANCIENT MAGUS' BRIDE VOLUME 6 IS FINALLY AVAILABLE! THANK YOU ALL!
I went for the DOKOMI anime convention in Düsseldorf, Germany.
NOW FOR AN ABRUPT CHANGE OF SUBJECT! THIS PAST MAY, I VISITED GERMANY.
I'M SURE I CAUSED MUCH CONFUSION AND TROUBLE FOR MANY PEOPLE, BUT I HAD A LOT OF FUN THERE!
Thank you to everyone who took care of me!
I REALIZED SOMETHING WHEN I GOT HOME, THOUGH.
Ugh. Doing all that laundry would be such a pain...!
Packing less with every trip.
AT A RESTAURANT IN ROTHENBURG, GERMANY...
※In Japanese
WHAT WOULD YOU LIKE TO DRINK?
APPLE JUICE?
GRAPE JUICE?
THEY'RE ALL DELICIOUS.
Listening to it, it sounded almost like Latin.
AT A BOOK STORE IN DÜSSELDORF, GERMANY.
HULLO. GUTEN TAG!
PLEASE!
HAVE A COOKIE!
Given to me for free when I bought a lot of reference books.
DANKE SCHÖN!
The counter was really high.
IT MADE ME FEEL LIKE ASIANS ARE VERY DIFFERENT.
5'1" TALL. BABY-FACED. BORN THE YEAR THE BERLIN WALL CAME DOWN.
DID THEY THINK I WAS A CHILD...?!
Mm. Sweet.
I ALREADY HAVE PLANS FOR WHAT TO TALK ABOUT NEXT VOLUME...
LIKE FINALLY GETTING TO VISIT THE U.K., AND MY EDUCATIONAL TRIP TO BRITISH HILLS※.
WELL, THEN, UNTIL OUR PATHS CROSS AGAIN IN VOLUME 7!

※British Hills is a wonderful, wonderful fragment of Ye Olde England located in Fukushima Prefecture, Japan.

SEVEN SEAS ENTERTAINMENT PRESENTS

The Ancient Magus' Bride
VOLUME 6

story and art by KORE YAMAZAKI

TRANSLATION
Adrienne Beck

ADAPTATION
Ysabet Reinhardt MacFarlane

LETTERING AND RETOUCH
Lys Blakeslee

COVER DESIGN
Nicky Lim

PROOFREADER
Shanti Whitesides
Jenn Grunigen

PRODUCTION MANAGER
Lissa Pattillo

EDITOR-IN-CHIEF
Adam Arnold

PUBLISHER
Jason DeAngelis

THE ANCIENT MAGUS' BRIDE VOL. 6
© Kore Yamazaki 2016
Originally published in Japan in 2016 by MAG Garden Corporation, Tokyo.
English translation rights arranged through TOHAN CORPORATION, Tokyo.

Seven Seas books may be purchased in bulk for promotional, educational, or business use. Please contact your local bookseller or the Macmillan Corporate and Premium Sales Department at 1-800-221-7945, extension 5442, or by e-mail at MacmillanSpecialMarkets@macmillan.com.

Seven Seas and the Seven Seas logo are trademarks of Seven Seas Entertainment, LLC. All rights reserved.

ISBN: 978-1-626923-50-8

Printed in Canada

First Printing: January 2017

10 9 8 7 6 5 4 3 2 1

FOLLOW US ONLINE: www.gomanga.com

READING DIRECTIONS

This book reads from *right to left*, Japanese style. If this is your first time reading manga, you start reading from the top right panel on each page and take it from there. If you get lost, just follow the numbered diagram here. It may seem backwards at first, but you'll get the hang of it! Have fun!!

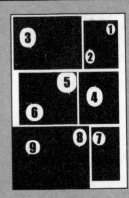

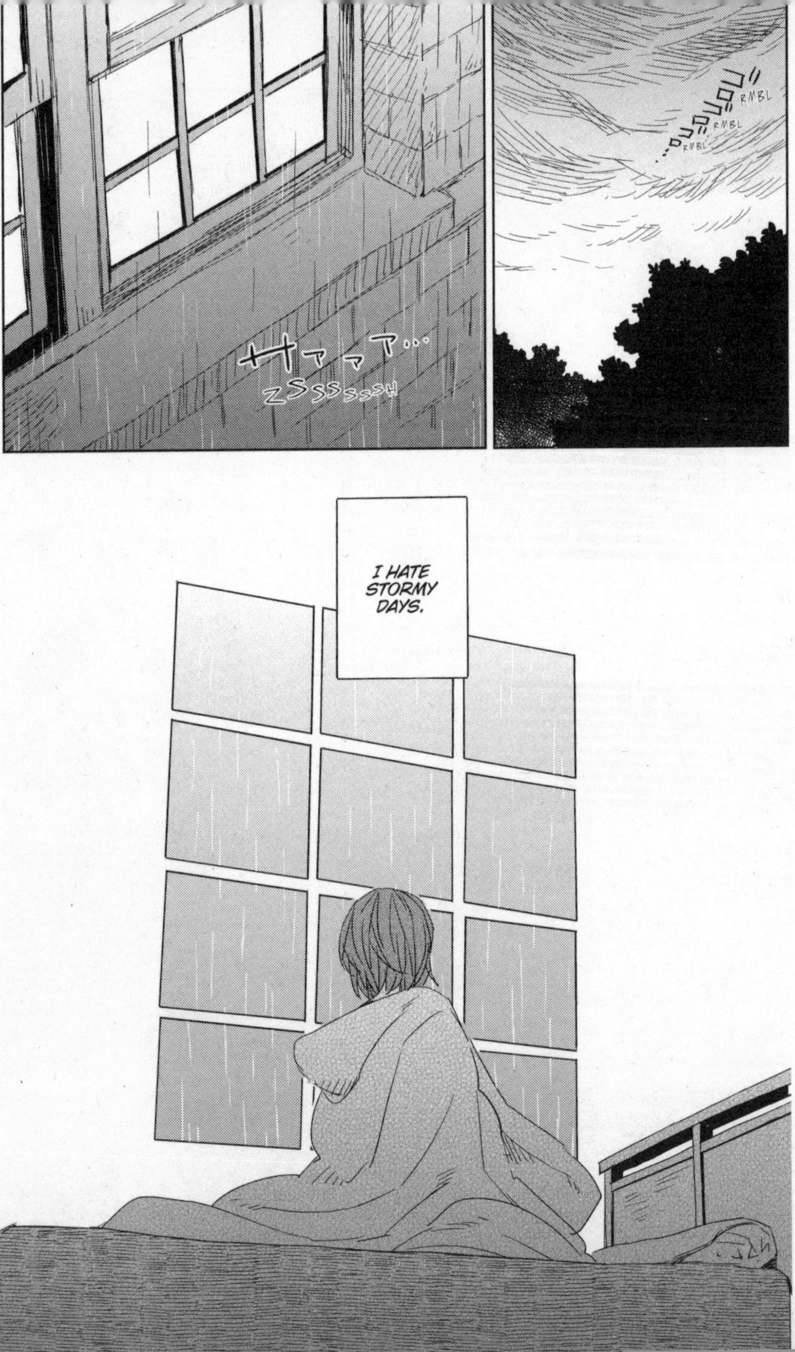
RMBL
RMBL
RMBL
ZSSSSSSH
I HATE STORMY DAYS.

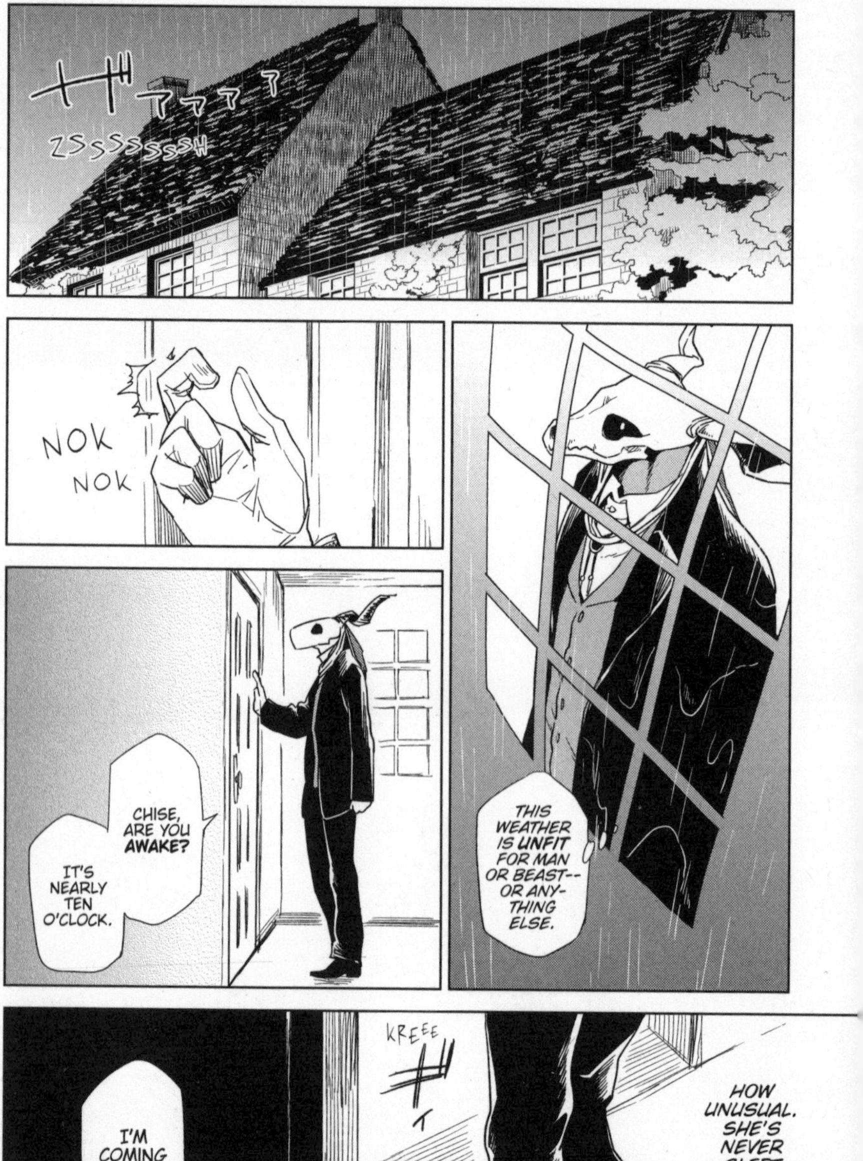
ZSSSSSSSH
THIS WEATHER IS UNFIT FOR MAN OR BEAST--OR ANYTHING ELSE.
NOK NOK
CHISE, ARE YOU AWAKE?
IT'S NEARLY TEN O'CLOCK.
HOW UNUSUAL. SHE'S NEVER SLEPT SO LATE BEFORE.
KREEE
I'M COMING IN.

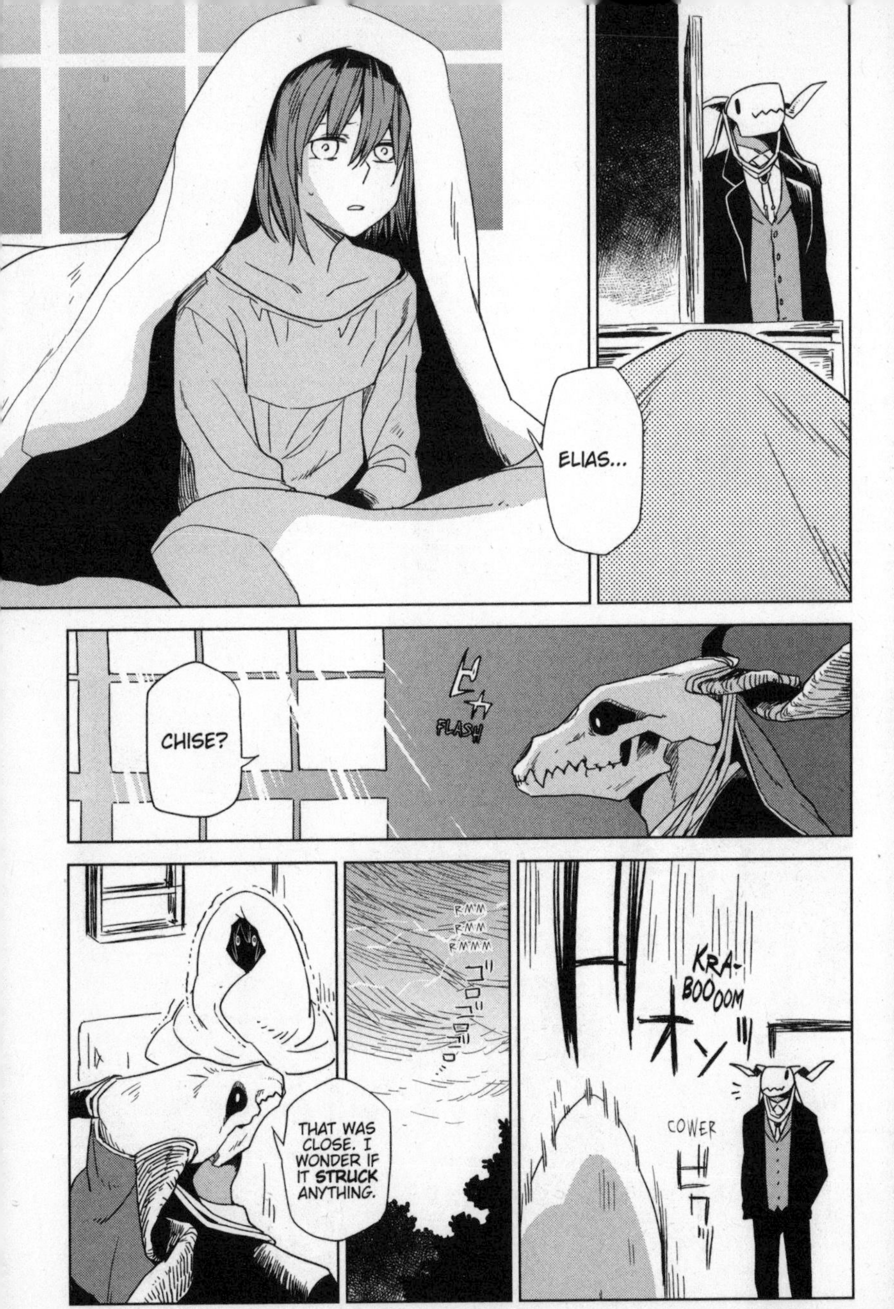
ELIAS...
FLASH
CHISE?
KRA-BOOOOM
COWER
R'M'M R'M'M R'M'M
THAT WAS CLOSE. I WONDER IF IT STRUCK ANYTHING.

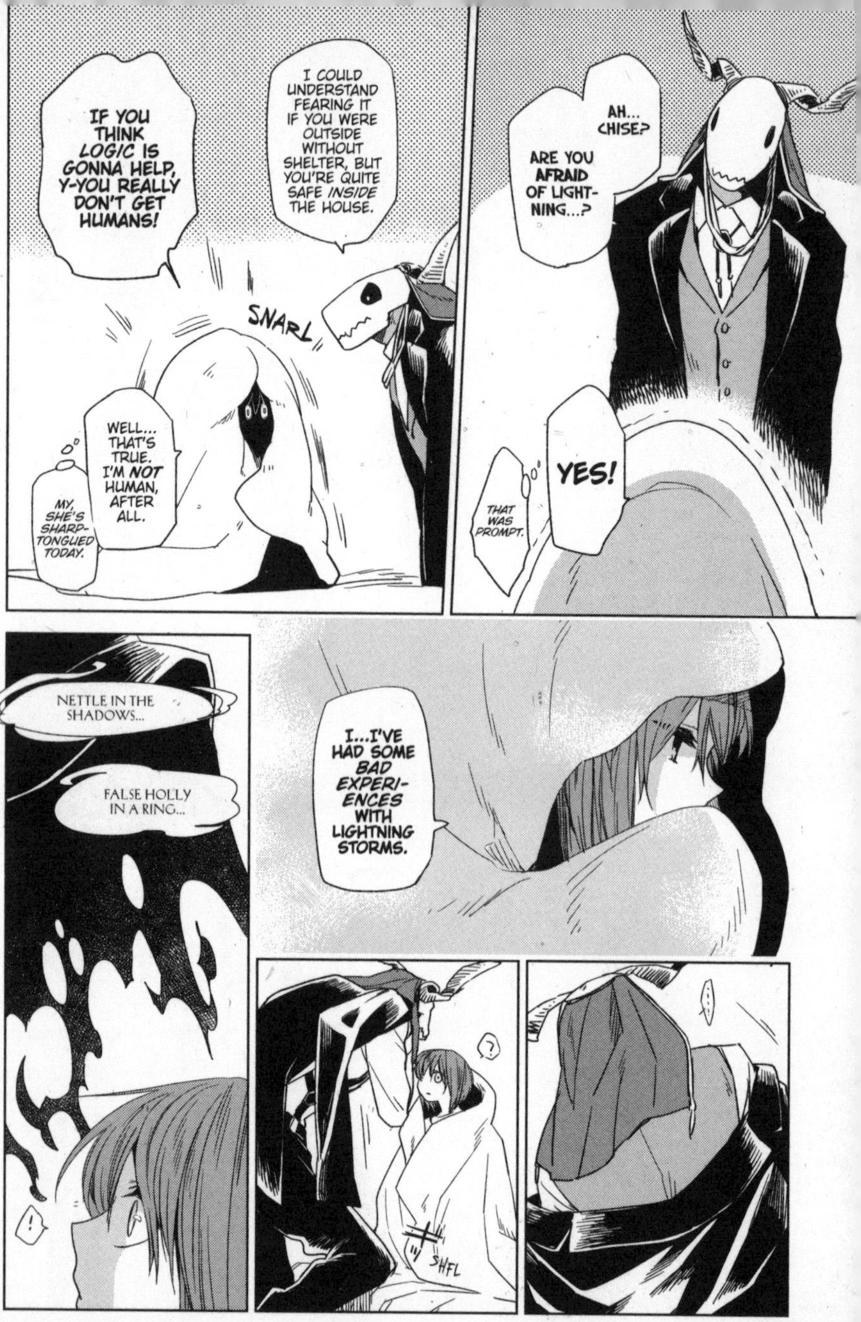
AH... CHISE?
ARE YOU AFRAID OF LIGHTNING...?
YES!
THAT WAS PROMPT.
I COULD UNDERSTAND FEARING IT IF YOU WERE OUTSIDE WITHOUT SHELTER, BUT YOU'RE QUITE SAFE *INSIDE* THE HOUSE.
IF YOU THINK *LOGIC* IS GONNA HELP, Y-YOU REALLY DON'T GET HUMANS!
SNARL
WELL... THAT'S TRUE. I'M *NOT* HUMAN, AFTER ALL.
MY, SHE'S SHARP-TONGUED TODAY.
I...I'VE HAD SOME *BAD* EXPERIENCES WITH LIGHTNING STORMS.
...
?
SHFL
NETTLE IN THE SHADOWS...
FALSE HOLLY IN A RING...
!

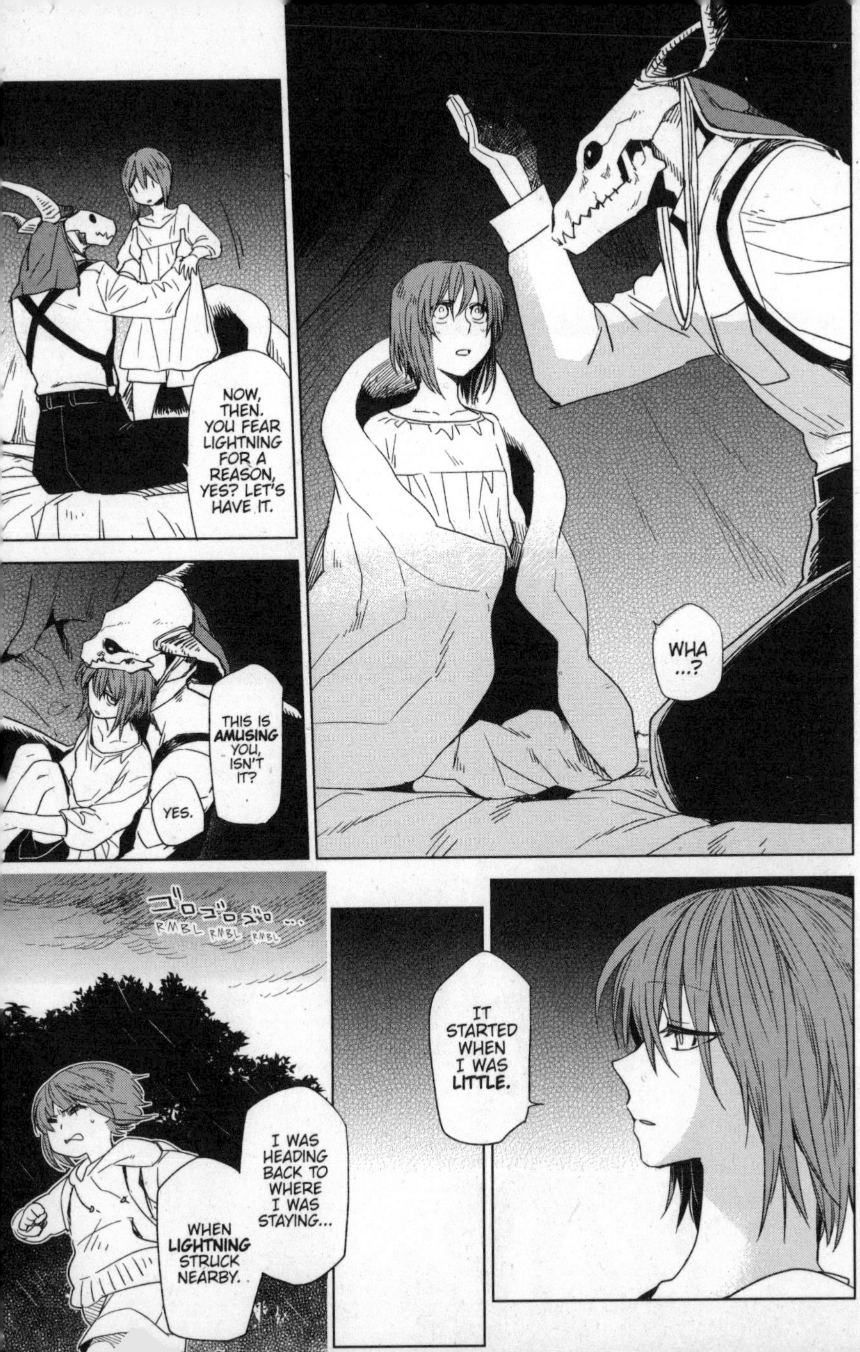
WHA ...?
NOW, THEN. YOU FEAR LIGHTNING FOR A REASON, YES? LET'S HAVE IT.
THIS IS **AMUSING** YOU, ISN'T IT?
YES.
IT STARTED WHEN I WAS **LITTLE.**
ゴロゴロゴロ...
RMBL RMBL RMBL
I WAS HEADING BACK TO WHERE I WAS STAYING...
WHEN **LIGHTNING** STRUCK NEARBY.

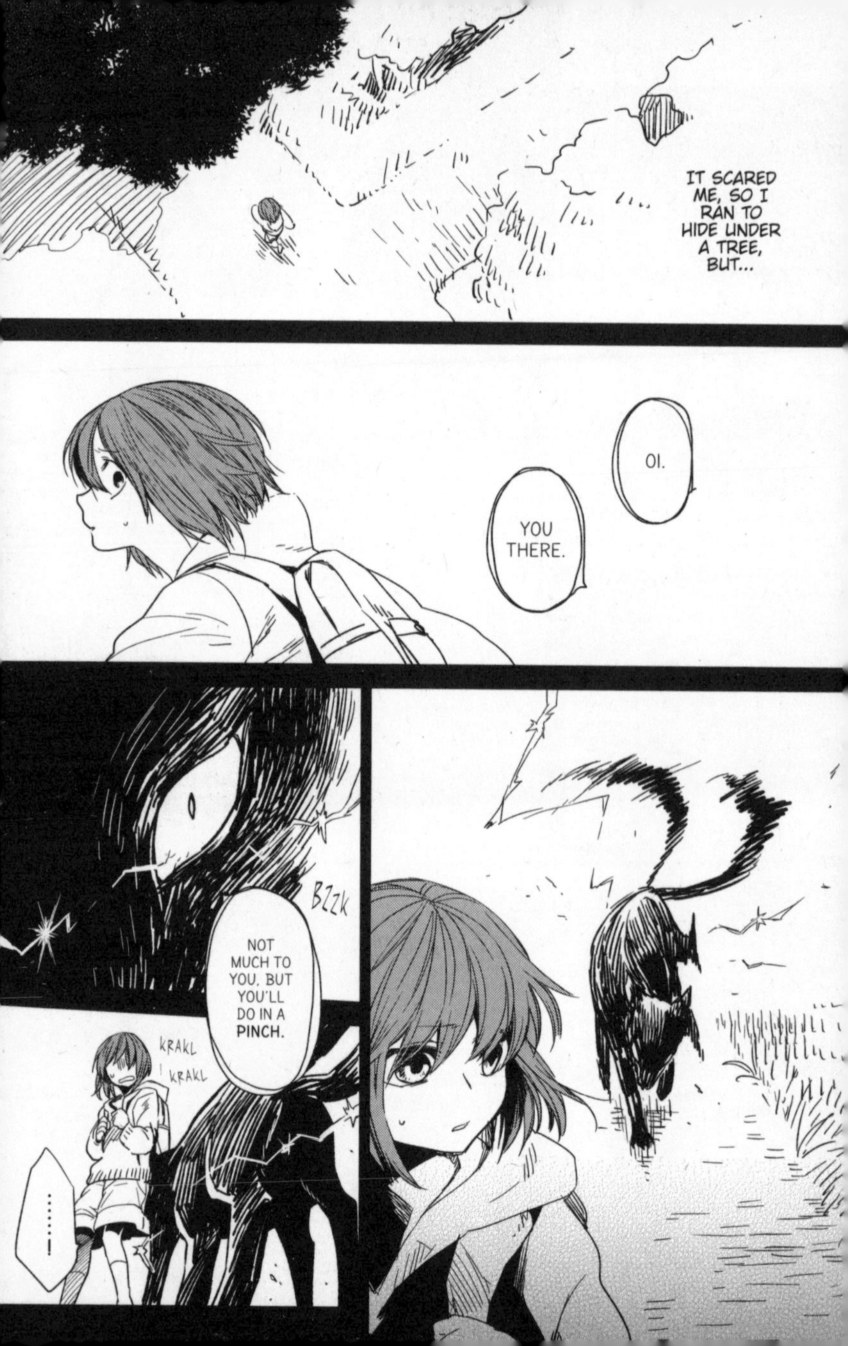
IT SCARED ME, SO I RAN TO HIDE UNDER A TREE, BUT...
OI.
YOU THERE.
BZZK
NOT MUCH TO YOU, BUT YOU'LL DO IN A PINCH.
KRAKL
KRAKL
......!

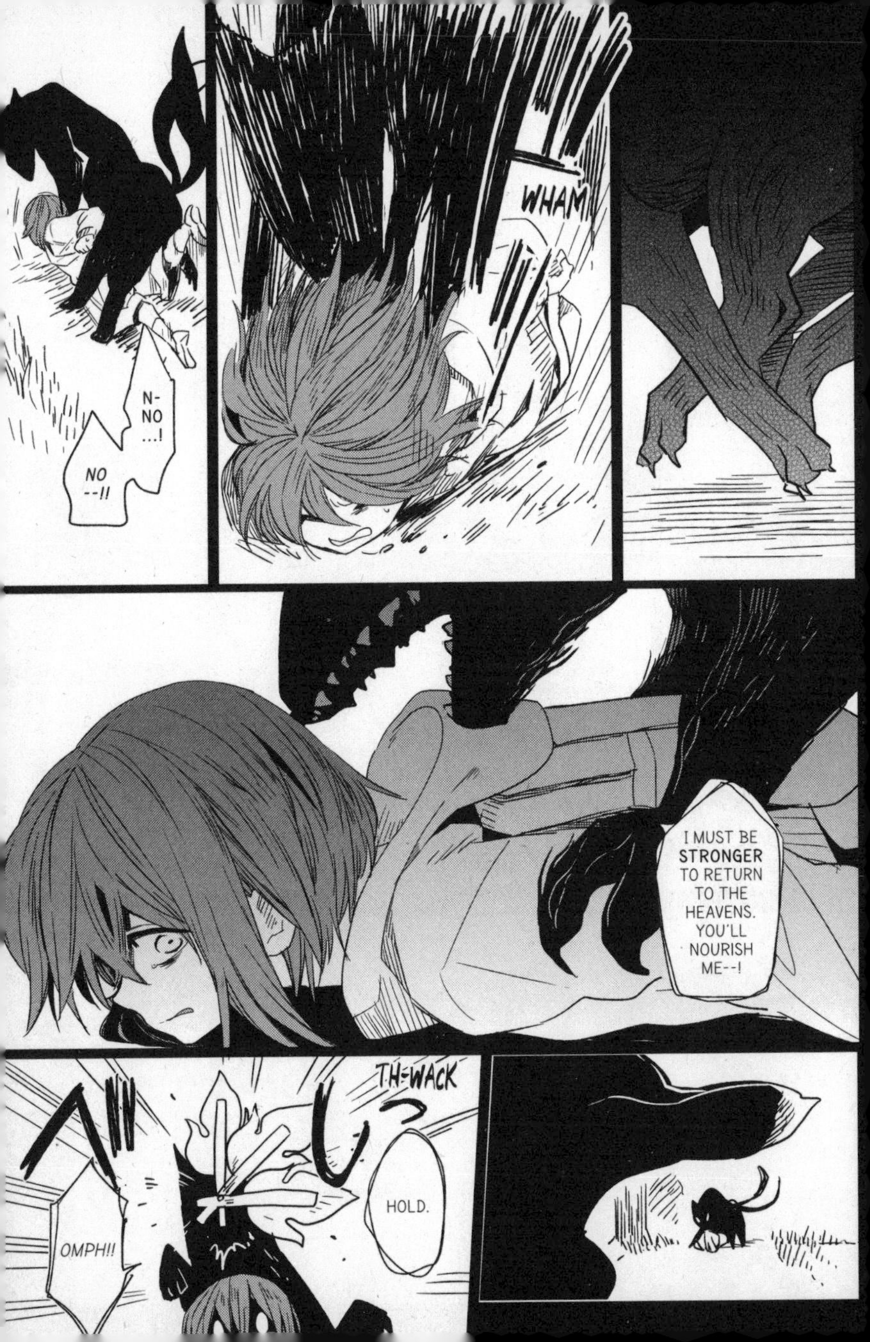
WHAM
N-NO ...!
NO --!!
I MUST BE **STRONGER** TO RETURN TO THE HEAVENS. YOU'LL NOURISH ME--!
TH-WACK
HOLD.
OMPH!!

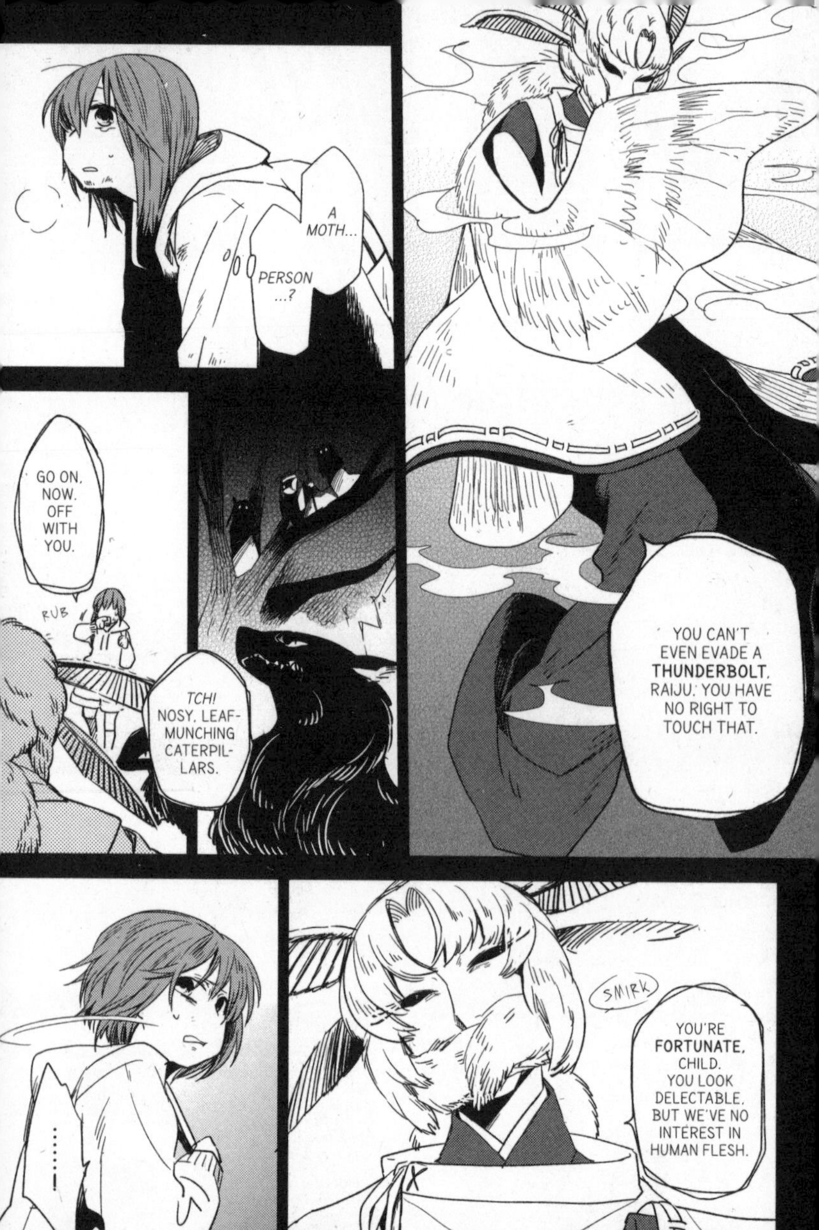
YOU CAN'T EVEN EVADE A **THUNDERBOLT**, RAIJU. YOU HAVE NO RIGHT TO TOUCH THAT.
A MOTH...
PERSON ...?
TCH! NOSY, LEAF-MUNCHING CATERPIL-LARS.
GO ON, NOW. OFF WITH YOU.
RUB
SMIRK
YOU'RE **FORTUNATE,** CHILD. YOU LOOK DELECTABLE, BUT WE'VE NO INTEREST IN HUMAN FLESH.
......!

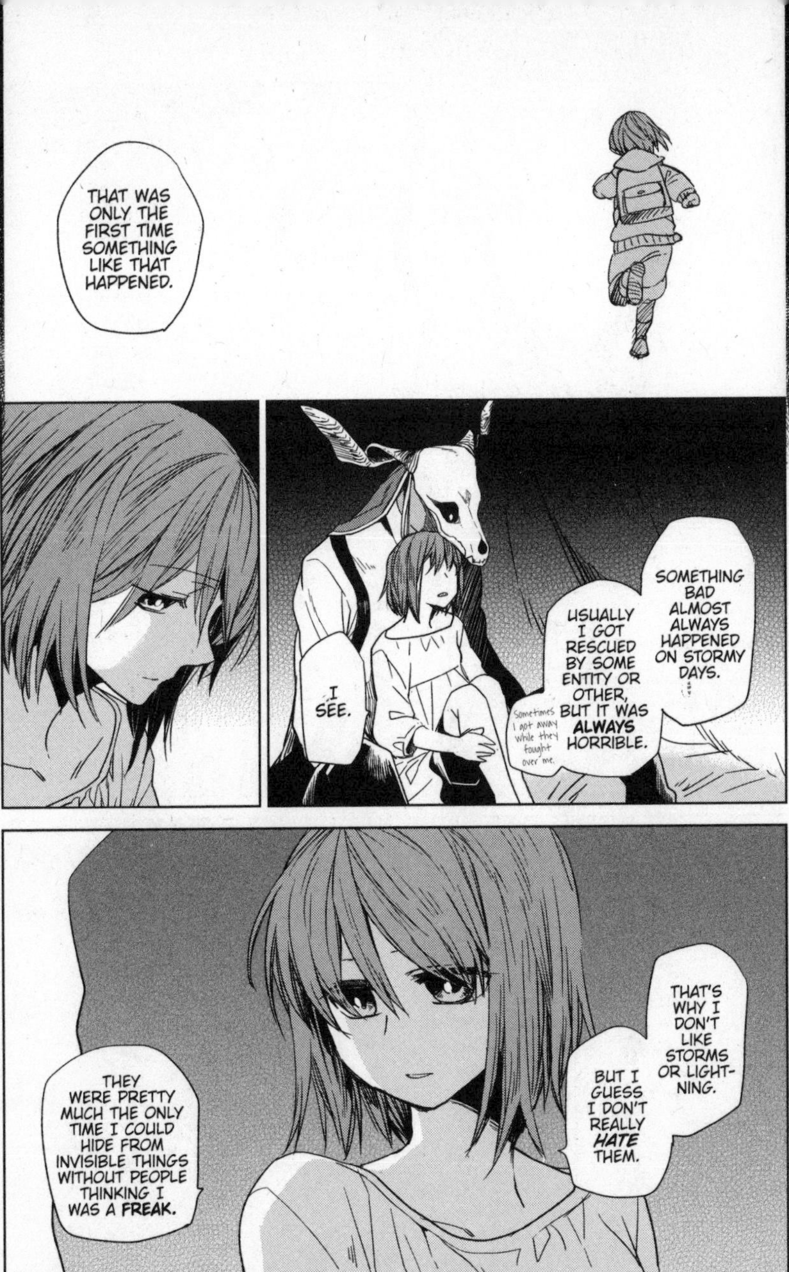
THAT WAS ONLY THE FIRST TIME SOMETHING LIKE THAT HAPPENED.
SOMETHING BAD ALMOST ALWAYS HAPPENED ON STORMY DAYS.
USUALLY I GOT RESCUED BY SOME ENTITY OR OTHER, BUT IT WAS ALWAYS HORRIBLE.
Sometimes I got away while they fought over me.
I SEE.
THAT'S WHY I DON'T LIKE STORMS OR LIGHT-NING.
BUT I GUESS I DON'T REALLY HATE THEM.
THEY WERE PRETTY MUCH THE ONLY TIME I COULD HIDE FROM INVISIBLE THINGS WITHOUT PEOPLE THINKING I WAS A FREAK.

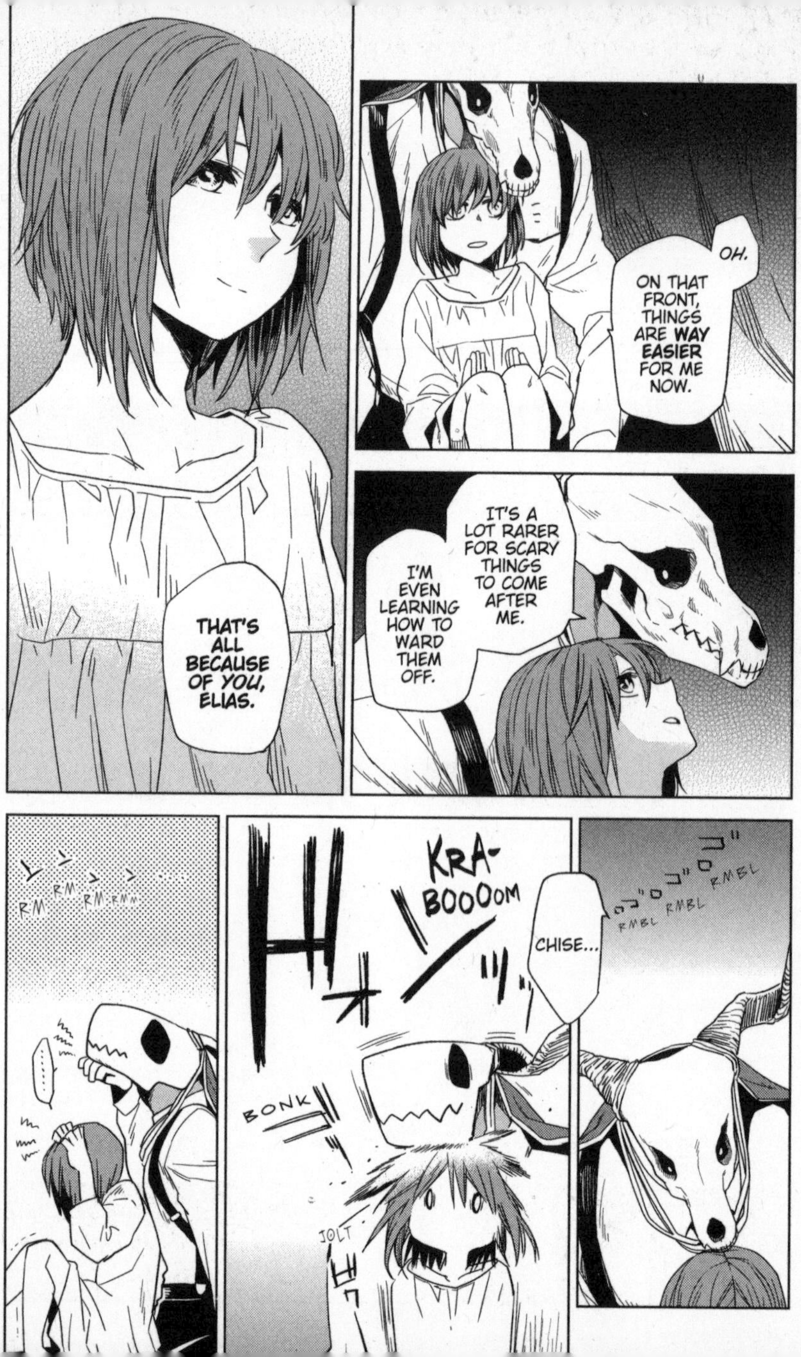
OH.
ON THAT FRONT, THINGS ARE WAY EASIER FOR ME NOW.
IT'S A LOT RARER FOR SCARY THINGS TO COME AFTER ME.
I'M EVEN LEARNING HOW TO WARD THEM OFF.
THAT'S ALL BECAUSE OF YOU, ELIAS.
RMBL RMBL RMBL
CHISE...
KRA-BOOOOM
BONK
JOLT
RM RM RMM
......

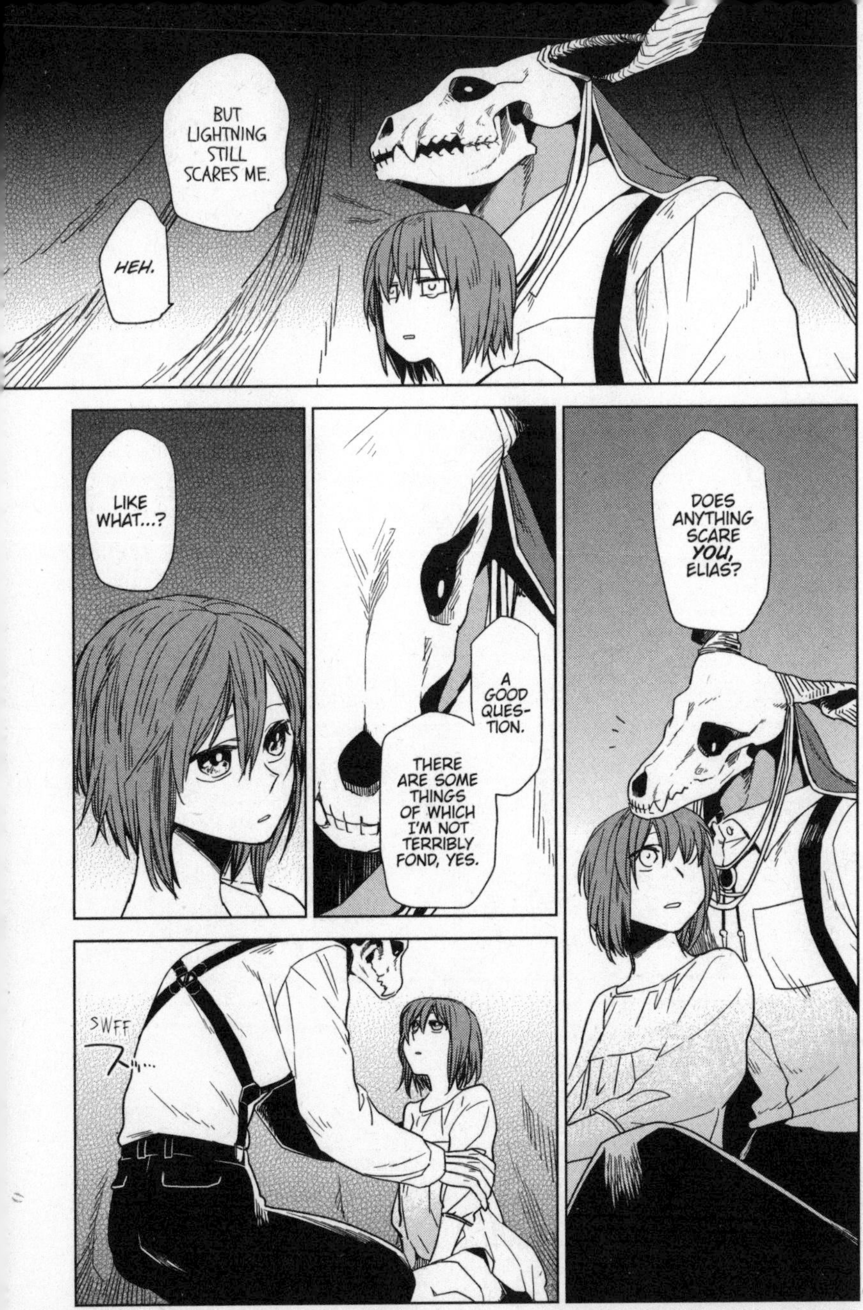
BUT LIGHTNING STILL SCARES ME.
HEH.
DOES ANYTHING SCARE *YOU*, ELIAS?
A GOOD QUES-TION.
THERE ARE SOME THINGS OF WHICH I'M NOT TERRIBLY FOND, YES.
LIKE WHAT...?
SWFF

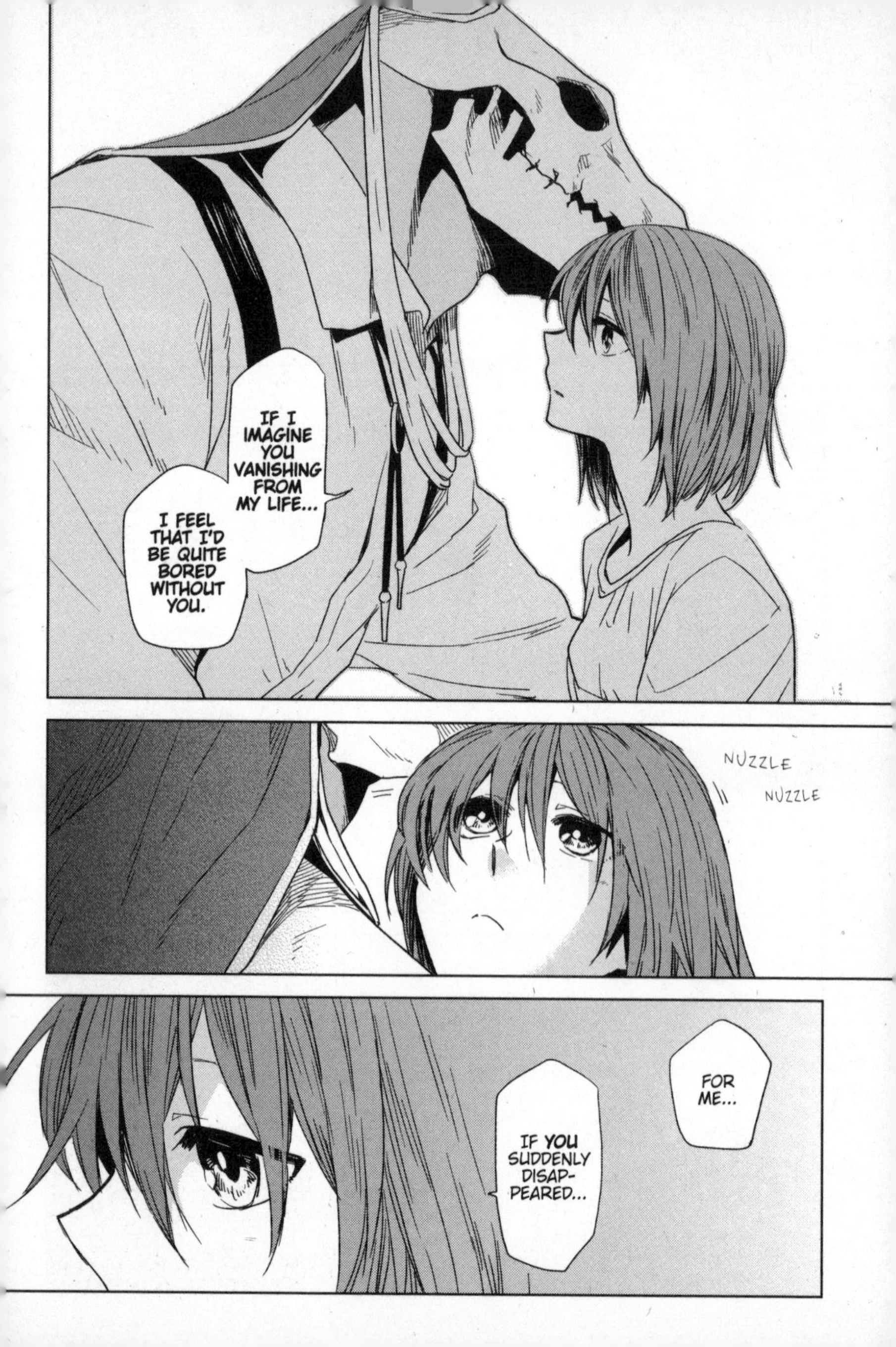
IF I IMAGINE YOU VANISHING FROM MY LIFE...
I FEEL THAT I'D BE QUITE BORED WITHOUT YOU.
NUZZLE
NUZZLE
FOR ME...
IF YOU SUDDENLY DISAP-PEARED...

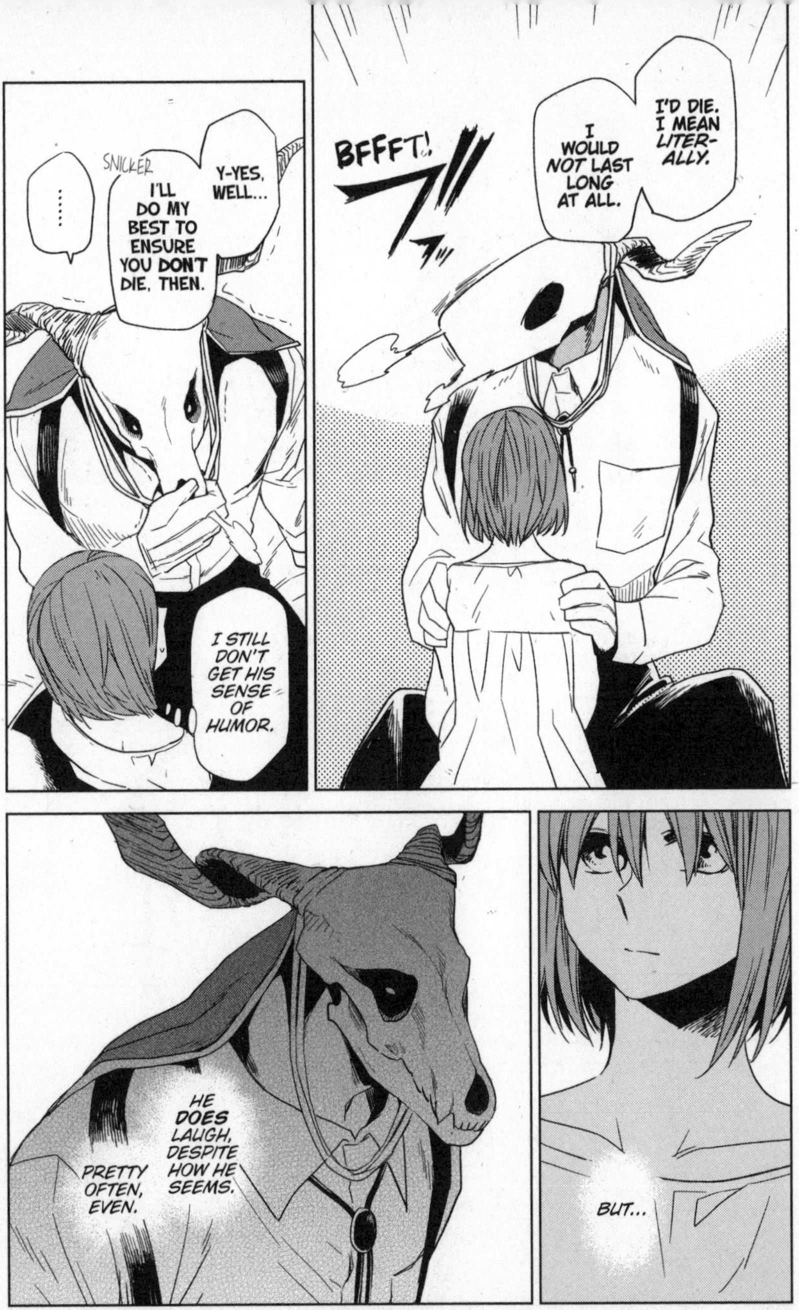
I'D DIE. I MEAN LITERALLY.
I WOULD NOT LAST LONG AT ALL.
BFFFT!
Y-YES, WELL...
I'LL DO MY BEST TO ENSURE YOU DON'T DIE, THEN.
SNICKER
......
I STILL DON'T GET HIS SENSE OF HUMOR.
BUT...
HE DOES LAUGH, DESPITE HOW HE SEEMS.
PRETTY OFTEN, EVEN.

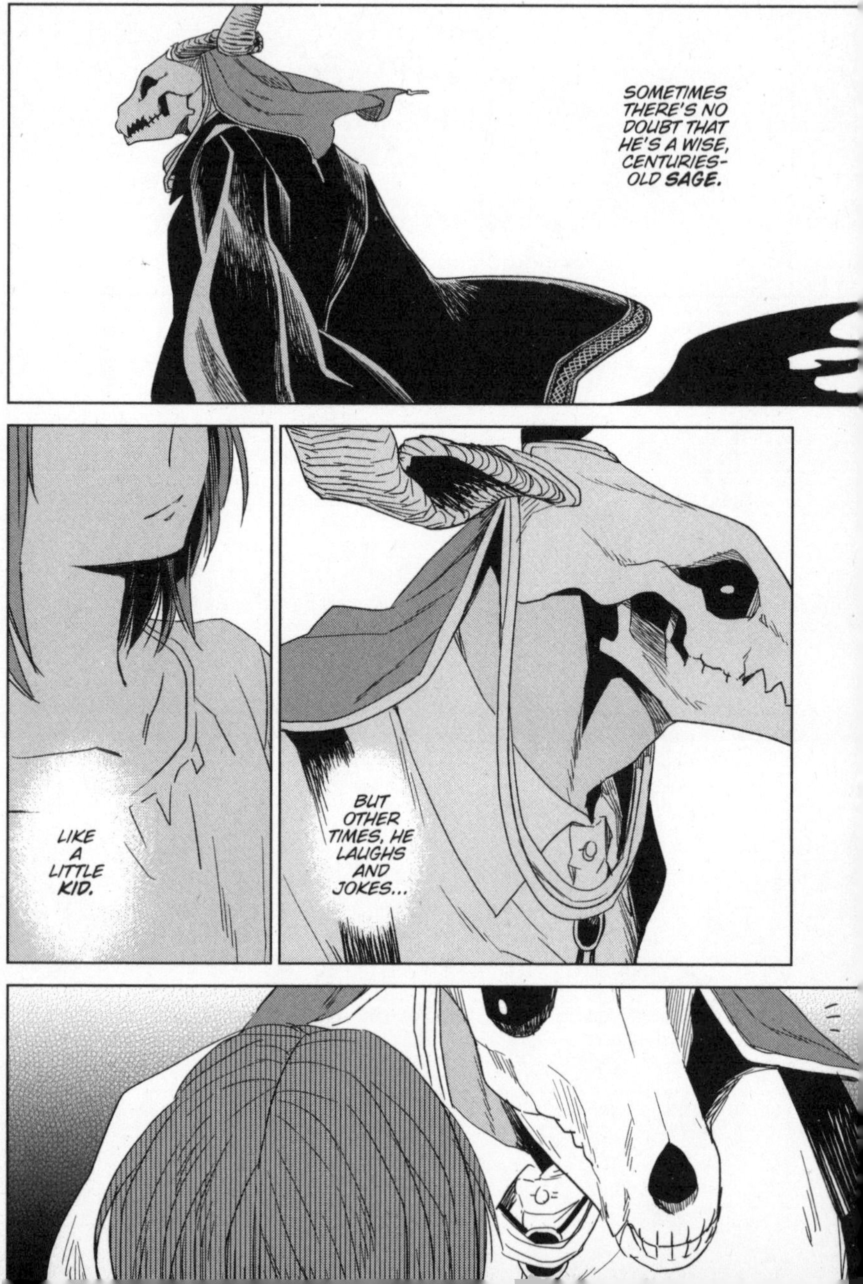
SOMETIMES THERE'S NO DOUBT THAT HE'S A WISE, CENTURIES-OLD SAGE.
BUT OTHER TIMES, HE LAUGHS AND JOKES...
LIKE A LITTLE KID.

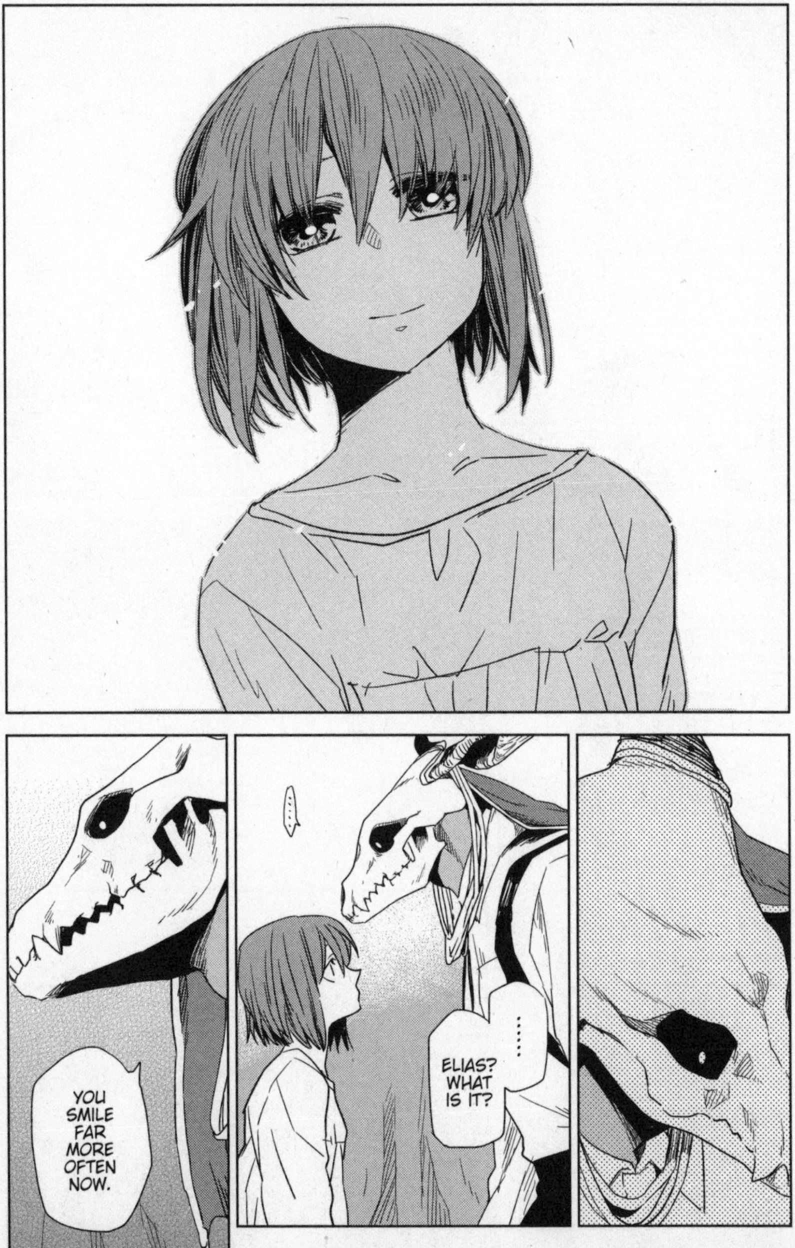
......
......
ELIAS? WHAT IS IT?
YOU SMILE FAR MORE OFTEN NOW.

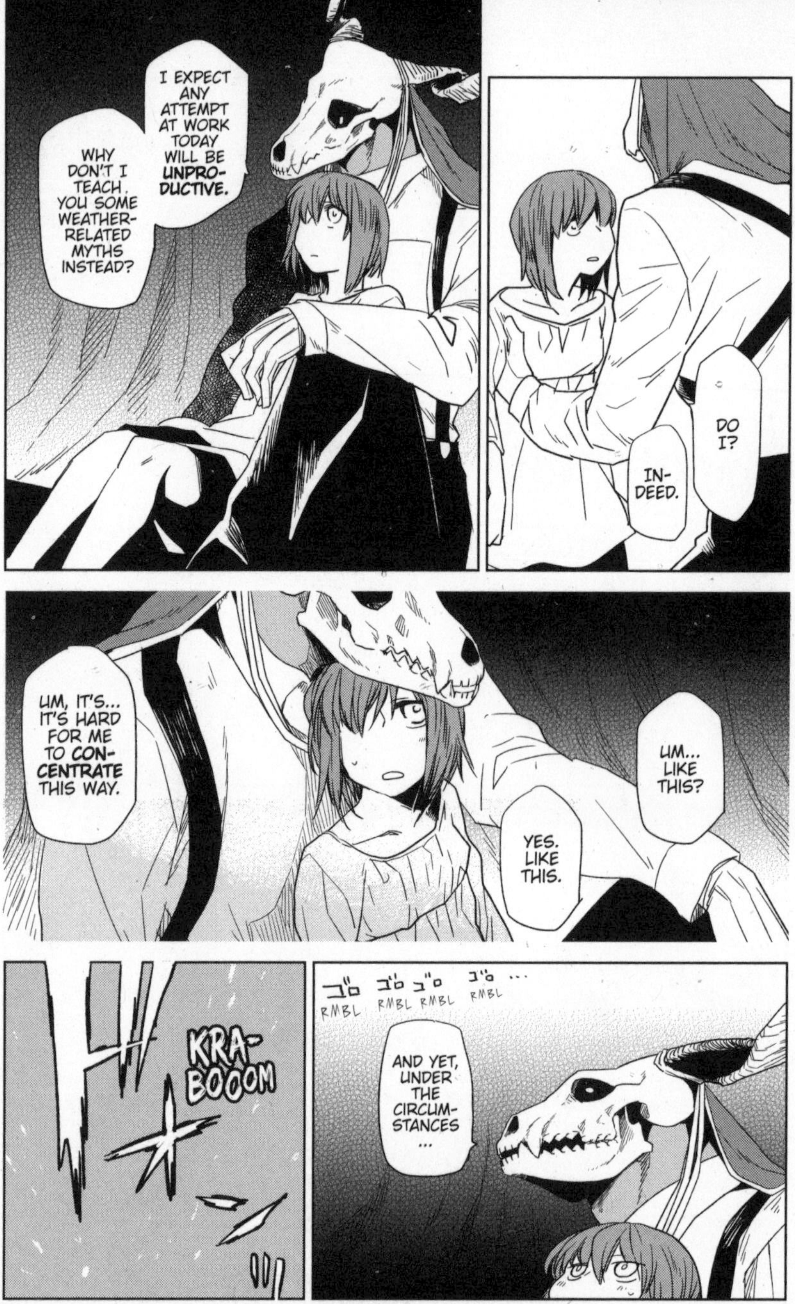

DO I?
IN-DEED.
I EXPECT ANY ATTEMPT AT WORK TODAY WILL BE **UNPRODUCTIVE.**
WHY DON'T I TEACH YOU SOME WEATHER-RELATED MYTHS INSTEAD?
UM... LIKE THIS?
YES. LIKE THIS.
UM, IT'S... IT'S HARD FOR ME TO **CONCENTRATE** THIS WAY.
ゴロ ゴロゴロ ゴロ…
RMBL RMBL RMBL RMBL
AND YET, UNDER THE CIRCUM-STANCES...
KRA-BOOOM

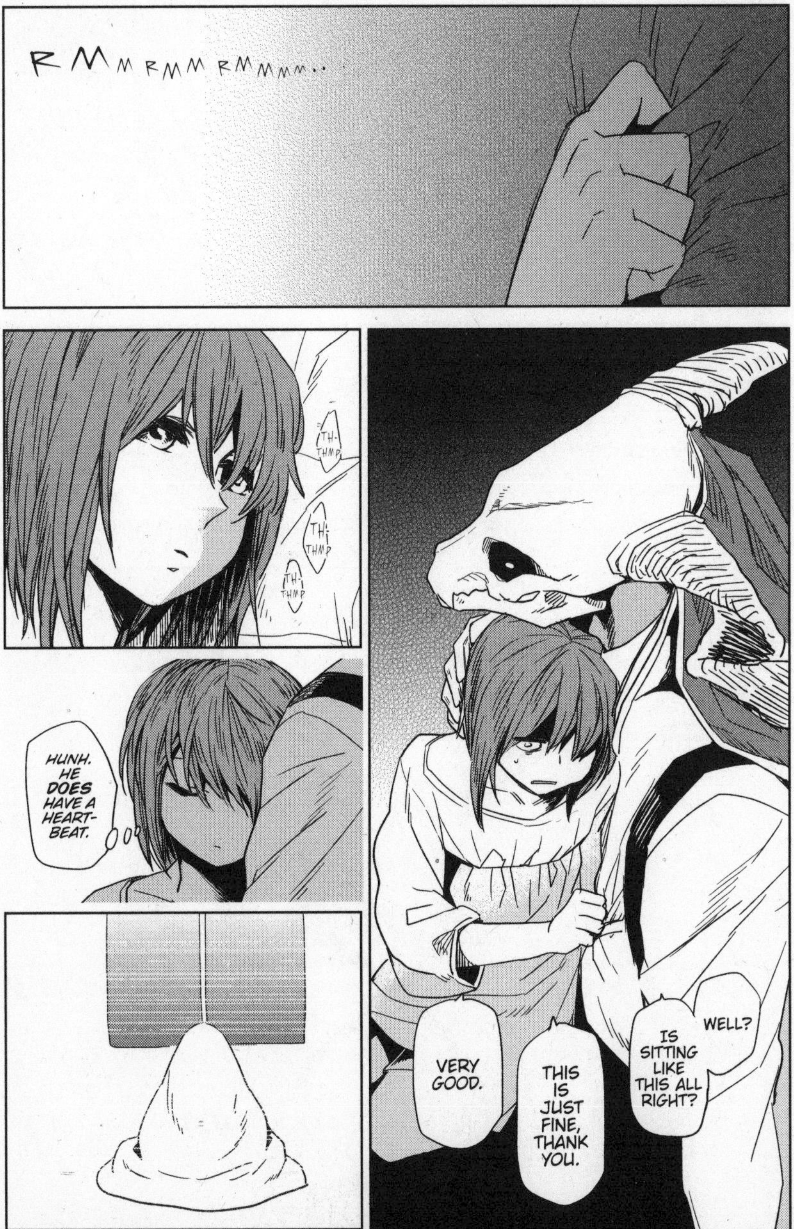
RMMRMMRMMMM..
WELL?
IS SITTING LIKE THIS ALL RIGHT?
THIS IS JUST FINE, THANK YOU.
VERY GOOD.
TH-THMP
TH-THMP
TH-THMP
HUNH. HE DOES HAVE A HEART-BEAT.

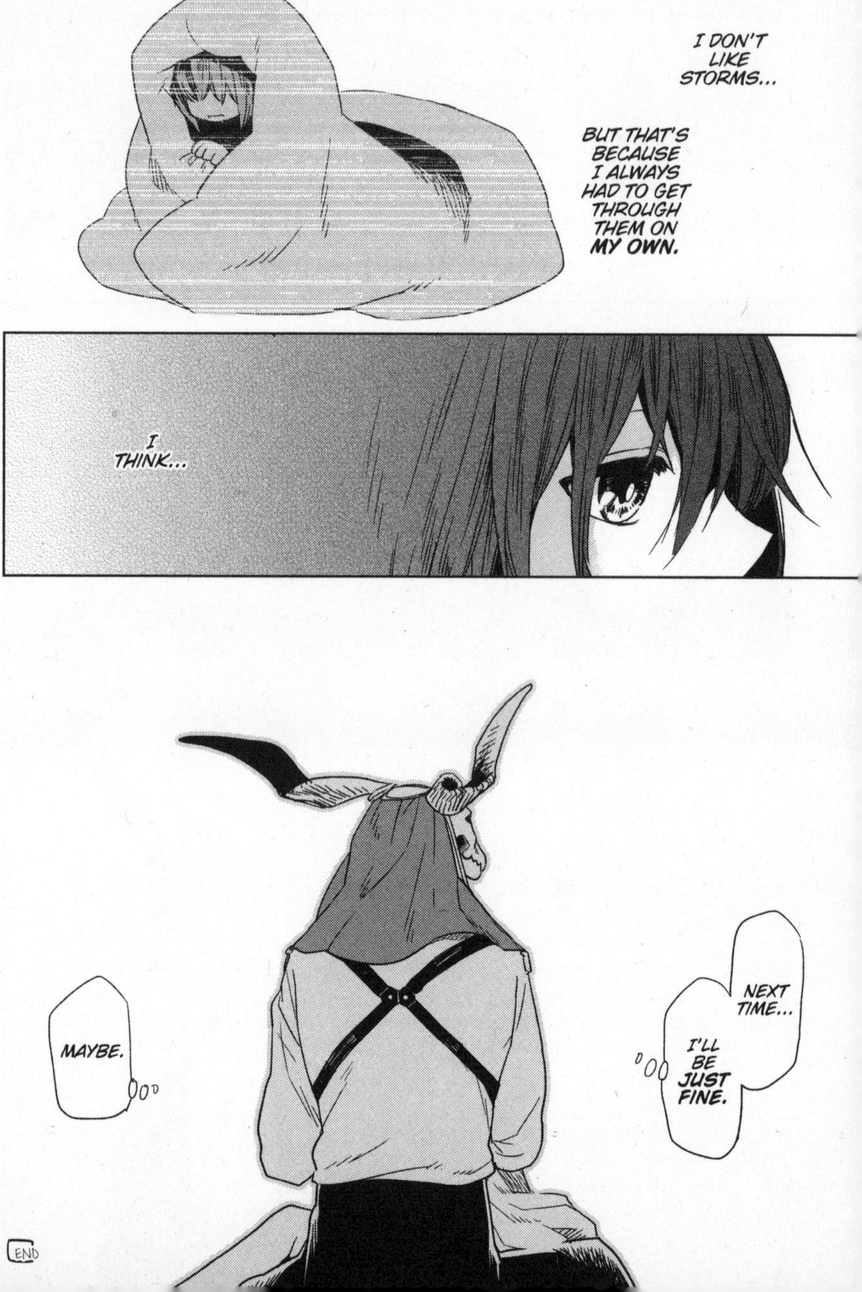
I DON'T LIKE STORMS...
BUT THAT'S BECAUSE I ALWAYS HAD TO GET THROUGH THEM ON MY OWN.
I THINK...
NEXT TIME...
I'LL BE JUST FINE.
MAYBE.
END

Thanks for picking up volume 6 of The Ancient Magus' Bride!!

Kore Yamazaki

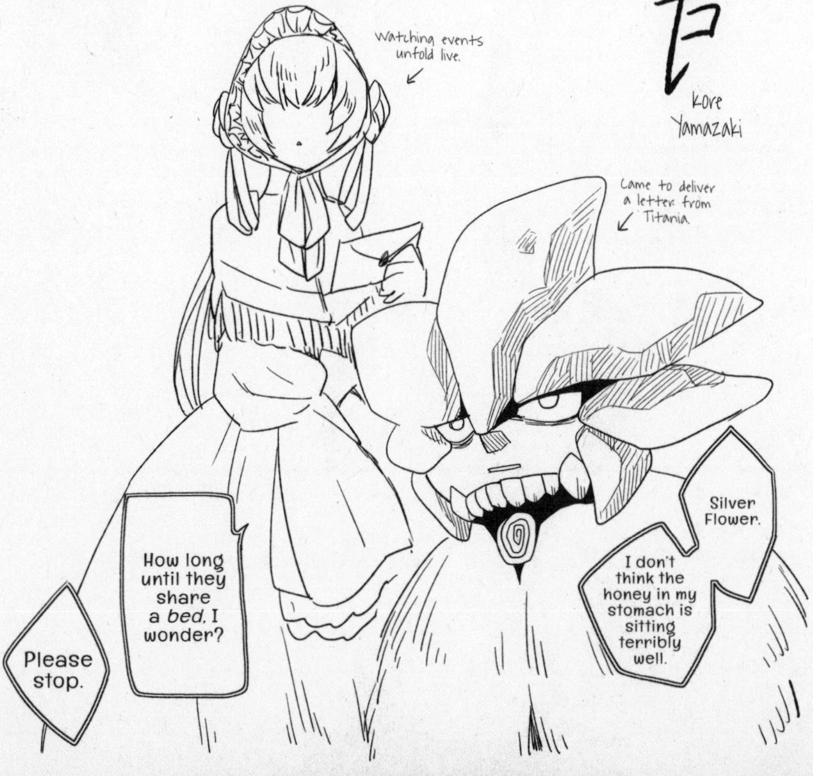
Watching events unfold live.
Came to deliver a letter from Titania.
Silver Flower.
I don't think the honey in my stomach is sitting terribly well.
How long until they share a *bed*, I wonder?
Please stop.

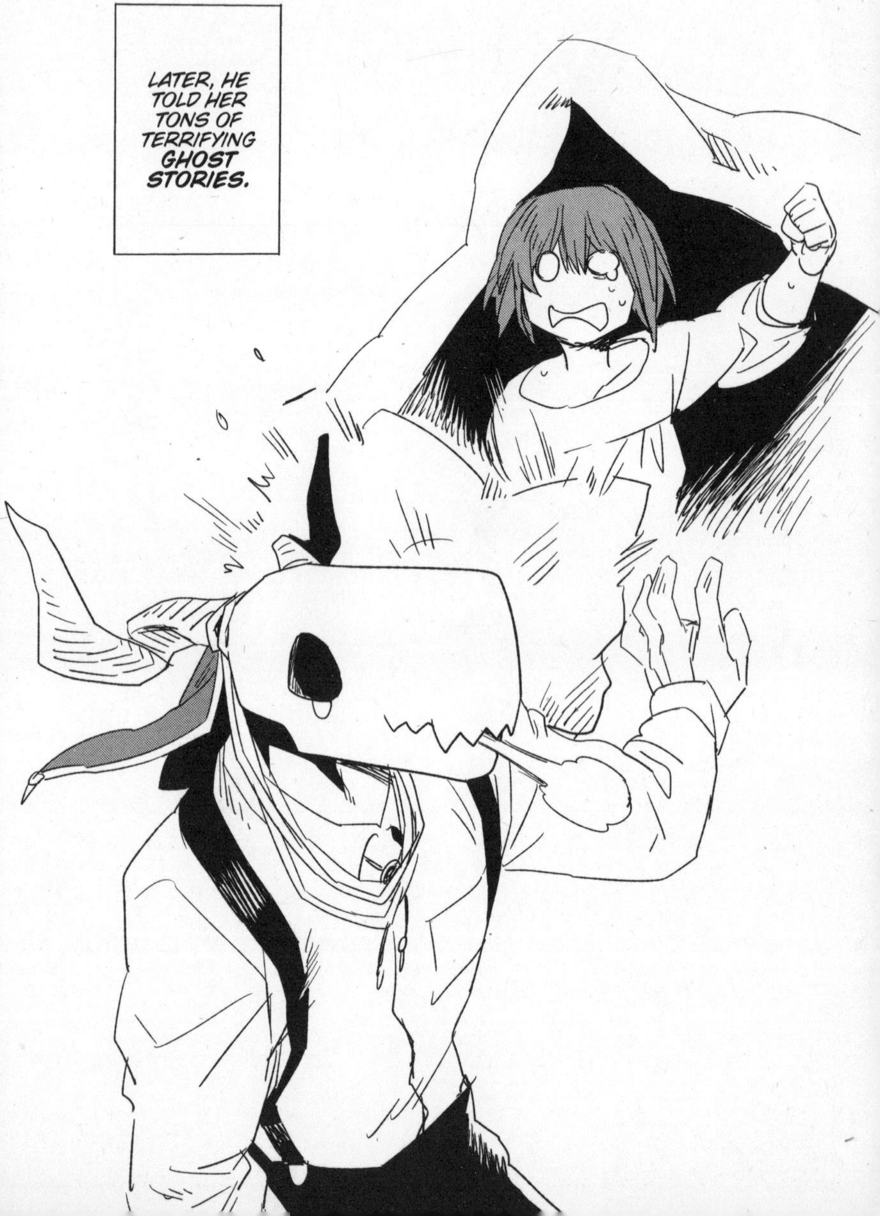
LATER, HE TOLD HER TONS OF TERRIFYING GHOST STORIES.